# Prophets in the Quran

*Comparative Islamic Studies*
Series Editor: Brannon M. Wheeler

This series seeks to examine the diversity of Islam by emphasizing both the global and historical variegation within Islamic traditions, and between Islamic and non-Islamic traditions. It is aimed primarily at undergraduates in the social sciences and humanities, though more specialized studies are also included. Books focus on changes due to historical developments, differences due to regional specificities, or salient aspects of particular traditions and societies. The goal is studies which show how prominent Islamic notions and artefacts contribute to an understanding of more generic concepts such as scripture, territory, authority or prophecy. Broad-based comparisons also address methodological issues related to the use of interdisciplinary and cross-cultural perspectives.

# Prophets in the Quran

An Introduction to the Quran and
Muslim Exegesis

Selected and translated by
**BRANNON M. WHEELER**

 **continuum**
LONDON • NEW YORK

**Continuum**

The Tower Building, 11 York Road, London, SE1 7NX

370 Lexington Avenue, New York, NY 10017-6503

First published 2002

**British Library Cataloguing-in-Publication Data**
A catalogue record for this book is available from the British Library.

ISBN 0-8264-4956-5 (hardback)
   0-8264-4957-3 (paperback)

**Library of Congress Cataloging-in-Publication Data**
Wheeler, Brannon M., 1965–
    Prophets in the Quran: An introduction to the Quran and Muslim exegesis
        p. cm.—(Comparative Islamic studies)
    Translation of selections from the Koran and from exegetical texts.
    Includes bibliographical references and index.
    ISBN 0-8264-4956-5—ISBN 0-8264-4957-3 (pbk.)
    1. Prophets in the Koran.   2. Koran stories.   I. Title.   II. Series.

BP134.P745 W48 2001
297.1'222—dc21

                                                     2001028582

Typeset by CentraServe Ltd, Saffron Walden, Essex
Printed and bound in Great Britain by Biddles Ltd, *www.biddles.co.uk*

# Contents

# Acknowledgments

Work on this book began many years ago, and will continue with the hope that future editions can be of greater benefit to readers. The impetus for this work comes from both students and friends who have expressed the need for an accessible introduction to and translation of the Quran. Such an ambition is not completely accomplished with this present book, but will continue to inspire my attention to further aspects of the Quran and its place in Islamic civilization. A goal of such proportions must always be a work in progress, and this book a temporary attempt to help myself and others make sense of an extremely significant phenomenon in human history.

Most of all, my students have contributed to this book. Students in large introductory courses, too numerous to name, continue to ask questions some of which this book begins to answer. Students from my seminars reading Arabic, Aramaic, and Hebrew texts from the Quran, Bible, and Jewish and Islamic exegesis have made specific contributions. I appreciate the efforts of Mustafa Elostaz, Jill Hutchins, John Matthies, Daryl Mutton, Magid Shihade, Ahmed Souaiaia, and Nick Tombs.

All of my colleagues at the University of Washington have been supportive of my teaching and research. The fascinating and far-flung interests of the many colleagues in Comparative Islamic Studies have encouraged my work on the Quran: Ilse Cirtautus (Turkic), Ahmad Karimi-Hakkak (Persian), Naseem Hines (Urdu), Pierre McKay (Arabic), Laurie Sears (Javanese), Carol Solomon (Bengali), and Farhat Ziadeh (Arabic) among others. I have gained in particular from the insights of those working with me in Comparative Religion. Marty Jaffee's work on late antique and medieval Judaism, Joel Walker's expertise in Syriac Christianity and pre-Islamic Iran, and Michael Williams' research in early Christianity and "biblical demiurgical myths." Scott Noegel and I taught together a course on "Prophets in Islam and Judaism" which has pushed my understanding of this topic far beyond anything I could have imagined on my own.

Colleagues at other institutions have supported me both directly and indirectly, especially in their willingness to discuss teaching strategies for the study of Islam and the Quran: Jonathan Brockopp, Art Buehler, Carl Ernst, Marcia Hermansen, Tazim and Zayn Kassam, Bruce Lawrence, and Jane McAuliffe. Suzanne and Jaroslav Stetkevych, both in their publications and in person, continue to be an inspiration. I have also derived great benefit from the several discussions of the interaction between the study of Islam and study of Judaism at the Western Jewish Studies Association meeting (1999) and the American Academy of Religion (2000), which has included contributions by Fred Astren, Michael Cook, Aaron Hughes, Kathy Kueny, Gordon Newby, and Steve Wasserstrom.

In part, the research and writing of this book was supported by the Natonal Endowment for the Humanities, the American Research Center in Egypt, and the American Institute for Maghreb Studies. The many scholars with whom I worked at the American Research Center in Egypt played an important role in my thoughts about this book: Shaykh Ahmed at the al-Azhar Library, Anne Broadbridge, Rick Colby, Emile Homerin, Tamir Mostafa, Stuart Sears, and Abdallah Shafer. The University of Washington also supported the completion of this book with released time from my teaching and administrative responsibilities.

Last but certainly not least is the support of my family: my sons Franklin, Zachary, and Jeffry, and my wife Deborah, whose interpretive acumen is two or three times my brain capacity. I dedicate this book to the rest of my family, but especially my grandmother Roberta Wheeler, all of whom have been waiting for me to write something which could better help them understand what it is I do.

# Introduction

In his book on the Stories of the Prophets, Ibn Kathir cites a striking passage in his discussion of Abraham, attributed to the Prophet Muhammad, and given on the authority of Ibn Abbas:

> Some of the companions of the Prophet Muhammad were sitting and waiting for him. He started to come out but when he got close to them he heard them saying something. He listened to their account, and one of them said something amazing, that God had taken a "friend" [khalil] from among his creation, and Abraham was his friend. Another said: "What is more amazing than that God spoke directly to Moses?" Another said: "Jesus was the spirit and word of God." Another said: "Adam was chosen by God." So the Prophet Muhammad came out and greeted them. He said: "I heard your words and your amazement that Abraham is the friend of God; that he is. That Moses is the speech of God; that he is. That Jesus is the spirit and word of God; that he is. That Adam is chosen by God; that he is. Only, I am the beloved of God, with no glory to myself; I am the first of those who intercede, with no glory to myself; I am the first who grasps the ring of the gate of Paradise. God will open it and cause me to enter, the poor and believers with me. I am the most noble of the first and the last on the Day of Resurrection, with no glory to myself."

This passage raises a number of questions concerning the relationship of the Prophet Muhammad to earlier prophets, figures familiar from the Bible and important in Judaism and Christianity. What is the link between the Quran and the Bible? How do Muslims use biblical references and allusions in their interpretation of the Quran? Why is Islam so closely tied to the same biblical stories as are Judaism and Christianity, and in what ways does the Islamic interpretation coincide with, contribute to, and abrogate other interpretations of these stories?

This book introduces the Quran through the eyes of its Muslim interpreters. Western scholars have often underestimated the significance of Muslim exegesis for an understanding of the Quran, and its relationship to Jewish and Christian interpretations of the Bible. The Quran itself is not organized according to subject or any chronological scheme, and its different parts are said to have been revealed at different times and in different contexts over more than two decades. Nor are the relationship among the different parts of the Quran, and the place of the Quran in defining Islam, obvious from the text of the Quran alone. It is in the context of Muslim exegesis, relating the revelation of the Quran to the Prophet Muhammad and the revelations to earlier prophets, that the themes and message of the Quran are delineated.

This book presents English translations of selected Quran passages and interpretations taken from classical Arabic commentaries on the Quran. The selections are organized by prophet, and ordered according to the chronology found in Muslim interpretation and roughly parallel to the order of the stories in the Bible, from Adam to Muhammad. Many of the interpretations collected here are attributed to the Prophet Muhammad and his followers, and are preserved and repeated in later Muslim scholarship continuing until the present. While these interpretations cannot represent the entire range of different perspectives Muslims have today and have had in the past on the Quran, they do provide a core of widely acknowledged and often cited perspectives. By focusing on the stories of the prophets, this book aims to highlight both the conjunction and the disjunction between the Quran as it is interpreted by Muslims and the Bible as it is interpreted by Jews and Christians.

## Quran and Its Study

The Quran is considered by Muslims to be the words of God, revealed to the Prophet Muhammad through the medium of the angel Gabriel, collected and preserved in written and oral form. The word "Quran" is mentioned some 70 times in the text of the Quran, though different names and words are also said to be references to the Quran. The term "Quran" is said to be derived from either the Arabic root q-r-ʾ meaning "read/recite" or the Arabic root q-r-n meaning "put together/assemble." Western scholars have also pointed out that the term may be related to the Syriac term *qeryana* meaning "Scripture reading/lesson" as used in Middle Eastern Christianity. There is an early Muslim tradition in which the Quran is identified with 55 different names in the text of the Quran.

Q 56:77–80 states that the Quran is a book sent down from God which only the pure may touch. Q 20:2 and 76:23 define the Quran as revelation, and Q 27:91, 16:98, and 17:45 describe it as a collection of revelations. In Q 12:1–3 the Quran is depicted as something revealed in Arabic, and in Q 9:111 it is compared to other revealed scriptures such as the Torah and the Gospel. Q 80:13–16 describes the Quran as an honored scripture written by scribes, and in Q 98:2–3 the Prophet Muhammad is said to be one who recited pure scriptures among which are established books. Q 26:196 states that the Quran is in the books of the former prophets.

The Quran is regarded by Muslims as more than just a book. Muslim Quran scholars preserve traditions that the Quran is pre-existent, that it intercedes for those who read it on the Day of Judgment, that it heals sickness, and can absolve people from sin. Certain surahs and verses in the Quran are singled out for their attributes, such as Surah al-Imran (Q 3) which is said to witness on the Day of Judgment for those people who read it. Other surahs are said to provide the protection of angels or cause the presence of God to descend upon the reader. There are reports given on the authority of Aishah that the Prophet Muhammad would recite the last two surahs of the Quran into his hands and then rub his hands over his body to relieve sickness.

The Quran is also recited and read in a variety of contexts. Recitation of a verse from the Quran is a part of the Muslim ritual prayer, and during Ramadan the entire Quran is recited in public and in private. There are intricate rules regarding the proper recitation of the Quran, and rules for handling the Quran as a physical object. Islamic law stipulates that the Quran may not be touched by a person not purified according to the stipulations of Islamic purity law. Some Muslim scholars maintain that it is not permitted for the Quran to be sold or for it to be owned by a non-Muslim person. Likewise, there are rules regarding the use of the Quran as decoration on food or clothing, or as graffiti.

Muslim Quranic Studies, or the "Sciences of the Quran" ['Ulum al-Quran], is central to the Islamic sciences and predicated on the importance of the Quran as a source for right belief and practice. This discipline is subdivided into a number of separate fields which include the study of the revelation of the Quran, its collection and description as a text, and its interpretation. According to many Muslim scholars, the Quran was taken from the "Preserved Tablet" (Q 85:21–22) in Paradise and brought down to the earthly heavens during the "Night of Fate" (Q 97:1) during the month of Ramadan. From there, the Quran was revealed to the Prophet Muhammad in intervals, so that he could memorize it, and because different parts of the Quran were addressed to specific circumstances occurring in the life of the Prophet

Muhammad. Other books including the Torah, the Gospel, and the Psalms are also considered to have been revealed, but only the Quran was revealed in discrete parts over the span of the Prophet Muhammad's mission.

There are differences of opinion among Muslim scholars regarding when and where all the parts of the Quran were revealed, and for what reasons a particular revelation occurred. Parts of the Quran were revealed to the Prophet Muhammad when he was in Mecca, Medina, in an outlying area, and even in Jerusalem or in Paradise according to some scholars. Some surahs, such as Surah al-Anʿam (Q 6), are considered to have been revealed all at once, and other surahs are said to have been revealed with the help of thousands of angels. At other times, the Quran was revealed to the Prophet Muhammad just a few verses at a time. Certain verses are considered to have been revealed more than one time, and some revelations are reported to have been abrogated or taken back by God after their revelation.

According to Muslim Quranic Studies, the collection of the text of the Quran took place in three stages. The first stage was during the lifetime of the Prophet Muhammad when his followers would memorize the revelations orally and record them in writing. Although many Western scholars have attributed the writing of the Quran to the Prophet Muhammad, Muslim scholars maintain that he was illiterate, and that during his life the Quran was not collected into a single book. Second, after the death of the Prophet Muhammad, during the time of the first Caliph Abu Bakr, all the various preserved pieces of the revelation were collected and put into writing. Zayd b. Thabit, a Companion of the Prophet Muhammad, is credited with this collection, verifying that there were two witnesses for every verse included in the collection of revelations. Third, during the time of the third Caliph Uthman b. Affan, the collected revelations were organized into a codex [mashaf], which was copied and sent to a number of cities as the official text of the Quran.

The text of the Quran is organized by surahs and verses. There are 114 surahs, each consisting of a number of verses. It is said that the order of the verses within the surahs was set by divine inspiration at the time of the Prophet Muhammad, but during Uthman's time the order of the surahs in the Quran was set. With the exception of the first surah, which is one of the shortest, the surahs in the Quran are arranged roughly longest to shortest. Muslims also divide the Quran differently according to its memorization and recitation, and there are some minor differences concerning the numbering of some verses, but the order of the surahs and the verses within them is fixed. Muslim scholars also recognize different "readings" of the Quran and variant codices, some of which are extant and still in use today.

## Interpretation of the Quran

The Quran was revealed to the Prophet Muhammad, though the text of the revelation is often addressed to the Prophet Muhammad's followers, his opponents, or a situation outside of his immediate purview. Many verses include God's command to the Prophet Muhammad to "Say" something to a particular group of people, and at times God seems to address directly people beside the Prophet Muhammad. Usually God refers to himself as "We" but also as "He" and "I" at certain times. According to Muslim scholars, the understanding of these references and the larger meaning of the verses is best obtained by understanding the contexts in which particular verses were revealed, and by identifying the situation and to whom a particular verse applies.

Muslim interpretation of the Quran relies first on the Prophet Muhammad himself for understanding the context and meaning of the revelations. This information is usually transmitted in the form of a report [hadith] from one or more of the Prophet Muhammad's followers who was present when the Prophet Muhammad said or did something. These hadith reports are then transmitted from the followers of the Prophet Muhammad (called "Companions") to their followers (called "Followers"), and so on for several generations of transmitters. Sometimes the hadith reports include a direct quotation from the Prophet Muhammad, but often the report only goes back to something said by one of the Companions or one of the Followers. Muslim scholars generally prefer a hadith report from the Prophet Muhammad over one from a Companion, and the report of a Companion over that of a Follower, but there are a number of other considerations which go into the critical study of hadith.

In addition to the hadith reports which indicate the circumstances of a revelation, there are also hadith reports transmitted from the Prophet Muhammad and his Companions that provide information on the stories in the Quran. For example, additional information about the life of Moses, not necessarily related to the time and place of the revelation of certain verses, might be given in a hadith report. Information which comes from the Prophet Muhammad, such as to whom a particular verse is revealed or the details of a particular Quranic story, is considered to originate with the Prophet Muhammad and be divinely inspired. Reports which go back only to a Companion or Follower can be considered to have originated with the Prophet Muhammad (though without a direct quotation), or they can be considered to have originated from another source such as pre-Islamic Arab culture, the Bible, or Jewish and Christian stories. Many of the Companions who are well known for their transmission of hadith reports about the Quran are said to have been converts from Judaism or Christianity and knowledgeable about the Bible and its interpretation.

Later generations of Muslims began to collect these hadith reports and organize them according to different subjects, including those that pertained to particular verses in the Quran. Some of the earliest written Quran interpretations come from the generation of the Followers, from figures such as Mujahid (d. c. 100 AH) whose commentary is not extant but cited by later interpreters. Muqatil b. Sulayman (80–150), of the next generation, wrote a Quran commentary based on first-hand information from twelve of the Followers among whom were prominent transmitters such as Ata b. Abi Rabah, Dahhak, Zuhri, Ibn Sirin, and Ikrimah. Sufyan al-Thawri (94–161) who also transmitted hadith reports from prominent Followers, is credited with writing a commentary on the Quran, cited in later Quran commentaries.

By the middle of the third Islamic century, scholars had assembled special collections of hadith reports going back to the Prophet Muhammad. Some of these collections, including that of Bukhari (d. 256), Muslim (d. 261), Ibn Majah (d. 273), and Tirmidhi (d. 279) became recognized as authoritative collections of prophetic hadith. Other collections of hadith, such as that of Abd al-Razzaq (d. 211) and Ahmad b. Hanbal (d. 241), are also regarded by later generations as authoritative works. Much of the first two and a half centuries of Quran interpretation is preserved in the monumental Quran commentary of Muhammad b. Jarir al-Tabari (224 or 225–310). Tabari's commentary is well known for its preservation of numerous hadith reports, not all of which are accepted by other scholars, which often provide various interpretations of the same verses. In part, this preservation of differing and even conflicting interpretations is due to the transmitted nature of the hadith reports. Tabari often provides his own opinion of which interpretations he favors, but like later scholars, he is hesitant to delete any hadith report which might preserve an earlier tradition given on the authority of the Prophet Muhammad or his Companions.

Later Quran commentaries rely heavily on the hadith reports collected in the third century and the foundation of Quran interpretation built by Tabari, including some of the best-known commentaries such as that of Qummi (d. 328), Tabarani (260–360), Abu al-Layth al-Samarqandi (d. 373 or 375), Tusi (385–413), Zamakhshari (467–538), Tabarsi (d. 548), Fakhr al-Din al-Razi (543–606), Qurtubi (d. 671), Ibn

Kathir (700–774), Suyuti (849–911), Kashani (d. 996), and Tabataba'i (1321–1403). In addition to preserving the hadith reports cited in earlier works, these later commentaries also cite the opinions of earlier scholars like Tabari. Many interpreters also give their own opinions derived from their reading of the Quran, a synthesis of hadith reports, or from other non-Quranic sources such as Jewish and Christian interpretation of the Bible. There is a certain coherence to these commentaries, such that they constitute a single tradition of "classical" Quran commentary, each building upon and preserving the scholarship of earlier generations, all linked back to the hadith reports from the Prophet Muhammad and his Companions.

## Stories of the Prophets

Quran commentaries were normally compiled and written according to the order of the surahs and verses in the text of the Quran. Although most of the major commentaries covered different aspects of the Quran in a general fashion, more specialized works began to appear, focusing on particular facets of the text such as language and orthography, specifying when and where verses were revealed, legal implications of verses, and the stories of the prophets. These more specialized works were also organized according to the order of the Quran, except for works on the stories of the prophets which were organized by prophet, in rough chronological order.

Some of the best-known works on the stories of the prophets were produced by scholars who had also written Quran commentaries. Both Tha'labi (d. 427) and Ibn Kathir wrote books on the stories of the prophets which are closely related to their larger Quran commentaries. Muslim historians, such as Tabari, Yaqubi (d. 284), and Ibn al-Athir (555–630) also wrote about the stories of the prophets in their world histories, which begin with Creation and the account of Adam and Eve. The first section of the biography of the Prophet Muhammad by Ibn Ishaq (85–150), not extant but cited extensively by later scholars, was one of the earliest written works focusing on the stories of the prophets, detailing their lives as a prelude to the life of the Prophet Muhammad.

The prophet-by-prophet and chronological structure of the stories contributed to a more accessible and less piecemeal interpretation of the Quran, and thus the genre of stories of the prophets has been more closely associated with sermons and popular Quran interpretation. It is likely that some of the earliest Quran interpretations, like those attributed to Wahb b. Munabbih, Ka'b al-Ahbar, and Ibn Abbas, originated as sermons or stories of the prophets rather than strictly comments on

particular verses of the Quran. Later works devoted to the stories of
the prophets, especially in Persian, were richly illustrated, picturing the
prophets in certain well-known scenes from the popular stories. In
the Muslim world today, one of the most popular formats for presenta-
tion of the Quran to children is through books and videos on the stories
of the prophets.

Within the Quran, different terms are used to refer to prophets.
Most common is *rasul* and its plural, which occur more than 200 times
and mean someone who "is sent" or a "messenger." Less common but
frequent is the term *nabi*, cognate with the Hebrew biblical term, which
means someone who "brings news" and occurs about 50 times in the
text of the Quran. With reference to Jesus the term *masih* is found eleven
times in the Quran, meaning the "messiah" or "Christ." Some Muslim
exegetes differentiate between a *rasul* as one who is supposed to bring
a revealed book and a *nabi* as a more generic prophet, but these
distinctions are not always consistent with the terminology used in the
Quran for different prophets.

The Quran itself (Q 2:136, 3:84, 4:136, 42:13) and later Muslim
creeds stipulate belief in all the prophets and the books revealed to
them without making distinctions among them. Ibn Sa'd (d. 230) reports
that the number of *rasul* including the Prophet Muhammad is 315, and
the total number of prophets is 1000. Other Muslim sources list the total
number of prophets as 224,000. The Quran mentions books revealed to
Abraham, and specifies the Torah, Gospel, Psalms of David, and Quran
as revealed books. A hadith report given on the authority of Abu Dharr
states that books were revealed to Adam, Seth, Idris, and Abraham in
addition to the revelation of the Torah, Gospel, Psalms and Quran.
Belief in the intercession of the prophets and their infallibility is also
mentioned in some Muslim creeds. Although not recognized by all
Muslims, many Muslims still go on pilgrimage today to the tombs of
certain prophets such as those of Hud in the Hadramawt and Shuayb
in Yemen.

The stories of the prophets constitute a significant portion of the
Quran, but the Quran does not tell the stories of the large numbers of
prophets claimed by some Muslim scholars. There are 25 prophets
mentioned by name in the Quran, though there are some disagreements
concerning the individual identities of all these. Among those men-
tioned by name are: Adam (mentioned 25 times by name), Idris (1),
Noah (43), Hud (7), Salih (10), Abraham (69), Ishmael (12), Isaac (17),
Jacob (16), Lot (27), Joseph (27), Shuayb (11), Job (4), Dhu al-Kifl (2),
Moses (137), Aaron (20), David (16), Solomon (17), Elijah (1), Elisha (2),
Jonah (4), Zechariah (7), John (5), Jesus (25), Muhammad (4). Other

Quran passages refer to prophets without mentioning names, but Muslim exegetes identify these prophets by name such as Khidr, Ezekiel, Samuel, Jeremiah, and Daniel. In the case of a few prophets, such as the one sent to the People of the Well (Q 25:38, 50:12), the prophets are not identified by name in the Quran, and the names given to the prophets are not well known outside of Muslim exegesis. There are also important characters mentioned by name in the Quran, such as Luqman and Dhu al-Qarnayn, who are not considered prophets but whose stories are nevertheless included in the stories of the prophets.

Most of the prophets in the Quran, mentioned by name or identified by Muslim exegetes, parallel characters from the Bible and its interpretation in Jewish and Christian traditions. Western scholars have proposed a number of explanations for these parallels, not all of which are mutually exclusive. One approach is to see the parallels as influences, to see the Quran and Muslim exegesis as derived or borrowed from the Bible and earlier Jewish and Christian biblical interpretation. This same explanation can also be used to account for later Jewish and Christian traditions which seem to be influenced by the Quran and Muslim exegesis. Another approach is to view parallels as originating from a common source. This works well for folklorists who see certain stories beginning as oral traditions predating both the Quran and the Bible, and it works well for Muslim scholars who claim that both the Quran and the Bible originate as divine revelation. A third approach is to eschew the question of origins and influence, and to instead regard all the different "versions" of a given story to be part of a larger composite "myth" which transcends any particular "telling" of it. This last approach allows for the comparison of different accounts, not to determine which is original or more correct, but rather to see how differences reflect the ideological and religious perspectives of those circulating the accounts.

Many of the stories of the prophets, as they appear in the text of the Quran, presume a certain familiarity with pre-Islamic traditions, especially the Bible as understood through Jewish and Christian interpretations. It is not unexpected that such a text would be cast in terms familiar to its intended audience, nor is this surprising to Muslim scholars who regard the revelation of the Quran as confirming the prophetic message of earlier revealed scriptures. The Quran and its interpretation are closely related not only to accepted Jewish and Christian traditions, but also to apocryphal and pseudepigraphical texts, and sometimes to otherwise not extant oral or written traditions. The origins of Islam and Muslim interpretation of the Quran are to be found in the context of and in continuity with the culture of the late antique

and ancient Mediterranean, including the rich traditions of Mesopotamia, Iran, and the Arabian Peninsula. In this sense, the Quran and its
exegesis provide a virtual encyclopedia of ancient and late antique
traditions, especially those related to the Bible.

It is important to recognize that Muslim exegetes themselves
acknowledge the relevance of the Quran and their interpretation of it to
Jewish and Christian interpretations of the Bible. Although some later
Muslim scholars discouraged reliance upon what are called *Israiliyyat*
or stories relating to the Israelites, much of the earliest Quran interpretation consists of such traditions. These Israiliyat traditions are sometimes related on the authority of the Prophet Muhammad, supplied by
Jewish and Christian converts to Islam, or compiled from what are seen
to be Jewish and Christian sources. Frequently, Muslim references to
the Bible and its interpretation originate as Muslim re-readings or
critiques of Jewish and Christian views. According to Muslim exegetes,
many passages in the Quran contain allusions and references which are
expected to be understood by those familiar with Jewish and Christian
traditions. Some Quran passages directly address Jews and Christians,
and challenge their interpretation of the Bible. It is through the exegesis
of these passages in particular that Muslims define their own identity
both in relation to a shared "biblical" past and in contradistinction to
exclusive Jewish and Christian claims to that past.

## Notes on Contents

This book is divided into 31 chapters, most of which are devoted to a
single prophet, though some include more than one prophet, and the
material on Moses is divided into three chapters. All chapters consist of
selections from the Quran and from Muslim exegesis, with the exception
of the chapter on Daniel, which has no Quran selection. The sequence
of the chapters corresponds to the order of the prophets as presented in
several of the major Quran commentaries and Stories of the Prophets
texts, although the exegesis included indicates that there is disagreement concerning this sequence.

Translations of the Quran are made from the Arabic text known as
the Hafs 'an Asim version, which was printed as the Egyptian standard
edition in 1924. Surah and verse divisions also follow the Egyptian
standard edition, as does the identification of surahs by number according to their order in that edition. Readers should be aware that there
are several different schemes used, not always consistently, for numbering verses in other published translations of the Quran.

The selection of Quran verses associated with each prophet is drawn from classical Muslim sources, though sometimes Muslim scholars disagree concerning the prophet or prophets to which certain verses refer. In most cases, these disagreements are represented in the exegesis included. Selections from different surahs are usually arranged according to their order in the Quran text, from lower to higher numbered surahs. In some cases Quran passages are arranged to reflect the narrative order of the story, and in some of the chapters passages are divided among the subdivisions of the story. These subdivisions and their headings are my own but often reflect those found in exegetical works.

There are many published English translations of the Quran, and the one provided here attempts to be literal and in plain English without losing the idiomatic sense of the language. Key Arabic terms are translated consistently with the same English words, and throughout names have been translated as the standard English equivalent usually familiar from biblical contexts. Sometimes a transliteration of the Arabic name is provided in square brackets when the Arabic is sufficiently different from the standard English equivalent. Some names in the genealogies of prophets have been left as transliterated Arabic when it is unclear what the biblical equivalent might be, or what is intended. Additional English words supplied to the translations of the Quran passages appear in square brackets. Occasionally, an Arabic term is provided in square brackets because of its wider resonance. For the same reason, and because of the uncertainty of its more precise semantic range, the term *hanif* is left untranslated throughout. The Arabic "Allah" is taken to be the Arabic *al-ilah* or "the God," and is translated throughout as "God." Punctuation is drawn from the syntax, the sense given to the text by the exegetes, and the text as recited.

Translations of the Quran exegesis are made from classical Arabic texts, all of which are listed in the "Works Consulted" section of the bibliography. Given the constraints of publication, it has been necessary to be selective, but this selection is intended to provide a representative and relatively broad sample of the Quran interpretation found in classical Arabic sources. The main sources consulted include Quran commentaries, histories, and collections of stories of the prophets, but there are occasional references to genealogical, geographical, and lexicographical works. These represent both Sunni and Shi'i scholarship, and some Mu'tazili works. The earliest references date to the time of the Prophet Muhammad, and the most recent Quran commentary consulted is that of the Shi'i scholar Tabataba'i who died in 1982 CE.

A glossary of interpreters and transmitters at the end of the book provides an overview of the sources for the exegesis found in the chapters. The glossary includes the names of those interpreters and transmitters who are cited by name as the source for particular exegetical comments. Most of the information is taken from the classical Arabic Islamic scholarship devoted to the details of the lives of the transmitters of hadith reports and other scholars of the Islamic sciences. Serious scholars of hadith criticism and Quran interpretation will need to consult the original sources in order to determine the exact chains of transmission and for more specific information about the particular transmitters of hadith reports in the glossary.

Throughout, diacritical marks have been omitted except for the ʿayn [ʿ] and hamzah [ʾ] where considered necessary. Likewise, the definite article al- has also been omitted from certain names. Readers familiar with Arabic should still be able to recognize and identify the original spelling. The ʿayns and hamzahs are indicated in the full name of the interpreters and transmitters in the Glossary. "Ibn" or "b." and "Bint" or "bt." refer respectively to the expressions "son of" and "daughter of"; this is a convention often used in names and genealogical information. All dates, except those in the "Suggestions for Further Reading" which are according to the Common Era (CE), are given according to the Muslim dating system commonly referred to as "Hijri" or *anno hegirae*, "in the year of the Hijrah" (AH). This is logical given that this book aims to introduce readers to Muslim interpretations of the Quran, and should help to underline the Muslim view of the Quran and its interpretation as originating with the Prophet Muhammad's prophetic mission. In addition, the dates for interpreters and transmitters provided by Muslim sources are given according to the Muslim dating system based on a lunar calendar and cannot always be translated accurately to Common Era dates.

An effort has been made to provide a broad range of interpretations for the various Quran passages cited, but also to present interpretations which are generally accepted by Muslim scholars. Of course, not all of the interpretations given are accepted by or known to all Muslim scholars, but all are taken from sources generally well recognized and respected. Certain interpretations are included to demonstrate not only the diversity of opinion in Muslim Quran commentary but also the remarkable extent to which such diversity is repeated and preserved by tradition and scholarship. Comments of text criticism, grammar, and other technical matters have not been reproduced, nor have most of the chains of transmission beyond the earlier transmitter. The translation of the exegetical comments is paraphrased at times, though care has been taken to produce accurate translation of quotations attributed to the Prophet Muhammad.

Readers may note that Muslim Quran interpretation is not always consistent in its interpretation of passages, the details of accounts, or the chronology of the prophets and their stories. This may be due to the interpreters' dependence on various sources of information, to the different settings in which interpretations were generated, and to the need to preserve a diversity of traditions. Later Quran commentaries, such as those of Ibn Kathir and Suyuti, regularly cite numerous divergent interpretations, often without comment as to one being more authoritative or correct than another. Muslim Quran interpreters generally do not view this diversity as indicating an insufficient explanation of the Quran or a lack of reliability among Quran interpreters, but rather as something which expands and enriches the possible understandings and applications of the revealed text.

It is important to acknowledge that the materials collected in this book do not constitute a study of Muslim Quran interpretation or a critical study of the Quran. Nor does this book present a comprehensive overview of the contents of the Quran. Such studies are available and necessary, but here the intention is to introduce readers to the Quran through a selection of the stories of the prophets, as these stories and related passages were (and continue to be) understood by Muslims. For this reason, readers are encouraged to look for general themes in the Quran passages and their interpretation. Are there patterns and phrases, found in the language of the Quran, which are repeated in several different stories and highlighted by Muslim interpretation? What can the recognition of such patterns disclose about the relationship of the Quran to the tradition of its interpretation? How is the Quran to be understood as a text revealed in a certain time and place but authoritative for all times and places?

Following the chapters is a bibliography which provides, among other things, references to primary Jewish and Christian sources which readers may compare with the Quran and its interpretation. These sources are not intended to be seen only or even primarily in terms of "influences" but rather can highlight some of the parallels between Muslim interpretation of the Quran and Jewish and Christian interpretation of the Bible. What these parallels indicate about the origins of certain motifs and narratives is beyond the scope of this book. Readers are encouraged, however, to consider how Muslim exegetes interpret these parallels. Are there particular motifs and details found in non-Quranic sources which Muslim interpreters appropriate to their interpretation of the Quran, and to what result? How do Muslim interpretations of the Quran re-read and critique Jewish and Christian interpretations of the Bible? What can the Muslim stories of the prophets, and the ways in which they agree with and are distinguished from Jewish and Christian stories, indicate about how the shared past of "biblical tradition" is integral to a definition of Islam?

On a broader level, it is hoped that knowledge of the Muslim interpretation of the Quran and the recognition of its close relationship with Jewish and Christian interpretation of the Bible will inspire readers to consider the relevance of Quran interpretation to Judaism and Christianity. Again, this is not primarily a question of Muslim influences on Jewish and Christian traditions, but rather an opportunity to ask how the Bible and its interpretation defines Christianity and Judaism, and how this is challenged by a Muslim appropriation of both the Bible and its interpretation for Islam's own self-definition. The nature of the Quran and its centrality in Islam do not require the exclusion of Jewish and Christian interpretation of the Bible. Do the Bible and its place in Judaism and Christianity necessitate an exclusion of the Quran and its interpretation?

# Adam and Eve

**Q 2:30** When your Lord said to the angels: "I am placing a vicegerent [khalifah] on the Earth." They said: "Will you place on [the earth] one who will spread corruption in it and shed blood, while we glorify your praise and sanctify you?" He said: "I know what you do not know." **31** He taught Adam all the names, then he presented them before the angels and said: "Tell me the names of these if you are right." **32** They said: "Glory to you, we have no knowledge except that which you taught us. You are the Knowing, the Wise." **33** He said: "Adam, tell them the names of these." When he had informed them of the names of these, he said: "Did I not say to you that I know what is hidden of the heavens and the earth? I know what you reveal and what you conceal."

## Iblis and Jinn

*Tabari:* In the days of the rule of Iblis, God created Adam, our father, the father of humanity. The reason for this is that the other angels did not know about Iblis being arrogant, so God wanted to expose this matter to them, to show them what had gone wrong with Iblis and why his authority and kingship came to an end. God said to the angels: "I am placing a vicegerent on the earth." They replied: "Will you place on it one who will cause corruption in it and shed blood?" (2:30). The angels said this because they had taken notice of what the Jinn had done who had lived on the earth previously. The angels said that they would praise God and exalt his name but God said: "I know what you do not know," meaning that he knew about Iblis' being arrogant and that Iblis intended to oppose his command, therefore God wanted the angels to see this.

*Tabari:* Iblis is the first to be given royal authority over the earthly heavens and the earth though he denied the divine authority of God, was arrogant, and therefore did not acknowledge the favor of God in giving him this office. God created Iblis beautiful and made him the keeper of Paradise, but he made himself out to be more important than his Lord and claimed lordship for himself. He called on the denizens of the earth and the skies to worship him. Therefore God transformed him into "stoned Satan" (3:36 and 19:98). He was driven out of the heavens and given the fire of Hell as a place of residence.

*Ibn Abbas:* Iblis was a keeper of Paradise and had authority to rule over the earthly heavens and the earth. There was an angelic tribe of Jinn, to which Iblis belonged, which governed everything between the heavens and the earth.

*Ibn Abbas:* Iblis belonged to a group of angels created from the fire of the Samum. His name was originally al-Harith. All of the angels in this group were created "from a blazing tongue of fire" (55:15). God created Adam from clay. The first to live on the earth were the Jinn, who caused corruption and shed blood, killing one another. God sent Iblis to them with an army of angels and there was a battle. Iblis banished the Jinn to the islands in the oceans and the edges of the mountains. After Iblis did this, he thought highly of himself and said: "I have done something which no one before has done." God knew that this was in the heart of Iblis but the angels who were with him did not know this.

*Rabi'a b. Anas:* God created the angels on Wednesday, the Jinn on Thursday and Adam on Friday. Some Jinn disbelieved and the angels went down to them on earth to fight them and this is how bloodshed came to be on the earth.

*Tabari:* Others say that Iblis was one of the Jinn on earth against whom the angels fought, but he was young. After he was taken to heaven he used to worship God with the angels, but when God commanded them to prostrate themselves before Adam, he refused. Another says that Iblis was sent by God to judge among the Jinn on the earth. He did so truthfully for 1000 years and was eventually called the "Arbiter" by God. Because of this, Iblis considered himself great and became arrogant, and among those to whom God had sent him as an arbiter, Iblis caused affliction, enmity and hate. Because of Iblis' instigation, these creatures fought among themselves on earth for 2000 years, causing so much bloodshed that their horses waded in their blood. This is what is meant by the statement of the angels: "Will you place on earth one who will spread corruption in it and shed blood?" (2:30). So God sent a fire to the earth that consumed the creatures there, but when Iblis saw this punishment he ascended to the heavens and worshipped with the angels until the time of the creation of Adam.

*Ibn Abbas:* Iblis used to be called ʿAzazil and was one of the most zealous and knowledgeable of the angels. This led him to pride. God created some creatures and said: "Prostrate yourselves before Adam" (2:34). They refused, so God sent a fire to consume them. Then God created other creatures and said: "I am creating a human being from clay (38:71), so prostrate yourselves before it," but they refused, so God sent a fire to consume them. Then he created this last group and said: "Will you prostrate yourselves before Adam?" They consented but Iblis belonged to those who refused to prostrate themselves.

*Ibn Kathir:* When God said he was placing a vicegerent on the earth he meant his intention to create Adam and his descendants who would follow one after another just as he says: "He is the one who makes you to be vicegerents [khala'if] on the earth" (6:165) and: "He makes you vicegerents [khulafa] of the earth" (27:62). When the angels protested it was not on account of Adam and his descendants but because previously there had been the Jinn and the Hinn on the earth.

## Creation of Adam

*Suyuti:* Adam is the father of humanity. Some mention that his name is a superlative derived from the word for skin [adim]. al-Jawaliqi says the names of all the prophets are non-Arabic except four: Adam, Salih, Shuayb, and Muhammad. Ibn Abbas says that he was named Adam because God created him from the skin [adim] of the earth. Some say that the name is originally Syriac and that it was later Arabicized. Tha'labi says "Earth" in Hebrew is *adam*, so he was named Adam. Ibn Abi Khaythamah says he lived 960 years. Nawawi says: It is well known in books of history that Adam lived 1000 years.

*Ibn Masud:* God sent Gabriel to the earth to get the clay to make Adam but the earth refused to give up the clay, so God sent Michael but again the earth refused. Finally the Angel of Death was sent and the earth refused but the Angel of Death scraped from the surface of the earth and made a mixture, taking some red, white, and black soil. Moisture was added so that the soil became sticky, then it was left until it became stinking.

*Ali b. Abi Talib:* The skin of the earth had both good and bad in it, which accounts for why some people are good and some are bad.

*Prophet Muhammad:* God created Adam from a handful of dirt which was taken from the entire earth, thus the children of Adam correspond to the earth in being red, black, white, and other colors, plain, rugged, pleasant or ugly.

*Tabari:* Adam's body was left lying around for 40 nights or 40 years. During this time Iblis used to come to it and kick it with his foot, and it would make sounds. This is what is meant by the verse "from *salsal* like potter's clay" (21:29). Iblis entered Adam's mouth then out his anus, then in the anus and out the mouth. Iblis said: "You are not an instrument for making sounds, so why were you created? If I am given authority over you, I will ruin you and if you are given authority over me, I shall destroy you."

*Tabari:* God created Adam with his own hands so that God could say to Iblis that he was exalting himself over that which God formed with his own hands. So God created Adam as a human and his body was from clay. The angels used to pass by him and kick him because they were frightened, the most frightened being Iblis. When Iblis would kick it, the body would make a sound as a potter's clay does. Iblis told the other angels not to be afraid because whereas God is solid, Adam is hollow.

*Tabari:* God breathed his spirit into Adam and it entered his head first, whereupon Adam sneezed. The angels said: "Say: Praise be to God, the Lord of the Worlds" (1:1), so Adam did. Then when God's spirit entered his eyes he saw the fruits of Paradise and when it entered his stomach he was hungry, so before the spirit reached his feet he tried to get up in haste to have the fruits of Paradise. This is the meaning of God's word: "Man was created of haste" (21:37). It is also said that Adam's body became flesh and blood as God's spirit moved through it, and when the spirit reached Adam's navel he looked at his body and was pleased and tried to get up but could not yet.

## Adam Taught Names

*Tabari:* There is disagreement about what the verse means by "names." Some say that Adam was taught the name of everything. Others say he was taught some specific names like the names of the angels or the names of his offspring. God taught Adam the names of essences, their actions, and their attributes. God taught Adam the names because when Adam was created the angels said among themselves that God can create whatever he wants, but whatever it is, the angels are more knowledgeable and more honored by God than anything else God creates. Therefore, God taught the angels a lesson this way. The angels, the heavens and the earth were tested by the creation of Adam as it says in Q 41:11: "Come willingly or unwillingly. They said: 'We come willingly.'"

*Ibn Abbas:* These are the names by which people know these things such as: human being, riding animal, earth, sea, mountain, mule, etc.

*Bukhari:* The Prophet Muhammad said: "God gathers all of the believers on the Day of Resurrection and they say: 'If only he would mediate for us to our Lord so that we could rest in this place of ours,' so they came to Adam and said: 'You are the father of humanity, God created you with his hands, he caused his angels to prostrate themselves to you, and taught you the names of all things.'"

*Ibn Kathir:* Moses said to Adam when they met in heaven: "You are Adam, father of humanity. God created you with his hands and breathed his spirit in you, caused his angels to prostrate themselves to you, and taught you the names of every thing." Likewise the people who are gathered on the Day of Resurrection will say this to him.

## Eve Created

*Ibn Abbas, Ibn Masud and others:* After Iblis was driven out of Paradise, Adam dwelled in Paradise and he used to walk around in it all by himself, without a spouse to live with him [7:189 and 30:21]. He fell asleep once and when he woke up there was a woman sitting at his head whom God had created from his rib. He asked her: "Who are you?" She said: "Woman." He said: "Why were you created?" She said: "For you to live with me." The angels were watching to see the extent of Adam's knowledge and asked him: "What is her name?" He said: "Eve" [Hawwa]. They said: "Why do you call her Eve?" He said: "Because she was created from something living" [hayya].

*Ibn Ishaq:* God made Adam sleep, as it is related by the People of the Book, on the authority of Ibn Abbas. God took a rib from one of the ribs on Adam's left side and put flesh in its place. Adam was asleep and did not wake up. God created his spouse Eve from his rib and fashioned her to be a woman so that Adam could live with her. When Adam awoke from his sleep he saw her at his side and said: "My flesh and my blood, and my spouse." He lived with her. When God gave him a spouse and made him a partner from himself, God said to him, face to face: "Adam, dwell, you and your spouse in Paradise. Eat what you want from its bounty but do not approach this tree or you will be among those who do wrong" (2:35).

## Fall of Iblis

**Q 7:11**   We created you, then shaped you, then we said to the angels: "Prostrate yourselves to Adam." They prostrated themselves, except for Iblis who was not one of those who prostrated themselves. **12** He said: "What prevented you from prostrating yourself when I commanded you?" He said: "I am better than he. You created me from fire and created him from clay." **13** He said: "Fall from here! You are not allowed to be arrogant here. Leave! for you are one of the small ones." **14** He said: "Grant me respite until the day they are called." **15** He said: "You are one of those who have respite." **16** He said: "Because you have thrown me out, I will certainly wait for them on your straight path. **17** "Then I will come to them from before them, behind them, from their right and their left. You will not find many of them to be thankful." **18** He said: "Leave from here! despised and expelled. I will fill Hell with all of those who follow you."

**Q 15:26**   We created the human from dried clay, from stinking slime. **27** The Jinn we created before, from the fire of the Samum wind. **28** When your Lord said to the angels: "I am creating a human from dried clay, from stinking slime. **29** "When I have fashioned him I breathed my spirit into him. Prostrate yourselves to him!" **30** So all of the angels together prostrated themselves **31** except for Iblis who refused to be with those who prostrated themselves. **32** He said: "Iblis, why are you not with those who prostrate themselves?" **33** He said: "I am not one to prostrate to a human being whom you created out of dried clay, from stinking slime." **34** He said: "Leave from here! You are stoned. **35** "The curse is upon you until the Day of Judgment." **36** He said: "My Lord, give me respite until the day they are called." **37** He said: "You are one of those who have respite **38** until the Day of the Appointed Time." **39** He said: "My Lord, because you wronged me, I will make it seem good for them on the earth and I will put all of them in the wrong **40** except your pure servants from among them." **41** He said: "This is a straight path for me. **42** "Over my servants you have no authority except those who follow you and those who do wrong. **43** "Hell is the promise for all of them. **44** "It has seven gates, and to each gate is a section assigned."

**Q 17:61**   When we said to the angels: "Prostrate yourselves to Adam!" and they prostrated themselves except for Iblis. He said: "Should I prostrate myself to one you created from clay?" **62** He said: "Do you see? This is the one you honor over me. If you discharge me until the Day of Resurrection then I will make worldly all but a few of his descendants." **63** He said: "Go! For those among them who follow you, Hell is your abundant reward. **64** "With your voice, arouse those who you can, assault them with your horsemen and foot soldiers. Share with them in possessions and offspring. Make promises to them." Satan promises them nothing but deception. **65** "You have no authority over my servants." Your Lord is sufficient as guardian.

**Q 18:50**   When we said to the angels: "Prostrate yourselves to Adam!" and they prostrated themselves except for Iblis who was one of the Jinn. He strayed from the command of his Lord. Will you take him and his descendants as protectors instead of me? They are enemies to you. Evil is the substitute for the those who do wrong. **51** I did not cause them to witness the creation of the heavens and the earth, nor their own creation. I do not take those who lead astray as faculties.

**Q 38:67**   Say: It is a great tiding **68** from which you turn away. **69** I have no knowledge of the high leaders when they discuss among themselves. **70** It is revealed to me only that I am a clear warning. **71** When your Lord said to the angels: "I am creating a human from clay. **72** "When I have fashioned him and breathed my spirit into him, fall down and prostrate yourselves to him!" **73** So all of the angels prostrated themselves, all together **74** except for Iblis who was arrogant. He was one of the unbelievers. **75** He said: "Iblis, what prevents you from prostrating yourself before that which I created with my hands? Are you arrogant or one of those on high? **76** He said: "I am better than he. You created me from fire and created him from clay." **77** He said: "Leave from here! You are stoned. **78** "My curse is upon you until the Day of Judgment." **79** He said: "My Lord, give me respite until the day they are called." **80** He said: "You are one of those who have respite **81** until the Day of the Appointed Time." **82** He said: "Then by your might I will certainly wrong them, all together **83** except your pure servants among them." **84** He said: "The truth, I say the truth. **85** "I will certainly fill Hell with you and with those who follow you, all together." **86** Say: I do not ask you for a recompense for it. I am not a pretender. **87** It is nothing but a reminder to the worlds. **88** You will certainly learn its message after a while.

*Tabari:* Iblis refused to prostrate himself before Adam as God commanded for he was being arrogant, one of the unbelievers, and then God said: "What prevents you from prostrating yourself before that which I created with my own hands?" (38:75). Iblis said: "I am better than he and I do not prostrate myself before a human being you have created from clay." Iblis said: "You created me from fire and you created him from clay." So God said: "Fall down from Paradise! It is not yours in which to be arrogant. Leave! you are one of the humble beings." God made Iblis a stoned satan.

*Umar b. Abd al-Aziz:* When the angels were ordered to prostrate, the first of them to prostrate was Israfil, so God gave to him the privilege that he would write the Quran on his forehead.

*Hasan al-Basri:* Iblis was the first to use analogical reasoning.

*Ibn Sirin:* The first to use analogical reasoning was Iblis. The sun was not worshipped nor was the moon except through analogical reasoning.

*Ibn Kathir:* The meaning of these verses is that Iblis makes a comparison between himself and Adam, sees that he is better than Adam, and that prevents him from prostrating before him despite the necessity of doing God's command and the fact that the rest of the angels were doing it. As for clay, it is of more benefit than fire because clay is staid, controlled, and deliberate whereas fire is inconstant, fickle, quick, and burns up.

*Ibn Kathir:* There is disagreement over which angels were ordered to prostrate themselves before Adam. According to most of the exegetes, it means the angels in general. But there is a report, given in Tabari on the authority of Dahhak, on the authority of Ibn Abbas, that it refers only to the "angels of the earth."

*Ibn Kathir:* The word of God concerning Iblis: "Fall from here" and "Leave here" indicates that he was in the heavens and was commanded to fall from there and to leave from the place and position which was for the worship of God alone, where the angels dwelled in obedience and worship of God.

## Test of Adam and Eve

**Q 2:34** When we said to the angels: "Prostrate yourselves to Adam," they prostrated themselves, except for Iblis who refused and was arrogant. He was one of the unbelievers. **35** We said: "Adam, you and your spouse dwell in Paradise. Eat what you want from its bounty but do not approach this tree or you will be among those who do wrong." **36** Satan caused them to fall from there and caused them to leave the state in which they had been. We said: "Fall! some of you are enemies to the others. For you, on the earth, is a place to settle and a comfort for a while." **37** Adam received words from his Lord. He forgave him for He is Relenting, Compassionate. **38** We said: "Fall from here, together! As for guidance that comes to you from me, whoever follows my guidance will have no fear nor will they grieve. **39** "Those who disbelieve and lie about our signs, they are the people of the Fire. They are in it forever."

**Q 20:115** We made a covenant with Adam before but he forgot and we did not find resolve on his part. **116** When we said to the angels: "Prostrate yourselves to Adam!" and they prostrated themselves except for Iblis who refused. **117** Then we said: "Adam, this one is an enemy to you and your wife. Do not allow him to make you both leave Paradise and be miserable. **118** "For you in it [Paradise] is such that you will not hunger or be naked. **119** "In it you will not thirst nor be under the sun." **120** Satan whispered to him and said: "Adam, shall I lead you to the Tree of Immortality, and to a kingdom that does not decline?" **121** So they both ate from the tree and their private parts appeared to them. They began to sew the leaves of Paradise around them. Adam disobeyed his Lord and did wrong. **122** Then his Lord chose him, forgave him and guided him. **123** He said: "Fall from here both of you, together!" Some of you [plural] are an enemy to others. As for the guidance which comes to you from me, whoever follows my guidance will not be misled nor be miserable. **124** Whoever rejects what I mentioned, for him is a confined life. We will gather him blind on the Day of Resurrection, **125** him saying: "My Lord, why did you gather me blind when I used to have sight?" **126** He said: "Just as our signs came to you and you forgot them, so you will be forgotten on this Day."

*Tabari:* This is the story of how Adam, to whom God had given the high rank of honor above the angels and to whom he allowed the enjoyment of Paradise, lost his place and was given the miserable life of the inhabitants of the earth: tilling, hoeing, and planting the soil. God prohibited the fruit of the one tree as a test and an affliction upon Adam and his descendants. Satan whispered to Adam and his spouse and they disobeyed God with the result that their secret parts, which had been concealed from them, became apparent.

*Wahb b. Munabbih:* The tree's branches were intertwined and it bore fruit which the angels ate to live forever, and it was this fruit that God prohibited to Adam and Eve. The tree is the most excellent in Paradise, and on earth: the acacia [talh] and the lotus tree [sidr].

*Muhammad b. Qays:* After Iblis came to Adam and Eve and convinced them that God only prohibited the tree because he did not want them to become like angels or live forever, Eve cut the tree and it bled. It is also said that she "bit" the tree, and it bled. The "feathers" (7:26) which covered Adam and Eve dropped off and they began to cover themselves with leaves.

*Abu al-Aliyah:* Adam and Eve ate of the tree. It was a tree which made whoever ate from it defecate but feces were not allowed in Paradise, so God drove Adam and Eve out of Paradise.

*Abu Hurayrah:* The Prophet Muhammad said: "In Paradise is a tree in the shade of which the stars course 100 years without cutting it: the Tree of Immortality."

*Ibn Abbas, Ibn Masud and others:* Iblis went to the snake which, at that time, was an animal with four feet like a camel. Iblis persuaded the snake to let him enter its mouth and take him into Paradise to Adam. This way Iblis was able to enter by the keepers of Paradise although God was aware of what was happening. Iblis proposed to every animal but they all refused until finally Iblis convinced the snake by telling it that he would protect it from the descendants of Adam. Iblis hid in the snake's mouth and spoke to Adam and Eve from inside of it. The snake used to be covered and walked on four legs but God made it naked and made it to crawl on its stomach. Because of this, people should kill snakes, breaking the covenant Iblis made with it.

*Wahb b. Munabbih:* The snake was like a Bactrian camel and was one of the most beautiful of animals created by God.

*Ibn Ishaq:* Iblis started off by crying for Adam and Eve, and they became sad when they heard him. They asked him why he was crying and he said: "I am crying for you because you will die and be forced to give up the luxury and plenty you are enjoying." Then Iblis went to them and whispered saying: "Adam, may I lead you to the Tree of Immortality and to a kingdom that does not decline?" (20:120). Meaning that they might become angels or live forever in Paradise.

*Wahb b. Munabbih:* Iblis left the snake and picked the fruit. He took it to Eve saying how sweet it smelled, how good it tasted, how beautiful its color. Eve ate of the fruit and then repeated the same arguments to Adam, who also ate it.

*Saʿid b. al-Musayyab:* Adam refused to eat from the tree but Eve gave him some wine to drink and when he was drunk she led him to the tree and he ate from it.

*Ibn Abbas, Ibn Masud and others:* Adam and Eve's secret parts became apparent to them after they ate from the tree. Previously only Iblis, from reading the books of the angels, knew that Adam and Eve had secret parts. At this time they were covered with "fingernail."

*Ibn Kathir:* Eve ate from the tree before Adam. There is a report in Bukhari on the authority of Abu Hurayrah, from the Prophet Muhammad: "If only the Israelites had not made meat to be bad, and if only Eve had not imposed her feminine wiles on her spouse."

*People of the Book:* The one who convinced Eve to eat from the tree was the serpent. It was the most beautiful and strong of animals. Eve ate on its advice and gave some to Adam to taste. Because of this, their eyes were opened and they learned that they were naked. They joined together fig leaves and made a covering.

*Wahb b. Munabbih:* Their clothes were of light, covering their genitals.

*Ubayy b. Ka'b:* The Prophet Muhammad said: "God created Adam to be a tall man with a lot of hair on his head like the top of a palm tree. When he tasted from the tree, his clothes fell from him. He was the first to have his nakedness revealed. When he looked at his nakedness, he began to be distressed in Paradise, so a tree took him by his hair and took it away. The Merciful called to him: 'Adam, are you fleeing from me?' When Adam heard the words of the Merciful he said: 'Oh my Lord, no, but I am ashamed.'"

*Ubayy b. Ka'b:* The Prophet Muhammad said: "Your father Adam was like a tall palm, 60 cubits in height, with a lot of hair, his nakedness covered. When he sinned in Paradise, his private parts were revealed to him and he left Paradise. A tree caught him and took him by his forelock and his Lord called to him: 'Are you running from me, Adam?' He said: 'No, I am ashamed for that which I have done.'"

*Wahb b. Munabbih:* Adam went inside of the tree to hide, and it was there that God called to him, and that Adam replied he was ashamed.

## Fall of Adam and Eve

*Tabari:* Adam fell to India. It is the land with the sweetest smell on earth because when Adam was cast down there some of the smell of Paradise clung to India's trees. Adam was cast onto a mountain in India called Nod [Nudh/Budh]. It is said that this mountain is the one whose peak is closest to heaven. Standing upon it Adam had his feet on the earth and his head in heaven and could hear the angels. Because of this, Adam's size was reduced. The snake was cast down to Isfahan or to the wilderness and Iblis to the seashore at al-Ubullah.

*Ibn Abbas:* Adam was cast down in India and Eve in Jeddah. Adam went in search of her until they met and Eve drew near to him [izdalafat] and therefore the place was called "Muzdalifah." They knew each other [taʿarifa] at ʿArafat and hence the name ʿArafat, and they united [jamaʿa] at Jamʿ, hence the name Jamʿ.

*People of the Torah:* Adam fell to India on a mountain called "Wasim" in a valley called Buhayl between al-Dahnaj and al-Mandal. Eve fell to Jeddah in the territory of Mecca.

*Ibn Abbas:* Adam was made to fall to earth, to a place called "Dahna" between Mecca and Taʾif.

*Hasan al-Basri:* Adam was made to fall in India, Eve in Jeddah, and Iblis in "Dastumisan" near Basrah. The serpent fell to Isfahan.

*Suddi:* Adam came down in India and with him was the Black Stone and a handful of the leaves of Paradise. He scattered them in India and the trees of perfume there grew from this.

*Tabari:* It is said that when Adam fell to earth he had a wreath on his head from the trees of Paradise and when he reached the earth the wreath dried up, its leaves scattered, and from them grew types of perfume. Others say: This was from the clothes that Adam and Eve sewed together from the leaves of Paradise. When these leaves dried they scattered and from them grew types of perfume. Others say: When Adam learned that God was casting him to earth he began to pass by every tree in Paradise and take branches from them. When he fell to earth these branches were with him. When they dried up their leaves scattered and this is the origin of perfume.

*Ibn Abbas:* When Adam left Paradise, there was nothing he passed by from which he did not take. It was said to the angels: "Let him take what he wants." When he came down, it was in India. The perfume which comes from India is from that which Adam brought out of Paradise.

*Abu al-Aliyah:* Adam left Paradise and took with him from there a rod from the trees of Paradise, and on his head was a crown or wreath from the trees of Paradise. He fell to India. From the wreath came all the perfume in India.

*Abu Musa al-Ashʿari:* When God caused Adam to leave Paradise, he provisioned him with some of the fruits of Paradise, and taught him how to make everything. All fruits come from the fruits of Paradise, except that fruits today change and those of Paradise do not.

*Tabari:* Adam caused some of the perfume of Paradise to come down with him. He also brought down with him the Black Stone which used to be whiter than snow, the rod of Moses which was from the myrtle of Paradise, ten cubits tall and equal to the height of Moses, myrrh, and incense. After that, anvils, mallets, and tongs were sent down to him. When Adam fell upon the mountain, he looked at a rod of iron growing on the mountain. He began to break up the trees which had grown old and dry with the mallet, then he heated that iron rod until it melted. The first thing he pounded out was a knife with which he used to work. Then he pounded out the oven, the one which Noah inherited, the one which boiled.

*Tabari:* When Adam fell he brushed his head on heaven and thus became bald, and passed on baldness to his children. The animals in the open fled from his tallness and became wild on that day. While Adam was on that mountain, standing, he heard the sounds of the angels and could smell the scent of Paradise. Therefore, his stature was reduced to 60 cubits [30 meters], and he was this tall until he died. The beauty of Adam was not found in any of his children except for Joseph.

*Tabari:* It is said that God provisioned Adam with 30 types of fruit when he caused him to fall to the earth. Ten with shells, ten with stones, and ten with neither shells nor stones. The fruits with shells include walnuts, almonds, pistachio nuts, hazelnuts, acorns, chestnuts, coco-nuts, pomegranates, and bananas. Those with stones include peaches, apricots, plums, dates, sorbs, lotus fruit, jujubes, and shahluj plums. Those with neither shells nor stones include apples, quinces, pears, grapes, mulberries, figs, citrus, breadfruit, ginger, and melon.

*Tabari:* It is said that from among the things which Adam brought out of Paradise with him was a bag filled with grains of wheat. It is also said that Gabriel brought wheat later, after Adam became hungry and asked his Lord for food. God sent Gabriel to him with seven grains of wheat. Gabriel put it in Adam's hand, and Adam asked Gabriel: "What is this?" Gabriel said to him: "This is what caused you to leave Paradise." Each of the grains weighed as much as 100,800 dirhems. Adam said: "What do I do with this?" He said: "Spread them in the earth." So he did and God caused them to grow immediately. Sowing in the earth thus became a custom for Adam's children. Then God commanded him to harvest it, to collect and husk it by hand. Then he commanded him to winnow it. Gabriel brought two stones to him and placed one of them on top of the other and ground the wheat. Then God commanded him to knead it, and commanded him to make bread in the ashes. Gabriel gave Adam a stone and iron. Adam struck them together and fire came out of them. He was the first to make bread from ashes.

*Ibn Abbas:* The tree which God forbade Adam and his spouse was grain. When they ate from it, their private parts became apparent to them. It was their fingernails that had covered their private parts. They began to cover themselves with the leaves of Paradise, fig leaves which they stuck together, one to another. Adam set out, taking refuge in the garden. A tree took hold of his head and God called out to him: "Adam, are you running from me?" He said: "No, but I am embarrassed, my Lord." He said: "Was all that I gave you and allowed you in Paradise not enough that you would do that which I had forbade you." Adam said: "No, my Lord, but I did not figure that one would swear by you falsely." This refers to the statement of Iblis mentioned in the Quran: "He assured them with an oath: 'I am one who gives good advice to you'" (7:21). God said: "By my might, I will certainly make you fall to the earth, and only by toil will you try to live." So God cast him down from Paradise, where they both had eaten of plenty, he cast him to a place without plenty to eat and drink. He was taught how to make iron, and commanded to plow. So he plowed, sowed, and watered until his crop ripened. Then he harvested it, thrashed, winnowed, ground, kneaded, baked bread, and ate it. Knowledge of these things did not reach Adam until God wanted it to reach him.

*Sa'id b. Jubayr:* God sent down a red ox to Adam, and he used it for plowing, wiping the sweat from his brow. This was the misery about which God had warned him.

*Ibn Kathir:* It is said that along with Adam came down anvils, tongs, mallets, and hammers. Those who say this include Ibn Abbas, who says: "Three things came down together with Adam: anvils, tongs, mallets and hammers."

*Anas b. Malik:* The Prophet Muhammad said: "Adam and Eve fell together naked, upon them the leaves of Paradise. The heat hit Adam until he sat and cried saying to Eve: 'Eve, the heat hurts me.' God said to Gabriel: 'Take him cotton.' He commanded her to spin it and taught her how. He commanded Adam to weave."

*Ibn Kathir:* Adam did not have sex with his wife while in Paradise until he fell from there on account of their eating from the tree. Each of them slept alone. One of them slept on the open ground and the other next to that one until Gabriel came and commanded Adam to produce his family. So he taught him how to produce it. After Adam had sex with Eve, Gabriel asked: "How did you find your wife?" He said: "Upright." This report is considered strange and does not go back to the time of the Prophet Muhammad.

## Curse of Adam and Eve

*Wahb b. Munabbih:* God cursed the earth from which Adam was created, changing fruits to thorns. Because Eve enticed Adam, pregnancy would be difficult and dangerous. Because the snake allowed Iblis to enter it, its feet were retracted into its belly and it was to eat from the earth, and be the enemy of the descendants of Adam. Wherever the snake encounters these descendants, it will hold onto their heel. Wherever they encounter the snake, they will crush its head.

*Muhammad b. Qays:* God asked Adam why he ate the fruit and he replied that Eve made him eat it. God asked Eve and she said the snake commanded her to do it. God asked the snake and he said: "Iblis made me do it." God cursed and banished Iblis. Because Eve caused the tree to bleed, she is to bleed every month. The snake is to have its feet cut off and slither on its face. Anyone who encounters the snake will crush its head with stones.

*Ibn Zayd:* When Adam blamed Eve for their sin, God said: "It is incumbent upon me to make her bleed once every month just as she made this tree bleed, and I will make her foolish though I created her smart, and I will make pregnancy and childbearing reprehensible though I had made pregnancy and childbearing easy." If it were not for the affliction that was set upon Eve, then the women of this world would not menstruate, they would be smart, and they would be pregnant and bear children in ease.

## Adam's Repentance

*Ubayy b. Ka'b:* The Prophet Muhammad said: "Adam said: 'Do you think, Lord, if I repent and return to you, that I might return to Paradise?' God said: 'Yes.' This is like the word of God [2:37]."

*Mujahid:* The Prophet Muhammad said that Adam said: "Oh God, there is no God but you, praise be to you and glory be to you, my Lord, I wronged myself, forgive me for you are the greatest of those who forgive. Oh God, there is no God but you, praise be to you and glory be to you, my Lord, I wronged myself, so show mercy on me for you are the greatest of those who show mercy. Oh God, there is no God but you, praise be to you and glory be to you, my Lord, I wronged myself, so accept my repentance for you are the Merciful who accepts repentance."

*Umar b. al-Khattab:* The Prophet Muhammad said: "When Adam committed his sin he said: 'Oh Lord, I ask you by the right of Muhammad, will you forgive me?' God said: 'How do you know about Muhammad, I have not yet created him?' Adam said: 'Lord, because when you created me with your hand and breathed into me from your spirit, I raised my head and saw what was written on the foundations of your throne: There is no god but God and Muhammad is the Apostle of God. I knew that you would not place his name there unless he is the most beloved of creation to you.' God said: 'You are right, Adam. He is the most beloved of creation to me. When you ask me in the right of his name, I will forgive you. If only for Muhammad did I create you.'"

*Abu Hurayrah:* The Prophet Muhammad said: "Moses challenged Adam and said to him: 'You are the one who caused people to leave Paradise, because of your sin, and caused them to be miserable.' Adam said: 'Moses, you are the one whom God singled out with his message and his words. Do you rebuke me for something God made incumbent upon me 40 years before I was created?'" The Prophet Muhammad said, three times: "Adam confuted Moses."

## Pilgrimage and Sanctuary in Mecca

*Ata b. Abi Rabah:* Adam's feet were on the earth and his head in heaven so that he was able to hear the angels talking and praying. He became familiar with this, so the angels complained and God lowered Adam down to earth. Adam missed what he used to hear from the angels and was lonely, and he complained about this to God. He was therefore sent to Mecca. Every place he stepped became a settled place, and everything between his steps became wilderness, until he ended up at Mecca. God sent down a jewel from the jewels of Paradise and it was in the place where the Ka'bah is today. The jewel used to be circumambulated until God sent down the Flood and the jewel was raised up to the heavens. God sent Abraham and he rebuilt the Ka'bah.

*Ibn Abbas:* God said to Adam: "The area around my throne is sacred to me. Therefore go and build me a House and circumambulate it just as my angels circumambulate my throne." God sent an angel to Adam who gave him knowledge of its place, and taught him the rites.

*Qatadah:* God put the House down together with Adam, while his head was in the heavens and his feet on the earth. The angels were in awe of Adam, but his size was reduced to 60 cubits and Adam was sad because he missed the voices of the angels and their praises. He complained about this to God who said: "Adam, I sent down a House for you to circumambulate, just as my throne is circumambulated, for you to pray there just as my throne is prayed at." Adam left and went to it. His steps were long and the interval between each step became wilderness. This wilderness continued to exist after that. Adam came to the House, circumambulated it, he and the prophets after him.

*Ibn Abbas:* God decreased Adam's size and Adam said that he used to be the neighbor of God in God's house, having no one but God to watch over him. He had plenty to eat and could dwell wherever he wanted. But then he was cast down to this holy mountain where he could still hear the voices of the angels, see them crowding around the throne, and could enjoy the sweet scent of Paradise. Then he was reduced to 60 cubits, cut off from the voices, the sight, and the scent of Paradise. God said: "Because of your disobedience, Adam, this has been done." When God saw the nakedness of Adam and Eve, he commanded Adam to slaughter a ram from the eight pairs of small cattle he had sent down from Paradise. Adam took the ram and slaughtered it, then he took its wool and Eve spun it. He and Eve wove it. Adam made a cloak for himself and a shift and veil for Eve. They put on that clothing. God then revealed to Adam: "I have a Sanctuary [haram] like that around my throne, so go there and build a House for me. Then crowd around it as you saw my angels crowd around my throne. There I will respond to you and your descendants, those who are obedient to me." Then Adam said: "My Lord, how can I do this, I have not the strength and have no guide?" So God chose an angel to go with him to Mecca. Whenever Adam passed by a meadow or place which pleased him, he said to the angel: "Let us stop here." The angel said to him: "This is your place." This happened until they reached Mecca. Every place they stopped became inhabited and cultivated, and every place he passed by became barren desert. So he built the House from five mountains: Mount Sinai, Mount of Olives, Lebanon, and al-Judi. He constructed its foundations from Mount Hira. When he finished with its building, the angel took him out to ʿArafat and showed him all the rituals of the Pilgrimage that people perform today. Then they returned to Mecca, and Adam circumambulated the House for a week. After this, Adam returned to the land of India and died upon Mount Nod.

*Ibn Abbas:* When Adam came down, he came down to India. He performed the pilgrimage from there 40 times on foot. Abu Yahya asked Mujahid: "Could he not have ridden?" Mujahid replied: "What thing could carry him? By God, his step was the distance of three days and his head reached the heavens." The angels complained about his breath. The Merciful One faulted him for this and made him small for 40 years.

*Ibn Umar:* While Adam was in India, God told him to perform the Pilgrimage to this House. So Adam went on the Pilgrimage from India and every place his foot stepped became a settled place and what was between his steps became wilderness, until he arrived at the House and circumambulated it. He completed all of the rites of the Pilgrimage, then he intended to return to India, so he set off. When he reached the two passes at ʿArafat the angels met him and said: "Your Pilgrimage was perfect, Adam." He was surprised. When the angels saw this they said: "Adam, we have been performing the Pilgrimage to this House before you were created, for 2000 years."

## Covenant with Adam's Descendants

**Q 7 : 172**  When your Lord took from the descendants of Adam, from their loins, their offspring, and made them testify for themselves. "Am I not your Lord?" They said: "Yes, we testify, lest we should say on the Day of Resurrection: 'We were not heeding this.'"

**Q 30 : 30**  Set your face to the religion, being *hanif*, the instinct of God with which he endowed people, for which there is no substituting for the creation of God.

**Q 33 : 7**  When we took from the prophets their covenant, from you, Noah, Abraham, Moses, and Jesus son of Mary. We took from them a solemn covenant.

**Q 53 : 56**  This is vowed from the first vows.

*Abu al-Darda:* The Prophet Muhammad said: "God created Adam, and when he created him he hit his back with his right hand. His descendants came out of his back white as if they were atoms. He hit his back with his left hand and his descendants came out black as if they were ashes. He said to those on his right: 'To Paradise.' To those on his left he said: 'To the Fire.'"

*Malik b. Anas:* Umar b. al-Khattab was asked about this verse [7:172]. Umar b. al-Khattab said: "I heard the Prophet Muhammad asked about this verse, and he said: 'God created Adam, then rubbed his back with his right hand and caused his descendants to come out of it. He said: I created these for Paradise, for the work of the people of Paradise they work. Then he rubbed his back and another group of descendants came out. He said: I created these for the Fire, for the work of the people of the Fire they work.'"

*Ibn Abbas:* The Prophet Muhammad said: "God took a covenant from the back of Adam on the Day of 'Arafat. He caused all of his offspring to come out of him, and spread them out in front of him."

## Adam's Death

*Tabari:* When Adam died it was Friday. The angels came to him, sent by God from Paradise, to embalm and wrap him, and they honored his son and heir Seth. Ibn Ishaq says: The sun and the moon were eclipsed for seven days and nights.

*Ibn Damrah al-Sa'di:* I saw a shaykh in Medina speaking, so I asked him about Adam's death. He said: "Adam, when he prepared to die, said to his sons: 'Sons, I desire the fruit of Paradise.' The sons went looking for it, and the angels received them. With them was his burial shroud and embalming supplies, and with them were axes, shovels, and baskets. The angels said to them: 'Children of Adam, what do you want and what do you seek?' They said: 'Our father is sick and he desires fruit from Paradise.' They said to them: 'Return, for your father is finished.' So the angels returned with the children of Adam, and when Eve saw them she recognized them. They took Adam, washed him, wrapped him, embalmed him, dug a hole for him, interred him and prayed over him. Then they put him in his grave, and wiped him. The angels then said: 'Children of Adam, this is your year.'"

*Ibn Abbas:* The Prophet Muhammad said: "The angels said: 'God is Great' [Allahu akbar] four times over Adam, Abu Bakr said it four times over Fatimah, Umar four times over Abu Bakr, and Suhayl four times over Umar."

*Ibn Kathir:* There is disagreement concerning the place of his burial. It is well known that he was buried at the mountain to which he fell in India. It is also said he was buried in Mount Abu Qays in Mecca. It is said that Noah, when it was time for the Flood, carried Adam and Eve in the Ark and reburied them in Jerusalem.

*Ibn Asakir:* His head is at the mosque of Abraham, his legs at the Dome of the Rock, and Eve died one year after him.

*Ibn Kathir:* There is disagreement concerning the extent of his life: Ibn Abbas and Abu Hurayrah say that his life span was written in the preserved tablet as 1000 years. This does not correspond with what is written in the Torah, that he lived for 930 years. It is possible that there is agreement between what the Prophet Muhammad said and what is in the Torah if what is in the Torah refers only to the time he spent on earth after the Fall, which would be 930 years according to a solar calendar and according to a lunar calendar 957 years. Add this to the 43 years he spent in Paradise before the Fall, as was mentioned by Tabari and others, and the total is 1000 years.

*Ibn Abbas:* When the verse of Debt was revealed, the Prophet Muhammad said: "The first one who disavowed was Adam, the first one who disavowed was Adam, the first one who disavowed was Adam. When God created Adam he rubbed his back and all his descendants until the time of the Day of Resurrection came out. Adam began to examine his offspring and saw among them a man who was shining. He said: 'Who is that, Lord?' God said: 'This is your son David.' He said: 'How long is his life?' God said: 'Sixty years.' He said: 'Add to his life.' God said: 'No, unless you subtract it from your life.' The life of Adam was 1000 years, so he added 40 years to David. God wrote this down in a book and the angels witnessed it. When the angels came to take Adam he said: 'I have 40 years remaining to my life,' and he was told: 'You gave it to your son David.' Adam said: 'I did not do this.' So God showed him the book and the angels witnessed it."

*Abu Hurayrah:* The Prophet Muhammad said: "God created Adam from the earth, then he made clay and left it until it was stinking slime, and God created him and formed him. Then he left him until the clay was dry like ceramic. Iblis used to pass by him and say: 'You have created a great thing.' Then God breathed his spirit into him and the first place the spirit went was his eyes and his nose. He sneezed and God was merciful to him. God said: 'Your Lord is merciful to you.' Then God said: 'Adam, go to those of the band and say to them: Do you see what you say?' So Adam said: 'Peace be upon you,' and they replied: 'Peace be upon you, the mercy of God and his blessings.' He said: 'Adam, this is your greeting and the greeting of your offspring. ' He said: 'Lord, what of my offspring?' He said: 'Pick a hand, Adam.' Adam said: 'I pick the right, my Lord. Both the hands of my Lord are right ones.' God spread out his palm and on it were the descendants of Adam, in the palm of the Merciful. A group of them had mouths of light, and one man surprised Adam with his light. Adam said: 'My Lord, what is this?' He said: 'This is your son David.' He said: 'Lord, how long a life did you give him?' God said: 'I gave him 60 years.' Adam said: 'Lord, give to him from my life so that his life will be 100 years.' So God did this. When the end of Adam's life had come, God sent the Angel of Death, and Adam said: 'But I still have 40 years of life.' The angel said to him: 'Did you not give it to your son David?' He disavowed this and his descendants disavowed it. He forgot and his descendants forgot."

*Abu Hurayrah:* The Prophet Muhammad said: "When God created Adam he rubbed his back and all of the creatures he created from the offspring of Adam until the Day of Resurrection, fell from Adam's back. He put between the eyes of each person a whiteness of light, then he returned them to Adam's back. Adam said: 'What are these?' God said: 'These are your offspring.' Adam saw a man, the whiteness between the eyes of whom was weak, so he said: 'Which is this?' God said: 'This is the man from the last of the communities of your descendants. He is called David.' Adam said: 'Lord, how long is his life?' God said: 'Sixty years.' Adam said: 'Lord, add to his life 40 years from mine.' When Adam's life had come to a close, the Angel of Death came to him and Adam said: 'Don't I have 40 years of my life remaining?' The angel said: 'Did you not give it to your son David?' So he disavowed it and his descendants disavowed it. Adam forgot and his descendants forgot. Adam sinned and his descendants sinned."

# Children of Adam and Eve

**Q 5:27** Recite to them the story of the two sons of Adam, in truth, when they each presented a sacrifice. One of them was accepted but the other was not. He [Cain] said: "I will certainly kill you!" He [Abel] said: "God accepts only from the upright. **28** "If you stretch out your hand against me, to kill me, I will not stretch out my hand against you, to kill you. I fear God, Lord of the worlds. **29** "I intend to let you take my sin and your sin, for you will be among the people of the Fire. That is the reward of those who do wrong." **30** His [Cain's] soul led him to the killing of his brother, so he killed him and became one of the losers. **31** God sent a crow which scratched in the earth to show him how to hide the exposed body of his brother. He said: "Woe is me for I was unable to be like this crow and hide the exposed body of my brother." He became regretful. **32** Because of this, we wrote for the Israelites that if someone kills another person, by himself or spreading corruption in the land, then it is as if he killed the whole people. If someone spares a life, then it is as if he spared the whole people. Our messengers have come to them with clear signs, yet even after that, many of them were transgressing on the earth.

## Cain and Abel

*Ibn Kathir:* It is reported that Adam used to marry the sons of one pregnancy to the daughters of another and that Abel wanted to marry the twin sister of Cain. Cain was older than Abel and his twin sister was more beautiful than Abel's. Cain wanted to possess her alone instead of her brother. Adam ordered Cain to give her in marriage to Abel but he refused, so he ordered both Cain and Abel to offer sacrifices. Adam went on a pilgrimage to Mecca and asked for the protection of the heavens over his sons, but the heavens refused. Then he asked the lands and the mountains but they refused. So Cain accepted the obligation of this protection. When they went to offer their sacrifices, Abel offered a fattened she-camel, for he was in charge of the livestock. Cain offered a bunch of produce from the undesirable part of his produce. A fire came down and consumed the sacrifice of Abel but left the sacrifice of Cain. Cain was angry and said: "I certainly will kill you to keep you from marrying my sister." Abel said: "God accepts only from the upright."

*Abu Ja'far al-Baqir:* Adam directed both of them in offering their sacrifices and the one from Abel was accepted but not the one from Cain. Cain said to Adam: "It was accepted from him because you instructed him but did not instruct me." So there was enmity between him and his brother over this. That night when Abel was late for shepherding, Adam sent his brother Cain to see why he was late. When Cain met up with his brother, Cain said to him: "God accepted it from you and did not accept it from me." Abel said: "God accepts only from the upright." Cain got angry because of this and hit Abel with a piece of iron that he had with him, and he killed him. It is said that he killed him with a rock that he threw at his head while he was asleep, crushing him. It is also said that he mauled him and bit him just as a predatory animal does, and then he was dead.

*Ibn Kathir:* Verses 28–29 indicate that Abel was created good and this is also established in Bukhari and Muslim, that the Prophet Muhammad said: "When two Muslims face one another with their swords, both the killer and the killed will be in the Fire." People asked: "This is right for the killer, but why for the killed?" He said: "Because he was bent on killing the other." Abel intended to leave the fight up to Cain, meaning that he would not be punished for fighting with his brother even though he was the one killed. Some people agree that on the Day of Resurrection the killed will call upon the killer so that the good deeds of the killer will not be enough to cancel out this injustice, and the misdeeds of the killed will be transferred to the killer.

*Ibn Abbas and Ibn Masud, and other Companions of the Prophet Muhammad:* With every boy born to Adam there was born a girl, and Adam used to marry the boy of one pregnancy to the girl of another. Two boys were born to him: Cain and Abel. Cain was in charge of agriculture and Abel was in charge of milk-producing livestock. Cain was the older of the two and his sister was more beautiful than the sister of Abel. Abel asked to marry the sister of Cain but he refused saying: "She is my sister and was born with me. She is more beautiful than your sister. It is more right that I marry her." His father ordered him to give her in marriage to Abel but he refused. So they both offered sacrifices to God to see who had more right to the girl. Adam was gone on that day, on his way to Mecca to look around. God said to Adam: "Adam, did you know that I have a House on the earth?" Adam said: "By God, no." God said: "I have a House in Mecca, so go to it." Adam said to the heavens: "Protect my two sons with a trust," but they refused. He said the same to the earth but it refused, and he said the same to the mountains but they refused. He said this to Cain and Cain agreed. Cain said: "You will go and return and find your family just as you left it." After Adam left, the two offered sacrifices. Cain had boasted to Abel: "I have more right to her than you for she is my sister and I am older than you. I am the heir of my father." When they made the sacrifice Abel sacrificed a fattened she-camel and Cain offered a bunch of grain. He found among the bunch a great ear, took it out of the bunch and ate it. The fire came down and consumed the sacrifice of Abel but left the sacrifice of Cain. He became angry and said: "I will certainly kill you so that you will not marry my sister." Abel said: "God accepts only from the upright. If you stretch out your hand against me, to kill me, I will not stretch out my hand against you, to kill you . . . his soul led him to the killing of his brother" (5:27–30). Cain wanted to kill Abel, so Abel tried to escape from him on the tops of the mountains. One day Cain came to him while he was shepherding his livestock on the mountain. Abel was sleeping. Cain lifted a rock and crushed his head with it. He died and Cain left him exposed, for he did not know how to bury him. God sent two crows that were brothers. The crows fought with one another and one of them killed the other. Then the one dug a hole for the other and covered it. When Cain saw this he said: "Woe is me, for I was unable to be like this crow and hide the exposed body of my brother" (5:31). When Adam returned he found that his son had killed his brother. This is related to God's word: "We offered safekeeping to the heavens and the earth and the mountains . . . but he is ignorant and does wrong" (33:72), referring to when Cain undertook the trust of Adam and then did not protect his family.

*Abdallah b. Uthman b. Khuthaym:* I went with Sa'id b. Jubayr to do the throwing of pebbles at Mina. He was veiled and leaning on my hand. When we turned toward the residence of Samurah al-Sawwaf, he stopped and related to me on the authority of Ibn Abbas: It was prohibited for a woman to marry her twin brother, but another of her brothers used to marry her. In each pregnancy there was a man and a woman. A beautiful woman was born and an ugly woman was born. The brother of the ugly one said: "I will marry your sister and you will marry my sister." He said: "No, I have more right to my sister." So they both offered sacrifices and the sacrifice from him who offered the ram was accepted but the sacrifice from him who was in charge of agriculture was not accepted. So the latter killed the former. This ram remained penned with God until he released it as a ransom for Isaac. He slaughtered it here on al-Safa on the rock of Thabir, at the residence of Samurah al-Sawwaf. It is to your right when you throw the pebbles.

*Ibn Ishaq:* It is said, on the authority of some of the scholars from the People of the First Book, that Adam used to have sex with Eve in Paradise before committing the sin. She bore him Cain and his twin sister and she had no craving or illness while pregnant, nor did she have pain when delivering them. She saw no blood in connection with them because of the purity of Paradise. After they both ate from the tree and committed disobedience, they fell to the earth and were content there. Adam had sex with her and she bore him Abel and his twin sister. She had cravings and illness with them, had pain in delivering them, and saw blood in connection with them. Eve used, it is said, to be pregnant only with twins, a boy and a girl. Eve bore for Adam 40 children, from his seed, a boy and a girl from twenty pregnancies. The man in each pregnancy could marry any of his sisters he wanted except for the twin sister who was born with him. She was not allowed for him. This was allowed because there were no other women at that time except for their sisters and their mother Eve.

Adam ordered his son Cain to marry his twin sister to Abel, and he ordered Abel to marry his twin sister to Cain. Abel was pleased and agreed with that but Cain refused, finding the idea reprehensible, thinking himself better than the sister of Abel. He desired his own sister instead of Abel having her. He said: "We are progeny of Paradise and they are progeny of the earth. I have more right to my sister." Some of the People of the First Book say that: The sister of Cain was one of the most beautiful of people, and Cain wanted to keep her from his brother. God knows best which one it was. His father said to him: "My son, she is not permitted for you," but Cain refused to accept this from his father and his father said to him: "Then, son, offer a sacrifice and your brother Abel will offer a sacrifice. Whichever of the two of you from whom God accepts the sacrifice, he has more right to her." Cain was in charge of sowing the earth and Abel was in charge of shepherding the livestock. Cain offered flour and Abel offered a first-born sheep from the sheep of his flock. Some say he offered a cow. God sent a white fire that consumed the sacrifice of Abel and left the sacrifice of Cain. In this way was a sacrifice accepted when God accepted it. When God accepted Abel's sacrifice, this being an indication of the decision of his right to the sister of Cain, Cain got angry. Arrogance overcame Cain and Satan overtook him. He followed his brother Abel while he was with his livestock, and he killed him. And this story of these two God related in the Quran to Muhammad: "Recite to them" meaning the People of the Book "the story of the sons of Adam, in truth, when they each presented a sacrifice. One of them was accepted . . ." (5:27) to the end of the story.

The People of the Torah allege that Cain, when he killed his brother Abel, was asked by God: "Where is your brother Abel?" He said: "I do not know, I am not his keeper." God said to him: "The voice of the blood of your brother is calling me from the earth. Now you are accursed from the earth which opened its mouth and accepted the blood of your brother from your hand. When you work the earth it will not give you back its produce and you will become a fugitive on the earth." Cain said: "My sin is greater than you will forgive, so today you have driven me from the face of the earth, and I will be concealed from before you and be a fugitive on the earth. All who meet me will kill me." God said: "It is not like this. There will be no seven-fold recompense for someone who kills another but for he who kills Cain, his recompense is seven-fold." God put a sign upon Cain so that all who found him would not kill him. Cain left from God's presence to the East of Eden, the garden.

*Abdallah b. Amir:* There were two sons of Adam who offered a sacrifice, one of which was accepted but not the other. One of the sons was in charge of cultivation and the other was in charge of livestock. Both of them were commanded to offer a sacrifice. The one in charge of the livestock offered the best, the fattest, and noblest of his livestock, that which he himself considered good. The one in charge of cultivation offered the worst of his produce: weeds and tares which he himself did not like. God accepted the sacrifice of the one in charge of the livestock but not the one in charge of cultivation. From this story is what God narrated in his Book: By God, the one killed was the stronger of the two men but the desire to avoid extending his hand against his brother prevented him.

*Ibn Abbas:* An issue in the matter of the two brothers is that there were no poor people to be given alms from the sacrifice, but that a man simply offered a sacrifice. While the two sons of Adam were sitting they said: "Let us offer a sacrifice!" When a man offered a sacrifice and God was pleased, he sent a fire that consumed it. If he was not pleased the fire was extinguished. So they both offered a sacrifice. One of them was a shepherd and the other was a farmer. The one in charge of livestock offered the best and fattest of his livestock. The other offered some of his produce. The fire came, descended between them and consumed the sheep but left the produce. The son of Adam said to his brother: "Should you walk among people, with them knowing that you offered a sacrifice which was accepted from you while my sacrifice was rejected? No, by God, the people will not look upon me and you and see you as better than I. I will certainly kill you." He said to his brother: "What is my sin? God accepts only from the upright."

*Hasan al-Basri:* The two men who are in the Quran: "Recite to them the story of the two sons of Adam in truth," were from the Israelites. They were not sons from the loins of Adam but the sacrifice took place among the Israelites, for Adam was the first person who died.

*Tabari:* Some say: Adam had sex with Eve 100 years after their fall to earth. She gave birth to Cain and his twin sister Qalima in a single pregnancy. Then Abel and his twin sister in a single pregnancy. When they reached maturity he intended to marry the sister of Cain who had been born with him in a single pregnancy to Abel but Cain prevented this. For this reason the two offered sacrifices and the sacrifice of Abel was accepted but not the sacrifice of Cain. Cain envied his brother and killed him on the slope of Hira, then Cain came down from the mountain, holding his sister Qalima by the hand. He fled with her to Aden in the land of Yemen.

*Ibn Abbas:* When Cain killed his brother Abel he took his sister by the hand and then brought her down from the mountain of Nod, to its foot. Adam said to Cain: "Go! You will always be afraid and not safe from the people you see." There was not a single one of his sons who did not try to kill him. A blind son of Cain's came accompanied by a son of his. He said to his blind son: "This is your father Cain." He shot at his father Cain and killed him. The son of the blind man said: "Father, you killed your father." The blind man raised his hand and slapped his son, and his son died. The blind man said: "Woe is me. I killed my father with my shot and I killed my son with my slap."

*Tabari:* It is mentioned that Eve bore Adam 120 pregnancies. The first of them was Cain and his twin sister. The last of them was Abd al-Mughayth and his twin sister Ummat al-Mughayth. As for Ibn Ishaq, it is mentioned on his authority that the total number of what Eve bore to Adam from his loins was 40, boys and girls from twenty pregnancies. He said: "We have received the names of some of them but not of others."

*Ibn Ishaq:* The names of fifteen men and four women have reached us. Among them are: Cain and his twin sister, Abel and Labudha, Adam's daughter Ashuth and her twin brother, Seth and his twin sister, Hazurah and her twin brother, when Adam was 130 years old, Adam's son Ayad and his twin sister, Adam's son Balagh and his twin sister, Adam's son Athati and his twin sister, Adam's son Tawbah and his twin sister, Adam's son Banan and his twin sister, Adam's son Shabu-bah and his twin sister, Adam's son Hayan and his twin sister, Adam's son Yahud and his twin sister, Adam's son Sandal and his twin sister, and Adam's son Baraq and his twin sister. Every man from among them was born with a woman in the pregnancy from the same womb in which they were carried.

*Sa'd b. Abi Waqqas:* I witnessed the Prophet Muhammad say: "There will be a trial and the one sitting in it is better than the one standing, the one standing is better than the one walking, and the one walking is better than the one running." Sa'd b. Abi Waqqas asked: "Did you see [in your prophetic vision] if Ali entered my house and stretched out his hand to kill me?" The Prophet Muhammad said: "Be like the son of Adam!" Others report that he said: "Be like the good son of Adam!"

*Ahmad b. Hanbal:* The Prophet Muhammad said: "A person is not killed unjustly except with a surety for his blood incumbent upon the first son of Adam, because he was the first to institute killing."

*Ibn Kathir:* Some people mention that when Cain killed Abel, he carried him on his back for a year. Others say that he carried him on his back for 100 years, and that this did not stop until God sent two crows.

*Ibn Kathir:* Those who saw this account in the book which is in the hands of the People of the Book are those who claim that it is in the Torah [Genesis 4:16–22]: that God marked Cain and watched over him, that he dwelt in the land of Nod to the east of Eden, and that they called him "Cain." That he had a son named Enoch, and to Enoch was Irad, and to Irad was Mehujael, to Mehujael was Methushael, to Methushael was Lamech. Lamech married two women: Adah and Zillah. Adah gave birth to a son whose name was Jabal. He was the first who dwelled in tents and had money. She gave birth also to Jubal [Nuwal]. He was the first to play the lyre and the flute. Zillah gave birth to a son whose name was Tubal-Cain [Shubaltayn] who was the first to work with copper and iron. The sister was named Naamah. In it, also is that [Genesis 4:25–5:32]: Adam had intercourse with his wife and she gave birth to a boy and called his name Seth. She said: This is because God has given me a replacement for Abel whom Cain has killed. To Seth was born Enosh. They say: The age of Adam on the day that Seth was born was 130 years, and he lived after that for 800 years. The age of Seth on the day Enosh was born was 105 years, and he lived after that for 807 years, and he had other sons and daughters besides Enosh. To Enosh was born Kenan when he was 90 years old, and he lived after that for 815 years and had other sons and daughters. When Kenan was 70 years old he begot Mahalalel and lived after that for 840 years, and had other sons and daughters. When Mahalalel was 75 years old he begot Jared and lived after that for 830 years, and had other sons and daughters. When Jared was 162 years old, he begot Enoch, and lived after that for 800 years, and had other sons and daughters. When Enoch was 75 years old he begot Methuselah and lived after that for 800 years, and had other sons and daughters. When Methuselah was 187 years old he begot Lamech, and after that lived for 782 years, and had other sons and daughters. When Lamech was 182 years old, he begot Noah, and lived after that for 595 years, and had other sons and daughters. When Noah was 500 years old he begot sons: Shem, Ham, and Japeth.

*Ibn Kathir:* The historians mention that Adam did not die until he saw the sons of the sons of the sons of his children, 1400 people.

## Seth

*Ibn Kathir:* The meaning of Seth is "gift of God" and he was named this because Adam and Eve sustained him after Abel was killed. It is said that the lineages of human beings all go through Seth and that the remaining children of Adam, other than Seth, became extinct. After Adam died he was succeeded by his son Seth who was a prophet, according to the report that Ibn Hibban relates in his collection of hadith reports, on the authority of Abu Dharr which goes back to the Prophet Muhammad, that 50 scrolls were revealed to him. When he was about to die, Seth was succeeded by his son Enosh, then after him Kenan, then Mahalalel. He is the one whom the Persians claim was king of the Seven Climes, the first to cut trees, build cities and strong fortresses. He was the one who built the city of Babel and the city of Sus. He vanquished Iblis and his army, and caused them to flee from the face to the edges of the earth and the peaks of its mountains. He killed a group of rebellious Jinn and ghouls. He had a great crown and used to speak to the people. His reign lasted for 40 years. When he died, Mahalalel was succeeded by his son Jared and when he was about to die he passed on his mantle to Enoch who is well known as Idris.

*Abu Dharr:* God sent down 104 scriptures, 50 scriptures to Seth.

*Ibn Ishaq:* When Adam was about to die, he called his son Seth and gave him his commission. He taught him the hours of the night and day, taught him the worship of the creatures in each of the hours of the night and day. He told him that each hour has a category of creatures which worship in it. Then he said to him: "Son, the Flood will be on the earth and last for seven years." He wrote his will and addressed it to Seth, who was the legatee of his father Adam. After the death of Adam, leadership became the responsibility of Seth. According to what was related on the authority of the Prophet Muhammad, God revealed to him 50 scriptures.

*Tabari:* When 150 years of Adam's life had passed, that is five years after Cain's killing of Abel, Eve bore him a son named Seth. The People of the Torah mention that Seth was born alone, without a twin. According to them, the interpretation of "Seth" is "Gift of God" meaning that he was a replacement for Abel.

*Ibn Abbas:* Eve bore Adam Seth and his sister Hazurah. He was called "Gift of God" derived from God on account of Abel. Gabriel said to her when she gave birth to him: "This is a gift of God in place of Abel." He is Seth in Arabic, Shath in Syriac, and Shith in Hebrew. He is the legatee of Adam. On the day Seth was born to Adam, Adam was 130 years old.

# Idris

**Q 19:56** Mention, in the Book, Idris, that he was truthful, a prophet. **57** We took him up to a high place.

### Idris

*Ibn Ishaq:* Jared married Barakna bt. al-Darmasil b. Mehujael b. Enoch b. Cain b. Adam when he was 162 years old. She bore him Enoch b. Jared. Enoch is Idris the prophet. He was the first of Adam's children to be given prophecy and the first to write with a pen. Jared lived 800 years after the birth of Enoch, and had more sons and daughters. So all of the years lived by Jared were 962, then he died.

*Tabari:* Some of the Jews say that Enoch, that is Idris, was born to Jared. God made him a prophet after 622 years of Adam's life had passed. Thirty scriptures were revealed to him. He was the first to write after Adam, to exert himself in the path of God, to cut and sew clothes, and the first to enslave some of Cain's descendants. He inherited from his father Jared that which his forefathers had bequeathed upon him, and had bequeathed to one another. All of this he did during the lifetime of Adam.

Adam died after 308 years of the life of Enoch had passed. Enoch summoned his people and admonished them. He commanded them to obey God and disobey Satan, and not to mix with the descendants of Cain. They did not follow him but group after group of the descendants of Seth went down to the descendants of Cain. It is written in the Torah that after 365 years of Idris' life and 527 years of his father's life had passed, God raised him up. After, his father Jared lived for another 435 years for a total of 962 years of life.

*Ibn Abbas:* In the time of Jared people made idols and some turned away from Islam.

*Ibn Kathir:* As for Idris, God praised him and attributed to him prophethood and truthfulness. He is Enoch. He is in the genealogical chain of the Prophet Muhammad, except according to one genealogist. He was the first descendant of Adam to whom prophethood was given after Adam and Seth. Ibn Ishaq says he was the first who wrote with the pen. There was a span of 380 years between him and the life of Adam. A group of people said: He is indicated in the report of Muʿawiyah b. al-Hakim when he asked the Prophet Muhammad about writing in the sand and the Prophet Muhammad said: "He was a prophet who wrote in it, and whoever agrees with his writing is thus." Many of the scholars allege that he was the first to speak about this, and they call him Thrice-great Hermes [Hermes al-Haramisah]. They say many lies about him just as they lied about other prophets, scholars, sages, and people who did things first.

*Bukhari:* It is mentioned on the authority of Ibn Masud and Ibn Abbas that Elijah is Idris. They take into consideration what is mentioned in the report of Zuhri on the authority of Anas b. Malik concerning the Night Journey: that the Prophet Muhammad passed by Idris and said to him: "Greetings, upright brother and upright prophet," but he did not say what Adam and Abraham said to him: "Greetings, upright prophet and upright son." If he were not in the chain of his ancestors then the opinion would be as the two of them said.

*Suyuti:* It is said that Idris was before Noah. Ibn Ishaq says that Idris was the first son of Adam to whom prophethood was given. He is Enoch b. Jared b. Mehaliel b. Enosh b. Kenan b. Seth b. Adam. Wahb b. Munabbih says that Idris was the grandfather of Noah, and he was called Enoch. The name is Syriac. It is also said the name is derived from the Arabic "studies" [dirasah] because of his studies of the scriptures. According to Samurah, Idris was a tall and white man with a huge stomach, a broad chest, and little body hair, but with a lot of hair on his head. One of his eyes was bigger than the other, and on his chest was a white spot but not from leprosy. When God saw the people of the earth, that many of them were not following the word of God, he raised Idris to the sixth heaven. Ibn Qutaybah mentions that Idris was raised when he was 350 years old. Ibn Hibban states that he was a prophet and messenger, and that he was the first to write with a pen. Ibn Abbas says that between Noah and Idris was 1000 years.

## Stars and the Sun

*Tha'labi:* He was named Idris because of his copious study [dars] of the books and scriptures of Adam and Seth, and his mother Ashuth. Idris was the first to write with a pen, the first to sew clothes and wear sewn clothing. He was the first one to study the stars and mathematics. God sent him to be the son of Cain and then raised him into the heavens. The reason God raised him into the heavens is what Ibn Abbas and others say, that he walked one day until the blaze of the sun set upon him. Holding the sun on his back he cried out to God for relief, so God sent the Angel of Death to rescue him from the heat and the weight of the sun. The Angel of Death lifted him on his wing into the heavens.

## Scriptures

*Abu Dharr:* The Prophet Muhammad said to me: "Abu Dharr, four [prophets] were Syrian: Adam, Seth, Noah, and Enoch. He was the first to write with a pen. God revealed to Enoch 30 scriptures."

*Tabari:* It is alleged that God sent Idris to all the people of the earth in his time, and that all the knowledge of those in the past was gathered together and added to him in 30 scriptures. The word of God: "This is in the first scriptures, the scriptures of Abraham and Moses" (87:18–10). "First scriptures" means the scriptures which were revealed to Adam's son "Gift of God" [Seth] and to Idris.

## High Place

*Ibn Kathir:* As for the word of God "We took him up to a high place" it is just as it is established in Bukhari and Muslim, in the report of the Night Journey: that the Prophet Muhammad passed by him, and he was in the fourth heaven.

*Ka'b al-Ahbar:* As for Idris, God revealed to him: "I will take you up one day, for I want to increase your work." A friend was sent to him from the angels and said: "God asked me to carry you to the heavens." Then he carried him between his wings until he ascended into the heavens. When he reached the fourth heaven the Angel of Death was there. The Angel of Death spoke to the angel who had been assigned to Idris. He said: "Where is Idris?" He said: "On my back." The Angel of Death said: "What a surprise. I was told to take the spirit of Idris in the fourth heaven, and I wondered: how can I take his spirit in the fourth heaven when he is still on the earth?"

*Ibn Abi Hatim:* Idris said: "Tell me, Angel of Death, how many years are left of my life?" He said: "I do not know until I look." So he looked and said: "You ask me about a man for whom there is nothing left of his life but a blink of the eye." So the angel looked under his wing to Idris. He had already taken him, but Idris did not know it.

*Mujahid:* Idris was taken up and did not die, just as Jesus was taken up. It means that he did not die until now, meaning that he was taken up to the heavens still living, then he was held there.

*Ibn Abbas and Dahhak:* He was taken up into the sixth heaven and died there.

*Hasan al-Basri:* He was taken into Paradise. As for the one who says he was taken up in the lifetime of his father, Jared b. Mahalalel, only God knows. Some claim that Idris did not come before Noah but in the time of the Israelites.

# Noah

**Q 7:59** We sent Noah to his people. He said: "My people, worship God, for there is no god for you other than he. I fear for you the punishment of an awful day." **60** The leaders of his people said to him: "We think you are in clear error." **61** He said: "My people, there is no error in me, but I am a messenger from the Lord of the worlds. **62** "I bring you the message of my Lord, and give you sincere advice. I know from God something you do not know. **63** "Do you wonder that a reminder from your Lord has come to you by the means of a man from among you, to warn you that you might fear God and receive his mercy?" **64** They rejected him but we delivered him and those with him in the Ark. We drowned those who rejected our signs. They were a blind people.

**Q 10:71** Recite to them the story of Noah, when he said to his people: "My people, if my being here and reminding you of the signs of God is hard upon you, I trust in God. Agree together about your affairs and among your partners, so that your affairs be not in turmoil. Then pass sentence on me and do not wait. **72** "If you turn back, I have asked for no recompense. There is no recompense except that which is from God. I am commanded to be one of those who submit." **73** They rejected him but we delivered him and those with him in the Ark. We made them viceregents but we drowned those who rejected our signs. See how those who were warned were punished.

**Q 11:25** We sent Noah to his people: "I am clearly warning you. **26** "Worship only God. I fear for you the punishment of a grievous day." **27** The leaders of his people who disbelieved said: "We think you are only a human being like us, nor do we think anyone follows you except those who are the lowest among us. Nor do we see any merit in you over us, but we think you are liars." **28** He said: "My people, do you think if I had a clear sign from my Lord, that he sent me mercy from himself, but it was hidden from you? Should we compel you when you are adverse? **29** "My people, I do not ask anything from you. There is no recompense except from God. I will not turn away those who believe. They are to meet their Lord but you I see as an ignorant people. **30** "My people, who would give me victory over God if I turned them away? Will you not remember? **31** "I am not saying to you that the treasures of God are with me, nor do I know the hidden, nor am I saying that I am an angel. I am not saying to those whom your eyes despise that God will not give them good. God knows what is in their souls. Then [if I did these things] would I be one of those who do wrong." **32** They said: "Noah, you have argued with us and prolonged our argument, so bring upon us that which you promised if you are one of the truthful." **33** He said: "God will bring it upon you, if he wishes, and you will be unable to resist. **34** "My advice would not benefit you, even if I intended to give you good advice, if God wishes to lead you astray. He is your Lord and to him you will return." **35** Or do these say: "He forged it." Say: "If I forged it then my sin is incumbent upon me, but I am free of what you are guilty." **36** It was revealed to Noah: "None of your people will believe except he who has already believed. Do not fret over what they are doing. **37** "Build the Ark under our eyes and inspiration. Do not address me concerning those who do wrong, for they will be drowned." **38** He began building the Ark, and every time the leaders of his people passed by him they ridiculed him. He said: "If you ridicule us now, we will ridicule you as you are ridiculing. **39** "You will learn on whom a punishment will come, shaming them. A lasting punishment will encompass them." **40** At length, our command came and the pits gushed forth. We said: "Ride on the Ark, pairs, two of everything, and your family, but not he against whom the word has already been issued, and he who believes." Only a few believed in him. **41** He said: "Ride in the Ark, in the name of God, whether it is moving or at rest. My Lord is Forgiving, Merciful." **42** The Ark sailed with them on waves like mountains. Noah called out to his son who had separated himself: "My son, ride with us and do not be with the unbelievers." **43** The son said: "I will take refuge on a mountain which will save me from the water." Noah said: "Today, no one can be safe from the command of God except the one to whom he shows mercy." The waves came between them and the son was one of those who were drowned. **44** It was said: "Earth, swallow your water! Sky, take up!" The water was taken away and the matter was concluded. The Ark rested on Mount Judi. It was said: "Away with the people who do wrong!" **45** Noah called upon his Lord, saying: "My Lord, my son is of my family. Your promise is the truth, and you are the most judicious of judges." **46** He said: "Noah, he is not of your family for his works were not upright. Do not ask me about that about which you have no knowledge. It is I who give you orders lest you be one of the ignorant ones." **47** Noah said: "My Lord, I seek refuge with you for asking you that about which I have no knowledge. Unless you forgive me and have mercy on me I will be one of the losers." **48** It was said: "Noah, come out of the Ark in peace from us, blessings upon you and the peoples who are [to descend] from those with you, peoples to whom we will grant pleasure but then a grievous punishment will befall them from us." **49** These are some of the stories of the hidden which we revealed to you, which neither you nor your people knew before this. Be patient. The end is for those who fear God.

**Q 21:76** Noah, when he called out to us before. We answered him and delivered him and his family from the great sorrow. **77** We caused him to be victorious over the people who rejected your signs, for they were an evil people. We drowned them, all together.

**Q 23:23** We sent Noah to his people. He said: "My people, worship God. There is no god for you other than he. Do you not fear God?" **24** The leaders of his people who disbelieved said: "This one is only a human like you, and he wants for you to consider him better than you. If God had wanted he could have sent angels. We have not heard this from our forefathers. **25** "He is only a man in whom is a Jinn, so be patient with him for awhile." **26** Noah said: "My Lord, give me victory because they are rejecting me." **27** We revealed to him: "Build the Ark under our eyes and inspiration. When our command comes and the pits gush forth, take on board pairs, two of everything, and your family, but not him against whom the word has already been issued. Do not address me concerning those who do wrong, for they are to be drowned. **28** "When you and those with you are on board the Ark, say: 'Praise God who saved us from the people who do wrong.' **29** "Say: 'My Lord, allow me to disembark blessed. You are the best to allow us to disembark.'" **30** In this are signs. We test.

**Q 26:105** The people of Noah rejected the messengers. **106** When their brother said to them: "Do you not fear God? **107** "I am a trustworthy messenger to you. **108** "Fear God and obey me. **109** "I do not ask you for recompense. There is no recompense except from the Lord of the worlds. **110** "Fear God and obey me." **111** They said: "Should we believe you when the lowly follow you?" **112** He said: "What is my knowledge about what they do? **113** "Their accounting is only with my Lord, if you could perceive. **114** "I do not turn away the believers. **115** "I am only a warner." **116** They said: "If you do not stop, Noah, you will be one of the stoned." **117** He said: "My Lord, my people rejected me. **118** "Make an opening between me and them. Save me and those who believe with me." **119** We saved him and those with him in the full Ark. **120** Then we drowned those who remained. **121** In this is a sign, but most of them are not believers. **122** Your Lord is the Mighty, the Merciful.

**Q 29:14** We sent Noah to his people. He stayed among them 1000 years except for 50 years. The Flood took them while they were doing wrong. **15** We saved him and the people of the boat. We made it a sign for the worlds.

**Q 37:75** Noah cried out to us, the best of those who answer. **76** We delivered him and his family from the great calamity, **77** made his seed to remain on the earth, **78** and left [this legacy] for him among the later generations. **79** Peace upon Noah in all the worlds. **80** Likewise do we reward those who do good. **81** He was one of our servants, the believers. **82** Then the others we drowned.

**Q 54:9**  Before them, the people of Noah disbelieved. They rejected our servant, saying: "He is possessed by a Jinn," and he was turned away. **10** He called upon his Lord: "I am overcome. Give me victory." **11** We opened the gates of the sky with water pouring forth. **12** We caused the earth to gush forth with springs. The waters met according to the command that had been issued. **13** We bore him on that of planks and caulk. **14** It flowed in our eyesight, a recompense to him who had been rejected. **15** We left it as a sign. Is there one who would be reminded? **16** How was my punishment and my warning? **17** We made the Quran easy to remember. Is there one who would remember?

**Q 71:1**  We sent Noah to his people: "Warn your people before a grievous punishment comes to them." **2** He said: "My people, I am a clear warner for you. **3** "Worship God, fear him, and obey me, **4** so he will forgive you your sins and delay your stated term. When the appointed time of God comes there cannot be a delay, if only you learned." **5** He said: "My Lord, I called my people night and day **6** but my call increases their flight. **7** "Every time I call them that you might forgive them, they put their fingers in their ears, cover themselves with their clothes, become obstinate, and are arrogant. **8** "So, I call to them aloud, **9** and I announce to them in public and in secret. **10** "Saying: 'Seek forgiveness from your Lord. He is Forgiving. **11** "'He will send the skies upon you with abundant rain, **12** expand your wealth and sons, and make you gardens and rivers. **13** "'What is it with you that you do not acknowledge the majesty of God? **14** "'For he has created you in different stages. **15** "'Do you not see how God has created seven heavens, in layers? **16** "'He made the moon to be a fire within them, and the sun to be a lamp. **17** "'God produced you from the ground. **18** "'You will return into it [the earth] and he will bring you out of it. **19** "'God made the earth spread out for you, **20** so that you might move about in it openly.'" **21** Noah said: "My Lord, they disobey me and follow him whose wealth and offspring increase only their loss. **22** "They have devised a great plan. **23** "They said: 'Do not abandon your gods: Wadd, Suwa, Yaghuth, Yaʿuq, and Nasr.' **24** "They have misled many. Do not increase those who do wrong except in being misled." **25** Because of their sins, they were drowned and are made to enter the Fire. They found none to help them in place of God. **26** Noah said: "My Lord, do not leave upon the earth any of the unbelievers in their homes. **27** "If you leave them, they will mislead your worshippers and will have only unbelieving and evil offspring. **28** "My Lord, forgive me, my parents, he who enters my house a believer, and all believing men and women. Only increase the perdition of those who do wrong."

## Genealogy and Age of Noah

*Ibn Kathir:* He is Noah b. Lamech b. Methuselah b. Idris b. Jared b. Mehalalel b. Kenan b. Enosh b. Seth b. Adam the father of humanity.

His birth was after the death of Adam by 126 years. According to the history of the People of the Torah, there were 140 years between the birth of Noah and the death of Adam. There were ten generations between them. God sent Adam when idols and false gods were worshipped. People legislated in error and disbelief. So God sent Noah as a mercy to his worshippers. He was the first messenger sent to the people of the earth. His people were called the "Banu Rasib." There is disagreement concerning his age when he was sent. It is said he was 50 years old, or 350 years old, or 480 years old. All three of these opinions are attributed to Ibn Abbas.

*Ibn Abi Hatim:* Abu Amamah heard a man say: "Messenger of God, was Adam a prophet?" The Prophet Muhammad said: "Yes." The man said: "How long was between him and between Noah?" The Prophet Muhammad said: "Ten generations."

*Tabari:* God sent Moses to his people, calling them to repentance, return to God, and doing the works which God had commanded in the scriptures he had revealed to Adam, Seth, and Enoch. Noah was sent when he was 50 years old.

*Suyuti:* al-Jawaliqi says the name Noah was originally not Arabic but was Arabicized. Kirmani adds that the meaning of the name in Syriac is "thankful." Hakim says that he was named Noah because he used to cry a lot to himself. His name is "Abd al-Ghaffar" [worshipper of the forgiving God]. Many of the companions of the Prophet Muhammad say he came before Idris. Others say he is Noah b. Lamech b. Methuselah b. Enoch (who is Idris). Tabarani says that Abu Dharr said: "Prophet of God, who was the first of the prophets?" He said: "Adam." I said: "Then who?" He said: "Noah. Between them was twenty generations." According to Ibn Abbas, between Adam and Noah was ten generations, this on the basis of a report: "God sent Noah at 40 years. He stayed with his people for 950 years calling them to God. He lived after the Flood for 60 years until most of the people were dispersed." Tabari mentions that the birth of Noah was 126 years after the death of Adam. Nawawi says that Noah lived the longest of the prophets.

*Awn b. Abi Shaddad:* God sent Noah to his people when he was 350 years old. He stayed with them for 1000 years less 50, and he lived after that for another 350 years.

*Ibn Abbas:* God sent Noah to them when he was 480 years old. Then he called them to God during his prophethood for 120 years. He rode on the boat when he was 600 years old, and then lived after that for another 350 years.

*Muhammad b. Qays:* In the time of Noah, all the places of the earth were claimed by someone.

## False Gods

*Ibn Abi Hatim:* Urwah b. al-Zubayr reports that Wadd, Suwa, Yaghuth, Ya'uq, and Nasr were children of Adam. Wadd was the oldest and most pious of them.

*Muhammad b. Qays:* These names were a group of upright people from among the descendants of Adam, and there were people who used to follow and imitate them. When they died their companions who used to imitate them said: "If only we had images of them, it would be better for us to worship them to remember them." So they made images of them but when they died others came after them, and Iblis came to them. He said: "If only you would worship them, the rain would fall on account of them." So they worshipped them.

*Ibn Abi Hatim:* They asked whether Yazid b. al-Muhallab was killed in the first country in which something other than God was worshipped. It was said: Wadd was an upright man. He was answerable within his community. When he died his people remained around his grave in the land of Babylon and felt pity for him. When Iblis saw their pity he appeared to them in the form of a human and said: "I saw your pity over this man. Are you able to make an image of him so that he can be in your place of assembly and you can remember him?" They said: "Yes." So they made an image of him. They put him in their place of assembly and began to remember him. When Iblis saw what they were doing he said: "Can each one of you make a stand for yourselves so that he can be in each of your houses so that you can remember him?" They said: "Yes." So in each house there was a likeness of him. Then their sons learned and saw what they were doing. They continued to do this, remembering this man until they took him for a deity and worshipped him in the place of God, their children and their children's children. He became the first thing that was worshipped in the place of God: Wadd.

## Ark

*Tabari:* God stayed among his people for 1000 years less 50 just as God says: "summoning them to God both openly and secretly." Generation after generation passed and they did not respond to him until three generations passed this same way. God intended to destroy them, and ordered Noah to plant a tree, so he did. When it grew and went in all directions, after 40 years, God ordered him to cut it down and make a boat from it. So he cut it down and began to work on the boat.

*Salman al-Farisi:* Noah worked on the boat for 400 years, the teak tree had grown for 40 years until it was 300 cubits tall, a cubit being the length of the arm to the shoulder.

*Qatadah:* It was mentioned to us that the boat was 300 cubits in length and 50 cubits wide. Its height was 30 cubits and it had a door on its side.

*Hasan al-Basri:* The length of Noah's boat was 1200 cubits and its width 600 cubits.

*Ibn Abbas:* The disciples said to Jesus, son of Mary: "If only you could send to us a man who had seen the Ark, and would tell us about it." He went with them until he came to a hill of earth. He took a handful of this earth in his palm and said: "Do you know what this is?" They said: "God and his messenger know." He said: "This is the grave of Ham b. Noah." He hit the hill with his rod and said: "Rise with God's permission!" Then Ham was standing there shaking the earth from his gray hair. Jesus said to him: "Is this how you died?" Ham said: "No, when I died I was a young man but I perceived that it was the Hour and then my hair turned gray." Jesus said: "Tell us about the boat of Noah." Ham said: "Its length was 1200 cubits and its width 600 cubits. It had three decks: one for domestic and wild animals, one for people, and one for birds. When the droppings of the animals became too much God revealed to Noah to tickle the tail of the elephant. He tickled and a male and female pig came from the elephant, and they consumed the droppings. When the mouse fell into the seams of the boat and began gnawing at them, God revealed to Noah to hit the lion between its eyes. A male and female cat came out and consumed the mouse." Jesus said: "How did Noah know that the land had dried?" Ham said: "He sent a raven to bring him the news, but it found a corpse and stayed there. Noah proclaimed that it should be feared, and therefore it does not live near houses. Then he sent a dove which returned with an olive leaf in its beak and some clay on its feet. Noah knew that the land was dry. Because of this the ring around the dove's neck is green, and Noah said it should be tame and protected, and therefore doves live near houses." The disciples said: "Messenger of God, why not set out with him for our people so he can sit with them and tell them?" Jesus said: "How could one without sustenance follow you?" Jesus said to Ham: "Return with God's permission!" and he returned to the dust.

*Ibn Abbas:* Noah constructed the boat on Mount Nod where the Flood began. The boat was 300 cubits in length, a cubit being that of the grandfather of Noah's father [Enoch], 50 cubits in width, and 30 cubits in height. It stuck out of the water six cubits and had three decks. He made three doors for each deck, one beneath the other.

*Ibn Ishaq:* The Jews allege that God commanded him to build the Ark from teak wood, to make it slanting, to seal it with pitch on the inside and out, to make its length 80 cubits, its width 50 cubits, its height 30 cubits, to make it with three decks: upper, middle, and lower, and to make windows in it.

## Flood

*Aishah:* The Prophet Muhammad said: "If God had shown mercy on anyone from among the people of Noah, he would have shown mercy to the mother of the child. Noah stayed with his people for 1000 years less 50, calling them to God, until the end of his time when he planted a tree which became great and grew in every direction. He cut it down and began working on a boat. People would pass by him and question him. He would say: 'I am making a boat.' They ridiculed him because of it: 'You are making a boat in the desert. How will it float?' He said: 'You will learn.' When he was finished the pits gushed forth much water in the streets. The mother became frightened, the one who loved her child very much, and she fled to the mountain, going up a third of it. When the water reached her she went up another third of the mountain. When the water reached her she went to the top of the mountain. When the water reached her neck she lifted her child up with her hand, but the water took him away. If God would have shown mercy on anyone, he would have shown mercy to the mother of the child."

*Ibn Ishaq:* Noah's people used to grab him and choke him until he was unconscious, so he said: "Oh God, forgive my people for they do not understand." The people continued to be disobedient, and sin became great in the earth because of them. Noah waited for generation after generation but not one came which was not worse than the one before it, the latest saying: "This was the same with our fathers and grand-fathers, he is possessed by Jinn." They did not accept anything from him, until finally Noah complained about this to God. Noah began work on the Ark, giving up on his people. He cut wood, forged iron, and readied the pitch and other materials, which only he knew how to make, for the Ark. His people began to pass by him, while he was working, and ridicule him because of it. They would say: "Noah, you have become a carpenter after being a prophet!" So God made the wombs of women infertile and they bore no children.

Noah built the Ark as God commanded him, and when he was finished with it God made the pits to gush forth as a sign between himself and Noah. God said: "When our command comes and the pits gush forth, take and carry on the Ark a male and female of everything." When the pits gushed forth Noah loaded up the Ark according to the command of God, pairs, two of everything in which was a spirit, and trees, male and female. He had his three sons with him: Shem, Ham and Japeth, and their wives, and six people from those who believed in him, altogether ten people: Noah, his sons and their wives. Then he loaded the animals as God had commanded him, but his son Yam remained behind for he did not believe.

*Ibn Abbas:* The first animal that Noah loaded on the Ark was the ant, and the last was the donkey. When he loaded the donkey and only its chest was inside, Iblis attached himself to its tail so that it was unable to lift its legs. Noah said: "Get going!" and the donkey tried to get up but could not. Finally Noah said: "Get going even if Satan is with you!" The words he said were a slip of the tongue but when Noah said it, Satan let the donkey proceed. The donkey went in and Satan with him. Noah said: "How did you get in here with me, enemy of God?" Satan said: "Did you not say: 'Get going even if Satan is with you!'?" Noah said: "Go away from me, enemy of God!" Satan said: "There is no way for you not to take me." It is alleged that he was in the back of the Ark.

When Noah was settled in the Ark, having loaded all those who believed in him, the sixteenth night of the month had passed, the month of the year in which Noah entered the Ark, after 600 years of his life. After Noah and all those with him were in the Ark, the fountains of the deep began to flow and the gates of the heavens were opened. Between the time God sent the water and the boat floating on the water was 40 days and 40 nights. The water carried them, increasing and growing higher, the Ark carrying them upon waves like mountains. Noah called out to his son who perished with those who perished. He was standing apart from those who believed in his Lord when Noah saw him and said to him: "Son, ride with us and do not be one of the unbelievers." The son said: "I will take refuge on a mountain which will protect me from the water." He was in the habit of taking refuge on the mountains when it was raining, and he thought that this was going to be the same situation. The water rose fifteen cubits above the mountains. All creation disappeared from the face of the earth, everything with a spirit and all plants. No creation remained except for Noah and those who were with him on the Ark, and except for Og the giant, as the People of the Book allege. Between God's sending of the Flood and the receding of the water was six months and ten nights.

*Ibn Kathir:* Some of the exegetes allege that Og b. Anaq, also called Ibn Anaq, was alive from before the time of Noah to the time of Moses. They say he was an unbeliever, a giant, and a tyrant. They say he was not rightly guided but he was the offspring of his mother, a daughter of Adam, out of wedlock. On account of his height he used to take fish from the depths of the sea and fry them on the face of the sun. He used to say to Noah while he was on the Ark: "What is that large bowl you have there?" It is mentioned that he was 3333 and a third cubits in height.

*Ibn Abbas:* God sent rain for 40 days and 40 nights. When the rain came, the wild animals, domestic animals, and birds all went to Noah and were subjected to him. He loaded them onto the Ark just as God had commanded. He also carried with him the corpse of Adam, putting it as a barrier between the men and women. They loaded on the Ark on the tenth of Rajab and left on the Day of Ashura of Muharram, and this is why people fast on the Day of Ashura. The water came out in two halves: half from the heavens and half from the earth. The water rose fifteen cubits above the tops of the mountains in the lands. The boat sailed with them and circumambulated the whole earth in six months, and did not stop until it reached the Sanctuary at Mecca. It did not enter but circled the Sanctuary for a week. Then the House built by Adam was lifted up, lifted out of the water, the Inhabited House [bayt al-ma'mur] and the Black Stone, onto Mount Abu Qubays. When the Ark had circled around the Sanctuary and traversed the earth, it came upon Mount Judi, a mountain with its base in the land of Mosul, and rested after six months. After the Ark came to rest on Mount Judi, it was said: "Earth, swallow your water!" and the earth sucked it up. The water which had come down from the heavens became the oceans which are seen on the earth today. The last of the water that remained from the Flood in the earth was water at Hisma. It remained on the earth for 40 years after the Flood, then it left.

## Pits and Oven

*Tabari:* The "oven" with water boiling over which God mentioned as a sign between him and Noah was the oven of stone which belonged to Eve and became Noah's.

*Hasan al-Basri:* It was an oven of stone which belonged to Eve and became Noah's. It was said to Noah: When you see the water boiling over the oven, you and your companions ride on the boat.

*Tabari:* There is disagreement concerning the location of the pits in the earth and the water boiling over which God made as a sign between him and Noah. Ibn Abbas says it was in India. Mujahid and Sha'bi say it was in the vicinity of Kufah. Qatadah says in Mesopotamia.

## People on Ark

*Ibn Abbas:* In Noah's boat there were 80 men, one of them was Jurhum. Noah took his sons in the boat: Shem, Ham, and Japeth, and his daughters-in-law, the wives of his sons. There were 73 of the sons of Seth also who believed.

*Sufyan al-Thawri:* Some people used to say there were 80 referring to the "few" mentioned by God in the Quran.

*Qatadah:* It was mentioned to us that on the boat was Noah, his wife, his three sons, and their wives, eight altogether.

*Hakim:* "Only a few believed with him" refers to Noah, his three sons, and his four daughters-in-law.

*Ibn Jurayj:* It was reported to me that Noah carried with him his three sons and the three wives of his sons, and the wife of Noah. Their number with their wives was eight. The names of his sons: Japeth, Ham, and Seth. Ham had sex with his wife on the boat, so Noah prayed that his seed be altered, and from him came the blacks.

*Ibn Ishaq:* It is alleged by the Jews that after Noah left the Ark he lived for 348 years. The total years of Noah's life were 1000 years less 50. Then God took him. It is said that only Shem was born to Noah 98 years before the Flood. Some of the Jews maintain that there was no procreation in the Ark and children were born to Noah only after he left the Ark.

*Ibn Kathir:* It is said that Noah did not have Shem, Ham, and Japeth until after the Flood, but before the boat there was his son Canaan who was drowned and Eber who died before the Flood. It is also mentioned that Ham had sex with his wife in the boat and Noah asked God to disfigure the character of his sperm. He had a son who was black, Canaan b. Ham, the ancestor of the Blacks. It is also said that he saw his father sleeping and his private parts were exposed, but he did not cover him up. Rather, his brothers covered Noah. And it was on account of this that his sperm was changed, and that his descendants would be servants to those of his brother.

*Ibn Abbas:* Born to Noah was Shem whose descendants were white and tanned, Ham whose descendants were black with a little white, Japeth whose descendants were red and brown, and Canaan who was drowned. The Arabs call him Yam.

*Samurah:* The Prophet Muhammad said: "Shem is father of the Arabs, Ham is father of the Ethiopians, and Japeth is father of the Romans." By Romans he meant the Greeks.

*Saʿid b. al-Musayyib:* Noah had three sons: Shem, Japeth, and Ham. All people came from these three sons. The sons of Seth are the Arabs, Persians, and Romans. The sons of Japeth are the Turks, Slavs, and Gog and Magog. The sons of Ham are the Egyptians, Blacks, and Berbers.

*Aʿmash:* "Only a few believed with him" means there were seven: Noah, three daughters-in-law, and three of his sons.

*Ibn Ishaq:* Noah took his three sons: Seth, Ham, Japeth, their wives, and six people who believed in him. There were ten of them counting Noah and his sons and their wives.

## Resting Place of the Ark

*Tabari:* It is said that God sent the Flood on the thirteenth of Ab, that Noah stayed on the Ark until the water had receded, and the Ark came to rest on Mount Judi in Qarda [Ararat] on the seventeenth day of the sixth month. When Noah left the Ark he took a place in Qarda in the land of Mesopotamia, and built there a city which he called "The Eighty" [Thamanin] because he had built there a house for all the people with him who believed in him, their number being 80. Today, this place is called "Market of the Eighty" [Suq Thamanin].

*Ibn Abbas:* Noah came down in a land and each of the men built a house. It was called "Market of the Eighty." All of the descendants of Cain were drowned. The forefathers between Noah and Adam were Muslim.

*Tabari:* Noah and his family became Muslim, so God revealed that he would never send a Flood to the earth again.

*Abd al-Ghaffar:* The Prophet Muhammad said it was on the first day of Rajab when Noah rode the boat. He and all with him fasted while the boat sailed with them for six months ending in Muharram. The boat came to Mount Judi on the Day of Ashura. Noah fasted and ordered all the wild and domestic animals with him to fast, thanking God.

*Ibn Jurayj:* The top part of the boat was for the birds, the middle part for the people, and the lower part for the predatory animals. Its height was 30 cubits. The Ark left from Ayn Wardah on Friday after the tenth night of Rajab had passed. It came to Mount Judi on the Day of Ashura. It passed by the House, circumambulating it seven times. God lifted the House from drowning. Then the Ark went to Yemen and returned.

*Abu Ya'ala:* Ibn Abbas reported that the Prophet Muhammad went on Pilgrimage and when he came to Wadi Asfan he said: "Abu Bakr, which wadi is this?" Abu Bakr said: "Wadi Asfan." The Prophet Muhammad said: "Noah, Hud, and Abraham passed by this wadi on their mounts and circumambulated the ancient House."

*Qatadah:* Noah left the Ark on the Day of Ashura of Muharram. He said to those with him: "Those of you fasting should complete the fast. Those of you not fasting should fast." It was also mentioned that the Ark departed on the tenth day of Muharram, and was in the water for 150 days. It came to rest upon Judi for a month, then the people were brought down on the tenth of Muharram, the Day of Ashura.

*Abu Hurayrah:* A group of people from the Jews passed by the Prophet Muhammad while they were fasting, on the Day of Ashura. He said:

"What is this fast?" The Jews said: "This is the day on which God saved Moses and the Israelites from drowning when Pharaoh drowned, and this is the day on which the Ark rested upon Mount Judi, so Noah and Moses fasted to thank God." The Prophet Muhammad said: "I believe in Moses and the fast of this day." So he ordered his Companions to fast.

*Ibn Majah:* Abdallah b. Amir heard the Prophet Muhammad say: "Noah fasted all the time except for the day of the Id al-Adha and the day of the Id al-Fitr."

*Tabarani:* Abdallah b. Amir heard the Prophet Muhammad say: "Noah fasted all the time except for the day of the Id al-Adha and the day of the Id al-Fitr. David fasted half of the time. Abraham fasted a third of the days of each month. He fasted for a time and then broke the fast for a time."

## After Noah's Death

*Ibn Kathir:* Tabari and Azraqi report that the grave of Noah is in the mosque of the Sanctuary at Mecca. This is more established than what is alleged by many of the historians who mention that he is in a town in a spot known today as Kurk Noah. The People of the Book allege that when Noah rode in the Ark he was 600 years old. Ibn Abbas says the same thing but adds: After this he lived 350 years. The Quran says that Noah stayed with his people after he was sent as a prophet but before the Flood for 1000 years less 50 years. Only God knows if he lived after that. If what Ibn Abbas says is sound, then he was sent as a prophet when he was 480 years old and he lived after the Flood for 350 years, in which case he would have lived a total of 1780 years.

# Hud

**Q 7:65** To Ad [we sent] their brother Hud. He said: "My people, worship God. There is no god for you other than he. Do you not fear God?" **66** The leaders of his people who did not believe said: "We see you are in folly, and we think you are one of the liars." **67** He said: "My people, there is no folly in me, but I am a messenger from the Lord of the worlds. **68** "I bring you the messages of my Lord. I am a sincere and trustworthy advisor to you. **69** "Or do you wonder that a reminder has come to you from your Lord in the hands of a man from among you, to warn you? Remember when he made you inheritors after the people of Noah and increased your stature in creation. Remember the benefits of God, that you might prosper." **70** They said: "Come to us so that we might worship God alone and renounce that which our fathers used to worship. Cause to come to us that with which you threaten us if you are one of the truthful." **71** He said: "Punishment and wrath have already befallen you from your Lord. Dispute with me concerning names you have devised, you and your fathers. God did not send down authority for this. Wait: I am waiting with you." **72** We saved him and those with him with a mercy from us. We cut off the roots of those who rejected our signs and were not believers.

**Q 11:50** To Ad [we sent] their brother Hud. He said: "My people, worship God. There is no god for you other than he. You are nothing but forgers. **51** "My people, I do not ask you for recompense. My recompense is only from the one who created me. Do you not comprehend? **52** "My people, ask your Lord for forgiveness, then turn to him. He will send the heavens upon you pouring rain, and add strength to your strength. Do not turn back as sinners." **53** They said: "Hud, you have not brought us a sign, and we are not ones to leave our gods on your word. We do not believe in you. **54** "We say only that some of our gods may have possessed you with evil." He said: "I call upon God to witness and you witness that I am free from those who associate with God **55** that which is other than he. Scheme against me together, then do not stop. **56** "I trust in God my Lord and your Lord. There is no moving creature whose forelock he does not hold. My Lord is on the straight path. **57** "If you turn away, then I have brought you that with which I was sent to you. My Lord will create a people other than you and you will not harm him in any way. My Lord has watch over all things." **58** When our decree came, we saved Hud and those who believed with him by mercy from us. We saved them from a severe punishment. **59** This was Ad who rejected the signs of their Lord, disobeyed his messengers, and followed the word of all who are giant and obstinate. **60** They were followed in this life by a curse. On the Day of the Resurrection, woe to Ad who rejected their Lord! Away with Ad! the people of Hud.

**Q 26:123**   Ad rejected the messengers. **124** When their brother Hud said to them: "Do you not fear? **125** "I am a trustworthy messenger to you. **126** "Fear God and obey me. **127** "I do not ask of you any recompense. My recompense is from the Lord of the worlds only. **128** "Do you build a sign to amuse on every high place? **129** "Do you take artifices so that you might be immortal? **130** "When you strike, you strike like giants. **131** "Fear God and obey me. **132** "Fear the one who bestowed on you all you know. **133** "He bestowed on you cattle and sons, **134** gardens and springs. **135** "I fear for you the punishment of an awful day." **136** They said: "It is the same to us whether you admonish us or are not one of the admonishers. **137** "This is only a creation of the ancestors **138** and we are not the ones to receive punishment." **139** They rejected him and we destroyed them. In this is a sign but many of them are not believers. **140** Your Lord is He, the Mighty, the Merciful.

**Q 41:15**   As for Ad, they were arrogant in the land by other than truth, and said: "Who is stronger than we?" But did they not see that God who created them is stronger than they? They continued to be ignorant of our signs. **16** So we sent upon them a violent wind in days of disaster as a taste of a punishment of humiliation in the life of this world. The punishment of the hereafter will be a greater penalty. They will not be helped.

**Q 46:21**   Remember the brother of Ad when he warned his people among the winding sand-tracts. There had been warners before him and after him: "Worship only God! I fear for you the punishment of an awful day." **22** They said: "Did you come to us to turn us from our gods? Bring that with which you threaten us if you are one of the truthful." **23** He said: "The knowledge is with God only. I bring you that with which I was sent, but I see you to be a people in ignorance." **24** Then, when they saw a cloud coming toward their valleys they said: "This cloud will rain on us." But no, it is that which you wished to expedite, a wind in which is a grievous punishment. **25** It will destroy everything by the command of its Lord. Then they will become so that nothing except their houses is seen. Thus do we reward the sinning people.

## Ad

*Ibn Kathir:* Hud was Hud b. Shelah b. Arpachshad b. Shem b. Noah. It is said that Hud was Eber b. Shelah b. Arpachshad b. Shem b. Noah. Tabari mentions that it is said that he was: Hud b. Abdallah b. Rabah al-Khalud b. Ad b. Uz [Aws] b. Aram b. Shem b. Noah. He was from a tribe who called themselves Ad b. Uz [Aws] b. Shem b. Noah. They were Arabs living in the winding sand-tracts [al-Ahqaf], which is a mountain of sand in Yemen between Oman and the Hadramawt, in a land looking out upon the sea which is called "al-Shihr." The name of their valley was "al-Mughith." The Ad here is the first Ad who worshipped idols after the Flood. They had three idols: Sada, Samud, and Haba. These were the first Ad whom God mentioned. They were the descendants of Ad b. Iram who used to establish pillars in the desert.

*Qurtubi:* Ibn Abbas says that Hud was the son of one of the Ad. It is said: He was "their brother" in tribe. It is said: He was a human being from the descendants of their father Adam. Ibn Dawud says: "their brother" Hud means their companion. Ad was one of the sons of Shem, son of Noah. Ibn Ishaq says: Ad was the son of Uz [Aws] b. Aram b. Shelah b. Arpachshad b. Shem b. Noah. Ibn Masud says: This was the "first Ad" and Hud was not Arab. It is possible that the name was Arabic derived from "Had" and "Yahud." Between Hud and Noah, according to what the exegetes mention, were seven generations. Ad was divided into thirteen tribes who settled down in the cultivated sand. They were the people of two gardens, cultivated fields, and buildings. Their lands were the most fertile of all the lands. God became angry with them and made their lands powerful. They stretched from the Hadramawt to the Yemen. They worshipped idols. Hud brought with him those who believed with him to Mecca after his people were destroyed, and there they stayed until their death.

*Tabari:* The descendants of Noah divided the earth among themselves after Noah. From among these descendants were people who disobeyed God, so God sent a messenger to them but they rejected him and continued in their sinful ways. So God destroyed them, then two peoples descended from Aram b. Shem b. Noah. One of them was Ad b. Uz b. Aram b. Shem b. Noah. It was the first Ad. The second was Thamud b. Gether b. Aram b. Shem b. Noah. They were the original ['aribah] Arabs.

*Ibn Kathir:* It is said that Hud was the first to speak Arabic. Wahb b.

Munabbih alleges that it was Hud's father who was the first to speak it. Someone else says: The first to speak Arabic was Noah. It is also said that it was Adam. Those who were before Ishmael were called the "Original Arabs," who were many tribes. Among them were the Ad, Thamud, Jurhum, Tasam, Amim, Midian, Amalek, Abil, Jasim, Qahtan, the Banu Yaqtan, and others. As for the "Arabicized Arabs," they are the descendants of Ishmael b. Abraham. Ishmael b. Abraham was the first to speak eloquent, classical Arabic. He took the Arabic speech from the Jurhum who had settled with his mother Hagar in Mecca.

*Suyuti:* Ka'b al-Ahbar says Hud was the most similar of all people to Adam. Ibn Masud says he was a strong man. Ibn Hisham says he is Eber b. Arpachshad b. Shem b. Noah. Others say he is Hud b. Abdallah b. Rabah b. Hawadh b. Ad b. 'Uz b. Aram b. Shem b. Noah.

*Tabari:* As for Ad, God sent them Hud b. Abdallah b. Rabah b. al-Khalud b. Ad b. Uz b. Aram b. Shem b. Noah. Some genealogists allege that Hud was Eber b. Shelah b. Arpachshad b. Shem b. Noah. The people had three idols they used to worship. One of them was called Sadda, another Samud, and the third al-Huba. Hud summoned them to acknowledge the oneness of God, and the worship of him alone without another, to leave the tyranny of people. But they rejected him.

*Wahb b. Munabbih:* The Ad were idolaters, worshiping idols instead of God. Among the idols was one called Sadda, another called Hirad, and another called Hubba. God send Hud to them as a prophet and he was from among them and was the best thinker among them. He was 30 years old when he commanded them to acknowledge the oneness of God, not to put other deities with him, and to cease from being tyrants to the people. He did not command them to do anything else, but they rejected him and called him a liar.

### Stature

*Qurtubi:* In reference to Q 7:69, the Ad were tall in stature and great in body size. Ibn Abbas says their height was 100 cubits and then God shortened them to 60 cubits. This was the extra which added to the character of their forefathers. It is also said that this verse means they were increased in size over the people of Noah.

*Wahb b. Munabbih:* The head of one of them was like a great dome. The eye of a man was enough to scare predatory animals, and their noses likewise.

*Ibn Hubayrah:* One man from the people of Ad took two doors from the Hijaz that, put together, 500 men from the Hijaz could not bear.

## Buildings of Ad

*Ibn Kathir:* With reference to Q 26:128, Hud is saying to them: "Do you build a sign to amuse yourselves in every exalted place, a high place with great buildings such as castles and the like? You amuse yourselves with the buildings because you have no need of them." This is because they lived in tents.

*Ibn Kathir:* With reference to Q 26:129, it is said that the "artifices" were castles. It is also said they were water towers or something for holding water.

## Iram

**Q 89:6**  Do you not see how your Lord dealt with Ad, **7** Iram with lofty supports, **8** the like of which were not produced in all the lands? **9** And Thamud who cut out rock in the valley? **10** And Pharaoh of the stakes? **11** Those who transgressed in the lands **12** and made much spoil within them. **13** Your Lord poured out upon them the scourge of a punishment. **14** Your Lord is Watching.

*Ibn Kathir:* There were many who lived in tents with tall and thick pillars. There are those who claim that Iram was a city which moved around the earth, sometimes in Syria, sometimes in Yemen, sometimes in the Hijaz, and sometimes elsewhere. Some people allege that Iram is a city made of gold and silver and that it moves about in the land.

*Yaqut:* It is said that Iram was a city unlike any other ever created. It was situated in Yemen between the Hadramawt and Sana'a. In it were castles of gold and silver and dwelling places under which flowed rivers. It is also said that the people gathered all the gold, silver, pearls, gems, and precious stones in the world and brought them to one place, and from these things were built the city of Iram. The length and width of the city was twelve parsangs on each side. In it were 300,000 castles all made of jewels. After the people of Ad were destroyed, the city disappeared and no person has ever entered it except for one man during the days of Mu'awiyah whose name was Abdallah b. Qilabah.

### Punishment

**Q 51:41**   For the Ad, when we sent against them a devastating wind. **42** There was nothing it met that it did not reduce to ruin.

**Q 53:50**   It is he who destroyed the first Ad, **51** and Thamud he left no trace of them, **52** and the people of Noah before. They were the worst of those doing wrong and transgressing.

**Q 54:18**   Ad rejected, then how was my punishment and warning? **19** We sent upon them a violent wind on a day of lasting bad fortune, **20** uprooting people as though they were the roots of palm trees torn up [from the ground]. **21** How was my punishment and warning?

**Q 69:6**   As for Ad, they were destroyed by an exceedingly violent wind. **7** He made it rage against them for seven nights and eight days in a row, so that you could see the people overthrown in it as if they were the roots of hollow palm trees toppled. **8** Do you see any of them remaining?

*Abu Kurayb:* God imposed a drought on the Ad for three years, and they suffered, so they sent a party to pray for rain. Harith b. Hassan al-Bakri says: I set out to meet the Prophet Muhammad when I passed by a women in al-Rabdhah [near Medina on the road to Mecca]. She said: "Will you carry me to the Prophet Muhammad?" I said yes and I carried her until we reached Medina. I entered the mosque and there was the Prophet Muhammad standing at the pulpit. Bilal b. Rabah was there armed with a sword, and there were black banners. I asked: "What is this?" They answered: "Amr b. al-As has returned from his raid." When the Prophet Muhammad came down from the pulpit I went to him and asked his permission to speak. He gave me permission, so I said: "Oh Messenger of God, at the door is a woman from the tribe of Tamim who asked me to carry her to you." He said: "Bilal: give her permission to enter." So she entered and when she sat down the Prophet Muhammad said to me: "Was there any animosity between you and the Tamim?" I said: "Yes but there was a turn of fate against them. If you see fit to place the desert between us and them, then do it." The woman said: "If someone harms you, Messenger of God, who will harm back for you?" I said: "I am like the scapegoat who bears sins. Did I carry you so that you might become an adversary to me? God forbid that I might be like the party of Ad." The Prophet Muhammad said: "What party of Ad?" I said: "You have forgotten that the Ad had a drought, so they sent people to pray for rain for them. They passed by Bakr b.

Mu'awiyah in Mecca, who gave them wine to drink, and whose two slave-girls sang for them for a month. Then they sent a man from there until he came to the mountains of Mahrah [in Yemen]. He invoked God and clouds came. Each time they came he would say: 'Go to such and such a place!' until a cloud came and a voice called to him from it: 'Take them as ashes, leave not one of the Ad!' The man heard this but kept it secret until the punishment came to the Ad."

*Abu Bakr:* The one who came to them went to the mountains of Mahrah, ascended and said: "Oh God, I have not come to you because of a prisoner I ask you to redeem nor for a sick person I ask you to heal, but to send rain upon the Ad as you used to irrigate for them." Clouds rose up for him and from them a voice called: "Choose!" He said: "Go to the tribe of so-and-so," and "Go to the tribe of so-and-so!" until the last of the clouds, a black one, passed. He said: "Go to the Ad!" A voice called from it: "Take them as ashes, leave not one of the Ad!" He kept this secret from the delegation of Ad while they were still drinking with Bakr b. Mu'awiyah. Bakr b. Mu'awiyah thought it reprehensible to tell them while they were still with him and eating with him. So he began to sing and then mentioned it to them.

*Ibn Ishaq:* When the drought befell the Ad, they said: Let us prepare a delegation to go to Mecca to pray for rain. They sent Qayl b. Anz and Luqaym b. Huzal b. Huzayl b. Utayl b. Sadd b. Ad the elder, and Marthad b. Sa'd b. Ufayr who was a Muslim [follower of the Prophet Hud] but kept secret his religion, and Julhumah b. al-Khaybari, the maternal uncle of Mu'awiyah b. Bakr the brother of his mother. Then they sent Luqman b. Ad b. so-and-so b. Sadd b. Ad the elder. Each of these men went out with a group of his relatives so that the number of their delegation was 70 men. When they arrived at Mecca they alighted with Mu'awiyah b. Bakr. He was within sight of Mecca, on the outskirts of the sanctuary. He received them and honored them for they were his uncles and in-laws. Huzaylah bt. Bakr was the sister of Mu'awiyah b. Bakr by his father and his mother just as was Lahdah bt. al-Khaybari to Luqaym b. Huzal b. Huzayl b. Utayl b. Sadd b. Ad the elder. She bore him four sons: Ubayd, Amr, Amir, and Umayr. They were with their uncles in Mecca, the family of Mu'awiyah b. Bakr. In the end, they were the only Ad that remained from the first Ad who were destroyed.

The party remained for a month, and when Mu'awiyah b. Bakr saw that their stay was to be long, having been sent by their people to seek aid against the trial which had befallen them, he was distressed. He had his two female singers sing a song reminding them of their responsibility.

Marthad b. Sa'd b. Ufayr said: "By God, you will not receive rain by your invocation of God, but only if you obey your prophet and return to him will you be given rain." In doing this he revealed his allegiance to the Prophet Hud, so Julhamah b. al-Khaybari ordered the others to restrain Marthad from accompanying the delegation into Mecca. After they had left for Mecca to pray for rain, Marthad went from the dwelling of Mu'awiyah until he caught up to them in Mecca before they asked God for anything. When he reached them he got up to pray while the delegation was together praying. He said: "Oh God, grant me only one request: Do not include me in anything for which the party of Ad asks you." Qayl b. Anz was the head of the delegation of Ad, and they prayed: "Oh God, give to Qayl whatever he asks of you, and take our request together with his." Qayl b. Anz prayed: "Oh our God, if Hud is truthful, give us rain for he has destroyed us." So God caused three clouds to appear: white, red, and black. A voice called from the clouds: "Qayl, choose for yourself and your people from these clouds!" He said: "I choose the black cloud because it is the cloud with the most water." The voice called to him: "You choose ashes which will not leave anyone of the Ad, no parent nor child will it leave, it will make you extinct, except for the tribe of Lawdhiyah the rightly guided." The tribe of Lawdhiyah were the sons of Luqaym b. Huzal b. Huzayl b. Huzaylah bt. Bakr who lived in Mecca with their uncles and were not with the Ad in their land. They were the other Ad.

God sent the black cloud, which Qayl b. Anz had chosen, against the Ad. It came toward them from a valley of theirs called al-Mughith. When they saw it, they thought it was a good sign. The first to see what was really in it, that it was a wind, was a woman from the Ad named Mahdid. When she understood what was in the cloud she screamed and then fell unconscious. When she regained consciousness the people asked: "What did you see, Mahdid?" She said: "I saw a wind in which there was something resembling fire. In front of it were men, leading it." God caused it to strike them for seven nights and eight days without ceasing. It destroyed every last one of the Ad. Hud and those who believed with him were in an enclosed area. Nothing hit him or those with him except that which was gentle to the skin and pleasing to the soul. The wind passed from Ad destroying all between heaven and earth, marking them with stones. The delegation of Ad left Mecca and passed by Mu'awiyah b. Bakr and his father. They stopped there, and while they were with him a man approached on a camel in the moonlight on the third evening after the smiting of Ad. He told them the news and they asked: "Where did you part company from Hud and his companions?" He said: "I separated from them at the shore of the sea." They doubted what he had told them until Huzaylah bt. Bakr said: "He tells the truth, by the Lord of Mecca. Muthawwib b. Yaghfur son of my brother Muʿawiyah b. Bakr is with them."

*Suddi:* When the Ad rejected Hud, God smote them with a drought which made them suffer. Hud asked God for this and God sent a barren wind against them, a wind which does not pollinate the trees. When they saw it, they said: "This is a passing phase of our rainy season." When it came closer to them they saw the camels and men that the wind was causing to fly about between the heavens and the earth. When they saw this, they returned to their houses. When they entered their houses, the wind entered after them and destroyed them therein. Then it drove them out of their houses and afflicted them "on a day of lasting bad fortune" (54:19). The wind continued to be a punishment upon them "for seven nights and eight days in a row" (69:7). It destroyed everything in its path, driving the people from their houses as God said: "Uprooting people" from the houses "as if they were the roots of hollow palm trees torn up" (54:20), uprooted from their bases and "hollow" (69:7). They became hollow and fell over. After God destroyed them, he sent black birds upon them; the birds carried them to the sea and cast them into it.

*Ibn Ishaq:* When the wind went out against the Ad from the valley, seven of them, one of whom was al-Khuljan, said: "Come and let us stand at the edge of the valley and turn back the wind." But the wind began to go beneath each one of them, carrying them then throwing them so that each broke his neck. It left them as God said: "Overthrown in it as if the roots of hollow palm trees torn up" (69:7). Only al-Khuljan was left. He turned to the mountain, took hold of it by the side and shook it. It shook in his hand. Hud said to him: "al-Khuljan, submit and be safe!" al-Khuljan said: "What will I get from your Lord if I submit?" Hud said: "Paradise." al-Khuljan said: "What is that I see in the clouds as if it were camels?" Hud said: "Those are the angels of my Lord." al-Khuljan said: "If I submit, will your Lord protect me from them?" Hud said: "Woe are you! Have you seen a king protect from his own army?" al-Khuljan said: "If only he would do as I wished." Then the wind came and took him with his companions.

*Tabari:* The wind continued to punish them for seven nights and eight days in a row. It destroyed everything in its path. It took them from their houses, God said: "So that you could see the people overthrown in it as though they were the roots of hollow palm trees torn up" (54:20).

*Ibn Kathir:* When the Ad saw this cloud, forming in the air like a cloud, they thought it was a rain cloud but it was a cloud of punishment. They thought it was a mercy but it was an affliction. They hoped it was good and hoped it would be the end of their drought. The punishment that befell them was from the violent wind which passed over them for seven nights and eight days, and not one of them remained. They resembled the roots of palm trees which had no tops because the wind came to each one of them and carried them up into the air, then it turned them on the top of their heads and shattered them, leaving a trunk without a head.

*Ibn Kathir:* It is established in Bukhari and Muslim, on the authority of Hakim, on the authority of Mujahid, on the authority of Ibn Abbas, that the Prophet Muhammad said: "I was victorious with an east wind, Ad was destroyed with the west wind."

## Hud after Ad

*Ibn Kathir:* It is related that Ali b. Abi Talib mentioned a description of the tomb of Hud in the cities of Yemen. Others mention that it is in Damascus. Some people allege that the tomb of Hud is in the Qibla wall of the mosque.

*Tabari:* God destroyed al-Khuljan and extinguished the Ad except for those who remained. God saved Hud and those who believed in him. It is said that Hud lived 150 years.

## Luqman

**Q 31:12** We gave to Luqman wisdom: Be thankful to God! He who is thankful will be thankful for himself. For he who does not believe: God is Sufficient and Praise-Worthy. **13** When Luqman said to his son, admonishing him: "My son, do not associate anything with God. Associating something with God is doing great wrong." **14** We have enjoined upon the human being [obedience] to his parents. His mother bore him in great travail, and his weaning took two years. Therefore be thankful to me and to your parents! To me is the ultimate goal. **15** If they [parents] try to impose upon you associating something with me, that about which you have no knowledge, do not obey them but be companions to them in this world, with justice, and follow the path of he who turns to me. Then, to me is the return of you all. I will tell you all what you did. **16** "My son: if there were something the weight of a mustard-seed, and it was in a rock or in the heavens or in the earth, God would bring it forth for God is Knowing of all small things.

**17** "My son: establish prayer, command what is just, forbid the wrong, and bear patiently that which befalls you. This is the steadfastness of daily life. **18** "Do not swell your cheek toward people nor walk insolently in the earth. God does not love all who boast arrogantly. **19** "Aim for moderation in your pace and keep your voice low. The worst of sounds is the voice of the ass."

*Tabari:* It is said that Marthad b. Sa'd, Luqman b. Ad, and Qayl b. Anz prayed in Mecca, and that they were told: "You are given what you desire, so choose for yourselves except that there is no way to immortality. There is no escape from death." Marthad b. Sa'd said: "Lord, give me piety and truth." He was given this. Luqman b. Ad said: "Give me life." But he was told: "Choose for yourself, except that there is no immortality: length of the existence of sheep droppings on a rugged mountain on which flows only a trickle of water, or seven eagles when the life of one eagle passes to another?" Luqman chose the eagles for himself, and his life was the length of seven eagles. He would take the fledgling as it came out of its egg, taking the male for its strength. When it died he would take another. He continued to do this until he arrived at the seventh. Each eagle lived 80 years. When only the seventh remained, a son of his brother said to Luqman: "Uncle, nothing remains of your life except the life-span of this eagle." Luqman said to him: "Nephew, this is Lubadh." Lubadh in their language meant fate. The eagle of Luqman expired and his life ended. The other eagles flew the next day from the top of the mountain but Lubadh did not fly off with them. These eagles of Luqman were never apart from him. When Luqman did not see Lubadh fly with the eagles he went up to the mountain to see what Lubadh was doing. Luqman found himself to be weak as he had not experienced before. When he reached the mountain, he saw his eagle Lubadh fallen from the other eagles. He cried: "Rise up, Lubadh!" Lubadh tried to get up but was unable, for his forefeathers had fallen out. So the two of them died together.

# Salih

**Q 7:73** To Thamud [we sent] their brother Salih. He said: "Worship God. There is no god for you other than he. A sign has come to you from your Lord. This is the she-camel of God, a sign for you. Leave her to eat of God's earth and do not touch her with evil intent or a grievous punishment will take you. **74** "Remember when he made you follow after Ad, gave you habitations in the earth. You take for yourselves its plains for your castles and hew houses from the mountains. Remember the benefits of God and do no harm in the earth." **75** The leaders from among his people who were arrogant said to those who were thought to be weak, those among them who believed: "Do you know that Salih is a messenger from his Lord?" They said: "We are believers in that which was sent by him." **76** Those who were arrogant said: "We reject that in which you believe." **77** So they hamstrung the she-camel and insolently defied the order of their Lord. They said: "Salih, bring what you promised us if you are one of the messengers." **78** The earthquake took them and morning found them prostrate in their homes. **79** So he [Salih] left them and said: "My people, I brought to you the message of my Lord and gave good counsel to you but you do not love those who give good counsel."

**Q 11:61** To Thamud [we sent] their brother Salih. He said: "Worship God. There is no god for you other than he. It is he who produced you from the earth and settled you in it. Ask him for forgiveness, then turn to him. My Lord is near, ready to answer." **62** They said: "Salih, you were a hope among us before this. Do you forbid us to worship what our fathers worshipped? We doubt that to which you invite us." **63** He said: "My people, do you see, if I have a sign from my Lord. He has sent me mercy from himself. Who can help me against God if I were to disobey him? What would you add to me beside perdition? **64** "My people, this is the she-camel of God, a sign for you. Leave her to eat from God's earth and do not touch her with evil intent or a swift punishment will take you." **65** But they hamstrung her, so he said: "Enjoy yourselves in your homes for three days. This is not an idle promise." **66** When our command went forth we saved Salih and those who believed with him by mercy from us, from humiliation that day. Your Lord is the Strong, the Mighty. **67** The scream took those who did wrong, and morning found them prostrate in their homes **68** as if they had never enriched themselves in them. Thamud rejected their Lord! Away with the Thamud!

**Q 15:80** The people of al-Hijr rejected the messengers. **81** We sent them our signs but they continued to turn away from them. **82** They hewed houses out of mountains, feeling secure. **83** The scream took them as they awoke. **84** What they were earning was not sufficient for them.

**Q 17:59** We refrain from sending signs lest they be rejected as did those who came before. We sent Thamud the she-camel, a visible sign, but they did wrong. We sent the sign only to frighten.

**Q 26:141** Thamud rejected the messengers. **142** When their brother Salih said: "Do you not fear God? **143** "I am a trustworthy messenger to you. **144** "So fear God and obey me. **145** "I do not ask of you any recompense. My recompense is from the Lord of the worlds only. **146** "Will you be left secure in what is here? **147** "Gardens and springs, **148** crops and palms with spathes near breaking? **149** "You hew houses out of mountains skillfully. **150** "Fear God and obey me. **151** "Do not obey the order of those who transgress, **152** those who despoil the land and are not upright." **153** They said: "You are one of those under a spell. **154** "You are nothing but a human being like us. Bring us a sign if you are one of the truthful." **155** He said: "Here is the she-camel. She has drinking rights and you have drinking rights on fixed days. **156** "Do not touch her with evil intent or the punishment of an awful day will seize you." **157** They hamstrung her and became regretful. **158** The punishment took them. In this is a sign but most of them are not believers. **159** Your Lord is the Mighty, the Merciful.

**Q 27:45** We sent to Thamud their brother Salih: "Serve God," when they became two factions fighting with one another. **46** He said: "My people, why do you seek to bring on evil before good? If only you would ask God for forgiveness you might receive mercy." **47** They said: "We augur an ill omen in you and those who are with you." He said: "Your ill omen is with God; you are a people in trial." **48** There were nine people in the city who despoiled the earth and were not upright. **49** They said: "Swear an oath by God that we will come to him and his people by night and say to his patron: We did not witness the destruction of his family, and we are telling the truth." **50** They plotted a plan, but we plotted a plan while they were not aware. **51** See how was the end of their plot: we destroyed them and their people, all together. **52** Such were their houses in ruin because of the wrong they did. In this is a sign for people who know. **53** We saved those who believed and were God-fearing.

**Q 41:17** As for Thamud, we guided them but they preferred blindness over guidance. The thunderbolt of the punishment of humiliation took them because of what they earned. **18** We delivered those who believed and were God-fearing.

**Q 54:23** Thamud rejected the warners. **24** They said: "A single man from among us should we follow? Then we would be in error and madness. **25** "Is the message sent to him, of all people among us? No, he is a liar, an insolent one." **26** They will know tomorrow who is the liar and insolent one. **27** We are sending the she-camel as a trial for them. Watch them and be patient! **28** Tell them that the water is to be apportioned between them, each drink by turn. **29** They called their companion and he took and hamstrung her. **30** How was my punishment and warning? **31** We sent against them a single scream and they became like dry sticks used for cattle. **32** We made the Quran easy to remember. Are there any who are to be reminded?

**Q 91:11** Thamud rejected by their disobedience. **12** The most wicked of them was sent. **13** The messenger of God said to them: The she-camel of God has her drink. **14** They rejected him and hamstrung her. So their Lord rumbled against them for their sin and flattened them. **15** He does not fear its consequences.

## Thamud

*Tabari:* As for the Thamud, they were insolent toward their Lord, they rejected him and despoiled the earth. So God sent to them Salih b. Ubayd b. Asif b. Masikh b. Ubayd b. Khadir b. Thamud b. Gether b. Aram b. Shem b. Noah as a messenger to call them to the oneness of God and the worship of him alone. It is said that Salih was b. Asif b. Kamashij b. Iram b. Thamud b. Gether b. Aram b. Shem b. Noah. God had lengthened the lives of the Thamud. They used to live in al-Hijr all the way to Wadi al-Qura between the Hijaz and Syria. The Jews allege that there is no mention of Ad or Thamud, Hud or Salih in the Torah, but their reputation among the pre-Islamic and Islamic Arabs was like the reputation of Abraham's people to him.

*Suyuti:* Wahb b. Munabbih says he is Ibn Ubayd b. Hayir b. Thamud b. Hayir b. Shem b. Noah. He was sent to his people when he reached puberty. He was a man more red than white, with lank hair. He stayed with his people for 40 years. Others say only that Salih was an Arab. When God destroyed the Ad, the Thamud lived after them. Then God sent Salih to them, as a young boy. He called them to worship God. There are no prophets between Noah and Abraham except for Hud and Salih. Ibn Hajar says the Quran indicates that the Thamud were after the Ad just as the Ad were after the people of Noah. Tha'labi says that he was Salih b. Ubayd b. Asif b. Mashij b. Ubayd b. Hadhir b. Thamud b. Ad b. Uz b. Aram b. Shem b. Noah. God sent him to his people when he was a boy. They were Arabs who settled between the Hijaz and Syria. He stayed with them for twenty years and died in Mecca when he was 58 years old.

*Ibn Kathir:* The Thamud were Arab and they were after the Ad but they did not heed the example made of the Ad. They did as the Ad did. God permitted them to build castles in the open places of the earth, for they were skilled in building.

## Sign

*Abu al-Tufayl:* The Thamud said to Salih: "Bring us a sign if you are truthful." Salih said to them: "Go out to a high place in the land." When they arrived it shook as a woman in labor shakes and then a she-camel emerged from the midst of the rock.

*Abd al-Aziz b. Rufay:* Another man related that Salih said to the Thamud: "A sign of punishment will be that tomorrow morning you will be red. On the second day yellow, and on the third day black." The punishment came to them in the morning and when they saw this they prepared themselves for death.

*Amr b. Kharijah:* I will relate to you what the Prophet Muhammad related to me about the Thamud. The Thamud were the people of Salih to whom God had given long life in this world. God lengthened their lives so that when one of them built a dwelling from mud, it would collapse while the man was still living. So they began to hew their houses from out of the mountains. They hollowed out the mountains and lived comfortably in them. The people said: "Salih, ask your Lord to give us a sign so that we might know that you are the messenger of God." So Salih called upon his Lord and he sent the she-camel to them. Her drinking was fixed on one day and their drinking on another. When it was the day for her to drink, they would leave her alone to the water but take her milk, filling every vessel, container and water skin. When it was the day of their drinking, they kept her from the water and she did not drink any of it, and they filled every vessel, container and water skin. God revealed to Salih: "Your people are hamstringing your she-camel." Salih told them that and they replied: "We are not doing this." Salih said: "No, but if you are not hamstringing her now, then about to be born to you is a son who will hamstring her." They said: "What is the sign of this son? By God, when we find him we will kill him." Salih said: "He is a boy with fair complexion, blue eyes, red hair and ruddy complexion."

In the city were two powerful elders. One of them had a son whom he did not want to let marry and the other a daughter for whom he could not find a match. A meeting was arranged between them. One of the two said to the other: "What keeps you from allowing your son to marry?" The other said: "I cannot find a match for him." The first said: "My daughter is a match for him, I will arrange a marriage with you." So he married her to him and they bore a son. Also in the city were eight people who despoiled the earth and were not upright, and when Salih said to them that a child from among you will hamstring the she-camel, these eight chose eight women who were midwives from the area. They designated authority for these women to go around the area and when they found a woman in labor they were to see what she bore. If it was a boy they were to kill him but if it was a girl they were to spare her. When they found that specific child, the women shouted and said: "This is the one intended by God's messenger Salih." They were supposed to take the child but his two grandfathers intervened and said: "If Salih intends this one, then we will kill him."

The child was an evil child, and he grew in a day what other children would grow in a week, and in a week he grew as much as other children would in a month, and in a month he grew as much as other children would in a year. Those eight people who despoiled the earth and were not upright gathered together with the two powerful elders and said: "Appoint this boy over us because of his status and the nobility of his grandfathers." So the group became nine, and Salih refused to sleep with them in the area but instead spent his nights in a mosque called the Mosque of Salih. When morning came he would go and admonish them. When evening came he would go back to his mosque and stay there the night.

The people intended to trick Salih, so they came upon a tunnel in the path of Salih and the eight of them hid inside of it. They said: "When he comes out toward us we will kill him, and we will come to his family by night." But God ordered the earth to close in on them. Others gathered and went to the she-camel while she was standing at her pool. The culprit said to one of them: "Bring her and I will hamstring her." So they brought her but he found this too difficult, so he refused to do it. Another was sent for but also found it too difficult, and each time someone was sent for, they found it too difficult a thing to do, until finally the culprit himself went to the she-camel, pulled himself up, hit her tendons and she fell as she tried to flee.

A man came to Salih and said: "Go to your she-camel, it has been hamstrung." So he went and they came out to meet him, asking his pardon: "Prophet of God, so-and-so hamstrung her, so it is not our fault." He said: "See if you can catch her calf. If you catch it, then perhaps God will lift the punishment from you." So they went out after it. When the calf saw its mother hurt, it went to a low mountain called al-Qarah and ascended it. They went after to seize the calf but God spoke to the mountain and it grew tall into the sky until even birds could not reach it. Salih entered the area and when the calf saw him he cried until his tears flowed like water. Then he approached Salih and groaned once, again, and a final time.

Salih said: "For each groan is the term of one day. Enjoy yourselves in your homes for three days. This is not an idle promise: the sign of the punishment is that on the first day your faces will become yellow, red on the second day, and black on the third day." The next day their faces were yellow as if smeared with saffron, small and big, male and female. When evening came they shouted together: "Only one day of the term has passed and the punishment is upon us." On the morning of the second day their faces were red as if dyed with blood. They shouted, clamored and cried, knowing it was their punishment. When the evening came they shouted together: "Two days of the term have passed and the punishment is upon us." On the morning of the third day their faces were black as if smeared with pitch. They shouted together: "The punishment is upon us." They wrapped themselves in death shrouds and embalmed themselves with aloes and acids. Their shrouds were leather. Then they threw themselves to the earth and began looking back and forth, to the heavens once and to the earth once, not knowing from where the punishment would come, from over them in the heavens or from under them in the earth. On the morning of the fourth day a scream came to them from the heavens, in which was the sound of every thunderbolt and the sound of everything on earth that has a sound. Their hearts stopped in their chests and they became prostrate in their homes.

*Ibn Jurayj:* When Salih said to them that a boy would be born at whose hands they would be destroyed, they said: "What would you have us do?" He said: "I order you to kill him." So they killed all the male children, all but one. When it came to that child they said: "If we had not killed our sons, then each one of us would have a son like this. This is the work of Salih." So they plotted among themselves to kill Salih, saying: "Let us go out as travelers and the people will see us as this, then we will return on such and such a night, wait for him at his place

of prayer, and kill him. The people will think only that we are travelers."
So they went under a rock and lay in wait but God made the rock fall
down on them and crush them. Some men who knew about this went
out to check on them and found them crushed. They returned to the
city shouting: "Servants of God, Salih ordered them to kill their sons
and now he has killed them." The people of the area gathered together
to hamstring the she-camel together but they could not do it except the
son of the tenth one.

*Abd al-Razzaq:* Hasan al-Basri reports that the calf of the she-camel
said: "My Lord, where is my mother?" Then he went into the rock and
disappeared into it. It is also said that the people followed the calf and
hamstrung it also.

*Ahmad b. Hanbal:* Abdallah b. Zam'ah says that the Prophet Muhammad gave a sermon and mentioned the she-camel. He mentioned the
one who hamstrung her. He said: "The most wicked of them was sent
[91:12]: A violent, strong and imposing man like Abu Zam'ah was sent
to the she-camel."

*Ibn Ishaq:* The Prophet Muhammad said to Ali b. Abi Talib: "Should I
relate to you who was the most wicked of the people? Two men. One
of them was the little red one of the Thamud who hamstrung the she-
camel, and the other is the one who hit you, Ali, there on your head so
that your beard became wet from it."

*Ibn Kathir:* When the sun rose a scream came to them from the heavens
over them and a terrible earthquake from the ground under them. Their
spirit poured out, their souls departed, all movement ceased, all sound
stopped, and they became prostrate in their homes, with no air nor
movement in them. There was not a single one left of them except for a
girl named Kaliyah who was the daughter of al-Salaq, also called
Dhariah. She strongly rejected and was an enemy to Salih. When she
saw the punishment that defeated the men she got up and ran like
something fast. She came to a group of Arabs and told them what she
had seen, what had happened to her people, and requested some water.
When she drank she died.

## Salih After Thamud

*Tabari:* Some scholars allege that Salih died in Mecca when he was 58
years old, that he had remained among his people for twenty years.

*Ibn Kathir:* It is said that Salih moved to the sanctuary of God and lived there until he died.

*Ibn Umar:* When the Prophet Muhammad came to the district of the Thamud he said: "Do not enter and visit these who were punished unless you are crying. If you are not crying, then do not enter and visit them, or what befell them will befall you."

*Jabir b. Abdallah:* When the Prophet Muhammad came to al-Hijr he praised God and then said: "Do not ask your messenger for signs. These people of Salih asked their messenger for a sign and God sent to them the she-camel. She used to return from this pass and set out from this pass and drink from their water on the day of her turn."

*Abu al-Tufayl:* When the Prophet Muhammad went on a campaign to Tabuk he stopped at al-Hijr and said: "People, do not ask your prophet for signs. These people of Salih asked their prophet to send them a sign, so God sent them the she-camel as a sign. On the day of her turn she entered from this pass and drank their water, and on the day of their turn they used to take water from it and then take from her milk just as much as they would take from their water before that. Then she would come out of the pass. But they became insolent against the command of their Lord and hamstrung her. God promised a punishment after three days. It was a promise from God and not a lie. So God destroyed all who were with them from the east to the west of the earth except for one man who was inside God's sanctuary. God's sanctuary protected him from the punishment of God." They said: "Who was that man, Prophet of God?" He said: "Abu Righal."

*Ibn Jurayj:* When the scream overtook them, God destroyed all who were with them from the east to the west, except for one man who was in the sanctuary of God. The sanctuary of God protected him from the punishment of God. It was said: "Prophet of God, who was he?" He said: "Abu Righal." When the Prophet Muhammad came to the district of Thamud he said to his companions: "Let not one of you enter this area nor drink from their water." He showed them the place where the camel had gone up to al-Qarah.

*Ibn Ishaq:* Abdallah b. Umar was with the Prophet Muhammad when they left Ta'if and passed by a grave. The Prophet Muhammad said: "This is the grave of Abu Righal also known as Abu Thaqif. He was from the Thamud but was praying in this sanctuary [at the time of the Thamud's destruction]. When he left the sanctuary the affliction which struck his people struck him in this place, and he was buried here. A sign of this is that buried with him is a golden bough. If you exhume and take it from him you will be smitten along with him." He said this before the people could request the bough from him.

# Abraham

**Q 6:74** When Abraham said to his father Azar: "Do you take idols for gods? I see you and your people in clear error." **75** Like this we showed Abraham the kingdoms of the heavens and the earth so that he might be one who had certitude. **76** When night fell he saw a star and said: "This is my Lord." But when it set he said: "I do not love things that set." **77** When he saw the moon rising he said: "This is my Lord." But when it set he said: "If my Lord does not guide me I will become part of the group of those who are misled." **78** When he saw the sun rising he said: "This is my Lord. This is the greatest." But when it set he said: "My people, I am free from your associating things with God. **79** "I set my face to the one who endowed the heavens and the earth, being *hanif*. I am not one of those who associates other things with God." **80** His people disputed with him. He said: "Do you dispute with me concerning God when he guides me? I am not afraid of what you associate with God. Only if my Lord wishes a thing to be. My Lord encompasses all with knowledge. Will you not be reminded? **81** "How should I be afraid of what you associate with God while you are not afraid to associate things with God without having any authority revealed to you? Which of the two sides has more right to security? if you have learned. **82** "Those who believe and do not clothe their faith with injustice, they are the ones who are secure. They are rightly guided." **83** That was our argument which we gave Abraham against his people. We raise whom we will in degrees. Your Lord is Wise, Knowing. **84** We gave him Isaac and Jacob. All together we guided. Noah we guided before, and among his descendants are David, Solomon, Job, Joseph, Moses, and Aaron. Like this do we reward those who do good. **85** Zechariah, John, Jesus, and Elijah are all of the upright. **86** Ishmael, Elisha, Jonah, and Lot, all together we favored above the worlds. **87** And from among their fathers, their offspring, and brothers we selected them and we guided them to the straight path.

**Q 41:37** Among his signs are the night, the day, the sun, the moon. Do not prostrate to the sun or the moon. Prostrate to God who created them, if it is he you are worshipping.

## Birth of Abraham

*Tabari:* Abraham was son of Terah b. Nahor b. Serug b. Reu b. Peleg b. Eber b. Shelah b. Canaan b. Arpachshad b. Shem b. Noah. There is disagreement concerning the location in which he was born. Some say his birthplace was Sus in the land of al-Ahwaz. Other say his birthplace was Babylon in the land of the Sawad. Others say it was in the Sawad in the region of Kutha. Others say his birthplace was in al-Warka in the region of al-Zawabi and the borders of Kaskar, and that his father moved him to the place where Nimrod was, in the region of Kutha. Others say his birthplace was in Haran but his father Terah took him to the land of Babylon. Most of the earlier scholars say that the birth of Abraham was in the era of Nimrod b. Cush. Most of the historians say Nimrod was an official of Azdahaq, the one, it is alleged by some, to whom Noah was sent in the land of Babylon and its surroundings. As for a group of the earlier scholars, they say that there was a king over Babylon, and he was called Zarha b. Tahmasfan.

## Nimrod

*Ibn Ishaq:* Azar was a man from the people of Kutha from the district of Sawad, the Sawad of Kufah. This is when Nimrod the Sinner was king of the east. He was called the Lion. His kingdom, according to what they allege, included the east and the west of the earth, and was in Babylon. His kingdom and the kingdom of his people was in the east before the kingdom of the Persians.

*Tabari:* It is said that no king ruled the whole earth nor were all the people gathered under a single king except under three kings: Nimrod b. Arghu, Dhu al-Qarnayn, and Solomon b. David. Some say that Nimrod was Dahhak himself.

*Ibn Masud:* The first who ruled the earth, east and west, was Nimrod b. Canaan b. Cush b. Shem b. Noah. The kings who ruled all the earth were four: Nimrod, Solomon b. David, Dhu al-Qarnayn, and Nebuchadnezzar [Bukhtnasar], two believers and two disbelievers.

*Ibn Ishaq:* When God wanted to send Abraham, friend of the Merciful, as proof to his people, as a messenger to his worshippers, there had not been any prophet between Noah and Abraham except Hud and Salih. When the time of Abraham drew close, the astrologers of Nimrod said to him: "Know that we have found in our learning about a boy to be born in this district of yours, called Abraham. He will break off from your religion and break your idols in such and such a month and such and such a year." When the year which the astrologers had described to Nimrod began, Nimrod sent to all the pregnant women in his district and imprisoned them with him, except for the mother of Abraham, the wife of Azar, for he did not know she was pregnant. This was because she was a young girl and the pregnancy could not be known from her stomach. There was no boy born to a woman in that month of that year that Nimrod did not order to be slaughtered. When the mother of Abraham found she was in labor, she went out at night to a cave that was close by. In it she gave birth to Abraham. She took care of his needs as one does for a newborn, then she blocked up the cave, and returned to her house. When she returned to the cave to see what had happened, she found him alive, sucking on his thumb. They allege that God provided Abraham what he needed, and that it came to him from his thumb. Azar asked the mother of Abraham about her pregnancy: "What happened?" She said: "I gave birth to a boy and he died." He believed her and was silent about it.

*Ibn Abbas:* A star rose over Nimrod which was brighter than the sun and the moon. Nimrod was afraid of this and called upon his magicians, soothsayers, prognosticators and physiognomists, and asked them about this. They said: "A man will emerge from your kingdom, and it is his destiny to destroy you and your kingdom." Nimrod lived in Babylon, near Kufah. He left his district and went to another district, forcing the men to leave with him, but leaving the women behind. He commanded them to slaughter any male child who was born. He killed their children. After this, however, he had a need come up that required him to go to the city, and he could not trust it to anyone but Azar, the father of Abraham. So he summoned him and sent him, saying to him: "See to it that you do not have marital relations with your wife." Azar said to him: "I am too strict in my religion for this." When Azar entered the district, he visited his wife and could not keep himself from having sex with her. He left with her to a district called Ur between Kufah and Basrah, and he put her in an underground passage, promising her food and drink, and that which was to sustain her.

## Abraham Discovers God

*Ibn Ishaq:* A day for Abraham was like a month growing up, and a month like a year. Abraham had not stayed in the cave but fifteen months when he said to his mother: "Take me out so that I can see." So she took him out in the evening and he looked and contemplated the creation of the heavens and the earth. He said: "The one who created me, provided for me, fed me, and gave me drink, is my Lord. I have no God but he." Then he looked in the sky and saw a star. He said: "This is my Lord." Then he watched it until it disappeared. When it set he said: "I do not like things that set." Then the moon rose and he saw its glow, and said: "This is my Lord." Then he watched it until it disappeared. When it set he said: "If my Lord does not guide me I will become part of the group of those who are misled." When the day broke and the sun rose, he saw the greatness of the sun, and he saw something that was greater than the light of all other things he had seen before. He said: "This is my Lord, this is the greatest." When it set he said: "My people, I am free from your associating things with God. I set my face to the one who endowed the heavens and the earth, being *hanif*. I am not one of those who associates other things with God" (6: 76–79).

*Ibn Abbas:* After a long time passed, the king said: "The opinion of the magicians was false. Return to your city." They returned and Abraham was born. Each of his days passed as if it were a week, and each week a month, each month a year in the time of his youth. The king forgot about this and Abraham grew without seeing anything of creation other than his father and mother. Abraham's father said to his companions: "I have a son whom I have hidden. Do you fear for him on account of the king if I am to bring him out?" They said: "No, bring him." So they set out and brought him. When the boy emerged from the subterranean passage he looked at the cattle, beasts, and creation and began asking his father: "What is this?" His father informed him that the camel was a camel, the cow was a cow, the horse was a horse, and the sheep were sheep. Abraham said: "These creatures cannot but have a Lord."

When he emerged from the subterranean passage it was after the setting of the sun. He raised his head toward the heavens and there was a star, which was Jupiter. He said: "This is my Lord" but when it disappeared he said: "I do not like things that set." He emerged at the end of the month and that is why he did not see the moon before the stars. When it was the next night, he saw the moon glowing as it rose. He said: "This is my Lord," but when it set, meaning disappeared, he said: "If my Lord does not guide me, I will be one of the people who is misled." When morning came he saw the sun shining and said: "This is my Lord, this is the greatest," but when it disappeared God said to him: "Submit." Abraham said: "I submit myself to the Lord of the worlds." Then he came to his people and said: "My people, I am free from your associating things with God. I set my face to the one who endowed the heavens and the earth, being *hanif*" (6:76–79).

## Abraham and the Idols

**Q 19:41** Mention, in the Book, Abraham. He was truthful, a prophet. **42** When he said to his father: "My father, why do you worship that which does not hear, does not see, and cannot enrich you with anything? **43** "My father, knowledge has come to me which has not come to you. Follow me. I will guide you on the even path. **44** "My father, do not worship Satan. Satan is disobedient to the Merciful. **45** "My father, I fear that a punishment from the Merciful will afflict you, and you will become a companion of Satan." **46** He [father] said: "Do you disdain the gods, Abraham? If you do not stop I will stone you. Get away from me for a long time." **47** He [Abraham] said: "Peace be upon you! I will ask my Lord to forgive you. To me he is Gracious. **48** "I will turn away from you and from that upon which you call besides God. I will call upon my Lord. Perhaps I will be, by my calling on my Lord, blessed." **49** When he turned away from them and from that which they worshipped besides God, we gave him Isaac and Jacob. Each of them we made to be a prophet. **50** We gave to them of our mercy and we made them to be high with a truthful tongue.

**Q 21:51** We gave Abraham his integrity before, and we knew him. **52** When he said to his father and his people: "What are these images to which you are devoted?" **53** They said: "We found our fathers worshipping them." **54** He said: "You and your fathers have been in clear error." **55** They said: "Have you brought the truth or are you one who plays?" **56** He said: "Rather, your Lord is the Lord of the heavens and the earth, the one who endowed them. I am witness to this. **57** "By God, I will plan against your idols after you turn your backs." **58** So he made them broken except for the biggest one of them, so that they might return to it. **59** They said: "Who has done this to our gods? He is one who does wrong." **60** They said: "We heard a youth mention them. He is called Abraham." **61** They said: "Bring him before the eyes of the people so that they might witness." **62** They said: "Are you the one who did this to our gods, Abraham?" **63** He said: "No, but the biggest of them did it. Ask them this if they are able to talk." **64** They turned to themselves and said: "You are the ones who do wrong." **65** Then they hung their heads in shame: "You know that these do not speak." **66** He said: "Do you worship besides God that which does not benefit nor harm you in any way? **67** "Uff upon you and that which you worship besides God. Do you not under-stand?" **68** They said: "Burn him and help your gods if you do anything." **69** We said: "Fire, be cold and peaceful for Abraham." **70** They intended to plan against him but we made them the losers.

**Q 37:83** From his [Noah's] party was Abraham. **84** He came to his Lord with a sound heart. **85** When he said to his father and his people: "What are you worshipping? **86** "Is it lies, gods other than God that you want? **87** "What do you think about the Lord of the worlds?" **88** He cast a glance at the stars, **89** and said: "I am sick." **90** So they turned their backs on him. **91** He turned to their gods and said: "Will you not eat? **92** "What is it that you do not speak?" **93** He turned upon them, striking with the right hand. **94** They hurried back to him. **95** He said: "Do you worship that which you have carved? **96** "God created you and what you do." **97** They said: "Build a furnace for him and throw him in the blazing hell-fire." **98** They intended to plan against him but we made them the most humiliated. **99** He said: "I am going to my Lord who will guide me."

**Q 9:114** Abraham asked God to forgive his father only on account of a promise he had made to him. When it became clear to him that he [his father] was an enemy of God, he freed himself from him. Abraham was tender-hearted, forbearing.

**Q 29:16** Abraham, when he said to his people: "Worship God and fear him. That would be best for you if you have learned. **17** "You worship merely idols instead of God, and you create lies. Those things which you worship instead of God have no power to provide for you. Seek sustenance from God, worship him, be thankful to him, and to him will be your return. **18** "If you disbelieve, peoples before you disbelieved. It is only incumbent upon the messenger to make public and clear." **19** Do they not see how God begins the creation, then renews it? This is easy for God. **20** Say: "Travel in the earth and see how God began the creation. Then God will cause another to be produced. God is Controlling of all things. **21** "He punishes whom he will and is merciful to whom he will. Towards him you are directed. **22** "You are not able to make weak, whether on earth or in heaven. You have no protector or helper besides God." **23** Those who reject the signs of God and the meeting with him, they will despair of my Mercy. To them is a grievous punishment. **24** There was no answer from his people except that they said: "Kill him or burn him." But God saved him from the fire. In this are signs for the people who believe. **25** He said: "You have taken idols besides God, out of regard among yourselves in this life. Then, on the Day of Resurrection some of you will reject others, and some of you will curse others. Your place is the Fire and you will not have any helpers." **26** Lot believed him. He said: "I will emigrate to my Lord. He is the Mighty, the Wise." **27** We gave to him Isaac and Jacob. We gave prophethood to his offspring, the Book, and we gave him his reward in this world. In the Hereafter he will be among the upright.

## Idols

*Ibn Ishaq:* Then Abraham returned to his father Azar, having turned his face to the right course. He had recognized his Lord and was free of the religion of his people, but he did not reveal this to them. He told his father that he was his son, and Abraham's mother said he was his son. She told Azar what had happened, and Azar was very happy about it.

Azar used to make the idols his people worshipped, so he employed Abraham to sell them. Abraham went with them and said: "Who will buy that which will harm but not benefit him?" No one bought them from him. When he was through, he took them to the river, put their heads in it, and said: "Drink!" mocking his people. He did this until his disrespect for the idols spread among his people and the people of his district, but this news did not reach Nimrod the king. At the time when Abraham decided to reveal his opposition to his people and the command of God, he "cast a glance to the stars and said: 'I am sick.'" So "they turned their backs on him" (37:88–90).

The people fled from him when they heard him say he was sick. Abraham only intended for them to leave so that he could do to their idols what he wanted. When they left, he went to the idols which they worshipped instead of God and set out food for them. He said: "Will you not eat? Why do you not speak?" Abraham approached the idols, "striking with his right hand" (37:93). Then he began to break them with an ax in his hand until only the greatest of the idols was left, and he tied the ax in its hand. Then he left. When his people returned, they saw what had been done to their idols and were afraid. They said: "Who has done this to our gods? He must be one who does wrong." They remembered and said: "We heard a youth mention them. He is called Abraham" (21:60). They meant: "We have never heard anyone saying anything like that, so he is the one who did this."

*Ibn Abbas:* The father of Abraham made idols and appointed his sons to sell them. He used to give them to Abraham, who would announce: "Who will buy that which harms him and does not benefit him?" His brothers returned having sold their idols and Abraham returned with his idols just as when he left. Then he called upon his father, saying: "My father, why do you worship that which does not hear, does not see, and cannot enrich you with anything?" (19:42). His father said: "Do you disdain the gods, Abraham? If you do not stop I will stone you. Get away from me for a long time" (19:46). This meant "forever."

Then his father said to him: "Abraham, we have a festival. If you were to come with us, our religion would amaze you." When the day of the festival came, they all went out to it, Abraham with them. When he was part of the way, Abraham threw himself down and said: "I am sick." He said: "My foot hurts." They sat down by his feet and he was laid out. When they went on he called out to the two people who remained behind: "By God, I will plan against your idols after you turn your backs" (21:57). They heard this from him, then Abraham returned to the house of the gods which was a great hall. Opposite the door of the hall was the biggest idol next to a smaller one, and a smaller one next to that. All the idols were arranged in descending size down to the door of the hall. The people had just prepared food and put it in front of the gods. They said: "When we return, the gods will have blessed our food and we will eat." When Abraham saw them and the food in front of them, he said: "Will you not eat?" When they did not answer, he said: "Why do you not speak?" He attacked them, hitting with his right hand. He took an iron bar and lopped off all of the idols' appendages. Then he hung the ax from the neck of the biggest idol. When the people returned for their food, they saw their gods and said: "Who has done this to our gods? He is one who does wrong." They said: "We heard a youth mention them. He is called Abraham" (21: 59–60).

### Fiery Furnace

*Ibn Ishaq:* When Abraham was brought and his people assembled before him in the presence of Nimrod, they said: "Are you the one who did this to our gods, Abraham?" He said: "No, but the biggest of them did it. Ask them this if they are able to talk" (21:62–63). Abraham continued: "He became angry because you worshipped these little ones with him, though he is the greatest of them, so he broke them." So the people left him alone and stopped saying that Abraham had broken them. They said: "We have wronged him, for it must have happened as he said." Knowing, however, that the idols could not harm nor be of benefit, nor be violent, they said: "You know that these do not speak" (21:65). They continued: "Tell us who did this to them, for they do not hit with their own hands, and we will believe you." He said: "Uff upon you and that which you worship besides God. Do you not understand?" (21:67). Abraham's people then argued with him about God, asking him to describe God, and telling him that their gods were better than the one he worshipped. He said: "Do you dispute with me concerning God when he guides me?" (6:80) up to the verse "Which of the two sides has more right to security? if you know" (6:81). He gave them parables and explained to them so that they might learn that it is more right to fear and worship God than those idols which they worshipped instead of him.

*Tabari:* Nimrod said to Abraham: "Have you seen your God, this one whom you worship and summon others to worship, the power of whom is greater than all others?" Abraham said: "My Lord is who gives life and causes death," and Nimrod said: "I give life and cause death," so Abraham said: "How do you cause life and death?" Nimrod said: "I will take two men who have been condemned to die according to my judgment. I will kill one of them and so I will have caused him to die. I will pardon the other and leave him be, so I will have made him live." Abraham said to him: "God causes the sun to come in the east, so can you make it rise in the west?" (2:258). He knew that it was just as Abraham was saying, Nimrod was confounded, and did not respond because he knew that he was not capable of that. God said: "He who rejected God was confounded" (2:258). Then Nimrod and his people gathered against Abraham and said: "Burn him and help your gods if you do anything" (21:68).

*Mujahid:* I recited this verse [21:68] to Abdallah b. Umar. He said: "Do you know, Mujahid, who it was who indicated that Abraham was to be burned in the fire?" I said: "No." He said: "A man from the nomads of Persia." I said: "Abu Abd al-Rahman, do the Persians have nomads?" He said: "Yes, the Kurds are the nomads of Persia, and it was a man from among them who indicated that Abraham was to be burned in the fire."

*Shuayb al-Jabaʾi:* The name of the one who said: "Burn him" was Haynun. God caused the earth to swallow him. He is tossing around in it until the Day of Resurrection.

*Ibn Ishaq:* Nimrod ordered the collection of wood. The people collected hard wood from different types of trees to the extent that whenever a woman of Abraham's district made a vow concerning something, she would say: "If this happens then I will gather wood for the fire of Abraham in which he is being burned." When they were ready to throw him into the fire, they lit it in each of the corners of the wood which they had gathered so that the fire roared. They came together to push him into it. The heavens and the earth and all that was created in it except the humans and the Jinn screamed to God in a single voice: "Our Lord, there is no one on your earth but Abraham who worships you,

and he is being burned in the fire. Give us permission to help him."
When they said this, God said: "If he calls for something from you or
asks for something, then help him. I give permission for this. If he does
not call out except for me, I am his protector. Leave it between me and
him. I will make him secure." So they threw him into the fire, and he
said: "Fire, be cold and peaceful for Abraham" (21:69), and it was as
God said.

### Dispute over God

**Q 2:258**  Did you not see the one who argued with Abraham about his Lord,
because God gave him dominion? Abraham said: "My Lord is the one who gives
life and death." He said: "I give life and death." Abraham said: "God causes the
sun to come from the east. Do you cause it to come from the west?" He who
rejected God was confounded. God does not guide the people who do wrong.

*Ibn Kathir:* This happened when Abraham was disputing with the king
of Babylon, Nimrod b. Canaan.

*Suddi:* This debate took place between Abraham and Nimrod after
Abraham came out of the fire. There was a great gathering with the
king on this day when the dispute took place between them.

*Qatadah:* The king brought out two men who were to be killed. He
ordered one of them to be killed, so he was killed. He ordered the other
to be pardoned and not killed. This is the meaning of the king saying
he gives life and death.

*Zayd b. Aslam:* Nimrod had some food and the people used to come to
him early in the morning for provisions. Abraham arrived in a big
group which was coming to get provisions when this dispute occurred
between them. Abraham did not take the food that was being given to
the people. Rather, he left with no food. When he got close to his
household, he headed for a mound of dirt and filled his vessel with it.
He said: "My family will be alienated from me when I approach."
When he arrived he put down his bags and went to sleep. His wife
Sarah got up and went to the vessels. She found that they were full of
good food. So she prepared the food, and when Abraham got up he
found this and said: "I brought you this?" She said: "Who else brought
it?" Then he knew that God was providing them with sustenance. God
sent an angel to the king ordering him to believe in God, but he refused.
Then he called him a second time but he refused, and a third time and

he refused. So he said: "Assemble your forces and I will assemble my forces." Nimrod assembled his armies at the time of the rising of the sun, and God sent a column of mosquitoes so thick that it covered the sun. God caused them to cover the armies, eating their flesh and blood, leaving only bones. One of the mosquitoes went up the nose of the king and stayed in his head for 400 years. He kept hitting his head with an iron rod until God finally allowed him to die from it.

## Hijrah to Holy Land

**Q 21:71** We delivered him and Lot to the land which we blessed for the worlds. **72** We gave him Isaac and Jacob in addition, and we made each of them upright. **73** We made them to be examples, guided by our command. We revealed to them to do good things, establish the prayer, give alms. They were worshipping us.

*Ibn Kathir:* When Abraham emigrated with his people, his wife was barren for she had not given him a single child, but with him was the son of his brother, Lot b. Haran b. Azar. God gave Abraham upright sons after this and gave prophethood and the Book to his progeny. Every prophet who was sent after Abraham was from his progeny, and every book which was revealed from the heavens was to the prophets after him. He left his city with his household and relatives, and emigrated to a land in which he could worship his Lord. The land to which he emigrated was Syria. This is the opinion of Abu al-Aliyah, Qatadah and others. Atiyah al-Awfi relates on the authority of Ibn Abbas that it was Mecca. Ka'b al-Ahbar alleges it was Haran. The People of the Book relate that he went from the land of Babylon: he, his father, Lot the son of his brother, his brother Nahor, Abraham's wife Sarah, and Malka the wife of his brother. They settled in Haran and Terah the father of Abraham died there.

*Suddi:* Abraham and Lot set out toward Syria, and Abraham met Sarah. She was the daughter of the king of Haran, but she had turned from the religion of her people.

*Ibn Kathir:* It is well known that Sarah was the daughter of Abraham's uncle Haran, whose name is related to the city Haran. There are some who claim that she was the daughter of his brother Haran, the sister of Lot, such as Suhayli on the authority of Naqqash. There are some who claim that marriage to the daughter of a brother was, at that time, legal but there is no indication of this. It is also well known that when Abraham left Babylon he took Sarah with him.

*People of the Book:* When Abraham arrived in Syria, God revealed to him: "I will give this land to those who come after you." So Abraham built an altar to God in thanks for this kindness. He also pitched his tent east of Jerusalem, then he set out, traveling to Taima, but there were people there: Qahat, Shadda, and Ghala. So he traveled to Egypt.

### King and Sarah

*Abu Hurayrah:* Abraham lied only three times. Two of them were when he said: "I am sick" (37:89) and "The biggest of them did it" (21:63). The third time was concerning Sarah. When he came to one of the giant kings, the king was told: "There is a man who has the most beautiful of wives." So the king sent for Abraham and asked him: "Who is this?" He said: "My sister." So Sarah came and he said: "Sarah, there is not, on the face of this earth, a believing man except for me and you. If this one asks you, tell you that you are my sister. Do not make a liar out of me."

The king sent for Sarah. When she entered he tried to touch her with his hand but it was taken back. He said: "May God help me, I will not harm you." Then she called upon God and he left. Then he tried a second time and his hand was taken back like the first time or even more strongly. He said: "May God help me, I will not harm you." Then she called upon God and he left. Then the king called some of his advisors and said: "You have not brought me a person but rather a devil." So he gave her Hagar as a servant.

*Abu Hurayrah:* The Prophet Muhammad said: "Abraham lied only three times: his statements when he said to his family 'I am sick' and 'The biggest of them did it' and his statement about Sarah: 'She is my sister.'"

*Ibn Kathir:* Some of the historians mention that the Pharaoh of Egypt at this time was the brother of Dahhak, the king infamous for his tyranny. He was an agent for Dahhak in Egypt. It is said that his name was Sinan b. Alwan b. Ubayd b. Awlaj b. Amalek b. Lud b. Shem b. Noah.

### Promised Land

*Ibn Kathir:* After this, Abraham returned from Egypt to the land of Taima, which was the Holy Land in which he had been before. With him were sheep, servants, much wealth, and Hagar the Egyptian. Lot took his share of the property according to what Abraham commanded, and he went to the land of Ghur. Zaghar was known as Ghur. He settled in the city of Sodom, the capital of the land at that time. Its inhabitants were unbelievers. God revealed to Abraham and commanded him to extend his sight, looking northward, southward, eastward, and westward, that all of this land would be given to him and those who succeeded him until the end of time, that his progeny would be more numerous than the sand of the earth. These words were meant to refer to the community of Muhammad, as the Prophet Muhammad said: "God caused me to visit the whole earth. I saw from the east to the west. He will cause all that I visited to come into the possession of my community."

## Annunciation of Isaac

**Q 11:69** Our messengers came to Abraham with good news. They said: "Peace." He said: "Peace," and did not hesitate to bring a roasted calf. **70** When he saw their hands not reaching for it, he was suspicious of them and formed a fear of them. They said: "Do not be afraid. We are messengers to the people of Lot." **71** His wife was standing, and she laughed. We gave her the good news of Isaac and after Isaac, Jacob. **72** She said: "Alas for me, am I to bear a child, being feeble? This husband of mine is an old man. This is a strange thing." **73** They said: "Are you amazed at the word of God? The mercy of God and his blessings upon you, people of the house. He is Praise-Worthy, Glorified." **74** When the apprehension left Abraham, and the good news reached him, he pleaded with us for the people of Lot.

**Q 15:51** Tell them about the guests of Abraham. **52** When they visited him they said: "Peace." He said: "We are afraid of you." **53** They said: "Fear not, we bring you good news of a knowing boy." **54** He said: "You give me good news though my years are many? What is your good news?" **55** They said: "We bring good news to you in truth. Do not be among the despairing." **56** He said: "Who despairs the mercy of his Lord except those who go astray?"

**Q 51:24** Has the report of the honored guests of Abraham come to you? **25** When they visited him, they said: "Peace." He said: "Peace, unknown people." **26** He left to his house and brought a fattened calf, **27** and placed it in front of them. He said: "Do you not eat?" **28** He formed a fear of them. They said: "Do not fear," and they brought him good news of a knowing boy. **29** His wife came forward with a clatter. She smote her face and said: "Barren old woman." **30** They said: "Thus your Lord said. He is the Wise, the Knowing."

*Ibn Kathir:* There were three angels: Gabriel, Michael, and Israfil. When they first arrived, Abraham thought they were guests, so he treated them as guests and prepared the best of his cattle for them. But when he offered them food, he did not see them eat. This was because angels have no need of food, but Abraham was afraid. When the angels announced they were sent to the people of Lot, Sarah became happy. She was serving the guests as was the custom among the Arabs, but she laughed when they announced the birth of a son, just as women do out of amazement. The son would be Isaac, the brother of Ishmael, a sound child. This indicates, just as Muhammad b. Ka'b states, that the one sacrificed was Ishmael, for Isaac could not have been the intended sacrificial victim after the good news of his son Jacob was known [11:71]. According to the People of the Book, the fatted calf was roasted and served with three rolls, fat, and milk. And, according to them, the angels ate, but this is not right. It is also said that they just appeared to be eating but that the food evaporated into the air.

## Discovery of Zamzam

**Q 14:35** When Abraham said: "My Lord, make this city secure. Keep me and my sons from worshipping idols. **36** "My Lord, they have misled many people. He who follows me is of me, but he who disobeys me, you are Forgiving, Merciful. **37** "My Lord, I have settled some of my offspring in a valley without produce, by your Sacred House, our Lord, that they might establish prayer. Fill the hearts of people with love toward them. Provide them with fruits so that they might be thankful. **38** "My Lord, you know what we hide and what we make known. Nothing is hidden from God, whether on earth or in the heavens. **39** "Praise be to God who gave me Ishmael and Isaac in my old age. My Lord is Hearing of prayer. **40** "My Lord, make me an establisher of prayer, and from my offspring, our Lord. Accept my invocation. **41** "My Lord, forgive me and my father, and all the believers on the day the reckoning is established."

*Bukhari:* Ibn Abbas said the first woman to wear a girdle was the mother of Ishmael. She wore it to cover her tracks from Sarah. Then Abraham came with her and with his son Ishmael, whom she was nursing, and settled them in the area of the House, beside a tall tree above Zamzam, today in the highest part of the mosque. There was no one in Mecca at that time, and there was no water. He left them there, leaving with them a basket of dates and a skin of water. Abraham turned to go home, but the mother of Ishmael followed him and said: "Abraham, where are you going, leaving us here in a valley in which there are no people and no things?" She said this again to him, but he did not turn back to her, so she said: "Did God order you to do this?" He said: "Yes." She said: "Then he will not allow us to remain weak." Then she turned back. Abraham continued until he reached the next mountain, where he turned to face the House and asked God in supplication to provide them with sustenance [14:37].

Hagar continued to nurse Ishmael and drink from the water. When the water dried up, she and her son were thirsty. When she saw the baby writhing out of thirst, she set out, not wanting to see him like this. She came upon Safa which was the closest mountain to the land where she was. She climbed it and then faced the valley, looking to see if there was anyone. She did not see anyone, so she came down from Safa and came to the valley floor. She lifted the edge of her dress and walked quickly until she had crossed the valley. Then she came to Marwah and climbed it. She looked to see if there was anyone, but she did not see anyone. She did this seven times.

The Prophet Muhammad said: "It is for this reason that people walk quickly between them" [Safa and Marwah, during the Pilgrimage].

When she approached Marwah, she heard a voice. She said: "Listen!" talking to herself. She listened and heard the sound again. She then said: "I hear. If you can help." When she did this, the angel was at the spot of Zamzam. He dug the ground with his heel, or with his wing, until the water appeared. She began to make a pool with her hands, spooning the water into her water skin. It was springing up every time she spooned it. The Prophet Muhammad said: "May God show mercy to the mother of Ishmael. If she had left Zamzam alone," (or he said: "If she had not spooned out the water,") "Zamzam would have been a flowing spring." She drank and nursed her baby. The angel said to her: "Do not be afraid of being weak. Here is the House of God. This boy and his father will build it. God does not allow his household to be weak."

At that time, the House was raised above the ground like a mound. Floods had come and taken away its right and left sides. She stayed there until a group from the Jurhum passed by. They were coming on the way from Kada. They alighted in the valley of Mecca when they saw birds flying around it. The said: "The birds must be circling water. We know this valley, and there is no water in it." So they sent one or two messengers, and when they found the water they returned and told the others about it. They came upon the mother of Ishmael by the water. They said: "Will you give us permission to settle here with you?" She said: "Yes, but you have no right over the water." They agreed. The Prophet Muhammad said: "This happened when the mother of Ishmael enjoyed social relations. They settled there and sent for their households to settle with them."

Ishmael became a youth. He learned Arabic from them, and they were amazed at him. When he attained maturity, they gave him one of their women in marriage.

## Well at Beersheba

*Ibn Ishaq:* I asked Zuhri: "What is the mercy which the Prophet mentioned to them?" He said: "Hagar the mother of Ishmael was from among them." It is alleged, God knows best, that Sarah was very sad when Ishmael was born to Hagar because her time of childbearing was over. Abraham had left Egypt for Syria. He was afraid of the king who was in Egypt, anxious about the evil he had done before. He settled in Beersheba in the land of Palestine, in the open country of Syria. Lot settled in al-Mu'tafikah, less than a day and a night's journey from Beersheba. God sent Abraham as a prophet. Abraham stayed there, it was mentioned to me, in Beersheba, dug a well there, and established a sanctuary [masjid]. The water of that well was pure and flowing. His flocks drank from there. Then, the people of Beersheba harmed him somehow, so he left there until he settled in another part of Palestine between al-Ramlah and Jerusalem, in a city called Qatt or Qitt. When he left from their midst, the water dried up and left. The people of Beersheba followed after him until they found him, regretting what they had done. They said: "We drove out a sincere man from among us." They asked him to return to them, and he said: "I will not return to a city from which I was driven out." They said to him: "The water which you used to drink, that we drank with you, it has dried up and gone." So he gave them seven goats from his flocks and said: "Take them with you. If you take them to drink from the well, the water will appear, flowing and pure as it was. Drink from it, but do not let a menstruating woman scoop water from it." They took the goats and when they stopped at the well, the water appeared there. They were again drinking from it because of what they did, until a menstruating woman came. She scooped water from the well, and the water of the well withdrew. It remains that way until today.

## Establishing the Sanctuary at Mecca

Q 22:26 When we appointed to Abraham the place of the House: "Do not associate anything with me. Purify my House for those who circumambulate, those who stand, and bow and prostrate. 27 "Announce the Pilgrimage to the people.

They will come to you on foot and on every camel, lean, from every deep mountain pass."

**Q 3:96** The first House appointed for the people was in Bakkah, blessed, a guidance for all the worlds. **97** In it are clear signs: the Place of Abraham. Whoever enters it is secure. Incumbent upon the people for God is the Pilgrimage to the House for those who are able to make the journey. If a person disbelieves, God is not in need of the worlds.

**Q 2:125** When we made the House a refuge for the people, a place of safety. Take the Place of Abraham as a place of prayer. We made a covenant with Abraham and Ishmael: "Purify my House for those who circumambulate, perform retreats, and bow and prostrate themselves." **126** When Abraham said: "My Lord, make this a secure city, provide for its people from the fruits, those of them who believe in God and the Last Day." He [God] said: "Those who disbelieve will enjoy themselves for a short time, then I will drive them into the punishment of the Fire, an evil end." **127** When Abraham raised the foundations of the House, with Ishmael: "Our Lord, accept from us. You are the Hearing, the Knowing. **128** "Our Lord, make us submit to you, and from our offspring a people submitting to you. Show us the rites and turn to us. You are the Relenting, the Merciful. **129** "Our Lord, raise from among them a messenger to recite to them your signs and teach them the Book and the Wisdom, to sanctify them. You are the Mighty, the Wise."

*Ibn Kathir:* God mentions that his servant, his messenger, his friend, the Imam of the *Hanifs*, progenitor of the prophets – Abraham – built the ancient House, and that it was the first mosque for the mass of people in which to worship God. God guided him to the place of the House, a place which had been specified since the time of the creation of the heavens and the earth. God ordered Abraham to build him a House which would be for the people of the earth just like the angels had a place of worship in the heavens. Every day 70,000 angels, never the same angel twice, worship God in the Inhabited House in the heavens.

*Bukhari and Muslim:* God made this city sacred on the day he created the heavens and the earth, and it is sacred to God until the Day of Resurrection.

*Ali b. Abi Talib:* Abraham was guided by revelation from God. The Ka'bah is directly below the Inhabited House, so that if the Inhabited House fell, it would fall on the Ka'bah. Just as the Inhabited House is a place of worship in the heavens, so is the Ka'bah on earth. Some of the early Muslims said that in every one of the heavens is a House in which the inhabitants of that heaven worship God. The Ka'bah is for the inhabitants of the earth.

*Suddi:* When God ordered Abraham and Ishmael to build the House, they did not know the location of it, until God sent a wind called "Khujuj" which had two wings and a head in the shape of a snake. It went before them to the area around the foundations of the first House. They followed it and began to dig until they uncovered its foundations. When they discovered the foundations, they prepared to build the corner. Abraham said to Ishmael: "My son, bring me a good rock so that I might place it here." Ishmael said: "My father, I am tired." So Gabriel brought the Black Stone from India. It had been white emerald, but when Adam fell with it from Paradise it became black from the sins of the people. In the meantime, Ishmael brought a stone but found that the Black Stone was already in the corner. He said: "My father, who brought this?" Abraham said: "One who has more energy than you."

*Ibn Abi Hatim:* Abraham and Ishmael built it from five mountains. Dhu al-Qarnayn, who was king of the earth at that time, passed by when they were building it. He said: "Who commanded you to do this?" Abraham said: "God commanded us to build it." He said: "I do not know anything about this." So five rams witnessed that God had commanded this. Dhu al-Qarnayn believed.

*Ibn Kathir:* The Ka'bah that Abraham built was very large. Then, later, the Quraysh rebuilt it and made it smaller than the foundations of Abraham on the north side which faced Syria. Ibn al-Zubayr then rebuilt it, in his time, according to what the Prophet Muhammad had indicated, as his aunt Aishah related it. When Ibn al-Zubayr was killed by al-Hajjaj in the year 73, al-Hajjaj wrote to the Caliph Abd al-Malik b. Marwan thinking that Ibn al-Zubayr had made these modifications according to his own design. So the Caliph ordered that the Ka'bah should be returned to how it was before Ibn al-Zubayr. A hole was made in the Syrian wall, the rock was brought out of the Ka'bah, and the wall blocked up again. The inside of the Ka'bah was filled with rocks which raised the eastern gate and blocked the western gate entirely. When they discovered that what Ibn al-Zubayr did was according to what Aishah had related, they regretted what they had done and wished they had left it alone. During his time, al-Mahdi b. al-Mansur asked Malik b. Anas about returning the Ka'bah to how it was under Ibn al-Zubayr. Malik said: "I am afraid that kings might take it as a toy," meaning that different kings might continue to rebuild it according to their own designs. So it was left as it was until today.

*Bukhari and Muslim:* Aishah says that the Prophet Muhammad said: "Did you not see your people when they rebuilt the Ka'bah, making it smaller than the foundations of Abraham?" She said: "Prophet of God, why not return it to the foundations of Abraham?" He said: "If your people had not been so recently beyond the time of Ignorance and disbelief, then I would have spent the treasure of the Ka'bah for the cause of God, I would have put its gate in the earth and put the Rock inside of it."

*Ibn Kathir:* It is said that Adam had previously pitched a tent [qubbah] over the spot, that Noah's Ark circumambulated it for about 40 days, but all of this is based on reports from the Israelites. We declare that they are not necessarily true or false, but they cannot be verified.

## Blessings of Mecca

*Ibn Kathir:* Abraham built the best of mosques in the best of locations, in a valley without cultivation, so he asked God to bless its inhabitants, to provide them with fruits because it had only a little water, and no trees, crops or produce. He asked God to make it a sacred and a secure place. God responded and gave him that for which he had asked. He also asked God to raise up a prophet from among them. God also responded and raised up for them a prophet, and what a prophet! The seal of his prophets and messengers, the one who perfected the religion of God and did not deviate from him in any way.

## Place of Abraham

*Ibn Kathir:* The Place of Abraham is a rock on which he stood when building the Ka'bah. His son gave him this rock. It had been attached to the wall of the Ka'bah since antiquity until the days of Umar b. al-Khattab who moved it a short distance from the Ka'bah so that the people praying there might not disturb those circumambulating the Ka'bah. Umar b. al-Khattab followed God in this. He coincided with his Lord in some things, one of them being his statement to the Prophet Muhammad: "Should we not take the Place of Abraham as a place of prayer?" God then revealed the verse: "Take the Place of Abraham as a place of prayer" (2:125). There used to be the footprints of Abraham remaining on the rock until the early days of Islam.

## Isaac or Ishmael as the Sacrificial Victim

**Q 37:99** He [Abraham] said: "I am going to my Lord who will guide me. **100** "My Lord, give me one of the upright." **101** We brought him the good news of a forbearing son. **102** When he reached the age of working with him, he said: "My son, I have seen in sleep that I am to sacrifice you. What do you think?" He said: "My father, do what you are commanded. You will find me, God willing, to be one of the patient." **103** When they both submitted to God, and he laid him on his forehead, **104** We called out to him: "Abraham! **105** "You have fulfilled the vision. Like this we reward those who do good. **106** "This was a clear trial." **107** We redeemed him with a great sacrifice. **108** We left him among the later generations. **109** Peace upon Abraham! **110** Like this do we reward those who do good. **111** He was one of our believing servants. **112** We brought him the good news of Isaac, a prophet, one of the upright. **113** We blessed him and Isaac. Of their offspring are those who do good and those who do clear wrong to themselves.

*Ibn Kathir:* Abraham had many sons but the best known were the two greatest sons who were prophets. The greatest of these two was the one who was the sacrificial victim: Ishmael the first-born son of Abraham, from his Egyptian wife Hagar. There are those who claim that the sacrificial victim was Isaac, but this is only transmitted from the Israelites who substituted and altered the Torah and the Gospel. They changed with their own hands what was revealed, that Abraham was ordered to sacrifice his first-born son. In another transmission it says "only" son. The text indicates that it was Ishmael. In the text of their book it is written that Ishmael was the son of Abraham when he was 86 years old, and that Isaac was only born after Abraham was past 100 years old. Therefore, Ishmael was the first-born, without doubt. He was the only son at the time of the sacrifice. He was the only son for thirteen years, and when his father left with him and his mother Hagar, he was carried by Hagar, as a small child, still being nursed, according to what is said in the Torah, when they were placed in the wilderness of the mountains of Paran. They are the mountains around Mecca. Abraham left them there, and was not with them for long, leaving them with little water. God surrounded them with his protection and blessings. God caused him to increase in forbearance, patience, and truth. Then he kept his prayers and kept his family away from punishment by calling upon them to worship the Lord of Lords.

*Ibn Ishaq:* Muhammad b. Ka'b reports that he mentioned the question of which son it was to Umar b. Abd al-Aziz who was Caliph at that time, when he was with him in Syria. Umar said to him: "This is something about which I do not have an opinion, but we will see." So he sent for a man who was with him in Syria, who was Jewish but then converted and was a good Muslim. He had been one of the scholars of the Jews. So he was asked: "Which of the two sons of Abraham was he commanded to sacrifice?" The converted Jew said: "Ishmael. The Jews know this but they are envious of you because it was your father about whom God made the order and who was steadfast when he was ordered to be sacrificed. They disavow this and allege that it was Isaac because Isaac is their father."

*Ibn Abbas:* The intended one was Ishmael. The Jews allege that it was Isaac, but the Jews are lying.

*Mu'awiyah:* A man said to the Prophet Muhammad: "Oh son of the sacrificed one." The Prophet Muhammad laughed.

*Ibn Abi Hatim:* I asked my father about the sacrificial victim. He said that it was Ishmael.

*Ibn Kathir:* Among those who say it was Isaac are: Ka'b al-Ahbar on the authority of Umar b. al-Khattab, Ali b. Abi Talib, Ibn Masud, Ikrimah, Sa'id b. Jubayr, Mujahid, Ata b. Abi Rabah, Sha'bi, Muqatil, Ubayd b. Umayr, Zayd b. Aslam, Zuhri, Ibn Abi Burdah, Makhul, Suddi, Hasan al-Basri, Qatadah, Abu al-Hudhayl. It is also the choice of Tabari, and this is surprising coming from him. And it is also in one of the transmissions of the opinion of Ibn Abbas. But, the sound opinion also, related by most of these, is that it was Ishmael. This is the opinion of Mujahid, Sa'id b. Jubayr, Sha'bi, Ata b. Abi Rabah, and one of the transmissions of the opinion of Ibn Abbas.

### Sacrifice Attempt

*Suddi:* Abraham tried to put the knife on the neck of his son but it would not cut anything. It is said that between the knife and his neck was like a sheet of copper.

### Ram

*Ibn Kathir:* It is well known that the ram was white of eye and horn. Abraham saw it tied to a sumac tree near Mount Thabir. Sufyan al-Thawri reports that Ibn Abbas said the ram had pastured in Paradise for 40 seasons. Sa'id b. Jubayr said that it had been kept in Paradise until Thabir split from it. Its wool was red.

*Ibn Abi Hatim:* Ibn Abbas also says that a ram came down to Abraham from Thubir, its eyes and horns intact, bleating. He sacrificed it. It was the ram which the son of Adam had sacrificed and was accepted from him by God.

*Mujahid:* He sacrificed it at Mina.

*Ubayd b. Umayr:* He sacrificed it at the Place [of Abraham].

*Ahmad b. Hanbal:* Safiyah bt. Shaybah says: A woman from the Banu Salim told me that the Prophet Muhammad sent for Uthman b. Talhah. She asked Uthman: "Did the Prophet of God not send for you?" He said: "The Prophet of God said to me: 'I saw the horns of the ram when I entered the House, but I forgot to order you to hide them.' So he hid them because he did not want anything to be in the House to distract people praying."

*Sufyan al-Thawri:* The horns of the ram were in the House until it was destroyed, at which time they were also destroyed.

*Ibn Abbas:* The horns were hung from the House, dried.

## Ten Words

**Q 2:124** When his Lord tested Abraham with the words which he fulfilled. He said: "I make you an example [Imam] for the people to follow." He said: "And also from my offspring?" He [God] said: "My covenant is not within the reach of those who do wrong."

**Q 53:37** Abraham who fulfilled [his obligations].

*Abd al-Razzaq:* Ibn Abbas says that the "words" (2:124) refer to God's trying of Abraham with respect to purification: five related to the head, and five related to the body. Related to the head are: trimming the mustache, rinsing the mouth, picking the teeth, snuffing, and combing the hair. Related to the body are: clipping the nails, shaving the pubic area, circumcision, plucking the armpit hairs, and washing with water any trace of feces and urine.

*Muslim:* Aishah says that the Prophet Muhammad said: "Ten are the instincts: trimming the mustache, letting the beard grow, picking the teeth, snuffing water, clipping the nails, washing the knuckles, plucking the armpit hairs, shaving the pubic area, and cleaning the excretory members with water." Mus'ab says: She forgot the tenth, but it is rinsing. Waki said: Cleaning the excretory members is washing the anus.

## Resurrection of the Birds

**Q 2:260**   When Abraham said: "My Lord, show me how you give life to the dead." He said: "Will you not then believe?" He said: "Yes, but to satisfy my heart." He said: "Take four birds and cut them into pieces. Then put a piece of each of them on every mountain, and then call to them. They will come to you quickly. Know that God is Mighty, Wise."

*Ibn Kathir:* The result of this is that God answered what Abraham had asked. He ordered him to prepare four birds, to tear their flesh and feathers, to mix them up piece by piece and then divide them into portions and place a portion of each on a hill. When Abraham did as God ordered him, God then ordered him to call the birds, by the permission of their Lord. When he called them, each member flew to its other members, and every feather came to its right wing until the body of each bird was whole. They came walking toward him so that he could clearly see that they were whole. It is also said that God ordered him to take the heads of the birds in his hand. When each bird came to him, he threw its head and it went and attached itself as it was supposed to be. Abraham obtained certain knowledge of the might of God to raise the dead, which he did not lack, but he wanted to witness this with his own eyes and gain eyewitness knowledge. So God answered him.

## Religion of Abraham

**Q 3:65**   People of the Book, why do you dispute about Abraham when the Torah and the Gospel were not revealed until after him? Do you not have understanding? **66** Ah, you are those who dispute concerning that about which you have knowledge. But why dispute concerning that about which you do not have knowledge? It is God who knows and you do not know. **67** Abraham was not a Jew nor a Christian, but he was *hanif*, Muslim, not one of those who associated others with God. **68** The nearest of people to Abraham are those who follow him, and this Prophet and those who believe. God is Protector of those who believe.

**Q 2:130**   Who turns away from the religion of Abraham except he whose soul is foolish. We chose him in this world. In the next world he is one of the upright. **131** When his Lord said to him: "Submit!" He said: "I submit to the Lord of the worlds." **132** Abraham bequeathed this to his sons, and Jacob: "My sons, God has chosen for you the religion. Do not die unless you are those who submit." **133** Were you witnesses when death appeared to Jacob, when he said to his sons: "What will you worship after me?" They said: "We will worship your God, the God of your fathers Abraham, Ishmael, and Isaac, and only God. We submit to him." **134** That was a community which passed away. To them is what they earned, and to you is what you earned. You are not to be asked about what they did. **135** They said: "Be Jews and Christians to be guided." Say: Rather, the religion of Abraham, being *hanif*. He did not associate anything with God. **136** Say: We believe in God, what was revealed to us, what was revealed to Abraham, Ishmael, Isaac, Jacob, the Tribes, what was given to Moses and Jesus, what was given to the prophets from their Lord. We make no distinction between any one of them. We submit to him. **137** If they believe as you believe, then they are rightly guided. If they turn back, then they are merely in schism. God will make you sufficient against them. God is the Hearer, the Knower. **138** [Our religion takes] the color of God. Who can give better color than God? We worship him. **139** Say: "Will you dispute us concerning God? He is our Lord and your Lord. To us is what we do, and to you is what you do. We are sincere in him." **140** Or do you say that Abraham, Ishmael, Isaac, Jacob, and the Tribes were Jews or Christians? Say: Do you know better than God? Who is doing more wrong than those who hide the testimony of him from God? God is Mindful of what you do.

**Q 16:120**  Abraham was a model [ummah], obedient to God, being *hanif*. He did not associate anything with God. **121** He was thankful for the favors of him who selected him and guided him on the straight path. **122** We gave him good in this world. In the next world he is among the upright. **123** We revealed to you: Follow the religion of Abraham, being *hanif*. He did not associate anything with God. **124** The Sabbath was made incumbent upon those who disagreed concerning it. Your Lord will adjudicate between them on the Day of Resurrection concerning that about which they disagreed.

**Q 4:125**  Who can be better in religion than one who submits his face to God, is a doer of good, follows the religion of Abraham, being *hanif*? God took Abraham as a friend.

***Ibn Kathir:*** God kept his friend from being a Jew or Christian, and made clear that he was *Hanif*, Muslim, and not one of those who associate things with God. God wanted others to follow Abraham because his was the right religion, the straight path. He established all of what his Lord commanded him, and for this God took him as a friend, his most beloved. Every book which was revealed from the heavens to one of the prophets after Abraham was to one of his descendants and followers. He had two great sons: Ishmael from Hagar and Isaac from Sarah, and Jacob, also known as Israel, was born to Isaac. This continued until prophethood among the Israelites was sealed with Jesus son of Mary. As for Ishmael, he became the various Arab tribes and there was no prophet among them equal to their seal which was Muhammad b. Abdallah b. Abd al-Muttalib b. Hashim the Qurayshi, the Meccan then the Medinan.

*Ibn Masud:* The Prophet Muhammad said: "People, God took me as a friend just as he took Abraham as a friend."

*Bukhari:* Ibn Abbas says that the Prophet Muhammad, when he saw the graven images in the Ka'bah, would not enter until they were wiped clean. He saw Abraham and Isaac pictured with divination arrows in their hands and said: "May God curse those who did that. By God, they never practiced divination with arrows."

*Ibn Mardaweh:* Ibn Abbas says: Some of the companions of the Prophet Muhammad were sitting and waiting for him. He started to come out but when he got close to them he heard them saying something. He listened to their account, and one of them said something amazing, that God had taken a "friend" [khalil] from among his creation, and Abraham was his friend. Another said: "What is more amazing than that God spoke directly to Moses?" Another said: "Jesus was the spirit and word of God." Another said: "Adam was chosen by God." So the Prophet Muhammad came out and greeted them. He said: "I heard your words and your amazement that Abraham is the friend of God; that he is. That Moses is the speech of God; that he is. That Jesus is the spirit and word of God; that he is. That Adam is chosen by God; that he is. Only, I am the beloved of God, with no glory to myself; I am the first of those who intercede, with no glory to myself; I am the first who grasps the ring of the gate of Paradise. God will open it and cause me to enter, the poor and believers with me. I am the most noble of the first and the last on the Day of Resurrection, with no glory to myself."

*Ibn Kathir:* God mentioned Abraham in many places in the Quran. It is said that he is mentioned in 35 places, and fifteen of these are in Surah al-Baqarah (Q 2) alone. He is one of the five great messengers mentioned by name in Surah al-Ahzab (Q 33) and Surah al-Tawbah (Q 9). Abraham is the most noble following the Prophet Muhammad.

*Bukhari and Muslim:* Ka'b b. Ujrah says: We asked the Prophet Muhammad how one should invoke prayers upon him. He said: "Say: 'Oh

God, prayers for Muhammad and the family of Muhammad just as you pray for Abraham and the family of Abraham. Blessings upon Muhammad and the family of Muhammad just as you bless Abraham and the family of Abraham. You are Praiseworthy and Gracious.'"

## Scripture of Abraham

**Q 53:36** Rather, he does not have information about the scriptures of Moses **37** and Abraham who fulfilled [God's commands].

**Q 87:18** These are the first scriptures, **19** the scriptures of Abraham and Moses.

*Tabari:* Abraham fulfilled that which was sent to him and that which was sent by him. There is disagreement about that which Abraham fulfilled. Some say it refers to Q 53:38: "No bearer of burdens is to bear the burden of another." Others say that it refers to Abraham's willingness to sacrifice his son. Still others say that he fulfilled all the laws of Islam. Others say that the things mentioned in Q 53:38–56 are to be found in the scriptures of Moses and Abraham.

*Ibn Kathir:* Abraham fulfilled all that which he was commanded. He established the properties of the faith and adherence to it. Abraham was not distracted from the command of God to establish good things, nor did he forget to establish the burden of the great in helping the weak.

## Death of Abraham

*Ibn Kathir:* It is said that Abraham was the first to trim his mustache, and that he was the first to wear pants. His tomb, the tomb of his son Isaac, and the tomb of his son Jacob are in the quarter which Solomon b. David built in the city of Hebron. It is the city known as "Khalil" today. This is something passed on from nation to nation, generation to generation, from the Israelites to our time now.

*Abu Hurayrah:* The Prophet Muhammad said: "In Paradise there is a castle, made of pearl, in which are no cracks or weakness. God prepared it for Abraham as a place of residence."

# Ishmael

**Q 19:54**  Mention, in the Book, Ishmael, that he was truthful in keeping his word, and a messenger, being a prophet. **55** He instructed his family in prayer and alms-giving, and was pleasing to his Lord.

**Q 38:45**  Remember our servants Abraham, Isaac and Jacob, having power and vision. **46** We chose them for the purpose of remembrance of the abode [of the hereafter]. **47** They are, according to us, among those who are pure in being chosen. **48** Mention Ishmael, Elisha, and Dhu al-Kifl, all of whom are among the chosen.

**Q 21:85**  Ishmael, Idris, and Dhu al-Kifl, all of whom are among the steadfast. **86** We caused them to enter into our mercy. They are among the upright.

**Q 4:163**  We have revealed to you just as we revealed to Noah and the prophets after him. We revealed to Abraham, Ishmael, Isaac, Jacob, and the Tribes.

**Q 2:136**  Say: We trust in God, what he sent down to us, what he sent down to Abraham, Ishmael, Isaac, Jacob, and the Tribes.

**Q 2:140**  Or do you say that Abraham, Ishmael, Isaac, Jacob and the Tribes were Jews or Christians? Say: Do you know better than God?

## The First to Speak Clear Arabic

*Ibn Kathir:* The genealogists mention that Ishmael was the first to ride a horse. Before that, they were wild, but he tamed them and rode them. He was the first to speak in proper and correct Arabic, and he learned this language from the Original Arabs who had settled with them in Mecca, the Jurhum, the Amalekites, and the people of Yemen, the Arab nations which preceded Abraham.

*Abdallah b. Amir:* The Prophet Muhammad said: "Take the horse and bridle it, for it is an inheritance from your father Ishmael."

*Abu Ja'far al-Baqir:* My father reports that the Prophet Muhammad said: "The first whose tongue spoke in clear Arabic was Ishmael, when he was fourteen years old."

## Family of Ishmael

*Suddi:* Abraham missed Ishmael and said to Sarah: "Allow me to go and see my son." She took from him a promise that he would not settle there, but would come back to her. He rode on al-Buraq, and went to visit. The mother of Ishmael had already died and Ishmael had married a woman from the Jurhum.

*Ibn Abbas:* When Hagar died, Ishmael got married to a woman from the Jurhum. Abraham came and asked about the dwelling of Ishmael. It was shown to him but he did not find Ishmael. Instead he found Ishmael's wife, coarse and rude. Abraham said to her: "When your husband comes home, tell him that an old man of such-and-such a description came and that he said to you: 'I am not pleased with the threshold of your door.'" He left and when Ishmael returned, she told him. He said: "That is my father and you are the threshold of my door." So he divorced her and married another woman from the Jurhum. Abraham came again and arrived at the dwelling of Abraham. He did not find Ishmael but instead he found his wife, compliant and generous. He said to her: "For where did your husband set off?" She said: "He set off for prey." He said: "What food do you have?" She said: "Meat and water." He said: "God, bless their meat and water three times." He said to her: "When your husband returns, tell him that an old man of such-and-such a description came and that he said to you: 'I am pleased with the threshold of your door, so keep it.'" When Ishmael returned, she told him. Then Abraham came a third time and the two of them raised the foundations of the House.

*Ibn Kathir:* Ishmael was married to an Amalekite woman, which his father rejected, so Ishmael rejected her also. Her name was Amarah bt. Sa'd b. Usamah b. Ukayl the Amalekite. Then he married another woman, and his father ordered him to keep her, so Ishmael kept her. Her name was al-Sayidah bt. Madad b. 'Amr the Jurhumite. It is said that this was his third wife. He had twelve sons. Muhammad b. Ishaq gives their names: Nebaioth [Nabit], Qedar [Qaydhar], Abdeel [Azil],

Mibsam [Misma'], Mishma [Misha], Massa [Mashsh], Dumah [Dusa], Hadad [Arrar], Jetur [Yatur], Naphish [Nabash], Tema [Tayma], Qedmah [Qaydhma]. The People of the Book call them the same in their book. They allege that they were twelve great messengers but they are wrong about this interpretation. All the Arabs of the Hijaz are descendants of Nebaioth and Qedar.

## Prophethood of Ishmael

*Ibn Kathir:* Ishmael was a prophet to the people of this place and what was around it, the tribes of Jurhum, the Amalekites, and the people of Yemen.

*Tha'labi:* God sent Ishmael as a prophet to the Amalekites and the tribes of Yemen. When the time of Ishmael's death was at hand, he bequeathed to his brother Isaac that Isaac should marry Ishmael's daughter to Esau, son of Isaac. Ishmael lived for 137 years and was buried in al-Hijr in the tomb of his mother Hagar.

## Death of Ishmael

*Ibn Kathir:* When Ishmael was about to die, he passed his inheritance on to his brother Isaac and married his daughter Nesmah to Isaac's son Esau. She bore the Romans, and it is said that they are the "Children of the Yellow" because of the yellow from Esau. She also bore him the Greeks. It is also said that among the descendants of Esau are the Ashban. Ishmael, the prophet of God, was buried in al-Hijr with his mother Hagar. On the day of his death, he was 137 years old.

*Umar b. Abd al-Aziz:* Ishmael complained to his Lord about the heat of Mecca. God revealed to him: "I will open for you one of the gates of Paradise in the place you are buried so that its spirit will flow over you until the Day of Resurrection."

# Isaac and Jacob

**Q 37:112** We brought you good news of Isaac, a prophet, one of the truthful. **113** We bless you and Isaac. Among their offspring are good and bad.

### Isaac and His Sons

*Suyuti:* He was born after Ishmael by fourteen years. He lived to be 180 years old. Abu Ali b. Miskawayh reports that the meaning of Isaac in Hebrew is "laughter."

*Abu Hurayrah:* The Prophet Muhammad said: "Honorable [karim], son of honorable, son of honorable, son of honorable, son of Joseph, son of Jacob, son of Isaac, son of Abraham."

*People of the Book:* When Isaac married Rebecca he was 40 years old. She gave birth to twins. One of them was named Esau. He is the father of the second Rome. The second one who came out was holding the heel of his brother, so he was named Jacob. He is Israel, the one who gave his name to the Israelites. Isaac loved Esau more than Jacob because he was his first-born, but their mother Rebecca loved Jacob more because he was the younger.

*Tha'labi:* When he was already past 60 years old, Isaac married Rebecca and she bore him Esau.

*Suddi:* Rebecca carried twins in one womb. When she was about to give birth, the twins were fighting with one another in her womb. Jacob wanted to come out before Esau, so Esau said: "By God, if you come out before me, then I will remain in the womb of your mother and kill her." So Jacob waited and Esau came out before him. He was named Esau ['Isa] because he rebelled ['asa] and came out before Jacob. The second was named Jacob [Ya'qub] because he came out second on the heel ['aqb] of Esau. Jacob was the older of the two in the womb but Esau came out before him.

When the two grew, Esau was more loved by his father and Jacob was more loved by his mother. Esau was a hunter, and when Isaac became old he was blind, and said to Esau: "My son, bring me some meat to eat, and then come close to me and I will give you the blessing my father gave to me." Esau was a hairy man and Jacob was smooth. So Esau went out to hunt, and his mother, having heard the conversation, said to Jacob: "My son, get a sheep, slaughter it, cook it, skin it, and put on its skin. Then go to your father and say to him: 'I am your son Esau.'" He did this and came to his father and said: "Father, eat!" His father said: "Who are you?" He replied: "I am Esau." His father touched him and said: "This is the feel of Esau but the smell is of Jacob." His wife said to him: "It is your son Esau, so bless him." He said: "Bring me your food." So he brought it and his father ate. Then he said to him: "Come closer to me." So he came closer to him, and he blessed him, that his descendants should be prophets and kings. Then Jacob got up and left and Esau came. Esau said: "My father, I have brought you the prey which you wanted." His father said: "My son, your brother Jacob has preceded you." So Esau was angry and said: "By God, I will kill him." His father said: "My son, I still have a blessing for you, so let me give it to you." So he came close to him and his father said: "May your descendants be as numerous as the sand and may no one else rule over them."

The mother of Jacob told him to go to his maternal uncle since Esau was seeking to kill him. So Jacob left, traveling in the night and hiding during the day. For this reason God called him "Israel" because he was the first to travel by night [isra bi-layl]. He came to his uncle. Now Isaac had ordered him not to marry a Canaanite woman but to marry one of the daughters of his uncle Laban b. Nahor. So when Jacob arrived he proposed marriage to Laban's daughter Rachel. Laban had two daughters: Leah was the older, and Rachel the younger. Laban said to him: "Do you have money so that I might marry her to you?" He said: "No, but I can serve you for a period of time until I earn what is due for your daughter." Laban said: "Her price is that you serve me for seven seasons." Jacob said: "You will marry Rachel to me since she is the younger. It is for her that I serve you." Laban said to him: "This is an oath between you and me." So Jacob shepherded for him for seven years. When he completed the stipulated time, Laban gave the older daughter Leah to him, and Jacob consummated the marriage with her in the night. When morning came he discovered that it was other than had been stipulated. Jacob came to Laban while he was in the council of his people, and said to him: "You have wronged me, for I worked seven years and you gave me other than my wife." Laban said to him: "Son of my brother, when has any people married the younger before the older? Serve me for another seven years and I will marry the other daughter to you." People used to be married to two sisters before Moses was sent and the Torah was revealed. So Jacob shepherded for him for seven more years and Laban gave him Rachel.

Leah gave birth to four tribes: Reuben, who was the oldest of them, Judah, Simon, and Levi. Rachel gave birth to: Joseph and Benjamin which, in Hebrew, is "powerful." He was named this because his mother died during his birth. Jacob also bore children through the handmaidens of his wives. Each one of them bore three tribes. Zilpah bore: Dan, Naftali, and Zebulun. Bilhah bore: Gad, Issachar, and Asher. The sons of Jacob were twelve men: two from Rachel, four from Leah, three from Zilpah, and three from Bilhah. They are those whom God called the "Tribes" [al-asbat] for each one of them gave birth to a tribe. The term "asbat" in Arabic means a twisted tree with many branches. The tribes of the sons of Israel were like those of the non-Arab peoples.

Jacob left his uncle during the night with his children, wives, and servants to the place of his father in Palestine in great fear of his brother Esau. But he did not see anything from his brother but goodwill. So he went down to his brother and they reunited until finally Esau left the land and moved around in Syria until he came to the coast. Then he crossed into Rome and made it his homeland. This became a homeland to him and his descendants.

*Ibn Ishaq:* Esau b. Isaac married the daughter of his uncle: Nasimah bt. Ishmael b. Abraham. She gave birth to Rome, son of Esau. All yellow people are from him. Esau lived during the time when people were called after their skin, so his offspring were called the "Yellow People."

*People of the Book:* Isaac lived for 100 years after the birth of Esau and Jacob. He died when he was 170 years old. His sons buried him in the tomb of his father in a great field.

## Prohibited Food

**Q 3:93** All food was allowed for the Israelites except that which Israel prohibited himself before the revelation of the Torah. Say: Bring the Torah and recite from it if you are truthful.

*Ibn Abbas:* Israel – that is, Jacob – was afflicted with sciatica in the night. It would disturb him and wake him from his sleep but it would go away in the morning. So he made a vow to God that if God cured him he would not eat sinews, and the offspring of his house would not eat sinews.

*Qatadah:* It was mentioned to us that the food which Israel prohibited himself was because he was afflicted with sciatica during the night so that he was not able to sleep. So he made a promise that if God cured him he would not eat sinews ever again. So his children promised to follow him in removing sinews from meat. What he prohibited himself before the revelation of the Torah was sinews.

*Qurtubi:* Jacob was returning from Haran, heading toward Jerusalem, at the time he was fleeing from his brother Esau. He was a strong man, and on the way he met an angel, and Jacob thought that he was a robber, so he wrestled with him. The angel injured Jacob's thigh and then ascended into the sky. Jacob looked and saw that his sciatic sinew was inflamed. In consequence of this, there was great pain. He could not sleep at night from the pain, and he passed the night screaming. So Jacob swore that if God cured him he would not eat sinews, and would not eat food in which there were sinews. He prohibited it himself. Following him, his children removed the sinews from meat.

*Dahhak:* The reason for the angel injuring Jacob was that Jacob had vowed that if God gave him twelve sons and he reached Jerusalem safely, that he would sacrifice the last of his sons. This was a redemption of his vow.

*Tabari:* A group of Jews came to the Prophet Muhammad and said: "Oh Abu al-Qasim, tell us what food Israel prohibited for himself before the revelation of the Torah." The Prophet Muhammad said: "I entreat you by the one who revealed the Torah to Moses, do you know that Israel-Jacob was very sick for a long time, so he made a vow to God that if God would cure him from this disease then he would prohibit his favorite food and drink? His favorite food was the meat of camel and his favorite drink was camel's milk." The Jews said: "By God, yes."

*Ibn Abbas:* A group of Jews went to the Prophet Muhammad and they said: "Oh Abu al-Qasim, we will ask about five things. If you tell us about them we will know that you are a prophet and follow you." He made them take an oath like the one Israel took from his sons when he said: "God is witness to what we say." He said: "Go ahead."
They said: "Tell us, what is the mark of the prophet?" He said: "His

eyes sleep but his heart does not sleep." They said: "Tell us, how does a woman produce both males and females?" He said: "The two semens meet. When the semen of the man is predominant over the semen of the woman, then it is a boy. When the semen of the woman is predominant, then it is a girl."

They said: "Tell us, what did Israel prohibit for himself?" He said: "He was afflicted with sciatica and he could not become better except by the milk of such and such" – (Ibn Hanbal said: some say "camel") – "so he prohibited its meat." They said: "You are right."

They said: "What is thunder?" He said: "One of the angels of God responsible for the clouds with his hand, or his hands, breaking from light which the clouds hold back when God commands." They said: "What is the sound that is heard?" He said: "Its sound."

They said: "You are right and only one thing remains and it is that which if you tell us it we will follow you: there is no prophet to whom an angel has not come with the message. Tell us, who is your companion?" He said: "Gabriel." They said: "This Gabriel descends in war and battle and is an enemy of ours. If only you had said Michael who descends in mercy and help." So God revealed: "Say: Who is an enemy to Gabriel? It is he who brought it down to your heart by the permission of God, confirming that which was between his hands, a guidance and good news to the believers" (2:97).

*Tirmidhi:* It is reported on the authority of Ibn Abbas that the Jews said to the Prophet Muhammad: "Tell us, what did Israel forbid himself?" He said: "He used to live as a nomad, and his sciatic sinew became afflicted, and he found nothing that would ease his pain except for camel meat and milk, so this he prohibited." They said: "You are right." It is also said that he made a vow that if he was cured of it, he would renounce the food and drink he loved best, and the food and drink he loved best was camel meat and milk.

*Wahidi:* This was revealed when the Prophet Muhammad said that he was following the religion of Abraham. The Jews objected: "How can this be when you eat the flesh of camels and drink their milk?" The Prophet Muhammad said: "This was lawful for Abraham, and is also lawful for us." The Jews said: "Everything we now consider unlawful was unlawful for both Noah and Abraham, and has thus come down to us." Then God revealed this verse [3:93].

*Fakhr al-Din al-Razi:* The Jews said to the Prophet Muhammad: "You claim that you are from the community of Abraham. If this is the case, then how can it be that you consume camel meat and its milk when this is prohibited in the religion of Abraham?" The Prophet Muhammad responded by saying: "This was allowed to Abraham, Ishmael, Isaac, and Jacob, except what Jacob forbid himself for a certain reason. This prohibition remained with his children." The Jews denied this, so the Prophet Muhammad ordered them to bring the Torah and requested that they find in it a verse which indicated that camel meat and its milk were forbidden to Abraham. They were incapable of doing this and were discredited. This was revealed to show that they were wrong about the claim of these things being prohibited to Abraham.

# Lot

**Q 7:80**   Lot, when he said to his people: "Do you commit obscenities which no one from all the worlds has before you? **81** "You commit with the men out of preference over the women. You are a transgressing people." **82** His people were not able to answer except by saying: "Drive them from your city, for they are people who are being pure." **83** We saved him and his people except for his wife who lagged behind. **84** We rained down upon them a rain. See how was the punishment of those who sin.

**Q 11:74**   When the fear had gone from Abraham and the good news had come to him, he pleaded with us for the people of Lot. **75** Abraham is forbearing, compassionate, and a penitent. **76** Abraham, do not ask for this, for the word of your Lord has already been issued. For them comes a punishment which cannot be turned back. **77** When our messengers came to Lot he was grieved and felt weak [to act as a protector] for them, so he said: "This is a day of distress." **78** His people came rushing to him. From before that time they used to practice evil things. He said: "My people, these are my daughters. They are more pure for you. Fear God and do not disgrace me with my guests. Is there not among you a man of integrity?" **79** They said: "You already know that we have nothing for your daughters. In truth, you know what we want." **80** He said: "If only I had the strength to suppress you or take myself to a strong support." **81** They [angels] said: "Lot, we are messengers from your Lord. They will not reach you. Depart with your family with a part of the night left but let none of you turn back, except your wife for what befalls them will befall her. Morning is their appointed time. Is not the morning near?" **82** When our word went out we made the cities upside down and rained down upon them stones from hardened clay in layers **83** marked by your Lord. They [stones] are not far from those who do wrong.

**Q 15:61**   When the messengers came to the family of Lot **62** he said: "You are an uncommon people." **63** They said: "We come to you concerning that about which they doubt. **64** "We bring to you the truth. We are truthful. **65** "Depart with your family with a part of the night left, and follow behind them. But let none of you turn back but continue to where you are ordered." **66** We decreed this to him, the order that the remnants of those would be found cut off in the morning. **67** The people of the city came expressing joy. **68** Lot said: "These are my guests. Do not disgrace me. **69** "Fear God and do not shame me." **70** They said: "Did we not forbid you from [speaking] on behalf of the worlds?" **71** He said: "These are my daughters if you must do something." **72** By your life they wander about in their drunkenness. **73** The scream took them at sunrise. **74** We made the cities upside down and rained down upon them stones from hardened clay. **75** In this are signs for those who do not understand by small signs. **76** The cities were on the established way. **77** In this is a sign for those who believe.

**Q 26:160** The people of Lot rejected the messengers. **161** When their brother Lot said to them: "Do you not fear God? **162** "I am a trustworthy messenger to you. **163** "Fear God and obey me. **164** "I do not ask you for recompense. There is no recompense except from the Lord of the worlds. **165** "From all of the world will you have sex with men, **166** turning away from that which your Lord created you as your wives? You are a transgressing people." **167** They said: "Lot, if you do not stop, you will be one of the outcast." **168** He said: "To me your actions are those of detestable people. **169** "My Lord, save me and my family from what they do." **170** So we saved him and his family, all together **171** except for an old woman who was with those who lingered behind. **172** The rest of them we demolished. **173** We rained down upon them an evil rain fit for those who were warned. **174** In this is a sign but most of them are not believers. **175** Your Lord is the Mighty, the Merciful.

**Q 27:54** Lot, when he said to his people: "Do you have indecent sex aware [that it is indecent]? **55** "Would you have lustful sex with men rather than women? You are an ignorant people." **56** His people gave no answer except: "Drive out Lot from your city, they are people who are pure." **57** We saved him and his family except for his wife. We fated her to be one of those who lingered behind. **58** We rained down upon them an evil rain fit for those who were warned.

**Q 29:28** Lot, when he said to his people: "Do you have indecent sex the likes of which no one before you in all of the worlds has had? **29** "Would you rather have sex with men and practice highway robbery, have wicked sex in your meeting hall?" His people gave no answer except: "Bring us the punishment of God if you are one of the truthful." **30** He said: "My Lord, give me victory over the despoiling people." **31** When our messengers came to Abraham with good news, they said: "We are to destroy the people of this city. The people of it have done wrong." **32** Abraham said: "Lot is there." They said: "We know who is there, and we will save him and his family except for his wife who is one of those who linger behind." **33** When our messengers came to Lot, he was grieved and was unable to protect them. They said: "Do not fear and do not be sad. We are to save you and your family, except for your wife who is one of those who linger behind. **34** "We are to bring down upon the people of this city a thunder from the sky because they are sinful." **35** We left of the city a sign showing people who understand.

**Q 37:133** Lot was one of the messengers. **134** We saved him and his family, all together **135** except for an old woman who was with those who linger behind. **136** We demolished the rest of them. **137** You pass by them by day **138** and by night. Do you not understand?

**Q 51:31** Abraham said: "Messengers, what is your business?" **32** They said: "We were sent to a people of sinners, **33** to bring to them stones of clay, **34** marked by your Lord, for those who transgress." **35** We caused all who were believers there to leave. **36** We found only one house of those who submit. **37** We left there a sign for those who fear the grievous punishment.

**Q 54:33** The people of Lot rejected the warning. **34** We sent a storm of rocks against them except for the family of Lot whom we saved at dawn **35** as a favor from us. Likewise do we reward those who give thanks. **36** Lot warned them of our violence but they disputed the warning. **37** They tried to seduce his guests but we effaced their eyes: "Taste my punishment and my warning!" **38** The lasting punishment came upon them in the early morning. **39** "Taste my punishment and my warning!" **40** We made the Quran easy to remember. Are there any who remember?

### Lot

*Tabari:* Lot was alive during the time of Abraham. He was Lot b. Haran b. Terah, the son of Abraham's brother, and his people were from Sodom. He was a person from the land of Babylon who, along with his paternal uncle Abraham in whom he believed and in whose religion he believed, migrated to Syria. With them was Sarah bt. Nahor. Some say she was Sarah bt. Haybal b. Nahor. Terah, the father of Abraham, was with them though he disagreed with the religion of Abraham. He remained opposing Abraham's religion until they arrived in Haran and then Terah, also called Azar, died. Abraham, Lot, and Sarah went to Syria and then to Egypt where they found the Pharaoh named Sinan b. Alway b. Ubayd b. Uwayj b. Amalek b. Lud b. Shem b. Noah. It is also said that the Pharaoh of Egypt in those days was the brother of Dahhak, that Dahhak had appointed him over Egypt. Then they all returned to Syria. It is mentioned that Abraham settled in Palestine and Lot settled in Jordan. God sent Lot to the people of Sodom. They were a people who disbelieved in God and were immoral.

*Ibn Kathir:* Lot was son of Haran b. Terah, also called Azar, the son of Abraham's brother. Abraham, Haran, and Nahor were brothers. It is said that this Haran was the one who built the city of Haran. Lot had emigrated with Abraham from his home and settled in the city of Sodom in the land of Gomorra. There was a people in that place who had lands with cities attached to them. These were the most reprehensible, evil, and unbelieving of people. They practiced highway robbery and had illicit sex in their meeting places. They were more immoral than any of the sons of Adam who had preceded them, having sex with other men and rejecting women. Lot called them to the worship of God alone and forbade them from doing the immoralities which God prohibited them, but they did not answer him and not a single man from among them believed in Lot. They did not renounce their ways but continued doing as they had, desiring the expulsion of their messenger from their midst. God kept Lot and his family, except for his wife, pure. He evacuated them from the city but left the others there forever.

## Sins of Lot's People

*Ibn Zayd:* When a person would pass by them on the road, they would rob him and do this heinous deed with him. The abominations were their heinous deeds which they did, taking and mounting riders who passed by.

*Ikrimah:* They used to molest the people of the road, taking from those who passed them.

*Aishah:* Concerning the verse "you commit abominations in your meeting halls," the abomination was farting.

*Mujahid:* The men used to have sex with one another in their meeting halls.

*Umm Hani:* The Prophet Muhammad said: "They used to take from the people of the road and ridicule them."

*Tabari:* Lot called them to the worship of God and forbade them by the order of God from the reprehensible things they did: practicing highway robbery, committing immoralities, and penetrating men in the rear. Lot threatened them with destruction because they continued to do these things and reject repentance.

## Number of Believers

*Tabari:* When God intended to destroy the people of Lot and give victory to his messenger Lot, he sent Gabriel and two other angels. It is said that the two other angels were Michael and Israfil, and that they came in the form of young men.

*Ibn Masud:* God sent the angels to destroy the people of Lot. They arrived in the shape of young men, and stopped with Abraham and sought to be his guests. When the awe on hearing the good news of his son left Abraham, the messenger told him that God had sent them to destroy the people of Lot. Abraham reasoned with them and argued with them.

*Sa'id b. Jubayr:* When Gabriel and those with him came to Abraham, they said: "We are to destroy the people of this city, for its people are doing wrong" (29:31). Abraham said to them: "Will you destroy the city if there are 400 believers in it?" They said: "No." Abraham said: "Will you destroy the city if there are 300 believers in it?" They said: "No." Abraham said: "Will you destroy the city if there are 200 believers in it?" They said: "No." Abraham said: "Will you destroy the city if there are 100 believers in it?" They said: "No." Abraham said: "Will you destroy the city if there are 40 believers in it?" They said: "No." Abraham said: "Will you destroy the city if there are fourteen believers in it?" They said: "No." So Abraham counted fourteen, including Lot's wife, and he stopped asking, satisfied he had saved the city.

*Ibn Ishaq:* Abraham asked the messengers who were sent to destroy the people of Lot: "Will you destroy the city if there are 300 believers in it?" They said: "No." Abraham asked: "How about 200 believers?" They said: "No." Abraham said: "How about 40 believers?" They said: "No." Abraham said: "How about fourteen believers?" They said: "No." Abraham continued in this way until he said: "What if you find in the city only one person who believes." They said: "No." Abraham said: "In it is Lot." They said: "We know who is there" (29:32).

*Ibn Abbas:* The angel said to Abraham: "If there are five people who pray in the city, the punishment will be lifted from them."

*Qatadah:* It has reached us that Abraham said to the angels that day:

"Do you think there are 50 Muslims among them?" They said: "If there are 50 among them, we will not punish them." He said: "40?" They said: "40." He said: "30?" They said: "30." This happened until he reached ten. They said: "If there are ten?" Abraham said: "There is no people who does not have at least ten good people in it." When Abraham learned of the condition of the people of Lot from the report of the angels he said to them: "Lot is there," out of concern for him. The angels said: "We know who is there, and we will save him and his family except for his wife who is one of those who linger behind" (29: 32).

***People of the Book:*** Abraham said: "Will you destroy it if there are 50 upright men in the city?" God said: "I will not destroy them if there are 50 upright people there." Then Abraham kept lowering the number until he reached ten, and God said: "I will not destroy them if there are ten upright people there."

## Angels in Sodom

***Hudhayfah:*** When the angels came to Lot he was working in the land. They had been told not to destroy the people until Lot bore witness to them first. They said to Lot: "We are to be your guests for a night." So he took them and walked for an hour, and said: "Do you know what the people of this city do? By God, I do not know a people more wicked than they on the face of the earth." He continued walking with them and said this a second time. Lot's wife, an evil old woman, saw them and went off to warn the others.

***Qatadah:*** The angels came to Lot while he was in his fields. God told the angels to let Lot bear witness against the people four times before they destroyed them. They said: "Lot, we wish to be your guests for a night." He said: "Have you heard about this people?" They said: "What about them?" He said: "I swear to God that this is the most wicked city on the face of the earth." He said this four times. So Lot bore witness against the people four times. They entered his house with him.

***Ibn Masud:*** After the angels left Abraham, they headed out toward the city of Lot. They went for half a day and when they arrived at the river of Sodom they met the daughter of Lot drawing water for her family. She was one of two daughters. The older was named Ritha and the younger was named Ra'ziya. They said to her: "Girl, is there a dwelling nearby?" She said: "Yes, but stand your ground and do not enter until

I come back." She was afraid for them on account of her people. She came to her father and said: "Father, I left two young men at the gate to the city. I have not seen faces of people as handsome as theirs. Do not let your people take them and rape them." Lot's people had forbade him to host any man as a guest. They had told him: "Leave them to us, and we will host the men." Lot brought the angels to his house but no one except the family of the house of Lot knew about it. But his wife went out and told the rest of the people: "In the house of Lot are men. I have not seen faces as handsome as theirs ever before." So the people came rushing over to Lot.

*Tabari:* When the people came to Lot, he said to them: "My people, do not disgrace me with my guests. Is there not among you a man of integrity (11:78)? Here are my daughters for you, for what you want to do." They said to him: "Did we not forbid you to host men as guests? You already know that we have no right to your daughters, and you know what we want." When they would not accept anything he offered, he said: "If only I had the strength to suppress you or take myself to a strong support" (11:80). He was saying if only he had some help to make him victorious over them or a clan who would keep them from him and keep them from what they wanted of his guests.

*Wahb b. Munabbih:* When Lot learned that his guests were angels of God, sent to destroy his people, he said to them: "Destroy them within the hour!"

## Destruction of Sodom

**Q 53:53** The overturned cities [mu'tafikah] he destroyed.

*Sa'id b. Jubayr:* When the angels came to Lot, Gabriel said to him: "Lot, we are to destroy the people of this city. Its inhabitants are doing wrong." Lot said to them: "Destroy them within the hour." Gabriel said: "Morning is their appointed time," then the following was revealed to Lot: "Is not the morning near?" (11:81). God commanded that Lot leave with his family while it was still night, and none of them was to turn around except Lot's wife. He left and when the hour came, Gabriel plucked up their land with his wing and raised it up until the people of heaven heard the crowing of the roosters and barking of the dogs. He turned them upside down and rained stones of baked clay upon them. The wife of Lot heard the commotion and said: "My people!" and a stone fell upon her and killed her.

*Shimr b. Atiyah:* Lot told his wife to keep his guests secret. When Gabriel and those with him visited him, she saw them in human form, the likes of which she had never seen before. She set out, running to her people. She went to the meeting hall saying that the people were in her hands. The people came hurrying, walking between a run and a trot. When they reached Lot he said to them what God said in his Book. Gabriel said: "Lot, we are messengers of your Lord. They will not harm you." Lot said: "I am in his hands." God effaced their eyes and they began searching around and feeling the walls because they could not see.

*Qatadah:* Lot's wife set out to tell her people when she saw the angels, saying: "He is hosting people, with faces more handsome and scent more pleasant than any people I have ever seen." So they hurried but Lot surprised them and held them back at the door, saying: "These are my daughters if you must do something" (15:71). They said: "Did we not forbid you from [speaking] on behalf of the worlds?" (15:70). They came upon the angels but the angels effaced their eyes. They said: "Lot, you have brought us sorcerers. We are under their spell just as you are until we awake in the morning." Gabriel carried the four cities of Lot, being in each city 100,000 people, and lifted them with his wing between the heavens and the earth until the people of the heavens could hear the sounds of their roosters. Then he turned them upside down, and God set them upside down.

*Mujahid:* Gabriel stuck his wing under the lower part of the land of the people of Lot and took them with his right wing. He took their flocks and cattle and raised them into the heavens.

*Qatadah:* It reached us that Gabriel took the city by the middle then flew it into the heavens so that the people of heaven could hear the yelps of their dogs. Then he demolished one part of it after another, then threw rocks at the people. There were three cities called Sodom, between Medina and Syria. It was mentioned that there were 4,000,000 people in the cities.

*Suddi:* When the people of Lot got up in the morning, Gabriel descended and uprooted the earth from the seven earths, and carried it until he reached the heavens, so that the people of the heavens could hear the barking of the dogs and the noises of the roosters. Then he turned it upside down and killed them, as God said: "The overturned cities he destroyed" (53:53), being that which was turned upside down when Gabriel destroyed it and uprooted the earth with his wing. Upon those who did not die when the earth fell God caused to rain down rocks while they were under the earth, and upon those who were scattered about on the earth.

*Muhammad b. Ka'b:* God destroyed Sodom and the cities around it. There were five cities: Zeboiyim [Sab'ah], Zoar [Sa'rah], Gomorrah [Amarah], Admah [Duma] and Sodom.

# Joseph

---

**Q 40:34** Joseph came to you before with messages but you continued to doubt that which he brought to you, to the point that he perished. You said: God will not send anyone as a messenger after him. Thus does God lead astray he who exceeds all bounds, and is in doubt.

**Q 12:1** Alif Lam Ra. These are the verses of the clear book. **2** We revealed it as an Arabic Quran so that you might understand. **3** We relate to you the best of the stories from what we revealed to you of this Quran. Before it you were heedless.

## Genealogy of Joseph

*Ibn Kathir:* Jacob had twelve sons who were the eponymous ancestors of the tribes of the Israelites. The most noble, the most exalted, the greatest of them was Joseph.

*Suyuti:* Hasan al-Basri says that Joseph was thrown into the pit when he was twelve years old. His father met him in Egypt when he was 80 years old, and he died when he was 120 years old. Some say that he was a messenger, according to the word of God: "Joseph came to you before with messages" (40:34). It is said that this is not Joseph b. Jacob but Joseph b. Ephraim b. Joseph b. Jacob. This is also repeated by others concerning the word of God "inheritance from the family of Jacob" (19:6), that the majority hold that this was Jacob b. Mathan, and that the wife of Zechariah was the sister of Mary bt. Imran b. Mathan. The opinion that this Joseph (husband of Mary) was Jacob b. Isaac b. Abraham is strange. This is also related to the claim that the Moses mentioned in Surah al-Kahf in the story of Khidr [18:60–82] is not the Moses of the Israelites but Moses b. Manasseh b. Joseph. It is said that he is son of Ephraim b. Joseph, but Ibn Abbas accused the one transmitting this opinion of lying in this matter. Even more strange is the opinion related by Naqqash and Mawardi that the Joseph mentioned in Surah Ghafir [40:34] is one of the Jinn which God sent as a messenger to the Jinn. Ibn Asakir reports that the Imran mentioned in Surah Al Imran (Q 3) is the father of Moses, not the father of Mary.

*Ibn Kathir:* The prophet Muhammad was asked: "Who is the most noble of people?" He said: "Joseph, the prophet of God, son of the prophet of God, son of the prophet of God, son of the friend of God."

## Dreams and Prophethood

**Q 12:4** When Joseph said to his father: "My father, I saw eleven stars, the sun and the moon, I saw them bowing down to me." **5** He said: "My son, do not relate your vision to your brothers for they will conspire against you. Satan is a clear enemy to humanity. **6** "Thus, your Lord has selected you and given you knowledge to interpret reports, and has perfected his blessing upon you and upon the family of Jacob just as he perfected it on your forefathers before: Abraham and Isaac. Your Lord is Knowing, Wise."

*Ibn Kathir:* There is a group of scholars who clam that Joseph was the only prophet among the sons of Jacob, and that the rest of his brothers did not receive revelations. It is evident from their actions and sayings in this story that this is the correct opinion. But, in support of the prophethood of his brothers is the verse: "Say: We believe in God, what he sent down to us, and what he sent down to Abraham, Ishmael, Isaac, Jacob, and the Tribes" (3:84). It is alleged that this refers to the Tribes, the peoples of the Israelites, for among them were found prophets to whom were made revelations from the sky.

*Ibn Kathir:* Joseph had his vision when he was young before he had reached maturity. The eleven stars symbolized the rest of his brothers. The sun and the moon symbolized his parents. They were all bowing down to him. When he woke up he told the dream to his father. His father knew that he was to obtain a high and exalted position in this world and the next, by the fact that his parents and brothers were bowing down to him in the dream. So he ordered him to keep the dream secret, and not to tell it to his brothers because they were jealous of him and would plot to do him harm.

*Jabir b. Abdallah:* A group of men from the Jews came to the Prophet Muhammad and one of them said to him: "Muhammad, tell me about the stars, the sun and the moon which Joseph saw, that were bowing down to him, what are their names?" The Prophet Muhammad was quiet and did not make any answer, then Gabriel revealed the names to him. The Prophet Muhammad said: "Will you believe if I tell you their names?" The Jew said: "Yes." So he said: "They are Harthan, Tariq, Dhiyal, Dhu al-Kitfan, Qabis, Wathab, ʿAmudan, Fulayq, Masbah, Daruh, Dhu al-Farʿ, Diyyaʾ, and Nur." The Jew said: "By God, those are their names."

*Abu Yaʿala:* When Joseph told his father about the dream, he said: "This is something dispersed which God united." The sun is his father and the moon his mother.

## Joseph and His Brothers

**Q 12:7** In Joseph and his brothers are signs for those who seek answers. **8** When Joseph's brothers said about him: "He is more loved by our father than we are, and we are a group. Our father is in clear error. **9** "Let us kill Joseph or cast him to the ground, so that the face of your father will be toward you, and after him you will be a community of the truthful." **10** One of them spoke saying: "Do not kill Joseph, but cast him into an empty pit so that one of the caravans might take him, if you are to take action."

*Mujahid:* The one who spoke was Simeon.

*Suddi:* The one who spoke was Judah.

*Qatadah and Ibn Ishaq:* The one who spoke was the oldest of them, Reuben.

**Q 12:11** They said: "Our father, why do you not trust us with Joseph, for we are concerned for his welfare? **12** "Send him with us tomorrow so that he might enjoy himself and play. We will protect him." **13** He [Jacob] said: "Your taking him will sadden me. I am afraid that a wolf might eat him while you are being heedless." **14** They said: "If a wolf should eat him, with us being in a group, then we are the losers."

*Ibn Kathir:* According to the People of the Book, Jacob sent Joseph after his brothers, following them. He lost his way on the road and asked a man about where his brothers were. This is another of their mistakes, for if Jacob was hesitant to send Joseph with them, why would he send him by himself?

**Q 12:15** When they took him and agreed to put him in an empty pit, we revealed to him [Joseph] that he would confront them with this matter when they were unaware. **16** They came to their father in the evening, crying. **17** They said: "Our father, we went quickly and left Joseph with our belongings, and a wolf ate him. You will not believe us even if we were being truthful." **18** They brought his shirt with false blood. He said: "Nay, you have enticed yourselves in this matter. Perfect patience I seek from God protecting me from what you describe."

### Revelation in the Pit

*Mujahid and Qatadah:* Joseph's brothers did not know of God's revelation to him.

*Ibn Abbas:* "When they were unaware" (12:15) means "you will tell them about what they did in a situation in which they will not recognize you."

### Joseph's Shirt

*Tha'labi:* The brothers returned in the evening so that they would be in darkness as a substitute for an apology, compounding their deception. When they told Jacob, he cried and said to them: "Show me his shirt." So they showed it to him. He said: "By God, I have not seen the likes of a day nor a wolf more mild-tempered than this which ate my son, for it did not rip or tear his shirt." He screamed and collapsed, and did not get up for a long time. When he got up, he cried, and then took the shirt and began to smell it and put it over his face and eyes.

*Sha'bi:* The shirt of Joseph has three verses: First, when they brought it to their father. They said: "A wolf ate him." He said to them: "If a wolf ate him, then his shirt should be torn." Second, when Joseph later rushed toward the door and the vizier's wife ripped his shirt from behind, the vizier knew that if Joseph had been stalking his wife, that the rip would have been in the front. Third, when Jacob cast the shirt over his face and became clear-sighted.

*Ibn Kathir:* The brothers slaughtered a lamb, took its blood, and put it on his shirt in order to pretend that Joseph had been eaten by a wolf. They said: "We forgot to tear the shirt, and our lie will be discovered." When the signs of doubt became apparent to them, their deed did not surprise their father because he already understood their enmity toward Joseph. According to the People of the Book, it was Reuben who suggested they put him in the pit so that he might later, when his brothers were unaware, return him to his father. But they sold him to the caravan. When Reuben returned at the end of the day to remove Joseph, he did not find him, so he screamed and tore his clothes. He put blood on the coat of Joseph. When Jacob learned of this, he tore his clothes, wore a black cloak, and was sad for many days.

*Ibn Abbas:* The reason for this trial of Jacob was that he had slaughtered a sheep while he was fasting. He asked a neighbor of his to eat it but he did not. So God tested him with the matter of Joseph.

## Arrival in Egypt

**Q 12:19** A caravan came and sent their water-carrier to draw a bucket. He said: "Good news, here is a boy." So they hid him as merchandise. God is Knowing of what they did. **20** They sold him for a small price, a few dirhems. They were among those who thought he was insignificant. **21** The one from Egypt who purchased him said to his wife: "Make his stay honored, for perhaps he will benefit us or we will take him as a son." Thus did we establish Joseph in the land so that we might teach him to interpret reports. God is Controlling of all his word but most people do not learn. **22** When he [Joseph] achieved his maturity, we gave him wisdom and knowledge. Thus do we reward those who do good.

*Tha'labi:* Ibn Masud and others say they sold him for twenty dirhems. Each of them took two dirhems. Mujahid says it was 22 dirhems. Ikrimah and Ibn Ishaq say it was 40 dirhems. They sold him for so little because they were among those who did not know his value.

*Ibn Abbas:* Joseph rested in the pit for three days. When the fourth day came, he prayed and Gabriel sent a caravan. It was a group of men from the tribe of Midian heading toward Egypt. They took the wrong road and strayed from it until they alighted near the pit. The pit was in a deserted area far from civilization, an area of shepherds and people passing through. The water there was salty but it was sweet after Joseph had been cast into it. When the caravan alighted, they sent a man from the Arabs of the people of Midian who was called Malik b. Da'ar to get some water for them. At the watering place was a well, so he lowered a bucket and it came up with Joseph hanging, ensnared. Malik told the others about finding Joseph and they said that he would become their merchandise.

Now Judah had been bringing food to Joseph every day, keeping it secret from his brothers. When he came that day just as he had been doing, he did not find Joseph in the well, so he waited. When Malik and his companions alighted with Joseph, Judah returned and told his brothers about this. They went to Malik and said: "This is our slave who has escaped from us." Joseph kept quiet because he was afraid they would kill him. Malik said: "I will buy him from you." So they sold Joseph to him, and in doing so the price they received was invalid because it is forbidden to sell a free person.

*Tha'labi:* It is said that the reason for the enslavement and selling of Joseph was that Abraham had entered Egypt at some time in the past. When he left, his party included their ascetics and slaves following after him barefoot for four parsangs, glorifying and making him great. Abraham did not dismount for them. Therefore God revealed to him: "Since you did not alight for the slaves and those walking barefoot with you, I will punish you by selling one of your descendants into this country."

## Egyptian Vizier

*Ibn Kathir:* The Egyptian who purchased Joseph was Aziz, a vizier in Egypt over the treasury. Ibn Ishaq says: His name was Potiphar b. Ruhayb. The king of Egypt in those days was Riyan b. al-Walid. He was an Amalekite. The wife of the vizier was called Ra'el bt. Rua'el. Others say her name was Zulaykha, but it is apparent that this was her nickname [laqab]. It is also reported by Tha'labi that she was Fakka bt. Yunis. Ibn Ishaq also reports, on the authority of Ibn Abbas, that the name of the Egyptian who purchased Joseph was Malik b. Za'ar b. Nuwayt b. 'Afqa b. Midian b. Abraham.

*Ka'b al-Ahbar:* Potiphar b. Ruhayb, who was great [aziz] in Egypt and its surroundings, purchased Joseph. He was in charge of the treasury of the great king. In those days, the king over Egypt and its surroundings was Riyan b. al-Walid b. Thawran b. Arashah b. Qaran b. Amr b. Amalek b. Lud b. Shem b. Noah. It is related that this king did not die until he believed in Joseph and followed him in his religion. Then he died while Joseph was still alive. The one who ruled after him was Qabus b. Mus'ab b. Mu'awiyah b. Numayr b. al-Salwas b. Faran b. Amr b. Amalek b. Lud b. Shem b. Noah. He was an unbeliever and Joseph called upon him to accept Islam but he refused to submit and become Muslim.

*Ibn Ishaq:* The most noble of people are three: Aziz, the Egyptian who said to his wife: "Make his stay honored." The woman who said to her father on behalf of Moses: "My father, hire him for it is good to hire one who is strong and trustworthy." Abu Bakr al-Siddiq when he was succeeded by Umar b. al-Khattab.

*Ibn Abbas:* When the caravan entered Egypt Joseph was sold to Potiphar by Malik for twenty dinars, a pair of shoes, and two pieces of white cloth.

*Wahb b. Munabbih:* The caravan entered Egypt with Joseph, displaying him in the market for sale. The people continued to raise his price until it reached his weight in musk and his weight in silk. Potiphar purchased him for this price from Malik.

## Joseph's Age

*Ibn Kathir:* There is disagreement concerning the age at which Joseph attained maturity. Malik, Rabi'a, Zayd b. Aslam and Sha'bi say when he reached puberty. Sa'id b. Jubayr says eighteen years old. Dahhak says twenty years. Ikrimah says 25 years. Suddi says 30 years. Ibn Abbas, Mujahid and Qatadah say 33 years. Hasan al-Basri says 40 years. There is also the verse "Until he reached maturity, and reached 40 years" (46:15).

**Q 12:23** The wife of the man in whose house Joseph stayed tried to seduce him. She closed the doors and said: "Come!" He said: "May God protect me. My master is he who has made my stay pleasant. Those who do wrong do not reap benefit." **24** She desired him, and he desired her if it had not been that he saw a proof of his Lord. It was thus that we might turn evil and obscenity from him. He was one of our pure servants. **25** The two of them went for the door, she ripped his shirt from behind, and they found her husband at the door. She said: "What is the price for him who intended evil against your household, only to imprison him or a painful punishment?" **26** He [Joseph] said: "It was she who tried to seduce me." A witness from her household testified to this: "If his shirt is ripped from the front, then she tells the truth, and he is one of the liars. **27** "If his shirt is ripped from the back, then she is lying and he is one of the truthful." **28** When he saw that his shirt was ripped from the back, he said: "It is one of your snares. Your snares are great. **29** "Joseph, forget about this. Ask forgiveness [addressed to the wife] for your sin, for you have been one who is at fault."

## Seven Pious People

*Ibn Kathir:* Joseph was a handsome youth but he was a prophet and a descendant of prophets, so his Lord kept him from obscenity and saved him from the wiles of women. He is the most pious of the seven pious people mentioned in Bukhari and Muslim on the authority of the Seal of the Prophets: "There are seven people whom God will cover with shade on a day when there is no other shade: a just leader, a man who remembered God when alone and his eyes shed tears, a man whose heart is attached to the mosque so that as soon as he leaves he wants to return to it, two men who love each other for the sake of God, a man who gives out alms secretly so that his left hand does not know what the right hand does, a youth who grows up in the service of God, and a man who when summoned by a beautiful woman says: 'I fear God.'"

## Witness

*Ibn Kathir:* The one who testified was a baby still in its crib. This is the opinion of Ibn Abbas. It is also said that it was a man related to Potiphar, or related to his wife. Among those who say it was a man are Ibn Abbas, Ikrimah, Mujahid, Hasan al-Basri, Qatadah, Suddi, Ibn Ishaq, and Zayd b. Aslam.

*Ibn Kathir:* The people of Egypt, even though they were idolaters, knew that there was one God who would forgive sins. This is the reason for the statement of her husband.

## Assembly of Women

**Q 12:30** The women of the city said: "The wife of Aziz is trying to seduce her servant from himself. He has caused her to be infatuated with love. We see that she is in clear error." **31** When she heard of their disgust, she sent for them and prepared a couch for them and brought each one of them a knife, and said [to Joseph]: "Go out to them!" When they saw him, they extolled him and cut their hands. They said: "God preserve us. This is no human but is none other than a noble angel." **32** She said: "There is the one concerning which you found blame in me. I did try to seduce him, but he resisted the temptation. If he does not do what is ordered of him, he will be imprisoned and will be among those who are small." **33** He said: "My Lord, prison is preferable to that for which they summon me, so unless you turn me away from their snare, I will give into them and be one of the ignorant." **34** His Lord answered him and turned him away from their snares. It is He who is the Hearing, the Knowing.

*Ibn Kathir:* She summoned the women and gathered them together in her house, and treated them as guests, giving them something which required being cut by knives, like fresh fruit, and giving each one of them a knife. She then went to Joseph and dressed him in the best of clothes, and ordered him to come out before them. He came out and was more radiant than the full moon.

## Joseph's Beauty

*Ibn Kathir:* In a report about the Prophet's Night Journey, he says: "I passed by Joseph and he had been given half the goodness." Suhayli and other scholars say that the meaning of this is that Joseph had half the beauty of Adam because God created Adam with his own hands, blew his breath into him, and he was the ultimate of human beauty. Because of this, the inhabitants of Paradise enter Paradise with the stature of Adam and beauty of Joseph. Joseph had the half that was the beauty of Adam. Between them there is none more beautiful, and likewise there are no two after Eve and Sarah, the wife of Abraham who resembled Eve.

*Ibn Masud:* The face of Joseph was like lightning. The woman gave him something to cover his face.

**Q 12:35** Then it occurred to them, after they saw the signs, to imprison him for a while. **36** Two young men entered the prison with him. One of them said: "I saw a vision in which I was pressing wine." The other: "I saw a vision in which I was carrying bread on top of my head, the birds eating from it. Tell us its interpretation, for we think you are one of those who do good." **37** He [Joseph] said: "Before food from which you derive nourishment comes, I will tell you its [vision's] interpretation, before it happens to you. This is part of that which my Lord has taught me. I have left behind the religion of a people who do not believe in God nor the next world, for they are unbelievers. **38** "I follow the religion of my fathers Abraham, Isaac, and Jacob. It is not for us to associate anything with God. This is by the grace of God upon us, and upon people even though most people are not thankful [for it]. **39** "My prison companions, are many lords, of various types, better than one supreme God? **40** "You worship, other than God, only names which you have contrived, you and your fathers, for which God has not sent down any authority. There is no dominion except to God, command except that you worship only him. This is the right religion, but most people do not know. **41** "My prison companions, one of you will serve wine to his lord. As for the other, he will be crucified and the birds will eat from his head. The matter about which you ask is thus decided."

## Joseph's Imprisonment

*Ibn Kathir:* It became evident to the people after having seen the signs of Joseph's innocence that he should be imprisoned for a time so that people might stop talking about the incident. They wanted to show that it was Joseph who was trying to seduce her, hence they imprisoned him unjustly. This was ordained by God as a protection from his beauty, to keep him far away from their assembly and their snares. Some of the Sufis say what was reported by Shafi'i from them: the one preserved is the one not found.

## Two Dreams

*Ibn Kathir:* It is said that one of Joseph's prison companions was the king's cup-bearer, and his name was Nabu. The other was his baker, the one who brought him food. His name was Mujalith. The king had accused them of some things and had thus imprisoned them. When they saw Joseph in prison, they were amazed at his guidance, his words and deeds, and his constant worship of his Lord. The exegetes say that they saw the vision during the first night. As for the cup-bearer, he saw that there were three rods which budded and produced grapes. He took them and pressed them into the cup of the king, and he drank. The baker saw that there were three baskets of bread on his head. Birds of prey came and ate the pieces from the upper basket.

**Q 12:42** He [Joseph] said to the one of the two whom he thought would be saved: "Mention me to your lord." But Satan caused him to forget to mention him to his lord. He [Joseph] lingered in prison for a few more years.

*Ibn Kathir:* "Mention me to your lord" shows that it is permissible to seek help and this does not contradict dependence on the Lord of Lords.

*Ibn Kathir:* "A few more years" means between three and nine. It is said: seven. It is said: up to five. It is said: less than ten. Farra says: It is said that "a few more" is ten and from twenty to 90. It is also said that it is 100 or 1000.

*Ibn Hibban:* Abu Hurayrah says that the Prophet Muhammad said: "God was merciful to Joseph for if he had not spoken the words: 'Mention me to your lord,' it would have been no time that he lingered in prison. God shows mercy to the oppressed if they seek refuge in God alone. God sent no prophet after him without the wealth of his people."

### King's Dream

**Q 12:43** The king said: "I see seven fat cows eating seven lean cows, and seven green ears of grain and others dry. Leaders, give me an opinion about my vision if you are those who can understand visions." **44** They said: "A muddle of dreams. We are not learned in the interpretation of dreams." **45** The one of the two [in the prison] who was saved and remembered after a time said: "I will tell you its interpretation, so send me! **46** "Joseph, truthful one, give us an opinion about seven fat cows eating seven lean, and seven green ears of grain and others dry, so that I may return to the people, so that they might know." **47** He [Joseph] said: "You will sow tirelessly for seven years. What you harvest, leave in the husks except for a little which you will eat. **48** "Then, after that, will come seven hard [years] eating up what came before them except for a little which you stored. **49** "Then, after that, will come a year in which the people will have abundant rain, in which they will press wine."

*People of the Book:* The king dreamed that he was on the bank of a river and from it came seven fat cows that grazed there. Then seven lean cows emerged from the river, grazed with the first cows and then ate them. The king woke up disturbed but then went to sleep again. He dreamed of seven green ears of grain in a single bunch. Then seven withered and dry ears ate the first, and the king woke up disturbed.

### The Confession

**Q 12:50** The king said: "Bring him to me." When the messenger came to him, he [Joseph] said: "Return to your lord and ask him: 'What is the condition of those women who cut their hands?' My Lord knows about their snares." **51** He said [addressing the women]: "What was the story when you tried to seduce Joseph?" They said: "God preserve us, we know of no evil against him." The wife of Aziz said: "Now the truth is made clear. I was the one who tried to seduce him. He is one of the truthful." **52** "This I say so that you might know I was not false to him in the absence, and God does not guide the snare of those who are false. **53** "I do not absolve myself. The soul of man incites to evil unless my Lord is merciful. My Lord is Forgiving, Merciful."

*Ibn Kathir:* It is said that the words (12:52–53) are the speech of Joseph. He is saying: "I seek restitution for this in order that Aziz might know that I was not false to him during my absence." It is also said that these are the speech of Zulaykha, saying: "I acknowledge this so that my husband might know that I was not false to him in this same matter," that it was a matter of seduction but nothing actually happened between them.

## Joseph's Position in Egypt

**Q 12:54** The king said: "Bring him to me. I select him to serve me." When he spoke to him, he [king] said: "Today, you are strong and trusted in this world." **55** He [Joseph] said: "Put me over the storehouses of the land. I am a keeper, knowledgeable." **56** Like this did we give strength to Joseph in the land, occupying a position in it where he pleased. We bestow our mercy on whomever we want. We do not waste the reward of those who do good. **57** The reward of the next world is better for those who believe and are certain.

*Ibn Kathir:* It is said that when Potiphar died, Joseph married his wife Zulaykha, finding her to be a virgin because her husband did not have sex with women. She bore Joseph two sons: Ephraim and Manasseh. The king of Egypt had confidence in Joseph. He treated the Egyptians with justice. The men and women loved him. It is related that on the day Joseph went before the king, he was 30 years old. The king addressed him in 70 languages, and each time Joseph answered him in that language.

*Ibn Ishaq:* The king of Egypt converted to Islam at the hands of Joseph.

## Joseph's Brothers Come to Egypt

**Q 12:58** The brothers of Joseph came and entered into his presence. He recognized them but they did not know him. **59** When he had supplied them with their provisions, he said: "Bring to me your brother from your same father. Do you not see that I pay full measure and I am the best provider of hospitality?" **60** He said: "If you do not bring him to me, you will have no measure from me nor will you approach me." **61** They said: "We will seek to win him from our father. We are those who do things." **62** He said to his servants: "Put their barter in their bags so they will find it when they carry it back to their household, so that they will return."

*Ibn Kathir:* It is said that Joseph put the goods back in the bags because he wanted his brothers to return when they found the goods in their own land. It is also said that he was afraid if he did not put the goods in, they would not return another time. It is also said that he did not want to take goods from them for food.

### Brothers Return to Jacob

**Q 12:63** When they returned to their father, they said: "Our father, more measures are kept from us, so send our brother with us that we might get more measures. We will take care of him." **64** He [Jacob] said: "Should I trust you with him with a result other than when I trusted you with his brother before? God is the best of protectors, and the most merciful of those who show mercy." **65** When they opened their baggage, they found their bartered goods returned to them. They said: "Our father, what more can we desire? These bartered goods of ours have been returned to us. We will provide for our family, protect our brother, and increase the measure by a camel-load. This is a simple measure." **66** He said: "I will not send him with you unless you make an oath in God's name that you will return him to me, unless you are all unable." They made an oath and he [Jacob] said: "May God be guarantor over what we say." **67** Then he said: "My sons, do not enter by one gate, but enter by various gates, not that I can help you from what God intends in any thing. There is no dominion but God's. In him do I trust. Let all those who trust trust in him." **68** When they entered in the way their father had commanded, it did not help them avoid what God intended in any way except it served a need in the soul of Jacob. He was full of knowledge from our teachings, but most people do not learn.

*Ibn Kathir:* Jacob ordered them to enter Egypt not by a single gate but through various gates. It is said that he only intended that they not be seen all at once because they were handsome and their form admirable. This is the opinion of Ibn Abbas, Mujahid, Muhammad b. Ka'b, Qatadah, Suddi, and Dahhak.

*People of the Book:* Jacob sent a present with them to Aziz: pistachios, almonds, pinenuts, terebinth, and honey. They also took the money which was returned with their baggage.

### Accusations of Theft

**Q 12:69** When they entered into the presence of Joseph, he gave refuge to his brother [Benjamin]. He [Joseph] said [to Benjamin]: "I am your brother. Do not be distressed because of what they [the other brothers] do." **70** When he supplied them with provisions, he put the cup-bearer's cup into the bag of his brother. Then a crier shouted: "You, in the caravan, are thieves!" **71** They [brothers] said, turning back towards them: "What are you missing?" **72** They said: "We are missing the chalice of the king. For the one who brings it will be a camel-load. I declare it." **73** They [brothers] said: "By God, you know we did not come to despoil the land, and we are not thieves." **74** They [Egyptians] said: "What is the penalty if you are liars?" **75** They said: "The one in whose bag it is found, he will be the penalty. Thus do we reward those who do wrong." **76** They began to search their baggage, before coming to the baggage of his brother. Then they removed it from the baggage of his brother. Thus did we cause a snare to be laid on Joseph's behalf. He could not take his brother, except by the law of the king, only by the will of God. We raise by degrees whomever we want. Over all, endowed with knowledge is the Knowing. **77** They said: "If he has stolen, he had a brother who stole before him." Joseph kept it secret in his soul and did not reveal it to them. He said: "You are the ones in a bad situation. God knows best what you describe." **78** They said: "Exalted one, he has a father who is an old man. Take one of us in his place, for we see that you are one of those who does good." **79** He said: "God forbid that we should take someone other than he with whom we found our property. If so, then we would be doing wrong."

*Ibn Kathir:* It is said that Joseph had stolen the idol of his grandfather, his mother's father, and broke it. It is also said that it was his paternal aunt who hung it from him, between his clothes when he was small, in the territory that belonged to Isaac. Then they removed it from between his clothes without him knowing what she had done. She merely wanted it to be with her, in her place for her comfort. It is also said that he took food from the house and fed the poor.

## Jacob's Sadness

**Q 12:80** When they [brothers] gave up all hope of him [Benjamin], they conferred in private. The eldest of them said: "Do you not understand that your father has made an oath with you, in the name of God, and before, in the matter of Joseph, you were neglectful? I will not quit the land except by the permission given me by my father or by the decision of God. He is the best of those who decide." **81** "Return to your father and say: 'Our father, your son was stolen. We testify only to what we know. We could not protect against the unseen. **82** '"Ask the district in which we have been, the caravan in which we returned. We are being truthful.'" **83** He [Jacob] said: "No, but rather you contrived this matter for yourselves. Patience is most fitting. Perhaps God will bring all of them back to me, for he is Knowing, Wise." **84** He took refuge from them and said: "How great is my sorrow for Joseph." His eyes became white from sadness. He was suppressed. **85** They [brothers] said: "By God, will you not cease to remember Joseph to the extent that you are so agitated and will be among those who are destroyed?" **86** He said: "I only complain of my sadness to God. I know, from God, what you do not know. **87** "My sons, go and inquire about Joseph and his brother. Do not give up all hope of God's spirit, for no one gives up hope from God's spirit except the community of unbelievers."

*Ibn Kathir:* "Perhaps God will bring all of them back to me" refers to Joseph, Benjamin, and Reuben. Jacob's eyes turned white from so much crying and he was suppressed with sadness and longing for Joseph. When his sons saw him in this state they said: "Will you not cease to remember Joseph to the extent that you wrack your body and weaken your strength?" Jacob had not revealed to them, or to anyone, but only to God, that he knew about the vision of Joseph which had not yet taken place. He knew that he and his sons had not yet prostrated themselves to Joseph as in the vision.

## Brothers' Exchange with Joseph

**Q 12:88**  When they entered into his [Joseph's] presence they said: "Exalted one, distress has hit us and our household. We bring paltry goods, but pay us a measure and be charitable to us. God rewards those who are charitable." **89** He said: "Do you realize what you did to Joseph and his brother when you were ignorant?" **90** They said: "Are you Joseph?" He said: "I am Joseph, and this is my brother. God has been kind to us. He who preserves and is patient, God does not deprive the reward of those who do good." **91** They said: "By God, God has chosen you above us. We have done wrong." **92** He said: "Today, let no blame be upon you. God forgives you, for he is the most merciful of those who show mercy. **93** "Take this, my shirt, and throw it over the face of my father. He will come to see. Then come with all of your household."

*Ibn Kathir:* The brothers, in asking Joseph to be charitable, asked him to return their brother Benjamin to them. It is said that they only had a few dirhems, or just a single pinenut or terebinth. Ibn Abbas says it was an empty sack and some string.

*Ibn Kathir:* Joseph ordered his brothers to take his shirt, the one that was on his back, and put it over the eyes of his father. It would return his eyesight to him, after it had left him from all his crying, by the permission of God. This was a miracle and one of the signs of the prophets.

## Reconciliation

**Q 12:94**  When the caravan left, their father said: "I sense the smell of Joseph, even if you think me a liar." **95** They said: "By God, you are in your old misleadings." **96** When the bearer of good news came he threw it [shirt] over his [Joseph's] face, and his sight returned. He said: "Did I not say to you that I know, from God, what you do not know?" **97** They said: "Our father, ask forgiveness for us, for our sins. We have done wrong." **98** He said: "I will ask my Lord to forgive you. He is the Forgiving, the Merciful."

*Ibn Abbas:* When the caravan left Egypt the smell of Joseph's shirt came to Jacob. He smelled his scent from a distance of eight days.

*Hasan al-Basri and Ibn Jurayj:* Between Joseph and Jacob was a distance of eight parsangs, and there had been, since their separation, 80 years.

*Ibn Kathir:* The time separating Joseph from his father is said to have been 80 years, or 83 years. Both of these are reported on the authority of Hasan al-Basri. It is also said 35 years. This is the opinion of Qatadah. Ibn Ishaq says that they mentioned he was gone from his father for eighteen years. The People of the Book allege that he was gone for 40 years. It is evident from the story that it was a short time. He was a youth of seventeen years, he was in prison for a few years, which was seven according to Ikrimah. Then he left and there were seven years of plenty and seven years of famine. It was during these years that his brothers came, in the next year that his brother Benjamin came, and the third year that he revealed himself to them.

*Bukhari and Muslim:* The Prophet Muhammad said: "Each night, our Lord descends to the earthly heavens and says: 'Is there anyone who wants to repent so that I might accept his repentance? Is there anyone who wants to ask so that I might give it? Is there anyone who wants to ask for forgiveness so that I might forgive him?'"

*Ibn Masud, Amr b. Qays, and Ibn Jurayj:* Jacob delayed forgiving them until the dawn.

*Muharib b. Diththar:* Umar b. al-Khattab used to come to the mosque and listened to the people, saying: "My God, you summoned me and I responded, you ordered me and I obeyed. This dawn, forgive me." He heard a voice when he was in the house of Abdallah b. Masud. Ibn Masud asked about this, and he said: "Jacob put off his sons until the dawn."

*Ibn Kathir:* In a report it is said: "Jacob put off his sons until Friday night." Tabari reports, on the authority of Ibn Abbas, that the Prophet Muhammad said, concerning "My Lord will forgive you," that he was saying: "'When Friday night comes.' This was the word of my brother, Jacob, to his sons."

## Israel Comes to Egypt

**Q 12:99**   When they entered into the presence of Joseph, he gave refuge to his parents and said: "Enter Egypt safely, if God wills." **100** He lifted up his parents onto the throne, and they fell down in prostration to him. He said: "My father, this is an interpretation of my dream from before. God has made it to come true. He was good to me when he took me out of prison, and brought you out of the wilderness, even after Satan had sowed enmity between me and my brothers. God is kind to whomever he wants. It is He who is the Knowing, the Wise. **101** "My Lord, you have given me dominion and taught me the interpretation of events. You bring forth the heavens and the earth, my guardian in this world and the next. Take me at death as one who submits, and attach me to the upright."

*Ibn Kathir:* Many of the exegetes mention that when Jacob, who is Israel, the prophet of God, drew near, Joseph wanted to go out and meet him. The king and his army rode with him, out of deference to the service of Joseph and the greatness of Israel the prophet of God. He called to the king that God would lift the drought from the people of Egypt and bless them. There was a great number who went out with Jacob. According to Ibn Masud it was 63 people. Abdallah b. Shawdhab says it was 83 people. Abu Ishaq says it was 390 people. When they left with Moses they were more than 600,000. In the text of the People of the Book they are said to have been 70 people.

## Parents of Joseph

*Ibn Kathir:* In reference to the verse: "He lifted up his parents onto the throne," it is said that his mother had already died, just as is the opinion of the scholars of the Torah. Some of the exegetes say that God brought her back to life. Others say that this was his aunt Leah, and the aunt took the place of the mother. Tabari and others say that it is evident from the Quran that his mother remained alive to this time, and this is preferable to what is conveyed by the People of the Book.

## Joseph's Death

*Ibn Kathir:* When Joseph saw all the good things that had happened to him, and that everything good that was to happen to him had happened, he asked God to take him in death, that is, when he did take him in death that he be regarded a Muslim, that he be counted among God's upright worshippers. It is said that he made this request when he was at his life's end, just as the Prophet Muhammad had asked, during the sufferings of his death, that his spirit be lifted to the truthful ones among the prophets and messengers. It is also said that Joseph asked for this when he was still healthy and sound, that this was allowed in their religion and law just as Ibn Abbas reports: No prophet asked for death before Joseph. In our law it is prohibited to ask God for death except in time of strife. Ali b. Abi Talib sought death when he faced severe strife and the fighting became intense. Bukhari also sought death when the situation became harsh for him, meeting with his opponents. But in the case of good living conditions, Bukhari and Muslim report, on the authority of Anas b. Malik, that the Prophet Muhammad said: "None of you should wish for death on account of a hardship that befalls him. As for the truthful one, perhaps he will become more truthful. As for the evil one, perhaps he will repent. Rather, he should say: 'By God, cause me to live as long as life is better for me, and take me when death is better for me.'"

*Ibn Ishaq:* The People of the Book say that Jacob settled in the cities of Egypt with Joseph, and stayed for seventeen years. Then he died. He bequeathed to Joseph that he should be buried with his fathers Abraham and Isaac.

*Suddi:* Joseph traveled with Jacob's body to Syria and buried it in a cave with his father Isaac and his grandfather Abraham.

*People of the Book:* The age of Jacob on the day he entered Egypt was 130 years. He stayed in the land of Egypt for seventeen years. The total of his life was thus 147 years. Jacob bequeathed to his sons, one by one, telling them what would come of them. He informed Judah that from him would issue a great prophet, Jesus son of Mary. When Jacob died, the people of Egypt cried for 70 days. Joseph ordered the physicians to prepare him and let him rest for 40 days. Then Joseph asked permission from the king of Egypt to leave with his father, to bury him with his family. He gave him permission and sent some of the great men of Egypt with him. When they arrived in Hebron, they buried him in the cave which Abraham purchased from Ephron b. Zohar (Sakhr). They performed a ceremony of mourning for him for seven days. Then they returned to Egypt and Joseph's brothers respected him and established themselves in Egypt. When it came time for Joseph to die, he bequeathed that they would carry him with them when they left Egypt and bury him with his forefathers. So they embalmed him and placed him in a coffin [tabut]. He remained in Egypt until Moses left with him.

He was buried with his forefathers. He died when he was 110 years old.

*Mubarak b. Fadalah:* Hasan al-Basri says that Joseph was cast into the pit when he was seventeen years old. He was away from his father for 80 years. After that he lived 23 years. So he died when he was 120 years old.

# Shuayb

**Q 7:85** To Midian [we sent] their brother Shuayb. He said: "My people, worship God! There is no god for you other than he. A sign has come to you from your Lord. Be fair in weights and measures, do not cheat the people their things, and do not make spoil in the earth after it has been restored. This is good for you if you are believers. **86** "Do not sit on every path threatening and blocking from the way of God those who believe in him, seeking to make it crooked. Remember when you were small and he made you great. Consider how the punishment will be of those who spoil. **87** "If a group of you believe in that with which I was sent, and a group does not believe, be patient until God decides between us. He is the best of judges." **88** The leaders from among his people who were arrogant said: "Shuayb, we will cast away from us you and those who believe in you, or you will return to our religion." He said: "Even if we are despisers? **89** "Should we concoct a lie against God? If we returned to your religion after God has rescued us from it? We have no way to return to it unless God, our Lord, wills it. Our Lord encompasses all things with his knowledge. We trust in God. Our Lord, decide between us and between our people, with truth, for you are the best of those who make decisions." **90** The leaders of his people who did not believe said: "If you follow Shuayb then you are ruined." **91** The earthquake took them and morning found them lying face down in their homes. **92** Those who rejected Shuayb were as though they had never enjoyed their homes. Those who rejected Shuayb were the ones who were ruined. **93** Shuayb left them and said: "My people, I brought you the message of my Lord, and advised you well. How can I lament a people who do not believe?"

**Q 11:84** To Midian [we sent] their brother Shuayb. He said: "My people, worship God. There is no god for you other than he. Do not use short weights and measures. I see you prosperous but I fear for you the punishment of an encompassing day. **85** "My people, be fair in weights and measures, do not cheat people their things, nor be insolent in the land as despoilers. **86** "What God leaves is best for you, if you were believers. I am not guardian over you." **87** They said: "Shuayb, do your prayers command you to make us leave that which our fathers worshipped, or doing with our property what we wish? Certainly you are forbearing and right-minded." **88** He said: "My people, see if I have a sign from my Lord. He gives me good sustenance from him. I do not want to oppose you, to forbid you from it. I only want rectification to the best of my ability. I have no success except with God. In him I trust and to him I turn. **89** "My people, do not let my dissent from you cause you to suffer and have happen to you what happened to the people of Noah, the people of Hud, or the people of Salih. The people of Lot are not far from you. **90** "Ask your Lord for forgiveness and then turn toward him. My Lord is Merciful, Loving." **91** They said: "Shuayb, we do not understand much of what you say. We see you to be weak among us. Were it not for your family connections, we would stone you. You have no great position among us." **92** He said: "My people, are my family connections of greater position to you than God? You put him behind your backs. My Lord encompasses all you do. **93** "My people, do what you can. I am doing [my part]. You will learn on whom punishment comes shaming him, and who is a liar. Beware, for I am watching with you." **94** When our decree came, we saved Shuayb and those who believed with him by mercy from us. The scream took those who did wrong and morning found them lying face down in their homes **95** as though they had never enjoyed their homes. Away with Midian just as Thamud had gone away!

## Midian

*Tabari:* God sent Shuayb to the descendants of Midian. Midian are descendants of Midian b. Abraham. Ibn Ishaq says: Midian is the name of a tribe like Tamim. It is said that Midian is the name of a person and that it is the name of a tribe or a land. Others say: It is reported that Midian was the son of the daughter of Lot. It is also said that his wife was the daughter of Lot. Ibn Ishaq alleges that Shuayb is he whom God mentioned as the one sent to them, from the descendants of this Midian. Shuayb was son of Mikil b. Issachar [Yashjar]. Ibn Ishaq says that his name in Syriac was "Yathrun."

*Tabari:* There is disagreement concerning Shuayb's genealogy. Ata b. Abi Rabah, Ibn Ishaq, and others say that Shuayb was son of Mikil b. Issachar b. Midian b. Abraham. His name in Syriac is "Beirut." His mother was Mik'ail daughter of Lot. Sharqi b. al-Qutami claims that Shuayb was Ephah b. Jashbub [Yawbab] b. Midian b. Abraham. Another claims that he was Shuayb b. Jazi b. Issachar [Ayfa] b. Levi b. Jacob b. Isaac b. Abraham. Shuayb is the diminutive of Sha'ab or Shi'b. Qatadah says he is Shuayb b. Jashbub. It is also said: Shuayb b. Safwan b. Ephah b. Thabit b. Midian b. Abraham. God knows.

*Ibn Kathir:* The people of Midian were an Arab people who lived in their city of Midian which is close to the land of Ma'an, on the edges of Syria, adjacent to the border of the Hijaz, close to the lake of the people of Lot. They came only a short time after the people of Lot. Midian is a tribe by which the people of the city are known. They are the descendants of Midian b. Abraham. Shuayb is their prophet. He is son of Mikil b. Jokshan [Yashjan], according to Ibn Ishaq. He says: it is said that in Syriac he is known as Jethro. Concerning this there is some speculation. It is said that he is Shuayb b. Issachar b. Levi b. Jacob. It is said: Shuayb b. Nuwayb b. Ephah b. Midian b. Abraham. It is also said: Shuayb b. Dayfur b. Ephah [Ayta] b. Thabit b. Midian b. Abraham. And other genealogies are offered.

*Wahb b. Munabbih:* Shuayb and Mulgham were among those who believed in Abraham on the day he was burned in the fire. Hagar was with him in Syria. He married the two daughters of Lot.

*Kisa'i:* Wahb b. Munabbih says: The letters of the Arabic alphabet are the names of the people of Shuayb: Abjad, Hawwaz, Huttiya, Kalaman, Sa'fas, and Qurishat. Qatadah says: They are the names of the people of the Tanglewood. It is also said that they are the names of the kings of the Amalekites, cousins of the people of Midian, but have no relation to Shuayb b. Zion b. Anka b. Midian b. Abraham.

*Sa'id b. Jubayr:* Concerning God's word "We see you to be weak among us" (11:91), it is said that Shuayb was blind.

*Tabari:* He was blind, just as his people said: "We see you to be weak among us" (11:91). It is said that he was the preacher of the prophets because he was accomplished in calling his people back to God. His people were disobedient to God by cheating in weights and measures.

*Ibn Kathir:* It was related that Shuayb cried out of love of God until he was blind, but God returned his sight to him. God asked: "Shuayb, do you cry out of fear of Hell? or out of your longing for Paradise?" Shuayb said: "Neither, but out of love for you. Whenever I look to you I do not care what is done to me." So God revealed to him: "Because of this, I will make Moses b. Imran to serve you."

## Miracles of Shuayb

*Ibn Kathir:* "A sign has come to you from your Lord" (7:85) meaning a sign, which was the coming of Shuayb with the message. The Quran does not mention any miracles he did. It is said that his miracles are what are mentioned by Kisa'i in his Stories of the Prophets.

## Sins of Midian

*Ibn Ishaq:* God sent to the descendants of Midian their brother Shuayb b. Mikil, calling them to obedience of God, leaving the evil of the earth, and an end to blocking the way of travelers. Shuayb said to them: "People, worship God alone without associating anything with him. No god requires your service except the God who created you, in whose hand is your benefit and loss."

*Suddi and Qatadah:* "Do not cheat the people their things" (7:85) means do not be unjust with the people, and do not diminish them their rights.

*Qurtubi:* The word of God: "Do not cheat the people their things" (7:85), cheating meaning lessening or shorting. In an item of commercial value it is having a flaw or defect or something to reduce its value, or adding or lessening the measure of something. All of this is invalid consumption of property. This was forbidden to the preceding generations and peoples according to the Sunnah of the prophets.

*Ibn Abbas:* In the land, before God sent Shuayb as a prophet, there was disobedience done and people allowing what is forbidden and the shedding of blood. This was their despoiling. When God sent Shuayb, he summoned the people to God so that the earth could be rectified. All prophets sent to their peoples seek to rectify them.

*Qurtubi:* God forbade them from sitting on the road and blocking the way of those who are obedient to God. There is disagreement among the scholars concerning the meaning of their sitting on the road. Ibn Abbas, Qatadah, Mujahid, and Suddi say that they used to sit on the roads open to Shuayb and would threaten anyone who wanted to go to him; they would block his way saying: "He is a liar, do not go to him." This is just as the Quraysh did with the Prophet Muhammad. This is evident from the verse. Abu Hurayrah says: This is forbidding highway robbery, and the taking of plunder. This is what they did. He relates that the Prophet Muhammad said: "I saw, on the night of my Night Journey, a piece of wood on the road by which no clothing except in pieces and nothing except shreds passed. So I said: 'What is this, Gabriel?' Gabriel said: 'This is like the people of your community who sit on the road and rob it.' Then he recited the verse: 'Do not sit on every path threatening . . .'" (7:86). Suddi also says: They were taking a 10 per cent tax. They were just like those today who take property from the people requiring them, by right of their economic position, by subjugation, to pay that which is not allowed to be required according to the laws of alms-giving and inheritance.

*Ibn Abbas:* The people to whom Shuayb was sent were an unjust people who would sit on the road and harass people, taking a 10 per cent tax from them. They were the first to establish this custom.

*Muhammad b. Ka'b:* It reached me that the people of Shuayb were punished for cutting dirhems. Then I found this in the Quran: "Do your prayers command you to make us leave that which our fathers worshipped, or doing with our property what we wish?" (11:87).

## Exchange

*Qurtubi:* Some say that this means Shuayb was following unbelief before faith in God, by the phrase: "You will return to our religion" (7:88). Zajjaj says: It is permitted that the return have the meaning of beginning. It is said: Return to me from so-and-so who is reprehensible, meaning change yourself, even if his previous condition was not reprehensible before that time.

*Ibn Abbas:* Shuayb was great in prayer. When the period of his people in unbelief was extended he gave up on their rectification. He called to them and said: "Our Lord, decide between us and our people, with truth, for you are the best of those who make decisions" (7:89). God answered his call and destroyed them with an earthquake.

*Ibn Kathir:* He forbade them first from being occupied with wealth which is connected to being stingy, and warned them of the negation of God's blessing upon them in their worldly dealings.

## Sarcasm

*Tabari:* The people said: "Shuayb, does your prayer command you that we should stop the worship which our fathers practiced, or that we should stop doing what we want with our belongings? Certainly you are forbearing and right-minded" (11:87). They said this in mocking and in ridicule: "Does your prayer, this to whom you pray, order you to prohibit us from worshipping all but your god? Should we abandon what our fathers before us, our ancestors, the first ones worshipped? Certainly we will only do what pleases you, abandoning the practices which you forbid so that we can please you."

*Ibn Kathir:* "Certainly you are forbearing and right-minded" (11:87). Ibn Abbas, Maymun b. Mihran, Ibn Jurayj, Zayd b. Aslam, and Tabari say: The people said this sarcastically.

## Earthquake

*Tabari:* The punishment which took those who rejected Shuayb was an earthquake. Those who rejected Shuayb and did not believe in him were destroyed, and their land became empty of them. Their houses were as if they had not yet settled into them nor ever lived in them before their destruction.

## Preacher of the Prophets

*Ibn Ishaq:* Yaqub b. Abi Salamah mentioned Shuayb, and the Prophet Muhammad said: "That one is the preacher of the prophets because of the eloquence of his calling his people to return to God. When they rejected him and threatened him with stoning and expulsion from their city, they rejected God, so the punishment of the Day of Shade took them. It was the punishment of an awful day."

*Yaqub b. Abi Salamah:* When the Prophet Muhammad used to mention Shuayb, he would say: "That one was the preacher of the prophets," because of the beauty of Shuayb's discourse in the dispute with his people.

## Tanglewood

Q 15:78 The people of the Tanglewood were those who do wrong. 79 So we exacted retribution from them. They both [people of Tanglewood and people of cities of Lot] were plain to see.

Q 26:176 The people of the Tanglewood rejected the messengers. 177 When Shuayb said to them: "Do you not fear God? 178 "I am a trustworthy messenger to you. 179 "So, fear God and obey me! 180 "I do not ask you for recompense. My recompense is from the Lord of the worlds only. 181 "Be fair in weights and do not be among those who cause others to lose. 182 "Weigh with accurate scales. **183** "Do not cheat the people their things, nor be insolent in the land as despoilers. **184** "Fear the one who created you and the disposition of the first ones." **185** They said: "You are one of those under a spell. **186** "You are nothing but a human being like us. We think you are a liar. **187** "Cause a piece of the sky to fall on us if you are truthful." **188** He said: "My Lord is most knowledgeable concerning what you do." **189** So they rejected him but the punishment of the Day of the Shade took them. It was a punishment of an awful day. **190** In this is a sign but most of them are not believers. **191** Your Lord is He, the Mighty, the Merciful.

*Suddi:* God sent Shuayb to Midian and to the people of the Tanglewood. The Tanglewood is a thicket of trees. Along with their unbelief in God was their cheating on weights and measures, so Shuayb called them to God and they rejected him. Then he said to them what is mentioned in the Quran, that which they rejected. They asked him about the punishment and God opened upon them one of the gates of Hell and the heat from it destroyed them. They found no benefit from shade nor water. Then he sent to them a cloud with a pleasant scent where they found the wind cool and pleasant. They called out about the shade to the others. When they had all gathered under the cloud, the men, women, and youths, God closed it over them and it destroyed them.

*Ibn Kathir:* There are exegetes, like Qatadah and others, who hold that the people of the Tanglewood are a different community than the people of Midian, but this position is weak. There are two things in support of it. The first of them is that the Quran says the people of the Tanglewood called the messengers liars but does not say that Shuayb was one of their brothers. Second, their punishment was the Day of Shade, and the punishment of the people of Midian was an earthquake or scream. In the first case, it is possible that God did not want to associate Shuayb with people who worshipped the Tanglewood, whereas it was not objectionable to identify him with their tribal affiliation. As for the second point, if one is to take the punishment of the Day of Shade as an indication that these were two separate communities, then one would need to take the mention of the earthquake and scream as indication that there were two other communities in addition.

*Suyuti:* It is said that Shuayb was the preacher of the prophets, sent as a messenger to two peoples: Midian and the people of the Tanglewood. Many agree that Midian and the people of the Tanglewood are the same people. Ibn Kathir says that the fact that they are both accused of cheating in weights and measures shows they are the same people. Suddi and Ikrimah say that God did not send any prophet twice except for Shuayb, once to Midian when God took them with a scream and once to the people of the Tanglewood whom God took with the punishment of the Day of Shade. Abdallah b. Umar says that the people of Midian and the people of the Tanglewood were two peoples and that God sent Shuayb to both of them. Ibn Kathir thinks this is strange and reports even further that there are those who think Shuayb was sent to three peoples, adding the People of the Well.

*Kisa'i:* Midian the son of Abraham lived a long life and married a wife from the Amalekites who bore him four sons: Nabeth, Japheth, Sahuh, and Anka. When they reached maturity they married, had children, and became a numerous people. They built for themselves a fortified city and called it Midian after their grandfather. Then came the people of the Tanglewood, who took the city, built their own homes, and mingled with the people of Midian who worshipped God while the people of the Tanglewood worshipped idols. Among the leaders of Midian was a man named Zion b. Anka who took a wife from the Amalekites, who bore him a son named Shuayb who was also called Jethro.

## Punishment of Shade

*Ibn Ishaq:* God gave authority over the people to the fire until it ripened them. Then he created for them a shade like a black cloud. When they saw it they gathered under it for its coolness to escape the heat, until they were all under it. Then God closed it on them and all of them together were destroyed, but God saved Shuayb and those who believed in him, by his mercy.

*Tabari:* When the people continued in their sin and mistakes, and Shuayb's reminders to them did not cause them to repent, nor did the warnings of God's punishments to them, God intended to destroy them, and he gave authority for this to happen.

*Ibn Abbas:* God sent fire and intense heat which took away their breath. They went into the hollows of their houses and the fire came into the hollows of their houses after them and took away their breath. So they fled from their houses to the wilderness, and God sent a cloud and it shaded them from the sun. They found it to be cool and pleasant, so the ones under the cloud summoned the others until all of them were gathered beneath it. Then God sent a fire down upon them. This was the punishment of the Day of the Shade.

*Qatadah:* Shuayb was sent to two peoples: to his people, being the people of Midian, and to the people of the Tanglewood, the Tanglewood being a twisted tree. When God intended to punish them he sent an intense heat upon them, and then it was as if he lifted the punishment with a cloud. Then, when the cloud drew near to them, they went out to it desiring its coolness. When they were under it, fire rained down upon them.

*Zayd b. Muʿawiyah:* The heat struck them while they were in their houses, and then a cloud was created which appeared to be shade, so they rushed toward it. When they were sleeping under it, an earthquake seized them.

*Mujahid:* The punishment of the Day of the Shade refers to the fact that this punishment cast a shadow over the people of Shuayb.

*Ibn Zayd:* God sent shade from a cloud and then commissioned the sun to burn everything on the face of the earth. All of the people left for the shade of this cloud. When all of them had gathered, God removed the shade from them and exposed them to the sun. They were burned just like locusts in the pan.

*Ibn Kathir:* It is mentioned that they were struck with intense heat, and God caused a strong wind to blow for seven days, and there was nothing that would relieve them, neither water nor shade nor entering into tunnels. So they fled from their dwellings into the wilderness. A cloud provided them shade. They all gathered under it seeking the relief of its shade. When all of them were there, God sent a flame and the earth shook with them, and a scream came to them from the sky. The wind brought about their destruction and burnt up their likenesses.

## Jethro

**Q 28:22** Then Moses turned toward Midian and said: "Perhaps my Lord will guide me on the right path." **23** When he arrived at the water of Midian he found a group of people around it watering [sheep], and he found apart from them two women, holding back [sheep]. He said: "What is your story?" They said: "We cannot water [the sheep] until the shepherds are done. Our father is a great old man." **24** He watered [the sheep] for them and then he took refuge in the shade, and said: "My Lord, I am in need of a good thing that you might send down to me." **25** Then one of the two women came to him, walking modestly, and said: "My father summons you to give you recompense since you watered [the sheep] for us." When he [Moses] came to him [the father] and told him the story [of his escape from Egypt], he [father] said: "Do not fear, we will protect you from the people who do wrong." **26** One of the women said: "My father, hire him, for the best whom you can hire is the strong and trustworthy." **27** He said: "I want to marry you to one of these two daughters of mine, on the condition that you work for me eight seasons. If you complete ten, then of that [extra] is yours. I do not want to make it difficult for you, so that, God willing, you will find me to be one of the truthful." **28** He [Moses] said: "That is between me and you, whichever of the two terms I complete, there will be no enmity upon me. May God be a witness to what we say."

*Ibn Kathir:* The exegetes disagree concerning the identity of the father-in-law of Moses. In the opinion of one of them he is Shuayb the prophet who was sent to the people of Midian. This interpretation is widespread among many of the learned ones. It is said by Hasan al-Basri and another person. Ibn Abi Hatim relates that Malik b. Anas reached the conclusion that Shuayb was the person described in the Moses story.

*Abu Ubaydah:* The one who hired Moses was Jethro, the nephew of Shuayb the prophet.

*Ibn Kathir:* Tabarani relates that someone came to visit the Messenger of God and he said to him: "Welcome to the people of Shuayb and the two sisters of Moses' houses." Others say: The father-in-law was only the cousin of Shuayb. It is said he was a believing man from the people of Shuayb. Others say: Shuayb was a long time before the time of Moses because Shuayb said to his people: "The people of Lot are not far from you" (11:89). The people of Lot were destroyed in the time of Abraham according to the text of the Quran. It is known that the period of time between Abraham and Moses was more than 400 years. Another person mentions that Shuayb lived a long time and that he – God knows – was protected from aging. If the father-in-law was Shuayb, then there is no doubt that his name would have been written in the text here. Found in the books of the Israelites is that the name of the father-in-law of Moses is Jethro. God knows. Abu Ubaydah says: Jethro is the cousin of Shuayb. The one to whom Moses was hired was a wealthy landlord in Midian.

*Ibn Kathir:* Some argue that the verse "The people of Lot are not far from you" (11:89) refers to being far off in time. It is also said that the meaning is they are not far from you in location and place. And it is said that this means they are not far from you in description and in hateful actions such as highway robbery and taking the belongings of people. All of these opinions are possible. They were not far from them in time, in place, and in description.

# Job

**Q 21:73** Job, when he called out to his Lord: "Distress has afflicted me. You are the most Merciful of the merciful ones." **74** We answered him and removed the distress that was with him. We restored his family to him, and another like them, a mercy from us, and a reminder for the worshippers.

**Q 38:41** Remember our servant Job, when he called out to his Lord: "Satan has afflicted me with distress and punishment." **42** Stamp your foot. This is cold water with which to wash and drink. **43** We gave his family to him, and another like them, a mercy from us and a reminder for thinking people. **44** Take some grass in your hand and hit with it. Do not break your oath. We found him steadfast, an excellent servant, for he returned.

## Genealogy

*Ibn Ishaq:* He was a man from Rome, Job b. Maws b. Reuel [Rawh] b. Esau b. Isaac b. Abraham.

*Ibn Kathir:* Some say that he is Job b. Maws b. Reuel b. Esau b. Isaac b. Abraham. Ibn Asakir relates that his mother was the daughter of Lot. It is also said that his father was one of those who believed in Abraham on the day he was thrown into the fire. It is known that he came after Abraham but before Moses. It is well known that he was a descendant of Abraham, based on the word of God: "Among his descendants are David, Solomon, Job, Joseph, Moses, and Aaron" (6:4) and it is sound to say that the "his" in this verse refers to Abraham and not Noah. It is also sound to say that his genealogy is from Esau b. Isaac and Isaac's daughter-in-law Leah, the wife of Jacob. It is also said that her name was Rahmah bt. Ephraim or Leah bt. Manasseh b. Jacob.

*Suyuti:* Ibn Ishaq says it is true that he was one of the Israelites but there is nothing established about his genealogy except that the name of his father was Abyad [white]. Tabari says he was Job b. Maws b. Reuel b. Esau b. Isaac. Ibn Asakir reports that his mother was a daughter of Lot and that his father was one of those who believed in Abraham, and that this was before Moses. Tabari says he was after Shuayb. Ibn Abi Khaythamah says he was after Solomon and was tried when he was 70 years old. His trial lasted for seven years, and it is also said thirteen years or three years. Tabarani relates that the length of his life was 93 years.

## Job's Mission

*Ibn Asakir:* The first prophet sent was Idris, then Noah, Abraham, Ishmael, Isaac, Jacob, Joseph, Lot, Hud, Salih, Shuayb, Moses and Aaron, Elijah, Elisha, Arfa b. Suwaylkh b. Ephraim b. Joseph b. Jacob, Jonah b. Mattai son of one of Jacob's sons, and then Job b. Razih b. Amos b. Eliphaz [Lefarz] b. Esau b. Isaac b. Abraham.

*Ibn Kathir:* Some of the exegetes and historians say that Job was a man with a lot of property, consisting of cattle, slaves, and a lot of land in the area next to Haran. Ibn Asakir adds that Job also had many children and a big family. But all of this was taken from him and his body was afflicted with different types of sores. There was not a single healthy member of his body except for his heart and tongue with which he used to remember God. Through all of this he was steadfast, and continued to remember God, night and day, morning and evening. His sickness continued for such a long time that the people around him began to loathe him, people stayed away from him, and they eventually drove him out of the city. No one would come near him except his wife who looked after him. She remembered his good treatment of her and his compassion for her. It is established that the Prophet Muhammad said: "The most afflicted of people are the prophets, then the upright, then those like them." He also said: "Each man is tried according to the strength of his religion. If his religion were to be more unyielding, then his trials would be increased." Job never lost his patience in all of this but was an example of steadfastness and because of this an example also of one who dealt with every type of trial.

There is disagreement concerning the length of his trials. Wahb b. Munabbih claims that he was tried for three years, no more and no less. Anas b. Malik says he was tried for seven years and some months. Humayd b. Abd al-Rahman says it was eighteen years.

*Wahb b. Munabbih:* The Israelites have stories about Job which have long accounts of how he lost his wealth, his children, and was afflicted on his body.

*Mujahid:* Job was the first to be afflicted with smallpox.

*Suddi:* The meat fell off him until only bones and sinews remained. His wife used to come to him with ashes and spread them out under him. When the sickness had afflicted him for a long time, she said to him: "Job, if you call upon your Lord, he will relieve you." He said: "I have lived for 70 years in health, can I not for the sake of God be patient for another 70 years?" She used to serve other people for wages in order to feed Job. But, after some time, the people stopped employing her service because she was the wife of Job, afraid that she might pass on his diseases and infect them. When she was not able to find anyone to employ her service, she decided to sell one of her braids for a lot of good food. She brought it to Job and he said: "Where did you get this?" She said: "I have served people for it." The next day she also could not find anyone to employ her, so she sold another of her braids for food and brought it to Job. He swore that he would not eat until she told him where she got the food. So she uncovered her head and when he saw her head with her hair cut short, he called to God: "Distress has afflicted me. You are the most Merciful of the merciful ones" (21:73).

*Ibn Abi Hatim:* Abdallah b. Ubayd b. Umayr says that Job had brothers, and they came one day and were not able to come close to him because of his smell. So they stood far away. One of them said to another: "If God had known someone better than Job, he would have tried him." Job became anxious because of what he had heard, so he said: "Oh God, if you know that I have never spent a night satiated but am known for being hungry, affirm me." So God affirmed this from the heavens, and the two heard it. Then Job said: "Oh God, if you know that I have no shirt but am known for being naked, then affirm me." So God affirmed this from the heavens and the two heard. Then Job said: "Oh God, by your might, I will never lift my head until you relieve me." So he did not lift his head until God relieved him.

*Anas b. Malik:* The Prophet Muhammad said: "The prophet Job was tried for eighteen years. People kept far away from him except for two of his brothers who were the most special of his brothers. They used to bring him food and show him kindness. One of them said to the other: 'Job must be the most guilty of sin of all people.' His brother said: 'Why is that?' The first said: 'For eighteen years his Lord has not shown him mercy and relieved him of his suffering.' So Job said: 'I do not know what you said but God showed that I was the matter which the two of you were discussing. So make mention of God and I will return to my house and be covered from you.'"

## Job's Relief

*Ibn Abbas:* God clothed him in clothing from Paradise, and when his wife came she did not recognize him. She said: "Servant of God, where has the one who was here, the afflicted one, gone? Perhaps dogs or wolves carried him off." He said: "I am Job." She said: "Do not make fun of me, servant of God." He said: "I am Job. God has returned my body." God returned to him his property and his children, two-fold.

*Wahb b. Munabbih:* God revealed to Job: "I return to you what was destroyed of your money, two-fold. Wash with this water, for it will heal you. Offer a sacrifice on account of your companions so that they might be forgiven, for they disobeyed me on account of you."

*Abu Hurayrah:* The Prophet Muhammad said: "When God relieved Job, he caused locusts of gold to rain down upon him. He began to take it with his hand and put it in his clothes. He was told: 'Job, are you satisfied?' Job said: 'My Lord, who can be more satisfied than from your mercy?'"

*Ibn Kathir:* God commanded Job to strike the earth with his foot. He did as he was commanded and God caused a spring of cold water to spring up. God ordered him to wash in it and drink from it. God caused his affliction to go from him, the sickness which had afflicted his body. God replaced the affliction with the soundness of Job's body, its perfect beauty, and gave him much wealth, and rained upon him locusts of gold. After this, Job lived for 70 years in the land of Rome, following in the *hanif* religion. He bestowed his legacy upon his son Humal, and after him he had another son named Bishr b. Job who is the one that many people allege is Dhu al-Kifl. This son was a prophet and he died at the age of 75.

*Tabari:* Job died when he was 73 years old.

*Mujahid:* On the Day of the Resurrection, God will use Solomon against the wealthy, Joseph against the slaves, and Job against the people of persecution.

# Dhu al-Kifl

**Q 21:85** Ishmael, Idris, and Dhu al-Kifl, all are among the steadfast. **86** We caused them to enter into our mercy. They are among the upright.

**Q 38:45** Remember our servants Abraham, Isaac, and Jacob, having power and vision. **46** We chose them for the purpose of remembrance of the abode [of the hereafter]. **47** They are, according to us, among those who are pure in being chosen. **48** Remember Ishmael, Elisha, and Dhu al-Kifl, all are among the chosen.

### Identity

*Suyuti:* He is the son of Job. Wahb b. Munabbih says that God sent Bishr b. Job, his son, after Job, as a prophet. He was called Dhu al-Kifl. God ordered him to call the people to monotheism. He lived in Syria his whole life until he died, at the age of 75 years. Kirmani records that he was Elijah. It is also said he was Joshua b. Nun, or that he was a prophet named Dhu al-Kifl. It is also said he was an upright man who kept the commandments and fulfilled them. It is said that he was Zechariah, based on the verse "Zechariah kept them [kaffala-ha]" (3: 37). Ibn Asakir says it is said that he is a prophet whom God keeps to do the undone work of other prophets. It is also said he was not a prophet but that Elisha followed him in fasting during the day and keeping vigil at night. It is said that he prayed 100 sets of bowing and prostrations every day. It is also said that he is Elisha, and that he had two names.

*Ibn Abi Hatim:* Abu Musa al-Ash'ari said from the pulpit: "Dhu al-Kifl was not a prophet but an upright man who prayed 100 times a day."

*Ahmad b. Hanbal:* It is related that Ibn Umar heard a report from the Prophet Muhammad that al-Kifl was one of the Israelites who were not abstaining from sins. A woman came to him and he gave her 60 dinars on the condition that he have sex with her. When he sat on her the way a man sits on his wife, she began to tremble and cry. He said to her: "What is making you cry? Do I cause you to despise me?" She said: "No, but this deed I have never done before, but I have a need." He said: "You are doing this but you have never done this before?" Then he got down and said: "Go with the dinars you have." Then he said: "By God, I will not disobey God and the guarantee [kifl] forever." He died that night. When morning came, written on his door was "God has forgiven al-Kifl."

*Ibn Kathir:* It is evident from his mention twice in the Quran, among these other prophets, that Dhu al-Kifl is a prophet, and this is well known. Others allege that he is not a prophet, but only an upright man. Tabari and Ibn Abi Najih relate, on the authority of Mujahid, that he was not a prophet but was only an upright man, that he vouched for the prophet of his people, that he adjudicated among them with justice.

*Tabari and Ibn Abi Hatim:* Dawud b. Abi Hind, on the authority of Mujahid, says that when Elisha was old he said: "If I were to appoint a man as successor over the people to guide them in my way, what would he do?" The people gathered and he said: "The one who follows me in three things will I appoint: fasting during the day, keeping vigil at night, and never being angry." A man stood up and said: "Me." He asked: "Do you fast during the day, keep vigil at night and are never angry?" He said: "Yes." He rejected him on that day, and likewise on the next. The people were quiet and then this man still stood up and said: "Me." So he appointed him as successor.

*Abdallah b. al-Harith:* One of the prophets said: "Who can keep for me vigil at night, fasting during the day, and not get angry?" A youth stood and said: "Me." The prophet told him to sit. Then he said the same thing the next day. The youth stood and said: "Me" and the prophet told him to sit. Then he returned and said the same thing a third time. The youth said: "Me." The prophet asked: "You keep vigil at night, fast during the day, and are never angry?" The youth said: "Yes." When this prophet died this youth sat in his place and adjudicated among the people, and was never angry.

*Tha'labi:* Some people say that Dhu al-Kifl was Bishr b. Job sent by God after his father as a messenger to the land of Rome. They believed in him and followed him. Then God ordered them to go on a Jihad but they refused and were weak. They said: "Bishr, we love life and do not want to die, and for this reason we do not want to disobey God and his messenger. If you would ask God to lengthen our lives and not cause us to die until we want, then we will serve him and go on Jihad against his enemies." Bishr said to them: "You ask me a great thing, and put upon me something extreme." Then he stood and prayed: "My God, you ordered me to bring the message, so I brought it. You ordered me to go on Jihad against your enemies and you know that I am not able by myself. My people have asked me for something about which you know better than I do. Do not put the guilt of another upon me. I seek your mercy from your displeasure, your forgiveness from your punishment." God revealed to him: "Bishr, I hear the petition of your people, and I have given them what they asked from me. Their lives will be long and they will not die until they want. They have a guarantee from me on this." So Bishr gave them the message of God and told them about what God had revealed to him, his guarantee [kafil] to them in this, just as God had commanded. So they called him Dhu al-Kifl [he of the "guarantee"]. Then the people began to have children and multiply and grow until the land became too small for them and their lives became restricted, and many of them were afflicted with harm. So they asked Bishr to pray to God to return to them their allotted lives. God revealed to Bishr: "Do your people know that it was their choice to choose for themselves?" Then they were returned to their normal life-spans and died at their appointed times. This is why Rome was so big to the extent that it is said that the world is their home, five-sixths of it is Rome. They were called "Romans" because they were related to their grandfather Rum b. Esau b. Isaac b. Abraham. Bishr b. Job, known as Dhu al-Kifl, settled in Syria until he died. He was 95 years old.

# People of the Well

**Q 25:38** Ad, Thamud, the People of the Well, and the many generations between them. **39** All of them we smote as examples, all of them we destroyed completely.

**Q 50:12** Before them, the community of Noah, the People of the Well, Thamud, **13** Ad, the Pharaoh, the brothers of Lot, **14** the People of the Tanglewood, and the community of Tubba rejected. All rejected the messengers and my promise was fulfilled.

## Location

*Ibn Abbas:* The People of the Well were the inhabitants of a district near the district of Thamud.

*Ibn Asakir:* The People of the Well were in Husawwar and God sent a prophet to them named Hinzalah b. Sifwan. They rejected and killed him. Ad b. Uz b. Aram b. Shem b. Noah and his children moved from the Well and settled in the Ahqaq. God destroyed the People of the Well and they dispersed to all parts of the Yemen. They spread about all of the earth until Jabrun b. Sa'd b. Ad b. Uz b. Aram b. Shem b. Noah settled in Damascus and built a city. He named it Jabrun. It is Iram of the pillars [dhat al-Imad]. There was no place established in the Hijaz bigger than what was in Damascus. God sent Hud b. Abdallah b. Riyah b. Khalid b. al-Khulud b. Ad to Ad, to the descendants of the Ad in Ahqaq. They rejected him, so God destroyed them.

*Ibn Abi Hatim:* Ibn Abbas says that the "Well" was a well in Azerbaijan.

*Sufyan al-Thawri:* Ikrimah says that the "Well" was a well into which they threw their prophet, meaning they buried him in it.

## Prophet

*Naqqash:* The People of the Well used to have a well from which they would get water to drink and irrigate all of their lands. They had a just and good king. When he died, they were very agitated but after a few days Satan appeared to them in the form of their king. He said: "I did not die, but I disappeared from you so that I could see what you would do." The people were very glad. Satan ordered them to build a partition between them and him. He told them that he would never die. Many of them believed in him and even worshipped him. God sent a prophet among them and he told them that this was Satan talking to them from behind the partition. He forbade them to worship him and ordered them to worship God alone without associating anything with him.

*Suhayli:* The revelations used to come to him during sleep. His name was Hinzalah b. Sifwan. The people rebelled against him, killed him and threw him in the well. The water dried up, they were struck with thirst, their trees dried up, their fruit fell off, and their houses were destroyed. Humanity was replaced with the wild, togetherness with separateness. They were destroyed and in their dwellings lived Jinn and wild beasts. Nothing is heard from this spot except the music of the Jinn, the roar of lions, and the howling of hyenas.

*Muhammad b. Ka'b:* The Prophet Muhammad said: "The first of people to enter Paradise on the Day of Resurrection is the black slave." This refers to when God sent a prophet to the people of a district and its people did not believe in him except for this black slave. Then the people revolted against the prophet, dug a well, and threw him into it. Then they put an enormous rock on top of it. This slave used to go and gather firewood upon his back. He used to come with his wood, buying and selling food and drink with it. He came to this well and lifted off the stone. God helped him with it, and he would lower down food and drink to the prophet. Then he returned the rock just as it was.

One day he was collecting firewood just as he was used to doing. He collected his wood, bundled it up, and left it. Later he went to move it after an hour had passed. He lay down and slept. While he was sleeping God caused seven years to pass. Then he went quickly around to his other portion and lay down. God caused another seven years to pass. Then he got up and gathered his load thinking that only an hour of the day had passed. He came to the district and sold his load. Then he bought food and drink just as he always did. Then he went to the well, to the place where it had been, he searched for it but could not find it. The prophet had reappeared to his people in the well and they had taken him out and believed in him.

Their prophet used to ask them about this black slave, what had happened to him. They said to him: "What do we know?" until God took the prophet. The black slave got up from his sleep after the prophet had died.

*Tabari:* It is not possible that this story [about the black slave] is related to the People of the Well mentioned in the Quran because God says that he destroyed the People of the Well, and in this story their prophet appears to them and they believe in him.

## Tubba

**Q 44:37** Are they better than the people of Tubba and those who were before them? We destroyed them because they were sinful.

*Ibn Kathir:* The people of Tubba are the people of Sheba. When God caused them to be destroyed, he razed their cities and scattered them among the lands. They were the Arabs from Qahtan as opposed to the Arabs from Adnan. They were Himyarites from Sheba. One of their kings was called Tubba and so they are called the people of Tubba and this is taken as a title just as is Khusrow the king of Iran, Caesar king of Rome, Pharaoh king of Egypt, and Negus king of Ethiopia. It is agreed that one of the kings of Tubba left Yemen and went to Samarqand. Its king was strong, had great authority, and a large army. Its kingdom had many cities and its subjects were numerous. He is the king who encamped at al-Hira, and it is agreed that he passed by Medina in the days before Islam. He intended to attack and kill its people but was prevented by a river. With this king were two rabbis from among the rabbis of the Jews who advised him and told him that there was no way into this city, that it was the place where a prophet would emigrate at the end of time. So the king took the two rabbis back to Yemen. When he passed by Mecca he wanted to destroy the Ka'bah but they prevented him from doing this also. They told him of the greatness of this House, that it was built by Abraham, that it would be a great thing at the hands of this prophet sent at the end of time. So the king circumambulated the Ka'bah and dressed it with fine clothes. Then he went to Yemen. He called the people of Yemen to convert to Judaism along with him. This was in the time when it was the religion of Moses before the sending of Christ. So the people of Yemen converted to

Judaism with him. It is said that the rabbis also said that "Ahmad" would be the name of the prophet sent at the end of time.

*Ibn Abbas:* It was asked whether Ezra was a prophet or not and whether Tubba was a cursed one or not. It is said that Tubba was an unbeliever but he submitted to God and followed the religion of Moses at the hands of one of the rabbis of the Jews at that time before the coming of Christ. He made Pilgrimage to the House in the time of the Jurhum and dressed it in fine clothes. He also sacrificed 6000 animals there to honor it. Then he returned to Yemen.

*Sa'id b. Jubayr:* Tubba clothed the Ka'bah. His name was As'ad Abu Kurayb b. Malikrab of Yemen. It is said that he was king over its people for 326 years. He died about 700 years before the coming of the Prophet Muhammad.

# Jonah

**Q 10:98** If there had been a city which believed, its faith would have brought it benefit, except the community of Jonah. When they believed we removed from it the punishment of disgrace in the life of this world, and allowed them to enjoy themselves for a while.

**Q 21:87** Dhu al-Nun when he left angry, thinking that we had no power over him. He called out from the depths of darkness: "There is no god other than you, glory be to you. I was one of those who do wrong." **88** We answered him and saved him from affliction. Thus do we save the believers.

**Q 37:139** Jonah was one of the messengers. **140** When he ran away to the ship, fully loaded, **141** he cast lots and was one of those who are refuted. **142** The fish swallowed him. He was blameworthy. **143** Were it not that he was one of those who glorified God, **144** he would have lingered in its belly until the Day of Calling Forth. **145** We cast him, naked, and he was sick. **146** We caused to grow over him a tree which spread. **147** We sent him to 100,000 or more, **148** and they believed. So we allowed them to enjoy themselves for a while.

**Q 68:48** Be patient for the decision of your Lord. Do not be like Dhu al-Nun, calling out when he was distressed. **49** Kindness from his Lord came to him so that he might be spit out naked while he was worthy of blame. **50** His Lord responded to him and made him one of the upright.

## Nineveh

*Ibn Kathir:* The exegetes say that God sent Jonah to the inhabitants of Nineveh, near the land of Mosul. He summoned them to God but they rejected him and continued in their unbelief. When this had gone on for a long time, Jonah removed himself from among them and invoked a severe punishment upon them after three days.

*Ibn Masud, Mujahid, Saʿid b. Jubayr, and Qatadah:* When Jonah left from their midst they were sure that the punishment would come down upon them from God, and they were repentant in their hearts. They regretted what they had done to their prophet. They put on sackcloth and removed the female animals from their young. Then God raged against them and they cried for help, beseeching him. The men, women, and children cried. Even the sheep, riding animals, and pack animals prayed: the camels and their young, the cows and their young, the sheep and their young. The great hour had come. But God removed the punishment from them.

*Ibn Kathir:* There is difference of opinion regarding how many people there were. According to Makhul it was 110,000. Tirmidhi, Tabari, and Ibn Abi Hatim relate the hadith of Abu al-Aliyah, that Ubayy b. Ka'b asked the Prophet Muhammad about the verse [37:147], and he said: "They were more than 120,000." Ibn Abbas says they were 130,000. Sa'id b. Jubayr says they were 170,000.

*Suyuti:* Jonah was the son of Mattai. Abd al-Razzaq states that it is the name of his people. Ibn Hajar records that it is said that he lived in the time of the small kingdoms of the Persians. Ibn Abi Hatim, on the authority of Abu Malik, transmits that he stayed in the belly of the fish for 40 days. Ja'far al-Sadiq says seven days. Qatadah says three. There are six different ways to pronounce the name Jonah in the Quran.

## Jonah and the Fish

*Ibn Kathir:* There is disagreement whether Jonah was sent before or after Dhu al-Nun, or if there were two different people. There are three opinions. The right one is the story of his going, angry because of his people, and riding a ship in the sea. When a storm hit them, the seas rolled, the ship was heavy and almost sank. The people drew lots among themselves to see who was the cause, that he might be thrown overboard. The lot fell on Jonah, the prophet of God, so they drew lots again, and a second time it fell on him. Then a third time and it fell on him again, so they knew that God had intended him in this matter. So God sent a great fish from the green sea to swallow him. God commanded the fish not to eat him as meat and not to bite him, for he was not his food. The fish took him and circled around all of the seas with him. It is also said that this fish was swallowed by another fish even bigger than the first. When he determined that he was in the belly of the fish, he thought that he was dead. But then he moved his limbs. He was alive, so he prostrated himself to God and said: "My Lord, I am prostrating myself to you in a place unlike any where you have been worshipped before."

*Ibn Kathir:* There is disagreement concerning the length of time Jonah lingered in the belly of the fish. Sha'bi says he was swallowed in the morning and spit out in the evening. Qatadah says he lingered in the fish for three days. Ja'far al-Sadiq says it was seven days. Sa'id b. Abi al-Hasan and Abu Malik say he lingered in the belly of the fish for 40 days. Only God knows how long he was in there.

*Ibn Kathir:* The fish circled the seas and took him to their depths. With him, the fish dove to the depths of the rolling sea. Jonah heard the other fish praising God and even the pebbles praising the Lord of the seven heavens, seven earths, and the ground that is between and under them.

*Salim b. Abi al-Ja'd:* The "depths of darkness" (21:87) refers to the fact that the fish which swallowed Jonah was swallowed by another fish, so there was the darkness of the two fish along with the darkness of the sea.

*Ibn Masud, Ibn Abbas, Amr b. Maymun, Sa'id b. Jubayr, Muhammad b. Ka'b, Hasan al-Basri, Qatadah, and Dahhak:* There was the darkness of the fish, the darkness of the sea, and the darkness of the night.

*Abu Hurayrah:* The Prophet Muhammad said: "When God wanted to imprison Jonah in the belly of the fish, he revealed to the fish: 'Take him but do not eat him as food nor chew him.' When the fish had taken him to the bottom of the sea, Jonah heard whispering. He said to himself: 'What is this?' God revealed to him in the belly of the fish: 'That is the beasts of the sea praising.' So he praised God while he was in the belly of the fish. The angels heard him praising and said: 'Our Lord, we hear a weak sound in the earth.' God said: 'That is my servant Jonah. He disobeyed me, so I imprisoned him in the belly of a fish in the sea.' They said: 'The upright servant, the one who lifted up to you, every day and night, upright deeds?' God said: 'Yes.' Thus they interceded on his behalf, and God ordered the fish to spit him on the beach."

*Anas b. Malik:* Jonah the prophet, when he began to pray these words, was in the belly of a fish: "Great God, there is no god other than you. To you belongs praise. I was one of those who do wrong." When this prayer was received under the Throne of God, the angels said: "Lord, a weak voice is heard from a strange place." God said: "Do you know what it is?" They said: "No, Lord, who is it?" God said: "My servant Jonah." They said: "Your servant Jonah, the one who does not cease to raise up good deeds which are received, and prayers which are answered? Our Lord, should you not show mercy for what he has done, and save him from this trial?" God said: "Certainly," and ordered the fish to put him on the beach naked.

*Ibn Kathir:* It was because of Jonah's praising of God, repentance and turning toward God that he was saved from the belly of the fish, otherwise he would have lingered there until the Day of Resurrection. When Jonah was spit onto the beach he was weak of body. Ibn Masud says he was like a chicken without feathers. Ibn Abbas, Suddi, and Ibn Zayd say he was like a child when it is born and has nothing.

*Ibn Kathir:* Some scholars say that the gourd grew over him abundantly, that its leaves were very soft, that it provided much shade, and that flies did not approach it. One could eat of its fruit from sun up to sun down, whether cooked or not, including the seeds and their shells. It gave great benefit and strengthened the brain and other parts of the body.

*Abu Hurayrah:* An animal would come in the morning and evening, and Jonah would drink of its milk. This was a mercy from God to Jonah, showing his kindness and goodness toward him.

*Sa'd b. Abi Waqqas:* I heard the Prophet Muhammad say: "The name of God, which when it is invoked he responds, when it is asked of him he gives it, is the invocation of Jonah b. Mattai." So I said: "Prophet of God, is this for Jonah alone or for all Muslims?" He said: "It is for Jonah in particular and for Muslims in general when they use the invocation."

*Ahmad b. Hanbal:* Sa'd b. Abi Waqqas said: I passed by Uthman b. Affan in the mosque and I greeted him. He saw me but did not return my greetings. So I went to Umar b. al-Khattab and said: "Commander of the Faithful, has something happened in Islam?" He said: "No, why?" I said: "I passed by Uthman while he was in the mosque and greeted him. He saw me but did not return my greetings." So Umar sent for Uthman and said to him: "What prevented you from returning the greetings of your brother?" He said: "I did not do this." So I [Sa'd] said: "I swear that you did." Then Uthman remembered and said: "May God forgive me, for when you passed by me I did not hear what you said because I was trying to remember something I heard from the Prophet Muhammad." I [Sa'd] said: "I will tell you it. The Prophet

Muhammad mentioned to us an invocation, then a Bedouin came and interrupted him. When the Prophet Muhammad went home, I followed him. On the way there I hit my foot on the ground. The Prophet Muhammad turned around to me and said: 'What is it, Abu Ishaq?' I said: 'Prophet of God, you mentioned something to us about an invocation and then you were interrupted by a Bedouin.' He said: 'Yes, it is the invocation of Dhu al-Nun when he was in the belly of the fish: "There is no god other than you, glory be to you. I was one of those who do wrong." If a Muslim says this to his Lord, there is nothing to which he will not respond.'"

## Virtues of Jonah

*Bukhari:* Ibn Abbas says that the Prophet Muhammad said: "It is not appropriate for a worshipper to say: 'I am better than Jonah b. Mattai.'"

*Tabarani:* Ibn Abbas says that the Prophet Muhammad said: "It is not appropriate for one to say: 'I am a better worshipper of God than Jonah b. Mattai.'"

*Muslim and Bukhari:* Abu Hurayrah reports the story of a Muslim who struck the face of a Jew when he said: "Moses is the one chosen above the worlds."

*Ibn Kathir:* Another says: "It is not appropriate for one to claim he is more virtuous than Jonah b. Mattai." This is just as it is recorded in some reports: "Do not find me more virtuous than the prophets, nor than Jonah b. Mattai."

# Moses in Egypt

**Q 19:51** Mention, in the Book, Moses. He was pure, a messenger, a prophet. **52** We called to him from the right side of the mountain. We allowed him to approach us safely. **53** We gave to him, from our mercy, his brother Aaron as a prophet.

*Ibn Kathir:* He was Moses b. Imran b. Qoheth b. Azar b. Levi b. Jacob b. Isaac b. Abraham.

### Pharaoh and the Israelites in Egypt

**Q 28:1** Ta Sin Mim. **2** These are the verses of the clear book. **3** We recite to you from the story of Moses and Pharaoh, in truth, for a community who believes. **4** Pharaoh exalted himself in the earth, and made its people into sects, weakening a group of them by slaughtering their sons and allowing their women to live. He was one of the despoilers. **5** We wanted to show kindness to those who had been weakened in the earth. We made them examples to be followed, and we made them heirs. **6** We empowered them in the land and by them showed Pharaoh, Haman, and their armies that which they feared.

**Q 7:137** We caused a people considered to be weak to inherit from the east and the west of the land which we had blessed. The good word of your Lord was fulfilled for the Israelites because they were patient. We leveled that which he [Pharaoh] made.

**Q 26:57** We expelled them from gardens and springs, **58** treasures, and honored position. **59** Thus we caused the Israelites to inherit these.

*Ibn Kathir:* At this time the Israelites were the chosen people. This tyrant king ruled over them and employed them as slaves in difficult work, killing their sons and allowing their women to live. The Pharaoh did this out of fear that among them would be found a boy by whose hands would be the cause of his destruction and the end of his state. So he ordered the killing of all the Israelite males, but this would not allow him to escape from the fate which God had decreed for him.

## Moses in the House of Pharaoh

**Q 20:38** When we revealed to your mother what we revealed: **39** "Cast him into the ark! Cast him into the sea! The sea will take him to the shore. An enemy to you and an enemy to him will take him." I will cause you to be beloved of me so that you will be raised under my watch. **40** When your sister went and said: "Should I point you to someone who will care for him?" We returned you to your mother in order that you might brighten her eyes, so that she would not be sad. You killed someone and we saved you from affliction. We subjected you to temptations and you stayed years with the people of Midian. Then you came according to fate, Moses. **41** I chose you for myself.

**Q 28:7** We revealed to the mother of Moses: "Nurse him, and when you are afraid for him, cast him in the sea. Do not fear and do not be sad. We are returning him to you, making him one of the messengers." **8** The family of Pharaoh found him with the result that he would be an enemy and distress to them. Pharaoh, Haman, and their armies were sinning. **9** The wife of Pharaoh said: "He brightens the eye of me and you. Do not kill him. Perhaps he might benefit us or we can take him as a son." They were not aware. **10** The heart of Moses' mother was empty and she almost disclosed him had we not bound her heart so that she would be one of the believers. **11** She said to his sister: "Keep track of him!" So she watched him from one side, and they were not aware. **12** We did not allow him to nurse up to that time. She [Moses' sister] said: "Should I point you to the family of a house which will care for him on your account? They will be true to him." **13** We returned him to his mother so that her eyes would be bright, that she would not be sad, and so that she would know that the promise of God is true. Most of them, however, do not know.

*Ibn Kathir:* When a lot of the Israelite males were killed, the Egyptians were afraid that they might annihilate all of the Israelites and then there would be no one to help them with hard work. So they said to the Pharaoh: "If this continues, when their elders die, and their boys have been killed, their women will not be able to do the work of their men." So the Pharaoh ordered the killing of children on alternate years. Aaron was born during a year when the children were not killed, and Moses was born during a year in which the children were killed. The Pharaoh had special people in charge of this, midwives who monitored the women. When they saw that an Israelite woman was pregnant they took note of her name. When it came time for her to give birth, only Egyptian women could be at the delivery. If the woman gave birth to a girl they left her alone. If she gave birth to a boy then some people would come and butcher the child with sharp knives, killing it.

When the mother of Moses was pregnant, she did not show her pregnancy like other women. When she gave birth to a boy she was very afraid but she loved him exceedingly. No one saw Moses who did not love him. Later, when she was in her house on the edge of the Nile, God told her to take an ark and make a cradle in it. She began to nurse her son, and when someone came to her and she was afraid, she would go and put Moses in this ark. He would go out on the water, but she would tie the ark with a rope at the house. On one day, someone came and she was afraid, so she put Moses in this ark and sent him on the water, but she forgot to fasten the rope. Moses went with the water, and it carried him until he passed the house of Pharaoh, where he was picked up. The ark was carried to the wife of Pharaoh, who was called Asiyah bt. Muzahim, who did not know what was in it. When she opened it she discovered a boy, the most beautiful of creation. God put love for Moses in her heart when she saw him. When the Pharaoh saw him, he wanted to kill him, afraid that it was one of the Israelites. But the Pharaoh's wife convinced him.

*Ibn Abbas and Mujahid:* Moses' mother, because of her sadness, almost disclosed that Moses was her son, but God strengthened her resolve.

*Ibn Kathir:* The mother of Moses ordered his sister, her daughter who was older, to follow Moses and bring back news. She was to ask about him at the edges of the city. Ibn Abbas says she followed to one side. Mujahid says she watched from far away. Qatadah says she watched him nonchalantly. He would not take a breast, and refused to accept it from anyone. So they took him out into the market hoping to find a woman suitable for nursing him. When Moses' sister saw him in their hands, she recognized him but she did not reveal this and they were not aware. It was in this way that God caused him to be returned to his mother, so that she might nurse him, that she might feel secure after having been scared.

*Ibn Abbas:* When the sister of Moses told them about someone to take care of Moses, they took her and questioned her about the matter. She said that she was seeking the pleasure of the Pharaoh, and desired him to benefit from the matter. So they took Moses to his mother. She gave him her breast and fed him. The people were glad and a messenger went to the wife of the king but she did not know that the mother of Moses was his real mother, only that he accepted her breast. Asiyah, the wife of the Pharaoh, asked the mother of Moses to live with her, but she refused. She said: "I have a husband, and children, and am not able to live with you, but I would love to nurse him in my own house." So the wife of the Pharaoh paid her for this service, giving her sustenance and good things.

*Tha'labi:* It is said that Asiyah, the wife of the Pharaoh, was an Israelite, that she was a sincere believer and worshipped God in secret.

## Moses Kills an Egyptian

**Q 28:14** When he [Moses] reached maturity, became strong and tall, we gave him wisdom and knowledge. Thus do we reward those who do good. **15** He entered a city when its inhabitants were not paying attention. In it he found two men fighting. One was from his group, and the other was from his enemy. The one from his group asked him for help against the one who was from his enemy. Moses struck him and finished him off. He [Moses] said: "This is the work of Satan. He is an enemy, clearly misleading." **16** He said: "My Lord, I have done wrong. Forgive me." God forgave him. He is the Forgiving, the Merciful. **17** He said: "My Lord, because of this favor you showed me, I will not support those who are guilty of crimes." **18** The next morning he was in the city afraid, looking this way and that, when the one who had asked for help the day before asked him for help [again]. Moses said to him: "You are clearly a loudmouth." **19** When he went to seize the one who was an enemy to both of them, he said: "Moses, do you intend to kill me just as you killed a person yesterday? You intend only to become a giant in the land, and do not intend to be one of those who are upright." **20** A man came from the farthest part of the city, running. He said: "Moses, the leaders are plotting against you, to kill you. Leave! I am one of your true advisors." **21** He left from there, afraid, turning this way and that. He said: "My Lord, save me from the people who do wrong."

*Mujahid:* When God gave Moses wisdom and knowledge it means that he gave him prophethood.

*Ibn Abbas:* Moses entered the city at dusk, or it was the middle of the day.

*Ibn Kathir:* Only Moses and the man he saved knew who Moses really was, so when he heard his name from the Egyptian man, he knew that what he had done was known. It reached the gate of the Pharaoh and he then knew about it also.

*Thaʿlabi:* Moses used to ride in the carriage of Pharaoh and dress like Pharaoh, so that people called him the son of Pharaoh. One day Pharaoh left on his carriage without Moses, and Moses was told that the Pharaoh had already left. So Moses rode off in his tracks and entered the city after noon when the shops were closed and no one was on the streets. He was walking in the streets by himself when he saw two men fighting. One of them was from the Israelites and the other was from the family of Pharaoh. The one who was from the Israelites was called al-Samiri, and the Egyptian was the Pharaoh's baker named Fatun. He had purchased a load of wood for cooking and ordered al-Samiri to carry it. al-Samiri refused and when Moses walked by al-Samiri called out to Moses for help against the Egyptian. Moses told the Egyptian to let him be, but the baker said to Moses: "It is only something in the service of your father," and he refused to listen to Moses. So Moses got angry and beat him to death, but he did not know that he had killed him. The man who came and informed Moses that Pharaoh was plotting to kill him was Hizqil, the Egyptian who believed [40:28].

## Moses in Midian

**Q 28:22** Then Moses turned toward Midian and said: "Perhaps my Lord will guide me on the right path." **23** When he arrived at the water of Midian he found a group of people around it watering [sheep], and he found apart from them two women, holding back [sheep]. He said: "What is your story?" They said: "We cannot water [the sheep] until the shepherds are done. Our father is a great old man." **24** He watered [the sheep] for them and then he took refuge in the shade, and said: "My Lord, I am in need of a good thing that you might send down to me." **25** Then one of the two women came to him, walking modestly, and said: "My father summons you to give you recompense since you watered [the sheep] for us." When he [Moses] came to him [the father] and told him the story [of his escape from Egypt], he [father] said: "Do not fear, we will protect you from the people who do wrong." **26** One of the women said: "My father, hire him, for the best whom you can hire is the strong and trustworthy." **27** He said: "I want to marry you to one of these two daughters of mine, on the condition that you work for me eight seasons. If you complete ten, then of that [extra] is yours. I do not want to make it difficult for you, so that, God willing, you will find me to be one of the truthful." **28** He [Moses] said: "That is between me and you, whichever of the two terms I complete, there will be no enmity upon me. May God be a witness to what we say."

## Leaving Egypt

*Ibn Kathir:* When that man told Moses about Pharaoh and his state gathering against him because of the killing, Moses left Egypt by himself. He was not accustomed to this sort of life because before, he had lived in luxury and ease in a position of leadership. He left looking around from side to side, asking God to deliver him from Pharaoh and his people. It is mentioned that God sent to him an angel on a horse which led him to the right way. When he asked God to guide him, God did this, and guided him to the straight path in this world and the next. He made him a true guide.

*Tha'labi:* When Moses was advised to leave the city after killing the Egyptian he did not know where to go. An angel on a horse with a spear in his hand appeared to him and said to him: "Follow me." So he followed him, and the angel led him on the road to Midian.

## Water of Midian

*Ibn Kathir:* There was a well in Midian which was visited by shepherds. When Moses saw the two women who were not able to water their sheep without being hurt by the other shepherds, he felt compassion and had mercy for them. He asked them why they did not visit the well with those others.

*Umar b. al-Khattab:* When Moses arrived at the water of Midian he found a group of men watering their sheep. When they were done they replaced a rock over the well which was not able to be lifted except by ten men. When Moses was with the two women holding back their sheep he said: "What is your problem?" They told him and he went to the stone and then lifted it up. Then all of the sheep drank until they were satiated.

*Muqatil b. Sulayman:* The father of the daughters was not able to water the sheep because of age. So Moses said to the two women: "Where is the water?" They led him to the water but there was a rock on the mouth of the well which only a whole group of people could lift. But Moses lifted it up by himself, with his own hands. Then he drew a bucket of water and poured it into the pool. Then he said a blessing.

*Zamakhshari:* It is reported that the shepherds used to place a rock on the mouth of the well which took seven men to lift. It is also said ten men, 40 men, and 100 men. Moses moved it all by himself.

## Shade

*Ibn Abbas:* Moses walked from Egypt to Midian without food except for plants and the leaves of trees, and he was barefoot. So when he reached Midian the soles of his feet were about to fall off. He sat in the shade and it was the best of what God had created. His stomach was stuck to his back from hunger, and the greenness of the plants was visible from inside his body.

*Zamakhshari:* It is said that what he intended was: "I am in need of the things of this world that you might send down to me, something of the other world, being protection from the people who do wrong," because his dominion and wealth had been with the Pharaoh.

*Ibn Masud:* I rode a camel for two nights until I reached Midian in the morning. I asked about the tree under which Moses sought shelter. It was a blooming, green tree. I guided my camel to it. My camel was hungry and so took some of it, chewed it for an hour, and then spat it out. So I prayed to God on behalf of Moses and then I left. The tree was a sumac tree.

## Father-in-law and Daughter

*Muqatil b. Sulayman:* Moses related to Shuayb all that had happened, concerning the enslavement of the Israelites, when he was born, how he was cast on the sea in the ark, the nursing after the ark, up to when he killed the Egyptian.

*Ibn Kathir:* When the two women returned so quickly with their sheep to their father he was skeptical about their situation because of their quick return. So he asked them about what happened to them. They told him about what Moses had done. Then he sent one of his daughters to invite Moses to meet her father. She walked shyly.

*Umar b. al-Khattab:* She came concealed by all of her dress, walking bashfully and speaking with her clothing over her face.

*Shuayb al-Jaba'i:* The names of the two daughters are Zipporah and Leah. The wife of Moses was Zipporah daughter of Jethro the priest of Midian. A priest is a rabbi.

*Ibn Abbas:* The man who hired Moses was named Jethro. He was the ruler of Midian.

*Muqatil b. Sulayman:* The names of the two daughters are Zipporah and Ebra. They were twins. The first was born half a day before the other.

*Ibn Ishaq:* The two daughters are Zipporah and Leah or Shurfa.

## Contract to Work for Wife

*Ibn Kathir:* One of the two daughters of this man walked behind Moses, and then said to her father: "Father, hire him" as a shepherd for the sheep. When she said: "It is a good thing that you hire one with true strength," her father said to her: "Did I teach you this?" She said to him: "He lifted the rock that only ten men could move. When I came with him I walked in front of him and he said to me: 'Be behind me! When there is a question about which way to go, throw a pebble at me so that I might know which way is the right path.'"

*Ibn Masud:* The most heroic of people are three: Abu Bakr when he was succeeded by Umar b. al-Khattab, the master of Joseph when he said: "Make his stay honored," and the wife of Moses when she said: "My father, hire him, for it is a good thing that you hire one who is strong and trustworthy" (28:26).

*Ibn Kathir:* The followers of Abu Hanifah use this verse [28:27] to indicate the soundness of a sale in which when one party says: "I sell you one of these two slaves for 100 dinars" and the other party replies: "I purchase it," it is sound. This verse is used by the school of Awza'i to indicate that when a person says: "I sell you that for ten coins or twenty at a later date," it is sound. The purchaser has the option to take one of the two choices. A report is found in Abu Dawud's book of Sunnah: If a person makes two sales contracts for one sale item, then he is responsible for the decrease or increase. This is according to this school. In the indication of this verse and this report, this school considers that this situation not be extended over a long time. Ahmad b. Hanbal and those who follow him find indication in this verse for the soundness of hiring a worker for food and clothing. Concerning this, the followers of Ahmad b. Hanbal observe what is transmitted by Ibn Majah in his book of Sunnah in his chapter on hiring a worker for the food of his stomach.

*Ali b. Rabah:* I heard Utbah b. al-Nuddar al-Sulami saying: We were with the Prophet Muhammad and he recited "Ta Sin Mim" until he arrived at the story of Moses and said: "Moses hired himself for eight years or ten years for the virtue of his wife and food for his stomach."

*Sa'id b. Jubayr:* A Jew from al-Hirah asked: "Which of the two time periods did Moses complete?" He was answered: "I did not know until I encountered the Rabbi of the Arabs. I went to Ibn Abbas and I asked him." Ibn Abbas said: "Moses completed the larger and better of the two. What the prophet of God says, he does."

*Ibn Abbas:* The Prophet Muhammad said: "I asked Gabriel: 'Which of the two periods did Moses complete?' He said: 'He completed the more complete of them.'"

*Ibn Kathir:* The Prophet Muhammad was asked: "Which of the two periods did Moses complete?" He said: "I do not know." Then the Prophet Muhammad asked Gabriel. Gabriel said: "I do not know." Then Gabriel asked the angel above him. He said: "I do not know." Then that angel asked God about what Gabriel had asked concerning what the Prophet Muhammad had asked. The Lord said: "He completed the best and the longest lasting," or he said: "The finest of the two."

## Rod

*Tabari:* The old man ordered one of his daughters to bring him a rod, and she did so. It was the rod that an angel in the form of a man had given to him. The daughter entered and retrieved the rod and brought it to him. When he saw it, he told her to get another one. She threw it down and tried to take another but that same one kept coming to her hand. He kept sending her back, but each time she would return with the same rod in her hand. When Moses saw this, he took the rod and shepherded the sheep with it. The old man regretted this because the rod had been entrusted to him. He went out to Moses and said to him: "Give me the rod." Moses said: "It is my rod," and would not give it to him. They disputed over the rod and then made a deal that the first man who came by would act as an arbitrator. An angel walked by and judged between them saying: "Put the rod in the ground. Whoever lifts it up, it is his." The old man tried but could not lift it. Moses grabbed it with his hand and lifted it up.

*Zamakhshari:* It is reported that Shuayb had in his possession the rod of the prophets. He said to Moses during the night: "Enter this house and take a rod from among these rods." He took the rod which Adam had taken from the Garden of Eden. It was passed down in a continuous line by the prophets until it was placed with Shuayb. Shuayb felt the staff, for he was blind, and took it back. He said: "Another one." But seven times only this one was put into his hand, so he knew that there was a certain quality to Moses.

*Ibn Yazid:* When the father married his daughter to Moses, he said to Moses: "Enter this house and take a rod that you can lean upon." So he entered and when he stood in the door of the house this rod flew toward him and he took it. The father said: "Return it and take another instead." So he returned it and went to take another when the same rod flew toward him. The father said: "Return it." This happened three times when he said: "I am not able to get any other rod today." So he turned to his daughter and said: "You are the wife of a prophet." The person who said this mentioned that the rod was a sign given to Moses by Gabriel.

*Zamakhshari:* When Moses prepared to go, Shuayb said to him: "When you reach the fork in the road do not go to your right. There is a pasture. There is nothing more in it except a dragon [tanin] who will frighten you and your sheep." The sheep went to the right and Moses could not control them. He followed them, and found an area grassy and fertile unlike anything he had seen. So he slept there. When the dragon arrived the rod fought the dragon and killed it, and then returned to Moses' side, bloody. When Moses saw the blood and the dragon having been killed he was satisfied. When Moses returned, Shuayb touched the sheep. He found their stomachs full of abundant milk. Moses told him and he was happy for he knew that there was a certain affinity to Moses and the rod.

## Speckled Sheep

*Utbah b. al-Nuddar:* The Prophet Muhammad was asked: "Which of the two periods did Moses complete?" He said: "The most obedient and fullest of the two." Then the Prophet Muhammad said: "When Moses wanted to depart from Shuayb he ordered his wife to ask her father to give her some sheep off which to live. So he gave her any of his sheep what would be born in that year not of one color. When a sheep passed, Moses would strike its side with a rod. All of the sheep gave birth to speckled young. Each sheep gave birth to two and three young, none among them had overly large or overly narrow milk-producing capacities, nor too short or too long of teats." The Prophet Muhammad added: "When you conquer Syria, you will find the remnants of that flock. It is in Samaria."

**Utbah b. al-Nuddar:** The Prophet Muhammad said: "Moses hired himself for the chastity of his wife and the food of his stomach. When he intended to depart from Shuayb, he instructed his wife to ask her father to give her from his sheep something off which to live. He gave to her what would be born of his sheep not of one color during that year. All that time all his sheep were a perfect black. Moses hurried off with his rod. He held it by one end and then put it near the water trough. Then he caused the sheep to come and gave them water. Moses stood facing the water trough. No sheep came by whose side he did not hit. All of them mated, their teats enlarged, and they gave birth to speckled young. Except for one or two sheep there was not among them overly large milk-producing capacities. Nor did they have overly narrow milk-producing capacities. Their backs were right, neither too narrow of teats or too long nor too short."

**Zamakhshari:** The father said to Moses: "I give to you from the litter of sheep every one of which is black and white." It was revealed to Moses in a dream: "Hit with your rod the water trough of the sheep." So he did it. Then he watered the sheep. Only those which were black and white emerged, so he got them according to his agreement.

**Anas b. Malik:** When the prophet of God Moses called upon his proprietor concerning the time period that was agreed upon between them, his proprietor said to him: "Every sheep that is born without a single color, it is born for you." So Moses stood and lifted a rope over the water. When the animals saw this they were startled and began to run around. All of the sheep gave birth to speckled young except for one. So Moses left with all of the sheep born that year.

## Revelation

**Q 20:9** Has the report of Moses reached you? **10** When he saw a fire and said to his family: "Stay here, I perceive a fire. Perhaps I will bring you a firebrand from it or find guidance at the fire." **11** When he approached it, he was called: "Moses, **12** I am your Lord. Remove your shoes. You are in the sacred valley of Tuwwa. **13** "I have chosen you. Listen to what is revealed. **14** "I am God. There is no god other than I. Worship me and establish prayer to remember me. **15** "The hour comes. I am about to reveal it for the recompense of every soul according to its efforts. **16** "Those who do not believe in it [the hour], but follow their own whims, do not let them turn you from it, lest you perish. **17** "What is that in your right hand, Moses?" **18** He said: "It is my rod on which I lean, with which I beat fodder for my sheep, and I have other uses for it." **19** He [God] said: "Throw it down, Moses!" **20** He threw it down and it was a snake, moving. **21** He [God] said: "Take it, and do not be afraid. We will return it to its original condition. **22** "Put your hand to your side. It will come out white without harm, another sign **23** in order that we may show you our greater signs. **24** "Go to Pharaoh. He has transgressed."

**Q 27:7**   When Moses said to his family: "I perceive a fire. I will bring you some news from it or a flaming firebrand so that you may warm yourselves." **8** When he came to it, he was called: "Blessed are those in the fire and around it. Glory to God, Lord of the worlds. **9** "Moses, I am God, the Mighty, the Wise. **10** "Throw down your rod." When he saw it moving as if it were a snake, he turned back but did not leave. "Moses, do not be afraid, for in my presence the messengers have no fear. **11** "If, however, one does wrong but then substitutes good for evil, I am Forgiving, Merciful. **12** "Put your hand in your clothes, and it will come out white without harm: it is among the nine signs to Pharaoh and his people." They were a sinful people.

**Q 28:29**   When Moses had completed the term and went with his family, he perceived a fire on the side of the Mountain. He said to his family: "Wait, for I perceive a fire. Perhaps I will bring you some news from it or a firebrand from the fire so that you may warm yourselves." **30** When he came to the fire, he was called from the right side of the valley, in a blessed spot, from a tree: "Moses, I am God, Lord of the worlds. **31** "Throw down your rod." When he saw it moving as if it were a snake, he turned back but did not leave. "Moses, approach and do not be afraid, for you are safe. **32** "Put your hand in your clothes, and it will come out white without harm. Put your hand back to your side without fear. These are two proofs from your Lord to Pharaoh and his leaders. They are a sinful people." **33** Moses said: "My Lord, I killed one of them and I fear that they will kill me. **34** "My brother Aaron is more eloquent than I in tongue, so send him with me as a helper to confirm me, for I am afraid they will reject me." **35** God said: "We will strengthen your arm with your brother and make both of you to be authorities. They will not touch you. With our signs you and those who follow you will overcome."

**Q 79:15**   Has the report of Moses reached you? **16** When his Lord called him from the sacred valley of Tuwwa. **17** "Go to Pharaoh. He has transgressed. **18** "Say to him: 'Would you be purified? **19** " 'That I might guide you to your Lord, should you fear him?' "

*Ibn Kathir:* They say that Moses had set out for the city and family of his birth. Having resolved his fear of Pharaoh and his people, he went with his family, and the sheep he had been given, leaving on a cold, dark, rainy night. They alighted at a spot when Moses saw something which looked like a fire shining far in the distance. He left his family behind and came to the side of the valley which was on the right, or the west side of the mountain. He found the fire in a green tree, and God called to him.

*Muqatil b. Sulayman:* The tree was a boxthorn. Surrounding it were other boxthorns and olive trees. The rod of Moses was a myrtle from one of the myrtles in Paradise.

*Tha'labi:* Mujahid and Ikrimah say that God told Moses to remove his shoes because the bottoms of his feet were on blessed ground. It had been made holy twice. Sa'id b. Jubayr says that this was out of hospitality. It was said to him: Walk on the ground barefoot just as one enters the Ka'bah out of respect for the blessing of the valley. It is also said that this meant for Moses to clear his mind and heart of the affairs of his family.

## Moses and Pharaoh

**Q 7:103** Then we sent, after them, Moses with our signs to Pharaoh and his assembly. They were doing wrong. See what is the punishment of those who despoil. **104** Moses said: "Pharaoh, I am a messenger of the Lord of the worlds. **105** "Truly, I speak only the truth for God. Signs from your Lord have come to you. Send out the Israelites." **106** He [Pharaoh] said: "If you bring a sign, then present it, if you are truthful." **107** He threw his rod and it was a serpent, clearly. **108** He removed his hand and it was white for those looking. **109** The leaders of the people of Pharaoh said: "This is learned magic. **110** "He wants to expel you from your land. What do you command?" **111** They said: "Summon him and his brother, and send messengers into the cities, **112** that every learned magician would come to you." **113** The magicians came to Pharaoh and said: "We have a price if we are to triumph." **114** He said: "Yes, you will be attendants." **115** They said: "Moses, will you throw or will we throw first?" **116** When they went, they mesmerized the eyes of the people, and caused them to be afraid of them. They came with great magic. **117** We revealed to Moses: "Throw your rod. It will consume what they have faked." **118** The truth took place and invalidated what they were doing. **119** They were defeated there and made to be small. **120** The magicians were thrown down prostrating. **121** They said: "We trust in the Lord of the worlds, **122** the Lord of Moses and Aaron." **123** Pharaoh said: "Do you believe in him before I give permission to you?" This is a deception which you conceived in the city, to drive its people out of it. You will know [the consequences]. **124** "I will cut off your hands and feet on opposite sides, then I will crucify you, all together." **125** They said: "We will be received by our Lord. **126** "Will you take vengeance on us only because we believed in the signs of our Lord when they came to us? Our Lord, pour patience upon us, and take us in death as those who submit."

**Q 10:75** Then, after them, we sent Moses and Aaron to Pharaoh and his assembly with our signs. They were arrogant and were a wicked people. **76** When the truth came to them from us, they said: "This is magic." **77** Moses said: "Do you say this about the truth when it has reached you? Is it magic like this? Magicians will not prosper." **78** They said: "Did you come to us to turn us from that which we found our forefathers following, in order that you two might be great in the land? We do not believe in you two." **79** Pharaoh said: "Bring me every learned magician." **80** When the magicians came, Moses said to them: "Throw that which you are throwing." **81** When they threw, Moses said: "What you bring is magic. God will void it, for God does not allow the work of despoilers to prosper. **82** "God, by his words, establishes the truth regardless of how much the wicked despise it." **83** None believed in Moses except a few of his people, out of fear of Pharaoh and his assembly, that they might persecute them. Pharaoh was exalted in the earth. He was one who transgresses.

**Q 17:101** To Moses we gave ten clear signs. Ask the Israelites. When he came to them, Pharaoh said to him: "I consider you, Moses, to be affected by magic." **102** He [Moses] said: "You know that these things have been sent down only by the Lord of the heavens and the earth as something to behold. I consider you, Pharaoh, to be doomed." **103** He [Pharaoh] intended to remove them from the earth, but we drowned him and those with him, all together.

**Q 20:49** He [Pharaoh] said: "Who is the Lord of you both, Moses?" **50** He [Moses] said: "Our Lord, the one who gave to everything its created form, and then guided it." **51** He [Pharaoh] said: "What is the condition of the first generations?" **52** He [Moses] said: "Knowledge of that is with my Lord, in a book. My Lord does not err, nor does he forget. **53** "He is the one who made the earth spread out for you, in which there are ways for you to travel. He sent down water from heaven which we use to produce separate pairs of plants. **54** "Eat, pasture your cattle. In this are signs for those who have intelligence." **55** From it [the earth] we created you, into it we will return you, and from it we will take you one final time. **56** We showed him [Pharaoh] all of our signs, but he rejected and denied them. **57** He said: "Have you come to expel us from our land with magic, Moses? **58** "We can bring the same to you with magic. Let us make an appointment between us and you. We will not fail to keep it, neither us nor you, in a fair place." **59** He [Moses] said: "Your appointment is the day of the celebration.

Assemble the people at morning." **60** Pharaoh took refuge and assembled his plan. Then he came. **61** Moses said to them: "Woe to you. Do not forge a lie against God, or he will destroy you with a punishment. The forger must be caused to fail." **62** They [Egyptians] disputed with one another but they kept it secret among themselves. **63** They said: "These two are magicians. Their intention is to drive you from your land with their magic, to do away with your exemplary way. **64** "Assemble your plan, then come in rows. Success today is to the one who has the upper hand." **65** They said: "Moses, will you throw first or will we be the first to throw?" **66** He said: "No, you throw first." Their ropes and their rods, it seemed to him on account of their magic, began to move. **67** Apprehension formed in Moses as a fear. **68** We said: "Do not be afraid. You are higher. **69** "Throw what is in your right hand. It will swallow what they created. What they had created is only the trick of a magician, and the magician will not succeed when he comes forward."

**Q 26:10** When your Lord called to Moses: "Go to the people who are doing wrong, **11** the people of Pharaoh. Do they not fear God?" **12** He [Moses] said: "My Lord, I fear that they might reject me. **13** "My chest will be constricted and my tongue will not be articulate. So send for Aaron. **14** "They also hold me responsible for a sin, and I fear that they might kill me." **15** He [God] said: "By no means. Both of you go with our signs. We are with you, listening. **16** "Go to Pharaoh and say: 'We are sent by the Lord of the worlds. **17** " 'Send the Israelites with us.' " **18** He [Pharaoh] said: "Did we not raise you in our midst as a child? Did you not stay in our midst for many years of your life? **19** "You did that deed which you did. You are one of the unbelievers." **20** Moses said: "I did it when I was misled. **21** "I fled from you because I was afraid of you. My Lord has given me wisdom, and has made me one of the messengers. **22** "This is the favor that you grant me, to enslave the Israelites?" **23** The Pharaoh said: "What is the Lord of the worlds?" **24** He [Moses] said: "The Lord of the heavens and the earth, and what is between them, if you had certain belief." **25** He [Pharaoh] said to those around him: "Do you hear?" **26** He [Moses] said: "Your Lord, and the Lord of your forefathers." **27** He [Pharaoh] said: "Your messenger who was sent to you is one of the insane." **28** He [Moses] said: "Lord of the east, the west, and what is between, if you had sense." **29** He [Pharaoh] said: "If you take a god other than me, I will make you prisoners." **30** He [Moses] said: "Even if I bring you something clear?" **31** He [Pharaoh] said: "Bring it, if you are being truthful." **32** He [Moses] threw his rod, and it was a serpent, clearly. **33** He drew out his hand, and it was white, for all those who see. **34** To the assembly around him [Pharaoh] said: "This is learned magic. **35** "He intends to expel you from your land with his magic. What do you command?" **36** They said: "Summon him and his brother. Send messengers into the cities, **37** so that every learned magician will come to you." **38** All of the magicians gathered at the appointed time on the set day. **39** It was said to the people: "Are you assembled? **40** "Perhaps we will follow the magicians if they triumph." **41** When the magicians came, they said to Pharaoh: "We have a price if we are to triumph." **42** He said: "Yes, you will be attendants." **43** Moses said to them: "Throw what you are throwing." **44** They threw their ropes and rods, and said: "By the might of Pharaoh, we are triumphant." **45** Moses threw his rod and it swallowed what they had created. **46** The magicians were thrown down, prostrating. **47** They said: "We believe in the Lord of the worlds, **48** the Lord of Moses and Aaron." **49** He [Pharaoh] said: "Do you believe in him before I give you permission? He who has taught you the magic is great to you. You will learn. I will cut off your hands and feet on opposite sides and crucify you, all together." **50** They said: "There is no harm, for we will be received by our Lord. **51** "We desire that our Lord will forgive us for our sins. We are the first of the believers."

**Q 79:20** Moses showed him [Pharaoh] the great sign. **21** He rejected it and disobeyed. **22** Then he turned his back, making efforts [against God]. **23** He gathered [his men] and made a proclamation. **24** He said: "I am your Lord, Most High." **25** God took him as an example in the Hereafter and in the first life. **26** In this is a lesson for those who fear God.

*Ibn Kathir:* Moses told them about the worship of God alone, without associating anything with him. The people said: "We have never seen any of our fathers following this religion. We only know of people who associate other gods with God."

## Tower of Babel

**Q 28:36** When Moses came to them with our clear signs, they said: "This is only magic. We have not heard of this from our forefathers." **37** Moses said: "My Lord knows who comes with right guidance from him, and to whom shall be the final abode [of the hereafter]. Those who do wrong will not prosper." **38** Pharaoh said: "Leaders, I do not know of a god for you other than myself. Kindle a fire for me, Haman, for clay brick. Build me a high tower so that I might see the God of Moses. I think he is a liar." **39** He and his armies were arrogant in the land. They thought that they would not return to us. **40** We took him and his armies and we cast them into the sea. See what the consequences are of those who do wrong. **41** We made them examples to follow into the Fire. On the Day of Resurrection they will not be victorious. **42** We caused a curse to follow them in this world. On the Day of Resurrection, they will be among the ugly ones.

**Q 40:36** Pharaoh said: "Haman, build me a tall tower so that I might have the means, **37** means to the heavens, to rise up to the God of Moses. I think he is a liar." Thus the evil of what Pharaoh did was an ornament to him. He was blocked from the path, and the plot of Pharaoh was nothing but ruin.

*Ibn Kathir:* Pharaoh ordered his vizier Haman to prepare baked clay, to make a lofty edifice for him. It was a very high tower. From this tower it was not possible to see anything higher in this world. With this, the Pharaoh wanted to show to his people that Moses was a liar concerning what he alleged about a god other than Pharaoh.

*Thaʿlabi:* God filled the gates of Pharaoh with kingship, authority, wealth, and pleasure which caused him to be feared by his subjects among the people of his kingdom, to the extent that he demanded their worship and they worshipped him. Along with this he was given a long life, great strength, and a powerful and numerous army. It is said that he could go for 40 days and nights without anything. He could eat and drink without spitting, blowing his nose, clearing his throat, coughing, with no pain in his stomach. His eyes did not get sore, he did not get sick. His nose did not run, and nothing bad seemed to affect him.

*Saʿid b. Jubayr:* Pharaoh ruled for 400 years and never encountered any hardship, as if during this time he never knew hunger, and no evil ever afflicted him. Everyone who met him loved him. One of his castles had 1000 stairs and God made subservient to him a special animal on which he would ride up to and down from this castle. When this thing happened with Moses, Pharaoh was afraid that his people would believe in Moses and put Moses in his place. So he commanded his vizier Haman to build a tower. Haman gathered workers, leaving no one from the building of this tower, 50,000 people. He built the tower non-stop, and God made it easy for him, so that he would be arrogant. It took seven years to build and when it was done it was more magnificent than anything since God's creation of the heavens and the earth. After it was finished, God revealed to Moses that he would destroy all that Pharaoh had wrought in a single hour. So God sent Gabriel, and Gabriel hit the tower with his wing, breaking it into three pieces. One of the pieces went into the sea, another went to India, and a third went to the far west.

*Dahhak:* God sent Gabriel and he hit the tower with his wing. He flung it on the soldiers of Pharaoh and killed thousands upon thousands of men.

## Israelites in Egypt

**Q 10:84** Moses said: "My people, if you believe in God, then in him put your trust, if you are those who submit." **85** They said: "In God we put our trust. Our

Lord, do not make us a trial for the people who do wrong. **86** "Save us with your mercy from the people who disbelieve." **87** We revealed to Moses and his brother: "Take, for your people in Egypt, houses and make your houses into places of worship, establish prayer, and give good tidings to those who believe." **88** Moses said: "Our Lord, you have given Pharaoh and his assembly ornaments and wealth in the life of this world. Our Lord, they mislead from your path. Our Lord, obliterate their wealth and harden their hearts so that they will not believe until they see the grievous punishment." **89** He [God] said: "Your prayer is answered. Establish yourselves and do not follow the path of those who do not know."

## The Egyptian Who Believed

**Q 40:23** We sent Moses with our signs and clear authority, **24** to Pharaoh, Haman, and Korah. They said: "A magician, a liar." **25** When he brought them the truth from us, they said: "Kill the sons who believe with him, and let their women live." The plots of those who disbelieve are only in error. **26** Pharaoh said: "Leave me to kill Moses, so that he might call upon his Lord. I fear that he might change your religion or cause spoil to appear in the land." **27** Moses said: "I have called upon my Lord and your Lord [for protection] from all who make themselves out to be great and do not believe in the Day of Reckoning." **28** A man who believed, from the family of Pharaoh, who had kept his faith secret, said: "Will you kill a man who says: 'My Lord is God,' when he has come to you with clear signs from your Lord? If he be a liar, then his lie is upon him, but if he be truthful, then some of that about which he warns you will befall you. God does not guide one who transgresses and lies. **29** "My people, you have dominion this day, are knowing in the land. Who will help us from the harm of God if it comes to us?" Pharaoh said: "I only cause you to see that which I see, and guide you on the path of good sense." **30** The one who believed said: "My people, I fear for you something like the Day of the Ahzab, **31** something like the fate of the people of Noah, Ad, Thamud, and those after them. God does not intend oppression for those who worship. **32** "My people, I fear for you a day of calling to one another, **33** a day when you will turn away and flee. You will have no defender against God. He whom God causes to be misled will have no guide. **34** "Joseph came to you before with clear signs, but you still doubt that which he brought to you, to the extent that when he died, you said: 'God will not send a messenger after him.' Thus God leads astray those who transgress, are skeptical, **35** those who dispute the signs of God without any authority reaching them, being very loathsome to God and those who believe. Thus does God seal every heart of those who make themselves out to be great, are giants." **36** Pharaoh said: "Haman, build me a tall tower that I might have the means, **37** means to the heavens, to rise up to the God of Moses. I think he is a liar." Thus the evil of what Pharaoh did was an ornament to him. He was blocked from the path, and the plot of Pharaoh was nothing but ruin. **38** The one who believed said: "My people, follow me. I will lead you to the path of good sense. **39** "My people, the life of this world is only temporary enjoyment, but the next life is the abode that lasts. **40** "He who does evil will only be rewarded with its like. Those who do upright deeds, whether male or female, and believe, they will enter Paradise and be sustained in it without measure. **41** "My people, what is it to me that I call you to salvation but you call me to the Fire? **42** "You call upon me to disbelieve in God, to associate things with him about which I have no knowledge. I call you to the Mighty, the Forgiving. **43** "There is no doubt that you are only calling me to one who has no right to be called in this world nor in the next. Our return is to God. The transgressors are companions of the Fire. **44** "You will remember what I say to you. My matter I give over to God. God has sight of the worshippers." **45** God took him from the evil they had intended, and the evil of the punishment encompassed the family of Pharaoh. **46** Over the Fire they are caused to pass morning and evening. The hour is established when the family of Pharaoh will enter into a more severe punishment.

*Ibn Kathir:* The man who believed was the son of the Pharaoh's paternal uncle. He kept his faith secret from his people, fearing for himself. Some of the people allege that he was Israelite, but this is far from the case and contradicts the general sense of the passage. The Prophet Muhammad said: "The best Jihad is a just word in front of an unjust authority."

*Ibn Abbas:* None of the Egyptians believed in Moses except for this man, the one who came from the farthest part of the city, and the wife of the Pharaoh.

*Daraqutni:* There was no one named "Simeon" except the believer from the household of the Pharaoh.

*Tabarani:* His name was "Khayr."

*Tha'labi:* Hizqil was one of the carpenters of Pharaoh. He was the one who had made the ark into which Moses had been placed after his birth when he was put into the sea. It is also said that he was the treasurer of Pharaoh and had been in charge of the treasury for 100 years. He was a sincere believer but kept his faith secret until Moses appeared. He was taken away and executed with the magicians. The wife of Hizqil was also a believer, and was a lady's maid for the daughter of Pharaoh.

*Ibn Abbas:* The Prophet Muhammad said: "During my Night Journey I passed by a pleasant scent. I asked Gabriel: 'What is that scent?' He said: 'That is the scent of the lady's maid of the family of Pharaoh and her children. One day the comb fell from her hand and she said: "In the name of God." The daughter of Pharaoh said: "You mean my father." Hizqil's wife said: "My Lord is not your father." So the daughter of Pharaoh told her father about this. When he heard he summoned her and her children. He said: "Who is your Lord?" She replied: "My Lord and your Lord is God." So Pharaoh ordered her and her children thrown into a giant oven of brass. She said to him: "I have one request of you." He said: "What is it?" She said: "Gather my bones and the bones of my children, and bury them." He agreed, then ordered her children to be thrown one at a time into the oven until the last of her children, which was an infant still nursing at her breast. The infant spoke: "Be steadfast, mother, for you are right." And the wife of Hizqil was cast into the oven along with the infant.' "

**Tha'labi:** It is said that Asiyah, the wife of Pharaoh, saw the wife of Hizqil killed by the Pharaoh. She was sitting at a window of the castle and saw how the lady's maid was punished and killed. When this happened, the angels strengthened Asiyah and bolstered her spirit, making her faith strong. When the Pharaoh came to her he began to tell her about the killing of the wife of Hizqil, and Asiyah said to him: "You are damned, Pharaoh. With what will God repay you?" He said to her: "Perhaps you are afflicted with the same Jinn as your companions?" She said: "I am not afflicted with Jinn, but I believe in God, my Lord, your Lord, the Lord of the worlds." Pharaoh summoned her mother and said to her: "Your daughter has been taken by the same Jinn which took control of the lady's maid." He said to her: "She will disbelieve in the God of Moses or she will taste death." She left her with her mother, and her mother asked her to agree with Pharaoh. She refused, saying: "You want me to disbelieve in God? By God, I would never do this." So the Pharaoh commanded her to be stretched between four stakes, and she was punished in this way until she died.

## Plagues

**Q 7 : 127** The leaders of the people of Pharaoh said: "Will you leave Moses and his people to spoil the land, to abandon you and your gods?" He said: "We will kill their sons and let their women live. We are victorious over them." **128** Moses said to his people: "Pray to God and be steadfast. The earth belongs to God, and he bequeaths it to whichever of his servants that he wants. The end result is for those who fear God." **129** They said: "We have suffered before you came and after you came." He said: "Perhaps your Lord will destroy your enemy and cause you to succeed them in the earth, so that he might see how you act." **130** We afflicted the family of Pharaoh for years with shortness of produce so that they might remember. **131** When plenty came, they said: "This is on our account." When evil befell them, they augured that it was Moses and he who was with him, except their omens were from God, but most of them do not learn. **132** They said: "Whatever sign you bring to us, to use as magic on us, we will not be believers." **133** So we sent upon them: flood, locusts, pestilence, frogs, and blood, signs clearly understood. But they were arrogant, were a sinning people. **134** When the plague fell upon them, they said: "Moses, call upon your Lord on our behalf, according to his promise with you. If you lift the plague from us, we will believe in you and send the Israelites with you." **135** When the plague was lifted from them, for a fixed term they had to reach, they broke their word. **136** We took retribution from them, we drowned them in the sea because they had rejected our signs and were heedless of them.

*Ibn Kathir:* There is disagreement about the meaning of the "flood" that God sent against the Egyptians. Ibn Abbas says it was a lot of rain which caused flooding of the crops and fruit, causing much death. Mujahid says it was water and pestilence. As for the locusts, they were what is eaten. Bukhari and Muslim cite the report: "We campaigned with the Prophet Muhammad seven times and ate locust." As for the "pestilence," Ibn Abbas says it was worms which came out of wheat. Hasan al-Basri says they were small black insects. Others say they were fleas. Tabari says they were insects resembling pestilence which camels eat.

*Mujahid:* The locusts ate the nails from their doors and the insides of the wood.

*Sa'id b. Jubayr:* When Moses came to Pharaoh he said to him: "Send the Israelites with me." So God sent a flood, which is rain, and something from the rain afflicted them which they feared was a punishment. They said to Moses: "Call upon your Lord to remove this rain from us. We will believe in you and will send the Israelites with you." So he called on his Lord but they did not believe nor send the Israelites with him. He caused to grow for them, in this year, things which were not planted before that, types of grains, fruit, and herbs. They said: "This is not what we were growing." God sent locusts upon them, and they consumed the herbs. When the people saw their remains among the herbs they knew that there was no crop left. They said: "Moses, call upon your Lord to remove these locusts from us. We will believe in you and send the Israelites with you." He called upon his Lord to remove the locusts from them, but they did not believe and did not send the Israelites with them. They fortified themselves in their houses and said: "We have protected ourselves." So God sent "pestilence" upon them, which is worms. Men would come out with ten sacks to mill and return with only three dry measures. They said: "Moses, call upon your Lord that he might remove this pestilence from us. We will believe in you and send the Israelites with you." He called upon his Lord, and he removed the pestilence from them, but they refused to send the Israelites with him. After this, Moses was sitting with Pharaoh, when he heard the croaking of the frogs. He said to Pharaoh: "What will you and your people do about this?" He said: "Perhaps this is a plot?" They continued sitting until men would be sitting with frogs up to their chins. When they wanted to talk, a frog would jump in their mouth. They said: "Moses, call upon your Lord, to remove these frogs from us. We will believe in you and send the Israelites with you." He called upon his Lord, and he removed the frogs from them, but they did not believe. So, God sent blood upon them. When they would go to get water from the rivers and wells they found that blood was in their containers. They complained to Pharaoh saying: "We are being tried with blood and have nothing to drink." He said: "You have been mesmerized by magic." They said: "Where are our magicians? We find nothing but blood in our containers." They came to Moses and said: "Moses, call upon your Lord to remove this blood from us. We will believe in you and send the Israelites with you." He called upon his Lord, and he removed it from them, but they did not believe and did not send the Israelites with him.

*Ibn Ishaq:* Because the Pharaoh would not listen to Moses, God afflicted them with plagues. First he sent a flood, then locusts, then pestilence, then frogs, then blood, all clearly understood signs. The flood was water which spread over the face of the land. It became stagnant and the people were not able to cultivate nor work the land, so that they were suffering from hunger. When this happened, they said: "Moses, call upon your Lord, by virtue of the covenant you have. If you will lift this punishment from us, we will believe in you and will send the Israelites with you." Moses called upon his Lord and he lifted it from them. But they did not do any of the things they had said. So God sent locusts against them. The locusts ate the trees, ate the nails made of iron out of their doors and infested all of their houses. They said what they said before, and Moses again called upon God who lifted it from them, but they did not do any of the things they had said. So God sent pestilence against them. It was said that Moses was commanded to walk to a mound and hit it with his rod. So he walked to a great mound of sand and hit it with his rod, and the pestilence came out of it. The pestilence overcame the houses, food, and prevented the people from sleeping.

They said what they had said before to Moses, he called upon God, God removed the pestilence from them, and they refused to do any of the things they had said. So God sent frogs against them. They filled their houses, their food, and their containers. No one could take a single cloth or piece of food and not find a frog in it. They said what they had said before to Moses. He asked his Lord, and he removed the frogs from them, but they refused to do any of the things they had said. So God sent blood against them. All the water of the people of Pharaoh became blood. They could not drink from any well or river, and everything they drew in containers was blood.

## Parting of the Sea

**Q 26:52** We revealed to Moses: "Go by night with my servants, for you will be followed." **53** Pharaoh sent messengers into the cities: **54** "These are a small band, **55** but they have angered us. **56** "We are a wary group." **57** We expelled them from gardens and springs, **58** treasures, and places of honor. **59** Thus we caused the Israelites to inherit these. **60** They followed them at sunrise. **61** When the two groups saw each other, the companions of Moses said: "We are to be overtaken." **62** He said: "No, my Lord is with me and he will guide me." **63** We revealed to Moses: "Strike the sea with your rod." It divided, and each [side] was like a great towering mountain. **64** Then we caused the others to approach. **65** We saved Moses and those with him, all together. **66** Then we drowned the others. **67** In this is a sign, but most of them are not believers. **68** Your Lord is He, the Mighty, the Merciful.

**Q 44:17** We tried their hearts, the people of Pharaoh. An honored messenger came to them: **18** "Return to me the servants of God. I am a trustworthy messenger to you. **19** "Do not make yourself out to be higher than God. I come to you with clear authority. **20** "I have taken refuge with my Lord and your Lord against your stoning me. **21** "If you do not believe me, then keep away from me." **22** He called upon his Lord: "These are a sinning people." **23** [God said]: "Leave by night, my servants, for you will be followed. **24** "Leave the sea calm, for they are an army to be drowned." **25** How many were the gardens and springs they left, **26** the fields of produce, noble position, **27** and pleasant things with which they had amused themselves? **28** It was thus, and we caused other people to inherit these. **29** Neither heaven nor earth cried for them, nor did they have any prospect. **30** We saved the Israelites from humiliating punishment, **31** from Pharaoh, for he was the most arrogant among those who transgress. **32** We chose them, with full knowledge, above the worlds. **33** We gave them signs in which was a clear trial.

*Ibn Kathir:* "Leave the sea calm" means leave it as it is, not changing it from being divided. This is the opinion of Ibn Abbas, Mujahid, Ikrimah, Rabi'a, Dahhak, Qatadah, Ka'b al-Ahbar, Abd al-Rahman b. Zayd b. Aslam, and others. When he left it in its divided condition, the Pharaoh rode into it and was finished. It is said that Gabriel appeared on the image of a horse. He passed right through the hands of Pharaoh quickly and he was dragged into the sea. Pharaoh was not able to do anything for himself. Then he saw that the army had also been dragged into the sea behind him. The sea surged around all of them, and then God ordered Moses to strike the sea with his rod. He struck it and the sea rushed back together, covering all of the Egyptians. Not a single person survived.

## Punishment of Pharaoh and His People

**Q 10:90** We caused the Israelites to pass through the sea. Pharaoh and his armies followed them, insolent and as enemies, until the drowning overtook him. Then he [Pharaoh] said: "I believe that there is no God other than he in whom the Israelites believe. I am one who submits." **91** Now, but you were disobedient before and were one of the despoilers. **92** Today we save you, your body, so that it might be a sign for those who come after you. Many people are heedless of our signs.

**Q 11:96** We sent Moses with signs and clear authority **97** to Pharaoh and his assembly. They followed the command of Pharaoh but the command of Pharaoh was not rightly guided. **98** He will bring his people forward on the Day of Resurrection, and will deposit them in the Fire. The resting place of those who are deposited is wretched. **99** They are followed by this curse in this [life] and the Day of Resurrection. Wretched is the help which will be offered.

**Q 43:46** We sent Moses with our signs to Pharaoh and his assembly. He said: "I am a messenger of the Lord of the worlds." **47** When he brought them our signs, they laughed at them. **48** We showed them signs, one greater than the one before, and we seized them with a punishment so that they might return. **49** They said: "Magician, call upon your Lord on our behalf, according to his promise with you. We will accept right guidance." **50** When we lifted the punishment from them they broke their word. **51** Pharaoh proclaimed to his people, saying: "My people, does not dominion over Egypt belong to me? these rivers flowing under me? Do you not see? **52** "Am I not better than this one who is contemptible and can barely express himself? **53** "Why are not bracers of gold bestowed upon him? or angels come with him in procession?" **54** He made his people afraid and they followed him, being a despoiling people. **55** When they provoked us we exacted retribution from them, and drowned them, all together. **56** We made them of the past and an example for others.

*Ibn Kathir:* They were drowned in the sea with a single scream, and not a single one of them remained. God mandated, upon the tongues of the believers who worship God and his messengers, a curse upon the people and upon their king Pharaoh, just as they are accursed in this world by the prophets and those who follow them. Pharaoh only repented when he saw that he was going to die.

*Ibn Abbas:* The Prophet Muhammad said: "Gabriel said to me: 'Did you not see me when I took the wall of the sea and shoved it into the mouth of Pharaoh, afraid that he would make amends for the sake of mercy?' "

*Ibn Abbas:* When God drowned Pharaoh he pointed his finger and raised his voice: "I believe that there is no God other than he in whom the Israelites believe" (10:90). Gabriel was afraid that the mercy of God would overcome his anger. So he began to take the walls of water with his wings and pound Pharaoh and his face, burying him.

*Ibn Abbas:* Some of the Israelites were doubtful that Pharaoh had died, and some of them even said that he had not died. So God ordered the sea to exhume him for them to see. They knew it was him by the insignia of his clothing.

*Ibn Kathir:* Some people read the verse [10:92] to mean that God saved his body so that the Israelites would know that he had died. He and his army died on the Day of Ashura.

*Bukhari:* Ibn Abbas says that when the Prophet Muhammad came to Medina he found the Jews fasting on the Day of Ashura. He asked them: "What day is this on which you fast?" They said: "It is the day Moses was victorious over Pharaoh." The Prophet Muhammad said to his followers: "You have more right to Moses than they do, so fast!"

# Moses and the Israelites

## Wilderness of Wandering

**Q 2:47**  Israelites, remember the blessings with which I blessed you, favoring you over all the worlds. **48** Fear the day when one will not help another in anything, when intercession will not be accepted, nor will just compensation be taken, nor will they be helped. **49** When we saved you from the people of Pharaoh who appointed you a harsh punishment, slaughtering your sons. In this was a great trial for you from your Lord. **50** When we divided the sea for you, saved you, and drowned the people of Pharaoh while you were watching. **51** When we appointed forty nights for Moses, and then you took the calf after he left, and you did wrong. **52** Then we forgave you, even after that, so that you might be thankful. **53** When we gave Moses the Book and the Furqan so that you might be rightly guided. **54** When Moses said to his people: "People, you have wronged yourselves by taking the calf for yourselves. Repent to your creator and kill yourselves. This is better for you, according to your creator." Then he absolved you, for he is Forgiving, Merciful. **55** When you said: "Moses, we will not believe in you until we see God openly." The thunder took you while you were watching. **56** Then we raised you up [or: sent you as prophets] after your death so that you might be thankful. **57** We gave the cloud to shade you and sent down the manna and quails: "Eat of the good by which we sustain you." They did wrong against us but were only wronging themselves. **58** When we said: "Enter this district, eat from its plenty what you want. Enter the gate prostrated and saying: 'hittah.' We will forgive your sins and will increase those who do good." **59** Those who did wrong changed the saying from that which was said to them. We sent down upon those who did wrong a plague from the heavens because they were despoiling. **60** When Moses prayed for water for his people, and we said: "Strike the rock with your rod." Twelve springs gushed forth from it, and each of the peoples knew their drinking place. "Eat and drink from the sustenance of God, and do not do evil despoiling the earth." **61** When you said: "Moses, we cannot endure one kind of food. Ask your Lord for us to bring forth for us that which the earth grows: potherbs, cucumbers, its garlic, lentils, and onions." He said: "Will you substitute that which is inferior for that which is better? Go down to Egypt, and there will be that for which you ask." They were struck with shame and misery. They called upon themselves the anger of God. This was because they were rejecting the signs of God and killing the prophets without right. This was because they rebelled and were transgressing.

### Blessings Given to Israelites

*Ibn Kathir:* According to Mujahid, Rabiʿa b. Anas, and Qatadah, God gave the Israelites kings, prophets, and books.

*Qatadah:* "We made you kings" means: servants for you and people to serve you.

*Tabarsi:* It is said that the prophets were those who came after Moses, being raised up among the Israelites until the time of Jesus, prophesying to them about the commands of their religion.

*Ibn Abbas and Mujahid:* The Israelites were "made kings" by the manna, the quails, the rock and the cloud.

*Abu al-Qasim al-Balkhi:* God made kingship and authority for the Israelites and spread out for them the luxuries which were fit for a king.

*Saʿid b. Jubayr and Abu Malik:* Being addressed here is the community of the Prophet Muhammad.

### Clouds

*Ibn Kathir:* These were white clouds which gave shade to the Israelites in the Wilderness of Wandering, to protect them from the heat of the sun.

*Ibn Abbas:* God shaded them in the Wilderness of Wandering with clouds.

*Mujahid:* These were not ordinary clouds but the clouds on which God will come on the Day of Resurrection, and they were only for the Israelites.

### Manna and Quails

*Ibn Abbas:* The manna came down to the Israelites upon the trees. They would go out early in the morning and eat from it what they wanted.

*Mujahid:* Manna is the gum of trees.

*Ikrimah:* Manna is something God sent down to the Israelites like thick juice. The quail was a bird like a bird in Paradise, bigger than the sparrow.

*Suddi:* When the Israelites entered the wilderness, they said: "Moses, how can we survive here, where is the food?" God sent down the manna. It would fall on the ginger trees. The quail were birds resembling but bigger than quails. One of the Israelites used to come and look at the bird. If it was fat, he would slaughter it. The people said: "This is food, but where is the drink?" God commanded Moses to strike the rock with his rod and twelve springs of water gushed forth from it. Each tribe drank from a spring. The people said: "This is drink, but where is the shade?" God caused a cloud to shade them. The people said: "This is shade, but where are the clothes?" Their clothes used to grow with them just as a young boy grows. The clothes would not tear. When they left the wilderness, the manna and quail were recalled, and they ate vegetables.

*Qatadah:* The manna used to come down in the camp, falling like snow, bright white from the milk and sweet from the honey. It fell from the breaking of dawn to sunrise. Each man would take from it measure enough for that day. When there was extra, it would spoil and not remain fresh except for on the sixth day and the Sabbath. On the sixth day there would be enough for that day and extra for the seventh day because the seventh day was a holiday on which no person was allowed to work nor seek after anything. All of this happened in the wilderness.

*Rabi'a b. Anas:* Manna was a drink which would come down to them like honey. It would rain down with water and then they would drink it.

*Wahb b. Munabbih:* Manna was fine bread like dust. The quail was a fat bird like a pigeon. They would come and the Israelites would collect them from Sabbath to Sabbath. The Israelites asked Moses for meat. God said: "We will feed them from the smallest meat known in the earth." He sent a wind upon them and the quail fell about their dwellings.

*Qummi:* After Moses crossed the sea with the Israelites, they stopped in the wilderness. The Israelites murmured to Moses saying: "You cause us to die by bringing us out of civilization, to a wilderness in which there is no shade, no trees, and no water." A white cloud came over them to shade them from the sun. At night, manna came down, falling on the trees, plants and rocks. After eating the manna, in the night a roasted bird would land on their tables. When they had eaten enough it would fly away. Moses also had a rock which he put in the middle of the people and struck with his rod, causing twelve springs of water to gush out.

## Moses on the Mountain

**Q 7 : 142**  We appointed for Moses thirty nights and completed it with another ten. The term with his Lord was completed in forty nights. Moses said to his brother Aaron: "Be my representative among my people. Be upright and do not follow the path of those who despoil." **143** When Moses came to the appointed place his Lord spoke with him. He said: "My Lord, show yourself to me so that I can see you." God said: "You cannot see me but look at the mountain. If it remains in its place, then you will see me." When his Lord revealed himself to the mountain, he made it crash down and Moses fainted. When he recovered he said: "Glory to you. I am repentant to you. I am the first of the believers." **144** God said: "Moses, I have selected you above other people by my message and my words. Take that which I give you and be one of those who are thankful." **145** We wrote for him on the tablets of all things, admonition and details of all things: "Take this with strength and order your people to take with its goodness. I will show you the abode of the sinful. **146** "I will turn away from my signs those who exalt themselves in the earth without right. Even if they see all the signs, they will not believe in them. Even if they see the way of right conduct, they will not take it as the way. If they see the way of error, they will take it as the way. They have rejected our signs and take no heed of them. **147** "Those who reject our signs and the meeting in the next world, their works are vain. How can they be rewarded except according to what they did?"

*Ibn Kathir:* The 40 nights took place during the month of Dhu al-Qaʿdah and the first ten days of Dhu al-Hijjah.

*Tabari:* After his Lord had spoken to him, Moses wanted to see God: "My Lord, show me yourself that I might see you." God said: "You will not see me but look at the mountain. If it remains in its place, then you will see me" (7:143). Angels surrounded the mountain and the angels were surrounded by fire, and angels surrounded the fire, and those angels were surrounded by fire. Then his Lord revealed himself to the mountain.

*Ibn Abbas:* He revealed to it something like the tip of his little finger, and he made the mountain crash down while Moses fainted. He did not recover from fainting until God wanted him to do so. Then God gave Moses the tablets. After that, no one was able to look at the face of Moses, so he wore a piece of silk over his face.

## Golden Calf

**Q 7:148** The people of Moses, after he left, took from their ornaments an embodied calf which bellowed. Did they not see that it could not speak to them nor guide them on the way? They took it but they were doing wrong. **149** When they fell on their hands and saw they had erred, they said: "If our Lord will not have mercy on us and forgive us we will be among the losers." **150** When Moses returned to his people, angry and grieved, he said: "You have done evil in my absence. Did you hurry to bring on the word of your Lord?" He threw the tablets and took his brother by his head and dragged him over, and Aaron said: "Son of my mother, the people thought I was weak and were on the verge of killing me. Do not cause the enemies to gloat over me nor consider me among the people who sinned." **151** Moses said: "My Lord, forgive me and my brother. Allow us to enter into your mercy. You are the most Merciful of those who are merciful." **152** Those who took the calf will be overwhelmed with anger from their Lord, and shame in the life of this world. This is how we reward those who fabricate falsehoods. **153** Those who do evil things and then repent afterward and believe, after this your Lord is Forgiving, Merciful. **154** When the anger of Moses was quieted, he took the tablets. In what was written on them [or: in the abrogation of them] was guidance and mercy for those who fear their Lord. **155** Moses chose seventy men from his people for our place of meeting. When they were taken by an earthquake, Moses said: "My Lord, if you had wanted, you could have destroyed them before, and me with them. Will you now destroy us for what the foolish among us did? This is nothing but your trial by which you cause to be misled whom you want and cause to be rightly guided whom you want. You are our protector. Forgive us and show mercy on us for you are the best of those who forgive. **156** "Promise for us that which is good in this world and the next, for we are following you." God said: "My punishment will afflict whom I want, but my mercy covers all things. I will promise it to those who do right, perform what is pure, and those who believe in our signs. **157** "Those who follow the messenger, the gentile [ummi] prophet about whom they find things written in their Torah and Gospel. He commands them to separate themselves from what is reprehensible. He allows them good things and forbids them impure things. He releases them from their burdens and yokes which are upon them. Those who believe in him, honor him, help him, and follow the light which is revealed with him, they are the ones who will prosper." **158** Say: "People, I am sent to you all as a messenger of

God, to whom belongs dominion over the heavens and the earth. There is no god other than he. He causes to live and causes to die, so believe in God and his messenger the gentile prophet who believes in God, his commands, and follow him so that you might be rightly guided."

**Q 20:80** Israelites, we delivered you from your enemy and we made a covenant with you on the right side of the Mountain. We sent down manna and quails for you. **81** Eat of the good things as your sustenance but do not transgress with it or my anger will envelope you, and those whom my anger envelopes are lost. **82** I am the one who forgives him who repents, believes, is upright, and is rightly guided. **83** "What made you impatient about your people, Moses?" **84** He said: "They are close behind me. I hastened to you, my Lord to please." **85** God said: "We have tested your people after you left. al-Samiri has misled them." **86** Moses returned to his people angry and sorrowful. He said: "My people, did not your Lord make you a good promise? Did the promise seem to take a long time or did you want that anger from your Lord would befall you, so you broke the promise to me?" **87** They said: "We did not break the promise to you concerning that which was in our control, but we were carrying the weight of the ornaments of the people, and we cast them as al-Samiri threw them. **88** "He brought out for us the embodied calf which bellowed. They said: 'This is your god and the God of Moses. He has forgotten.'" **89** Could they not see that it could not return a word to them and that it had no power for them, harm or benefit? **90** Aaron had said to them before this: "My people, you are being tested with this. Your Lord is Merciful, so follow me and obey my command." **91** They said: "We will not cease to devote ourselves to it until Moses returns to us." **92** Moses said: "Aaron, what held you back when you saw they were misled? **93** "Do you not follow me, did you disobey my order?" **94** He replied: "Son of my mother, do not take me by my beard and my head. I was afraid that you might say: 'You created a division among the Israelites and did not keep my word.'" **95** Moses said: "What is your story, al-Samiri?" **96** He replied: "I saw that which they did not see. I took a handful from the trace of the messenger and threw it just as my soul suggested to me." **97** Moses said: "Be gone! In this life you will say 'Do not touch me,' and for you is a promise which will not be broken: Look at your god to whom you are devoted. We will burn it and then throw it into the sea scattered." **98** Your god is God, there is no god other than he, encompassing of all things in knowledge.

*Suddi:* Gabriel came to Moses, to take him to God. He came on a horse, and when al-Samiri saw him he did not recognize him. It is said that his horse was the horse of life. When al-Samiri saw the horse, he said: "This is something." So he took some dust from the hoof of the horse. Moses set out and designated Aaron as his deputy over the Israelites. He promised them it would be 30 nights, but God completed this with ten more. Aaron said: "Israelites, spoils are not allowed for you. The jewelry of the Egyptians is spoils. Gather it together, dig a hole, and bury it therein. When Moses returns, if he allows it, you can take the jewelry back out, otherwise they are things you cannot use." So they gathered together all the jewelry in that hole and al-Samiri came with a handful of that dust and threw it into the hole. God caused to come forth from the jewelry "an embodied calf which bellowed" (20:88).

The Israelites figured the time Moses had promised, counting each night as a day and each day as a day. When they reached ten, the calf came out. When they saw it, al-Samiri said: "This is your god and the God of Moses. He has forgotten" (20:88). He said: "Moses left his god here and went searching for him." They occupied themselves with the calf and worshipped it. It bellowed and walked. Aaron said to them: "Israelites, you are merely being seduced." He said: "You are being tested with this," meaning the calf. "Your Lord is Merciful, so follow me and obey my command" (20:90). Aaron stood and the Israelites who were on his side did not fight the others.

Moses was speaking with his God when God told him about the incident with the calf. Moses said: "Lord, this al-Samiri commanded them to take the calf, but did you see who breathed the spirit into it?" His Lord said: "I did." Moses said: "Lord, then you have misled them."

*Ibn Abbas:* al-Samiri was a man from the people of Bajarma, from a people who worshipped cows. The love for the worship of cows was inside of him though outwardly he professed submission to God among the Israelites. When Aaron was in charge among the Israelites and Moses had gone to his Lord, al-Samiri said to Aaron: "You have been carrying the burden of ornaments of the people of the Pharaoh. Purify yourselves from it since it is unclean." He lit a fire for them and said: "Throw into the fire those ornaments you have with you." The people began to bring what they had and threw it in. Then al-Samiri saw a trace left by the horse of Gabriel. He took some dust from the trace of the hoofprint, came up to the hole, and said to Aaron: "Prophet of God, should I throw what is in my hand?" Aaron said yes, only thinking that it was some of what others were bringing, goods and jewelry. He threw it in and said: "Be an embodied calf which bellows!" This was a trial and cause for division. The Israelites occupied themselves with the calf and loved it with a love unlike anything before. God said: "He has forgotten" (20:88) meaning that al-Samiri left the state of submission to God in which he had been.

*Ibn Abbas:* God had written on the tablets exhortation, particulars of all things, guidance, and mercy. When Moses threw them down, God recalled six of the seven parts and left only one seventh.

## Punishment for the Golden Calf

*Ibn Abbas:* The command of Moses to his people was a command from God that they kill themselves. Those who worshipped the calf were sitting, and those who did not worship the calf were standing. They took daggers in their hands and an intense darkness fell upon them. They began to kill one another. When the darkness was raised, more than 70,000 were killed. All those who were killed were absolved, and all those who remained were absolved.

*Ibn Ishaq:* When Moses returned to his people, he burned the calf and scattered it into the sea, and left with a group of those whom he chose from his people. Thunder took their lives, and then they were raised up again. Moses asked his Lord for absolution on behalf of the Israelites for worshipping the calf. God said: "Only if they kill themselves." The people said to Moses: "We cannot bear the command of God." So Moses ordered those who had not worshipped the calf to kill those who were worshipping it, while they were sitting in their enclosures. The people unsheathed their swords and began to kill them. Moses cried while the women and young men came to him asking pardon for the people. He pardoned them and then ordered the people to withdraw their swords.

*Ibn Abbas:* When Moses returned he took the calf and slaughtered it. Then he filed it down and flung the remains into the sea. There was no flowing sea into which something of the calf did not fall. Moses said to them: "Drink from the water." So they drank. Whoever loved the calf, the gold they drank would appear on them. God refused to accept the repentance of the Israelites except on the condition that they fight with one another. Those who worshipped the calf and those who did not worship it hit one another with swords. Whoever was killed from the two groups was a martyr. This continued until many were killed and they were on the verge of annihilation, until the killing reached 70,000 people. Moses and Aaron called to God: "Our Lord, the Israelites are annihilated. Our Lord, the remnant, the remnant." He ordered them to put down their weapons, and forgave them.

*Qummi:* Moses said to his people: "Every one of you go to Jerusalem [bayt al-maqdis] with a knife, iron bar or sword. When I mount the pulpit of the Israelites, be ready with your faces veiled so that no one will recognize his friend and kill someone else." They gathered together 70,000 men who had worshipped the calf and went up to Jerusalem. When Moses mounted the pulpit they began to kill each other. They continued until Gabriel came down and told Moses to stop the killing. Ten thousand were killed.

## Seventy Chosen

*Ibn Ishaq:* When Moses returned to his people he saw that they were worshipping the calf. He burned the calf and scattered the ashes into the sea. Then Moses chose seventy of the best men from among them. He said: "Turn toward God and repent to God for what you have made. Ask God for forgiveness for those of your people whom you left behind." They fasted, purified themselves, and purified their clothing. Moses went with them to Mount Sinai at the time appointed by his Lord. The seventy went out to meet God and said: "Moses, ask your Lord that we might hear the words of our Lord." He said: "I will." When Moses went up to the mountain, a cloud descended and covered all of the mountain. Moses entered into it and said to his people: "Approach!" When Moses would speak with God a brilliant light would come upon his forehead, and no human being was able to look at him, so he covered his face with a veil. The people approached, entered into the cloud, and fell prostrate. They heard God while he was talking with Moses, giving him things to command and forbid: "Do this and don't do that." When the orders stopped the cloud rose from Moses and the seventy said to Moses: "We will not believe in you unless we see God openly" (2:55). So an earthquake, which was thunder, took their lives. All of them died and Moses stood imploring his Lord: "If I selected the seventy best men from among the Israelites, and I return to the rest and not a single one of the seventy is with me, then how can they trust and believe in me after that?" Moses did not stop pleading with God until God returned their souls to them. He asked for forgiveness on behalf of the Israelites for worshipping the calf, and God said not unless they kill themselves.

*Rabi'a b. Anas:* These were the seventy which Moses had chosen. They went ahead with him. When they heard the conversation between God and Moses they said: "We will not believe in you unless we see God openly" (2:55). They heard a sound and were struck by the thunder.

*Urwah b. Ruwaim:* Some of them were struck by thunder while the others watched. Then these were raised up while the others were struck by thunder.

*Suddi:* The people died and Moses stood crying. He called upon God saying: "Lord, what will I say to the Israelites when I come to them and the best of them have been destroyed?" God revealed to Moses that these seventy were among those who worshipped the calf. Then God revived them and they were living, the men looking at one another wondering how they were alive. They said: "Moses, pray to God for anything you ask he gives you. Ask him to make us prophets." So he prayed to God and God made them prophets, for that is his word: "Then we raised you up after your death" (2:56) but he made one letter precede and another go behind, changing it from "sent you as prophets" to "raised you up after death."

*Abd al-Rahman b. Zayd b. Aslam:* When Moses returned from the meeting with his Lord with the tablets on which the Torah had been written, he found the Israelites worshipping the calf. He commanded them to kill themselves and repent to God. He said: "On these tablets is the book of God which contain things God commands you to do and forbids you from doing." They said: "Who will take this on your word alone? Not until we see God openly, until we perceive God upon us saying: 'This is my book, take it.' Why does he not talk to us as he talks to you, Moses?" The anger of God came against them as thunder and all of them died together. Then God resurrected them after their death. Moses then said: "Take the book of God!" They said: "No." He said: "What has just happened to you?" They said: "We were dead and then we were living." Moses said again: "Take the book!" They said: "No." So God sent an angel who lifted the mountain over them, saying: "Do you know this?" They said: "It is Mount Sinai." The angel said: "Take the book of God or we will throw it down upon you." So they took the book of God as a covenant.

## Tabernacle

*People of the Book:* God commanded Moses to make a tent out of the wood of cedar, skin of cattle, and the wool of sheep. He commanded it to be ornamented with dyed silk, gold and silver. It had ten canopies, each one as tall as 28 cubits, with a width of four cubits. It had four doors and ropes of silk and dyed raw silk. Inside were shelves and slabs of gold and silver. In each corner were two doors, the outer door being big. The cover was of dyed silk. God also ordered the Ark to be made of cedar wood which was two-and-a-half cubits in length, two cubits in width, with a height of one-and-a-half cubits. It was gilded in pure gold inside and out. It had four rings on its four corners. On its lid it had Cherubim of gold. God ordered a table to be made out of cedar wood, two cubits long and a cubit and a half wide. It had edges and legs of gold. It had four rings of gold on each side. There was stitching of gold in the wood, something like pomegranates. They were to make a bowl and utensils for the table, and fashion a Menorah out of gold with six candle-holders of gold, three on each side with three lights on each candle-holder. This tabernacle was erected on the first day of their year, being the first day of al-Rabi'. The Ark of the Covenant was also assembled according to the description: "The Ark came to them, in which was the Presence from their Lord, the remains of what was left of the family of Moses and family of Aaron, born by angels. In this is a sign for you if you believe" (2:247).

*Ibn Kathir:* This is a simplification of what is written in the Torah. In it are their laws and the descriptions of their sacrifices and rites. In it is also that the Tabernacle was in existence before their worship of the Golden Calf which was before their coming to Jerusalem. It was for them like the Ka'bah in which and to which they prayed. They also made sacrifices there. When Moses entered, a pillar of cloud would descend upon its entrance. God would speak to Moses from this pillar of cloud, and he glowed while he talked with God. God gave him commands and prohibitions while standing on the Ark upright between the Cherubim.

While the Israelites were in the Wilderness of Wandering they prayed toward the Tabernacle. It was the direction of their prayer and their Ka'bah, and their prayer leader was Moses. His brother Aaron performed the sacrifices. When Aaron died, Moses caused this duty to pass to those who were close to their father, and it remained that way. When they arrived in Jerusalem they erected this Tabernacle on the Rock in Jerusalem, and used to pray toward it. When it was gone, they prayed toward its place, being the Rock. This was the direction of prayer of the prophets until the time of the Prophet Muhammad. The Prophet Muhammad prayed in this direction before the Hijrah, with the Ka'bah directly in front of him. After the Hijrah he ordered prayer toward Jerusalem for sixteen, or it is said seventeen, months. Then the direction of prayer was changed to the Ka'bah, which is Abraham's direction of prayer, in Sha'ban of year 2 in the time of the Afternoon prayer. It is also said it was changed at the time of the Noon prayer.

*Umar b. al-Khattab:* When the mosque of the Prophet was expanded, he said to all of those building it: "People, do not imitate them. Make it red or yellow."

*Ibn Abbas:* Do not ornament it as the Jews and Christians ornamented their places of worship.

## Twelve Springs from the Rock

**Q 7:160**  We divided them into twelve tribes of peoples and we revealed to Moses, when his people asked him for drink, to strike the rock with his rod. Twelve springs gushed from the rock. Each people knew its drinking place. We covered them with clouds and sent down to them the manna and quails: "Eat of the good things we provide you as sustenance." They did not wrong us but they only wronged themselves.

*Ibn Abbas:* God placed a square rock in the midst of the Israelites, and commanded Moses to strike it with his rod. Twelve springs gushed forth from it, three springs in each direction. Each tribe knew the spring from which to drink. Wherever they went they found this with them in the place where it first was.

*Atiyah al-Awfi:* God gave them a rock like the head of a bull. It was carried on a bull. When they stopped at a place, they would put it down, Moses would strike it with his rod, and twelve springs would gush forth. When they moved on, they carried it on a bull and abstained from water.

*Uthman b. Ata al-Khurasani, on the authority of his father:* The Israelites had a rock. Aaron would hold it and Moses would strike it with a rod.

*Qatadah:* It was a mountain-like rock from the mountain [Sinai]. They carried it with them until they stopped at a place, where Moses would strike it with his rod.

*Zamakhshari:* It is said that it was marble and one cubit by one cubit. It is said that it was like the head of a person. It is said that it was from Paradise and its length was ten cubits longer than the height of Moses. It had two boughs shining in the darkness. It was carried on a donkey. It is also said that it fell with Adam from Paradise and was passed down until it was deposited with Shuayb who gave it to Moses along with the rod. It is said that it is the rock upon which Moses put his clothes when he was bathing. Gabriel told him: "Lift up this rock. If you have the strength then there is a miracle in it for you." So Moses carried it in his nosebag.

*Hasan al-Basri:* Moses was not commanded only to strike the rock. This is apparent in the miracle. He would strike the rock with his rod and it would gush forth. Then he would strike it and it would dry up. The Israelites said: "Moses only does this when we thirst." Once God revealed to Moses to speak to the rock and then it gushed forth, but not to touch it with his rod so that they might believe.

## Entering the Holy Land

**Q 5:20**  When Moses said to his people: "My people, remember the blessings which God gave you, when he made prophets among you, made you kings, and gave you that which he had not given to anyone else in the worlds. **21** "My people, enter the holy land which God promised to you. Do not turn back or you will be overthrown as losers." **22** They said: "Moses, in this land are a people of giants. We will not enter it until they leave it. If they leave it, then we will enter." **23** Two of those who feared God and upon whom God had bestowed blessings said: "Enter at the gate. When you have entered it, you will overtake it. Put your trust in God if you are believers." **24** They said: "Moses, we will not enter it as long as they remain in it. Go, you and your Lord, and fight. We will be sitting here." **25** He [Moses] said: "My Lord, I have no control except over myself and my brother. Make a separation between us and this sinful people." **26** He [God] said: "It [the land] will be forbidden to them for forty years, and they will wander in the earth. Do not be troubled because of this sinful people."

*Ibn Kathir:* God commanded them to enter the holy land when they left Egypt, the land which was their inheritance from their father Israel. They were to battle the unbelieving Amalekites who were in it. But the Israelites shirked from fighting them, were weak, and nearsighted, so God cast them into the wilderness as a punishment.

*Ibn Abbas, Suddi and Ibn Zayd:* "Enter the holy land" refers to Jerusalem.

*Zajjaj and Farra:* The holy land refers to Damascus, Palestine and part of Jordan.

*Qatadah:* The holy land is Syria.

*Mujahid:* The holy land is the land of the Mountain [tur] and that which surrounds it.

*Tabarsi:* "The holy land which God promised to you" (5:21) refers to that which was written on the preserved tablets, the land that was for them. When Moses said: "My Lord, I have no control except over myself and my brother," (5:25) God revealed to him that they would wander in the earth for 40 years, and only he who did not disobey God in this would be excluded from the people. They remained in the Wilderness of Wandering for 40 years. There were 600,000 warriors whose clothes would not tear and which grew with them. God sent down the manna and quails. All of the representatives who had gone into the land died except for Joshua b. Nun and Caleb. The rest of them died but their offspring flourished and they went to war against Jericho and conquered it.

## Og

*Tabari:* God commanded them to journey to Jericho, in the land of Jerusalem [ard bayt al-maqdis]. They continued until they were near it, and Moses sent out twelve representatives, one from each of the tribes of the Israelites. They set out intending to bring news of the giants. One of the men from the giants, called Og, met them and took the twelve of them and put them in his belt. On his head was a load of wood. He went with them to his wife and said: "Look at these people who claim they intend to fight us." He flung them in front of her and said: "Should I grind them with my foot?" His wife said: "No, but free them so that they will report to their people what they saw." He did this and when the group left, they each said to one another: "If you tell the Israelites about the people here, they will forsake the prophet of God, but we can keep it secret and only tell the two prophets of God, and they will decide what to do." They all made a pact to keep it secret. Then they returned and ten of them broke the agreement, telling their brothers and fathers about what they had seen of Og. Two of them kept the secret, went to Moses and Aaron and gave them the news. This is when God said: "God made a covenant with the Israelites and we sent twelve representatives from among them" (5:12). Moses said to them: "My people, remember the blessings which God gave you, when he made prophets among you, made you kings" (5:20), each man ruling himself, his family, and his possessions. "My people, enter the holy land which God promised to you" (5:21), saying God commanded you to do it, "Do not turn back or you will be overthrown as losers" (5:21). They said, from what they had heard from the ten representatives: "In this land are a people of giants. We will not enter it until they leave it. If they leave it, then we will enter." Two of those who feared God and upon whom God had bestowed blessings (5:22–23) refers to the ones who had kept the secret, being Joshua b. Nun the servant of Moses and

Caleb b. Jephunneh, and it is also said Caleb b. Jephunneh, the brother-in-law of Moses. They said: "Enter at the gate." The Israelites said: "Moses, we will not enter it as long as they remain in it. Go, you and your Lord, and fight. We will be sitting here" (5:24). Moses was angry and called out: "My Lord, I have no control except over myself and my brother. Make a separation between us and this sinful people" (5:25). The impatience of Moses was Israel's impatience, for God said: "It [the land] will be forbidden to them for forty years, and they will wander in the earth" (5:26). When this wandering was cast upon them, Moses was regretful. His people who were obedient with him came and said to him: "What have you done to us, Moses?" When he was regretful, God revealed to him: "Do not grieve," that is, do not be sad about the people whom you called "sinful." So he was not sad.

*Nawf:* The height of Og was 800 cubits. The height of Moses was ten cubits and his rod was ten cubits. Moses jumped into the air ten cubits and hit Og, hitting his anklebone, and Og fell down dead. He was a bridge for the people to cross.

*Ibn Abbas:* The rod of Moses, his jump, and his height were each ten cubits. He hit the anklebone of Og and killed him. Og was a bridge for the people over the river. It is said that Og lived for 3000 years.

*Ibn Abbas:* The twelve representatives told Moses about the giants, that one of the giants named Og had seen them and taken them in his sleeve with some fruit which he was carrying from his garden. He brought them to the king and scattered them between his hands. He said to the king in amazement: "These people want to fight us." The king said: "Return to your master and tell him about us." Mujahid adds: "Say: it is not possible to carry their fruit. A bunch of their grapes would take five men with a trellis. Five men could fit inside the skin of half a pomegranate."

*Ibn Kathir:* There is consensus among the learned transmitters of reports that Og b. Anaq was killed by Moses. If he had killed him before the wandering, then the Israelites would not have feared the Amalekites. So this indicates that he killed him after the wandering. It is said: there is agreement that Balaam b. Beor [Ba'awra] was the tallest of the giants who called on Moses. The dead body of Og served as a bridge for the people to cross.

## Sin of Israelites and Moses

*Tabarsi:* It is said, concerning the request of Moses for a separation between himself and the Israelites, that there are two opinions. One of them, related on the authority of Ibn Abbas and Dahhak, is that he asked God to judge and make a decision concerning the disobedience of the Israelites which was the punishment of wandering. The other, given on the authority of Shuayb al-Jaba'i, is that he asked God to distinguish between him and them in the afterlife, that they would be in Hell and he and Aaron would be in Paradise. If he had asked God to destroy them, then they would have been destroyed.

*Tabarsi:* Many of the exegetes say that Moses and Aaron were with the Israelites in the Wilderness of Wandering. It is said also that both of them were not in the wilderness because the wandering was a punishment and they were punished one year for each day they worshipped the Golden Calf, and the prophets were not punished.

*Zajjaj:* When the Israelites were in wandering God allowed it to be easy on Moses and Aaron just as the fire was made easy on Abraham. He made it cold for them and peaceful. Moses died in the wilderness and Joshua who inherited leadership after Moses conquered the land. Joshua was the son of the brother of Moses. He inherited from Moses and was the prophet after him.

*Mujahid and Hasan al-Basri:* Moses did not die in the wilderness but he conquered the land.

*Qatadah:* None of the people entered the land of the giants except for Joshua b. Nun and Caleb b. Jephunneh, two months after the death of Moses. The children of Joshua and Caleb entered the land with the people.

*Ibn Kathir:* Moses called this punishment upon the Israelites because they refused to fight for God and enter the land. For a period of 40 years they were in the Wilderness of Wandering, constantly on the move with no guidance to leave the wilderness. There were many amazing and unusual things including their being covered with the cloud, the sending down of the manna and quail, and the flowing of the water from the massive rock which they carried around with them on an animal. When Moses hit it with his rod twelve springs would gush forth, one flowing for each tribe. There were other miracles by which God helped Moses b. Imran. There the Torah was revealed and the laws made for the Israelites. They built the Tent of Meeting, called the "Tent of Time" [qubba al-zaman]. Aaron died and then 30 years after him Moses died. God established Joshua b. Nun as a prophet among the Israelites, as a successor to Moses b. Imran. Most of the Israelites died there during that time. It is said that none of them remained except for Joshua and Caleb and those who were their descendants.

## People of Moses

**Q 7:159**  Of the people of Moses there is a group who are guided by the truth and act justly according to it.

## Jabars and Jabalq

*Yaqut:* Jabars is a city in the extreme east. The Jews say: The offspring of Moses fled there during the war of Saul or the war of Nebuchadnezzar. God caused them to travel there and caused them to settle in that place. No one joined them there, and they are the remnants of those who submitted to God. The land was folded for them, and the night and the day were made equal for them until they ended up at Jabars, where they settled. No one but God knows their number. Once, when one of the Jews went to them, they killed him. They said: "You may not join us, for you have corrupted your customs." Therefore they considered it lawful to shed his blood for this. Non-Jews mention that the people of Jabars are the remnants of the believers from Thamud, and in Jabalq are the remnants of the believers of the people of Ad.

*Ibn Abbas:* Jabalq is a city in the extreme west. Its people are the descendants of Ad. The people of Jabars are the descendants of Thamud. In each of the two cities are the remnants of the children of Moses, each one from both of the two communities.

## Beyond China

*Qurtubi:* These are the people beyond China, beyond the river of sand, who worship God in truth and justice, who believe in Muhammad, renounce the Sabbath, and face our direction of prayer. No one of them has come to us, and none of us to them. It is related that when the conflict took place after Moses, there was a group of the Israelites who followed the truth. They were not able to remain in the midst of the Israelites, so God took them out to an edge of his earth, in seclusion from creation. He made for them a subterranean passage in the earth and they walked in it for a year and a half until they came out beyond China. They follow the truth until now. Between humanity and them is a sea because of which people cannot reach them.

*Ibn Jurayj:* This refers to the Israelites when they killed their prophets and disbelieved. They were twelve tribes. One of the tribes was absolved from what the others did, and they were excused from punishment. They asked God to make a division between themselves and the others. God opened a tunnel for them in the earth and they traveled in it until they came out beyond China. There they were Muslims before Islam who prayed toward our direction of prayer.

## Beyond Spain

*Sha'bi:* The servants of God were beyond Spain the same distance it is between us and Spain. Their pebbles are pearls and sapphires, their mountains are gold and silver. They do not grow food, harvest, nor know how to work. They have a tree outside of their doors on which are broad leaves which are used as their clothing, and a tree at their doors on which is fruit from which they eat.

## Followers of Moses

*Qazwini:* Gabriel said to the Prophet Muhammad: "Between you and between them is a journey of six years going and six years returning. Between you and them is a river of sand which flows like arrows, and it stops only on the Sabbath. But ask your Lord." So the Prophet Muhammad called upon God and Gabriel protected him. God revealed to Gabriel to give the Prophet Muhammad what he asked. So he rode on Buraq and went step by step. When he was before the people, he greeted them and they asked: "Who are you?" He replied: "I am the Gentile Prophet." They said: "Yes, you are the one about whom Moses spoke, that your community, had they not sinned, would have reached the angels."

The Prophet Muhammad said: "I saw their graves at the doors of their houses and I asked them: Why is this?" They said: "So that we will be reminded of death in the morning and evening. If we did not do this, then we would only be reminded from time to time." The Prophet Muhammad asked: "Why are all your buildings equal?" They said: "So that we would not honor some over others, so that some of us would not block the view of others." The Prophet Muhammad asked: "Why do I not see among you any authority or judges?" They said:

"Should we divide some of us over others of us? We give the truth ourselves, so there is no need for one of us to enforce justice among ourselves." The Prophet Muhammad asked: "Why are your shops empty?" They said: "We grow everything and harvest everything. Each man takes from us what is sufficient and gives what remains to his brother." The Prophet Muhammad asked: "Why did I see some of your community laughing?" They said: "Because one of them has died." He asked: "So why are they laughing?" They said: "Out of joy because he was taken by God's unity." The Prophet Muhammad asked: "What are those people crying about?" They said: "A child was born to them and they do not know which religion it will take." He asked: "When a male child is born to you, what do you do?" They said: "We fast for God for a month out of thanks." He asked: "And if a female child is born to you?" They said: "We fast for God for two months out of thanks because Moses told us that the perseverance of a female is a greater reward than the perseverance of a male." The Prophet Muhammad asked: "Do any of you fornicate?" They said: "If anyone were to do that, the sky would rain down upon him from above, and the ground sink from under him." The Prophet Muhammad asked: "Do you practice usury?" They said: "The one who practices usury is the one who does not trust in the sustenance of God." The Prophet Muhammad asked: "Do you get sick?" They said: "We do not sin and do not get sick. If your community gets sick, then it is an expiation for their sins." The Prophet Muhammad asked: "Do you have predatory animals?" They said: "Yes, they pass us by and we pass by them but they do not harm us."

## Cow Sacrifice

**Q 2:67** When Moses said to his people: "God commands you to sacrifice a cow." They said: "Do you take us for fools?" He said: "I take refuge in God from being one of the ignorant." **68** They said: "Ask your Lord to distinguish for us what cow it is." He said: "He says that it is a cow not too old and not too young but of an age between these. Do what you are commanded." **69** They said: "Ask your Lord to distinguish for us the color of the cow." He said: "He says that it is a yellow cow, all of the same color, fine to those who see it." **70** They said: "Ask your Lord for us to distinguish for us which cow it is. All cows are similar to us and we are seeking guidance, if God wills." **71** He said: "He says: a cow not yoked to till the earth nor water the fields, whole and without blemish." They said: "Now you bring the truth." Then they sacrificed it but almost did not do it. **72** When you killed a person and you disputed concerning it but God brought forth what you were hiding. **73** We said: "Hit the body with a piece of the cow." Thus God brings the dead to life and shows you his signs so that you might understand.

## Red Cow

*Ibn Abbas:* There was an Israelite man with a lot of money. He was an old man, and had nephews who wanted him to die so that they could inherit from him. One of them intentionally killed him during the night and flung his body in the middle of an intersection. It is also said that he put the body at the door of another man. When morning came the people disputed with one another about this. The nephew of the dead man came and began to cry. The people said: "Why do you dispute among yourselves? Why not go and get the prophet of God?" So the nephew went and complained about this matter of his uncle to the prophet of God. Moses said: "God requests that the man with know-ledge of this killing come forth or else we will make his identity known." Not one of them knew about it, so they asked him to seek judgment from his Lord.

Moses asked his Lord about this and God commanded them to sacrifice a cow: "God commands you to sacrifice a cow." They said: "Do you take us for fools?" meaning "We ask you about this killing and you tell us this." If they had taken any cow and sacrificed it, it would have sufficed, but they made it difficult, so God made the task more difficult for them. They asked about its description, its color, and its age, so God made these things incumbent upon them.

Moses commanded them from God to hit the dead man with a piece of the cow. It is said that it was with the meat, that it was the bone attached to the cartilage, or with the meat which is between the shoulders. When they hit him with it, God resurrected him. He got up and Moses asked: "Who killed you?" He said: "My nephew killed me." Then he returned to being dead just as he was.

## City by the Sea

**Q 7:163** Ask them about the district which was settled by the sea, when they transgressed the Sabbath, for their fish would come to them openly on their Sabbath but when it was not the Sabbath the fish would not come. Thus did we try them, for they were sinners. **164** When a group from among them said: "Why do you preach to a people whom God will destroy or punish with a severe punish-ment?" They said: "Out of duty to your Lord, and perhaps they will fear him." **165** When they forgot what had been mentioned about it, we saved those who forbade evil but we took those who were doing wrong with a harsh punishment, for they were sinners. **166** When they were insolent in doing that which was forbidden, we said to them: "Be apes, despised."

**Q 2:65**  You knew about those from among you who transgressed the Sabbath. We said to them: "Be apes, despised."

**Q 5:78**  Those Israelites who disbelieved were cursed by the tongue of David and Jesus son of Mary, for they were disobeying and transgressing.

*Qurtubi:* This means for the Prophet Muhammad to ask the Jews about who they [the people of the city by the sea] were, their forefathers and how God changed them into apes and pigs. This was a mark of the truth of the Prophet Muhammad since God instructed him in these matters about which he had not studied. The Jews used to say: "We are the children of God and his most beloved because we are from the descendants of Abraham, Israel, Moses and the descendants of Ezra. We are their children." God said to the Prophet Muhammad: "Ask them, Muhammad, about the city, as to its punishment."

*Malik b. Anas:* The fish used to come to them on the Sabbath, and when it was evening they left and nothing was seen of them until the next Sabbath. On account of this, a man from among them took a sewn cloth and a peg and then trapped one of the fish in the water on the Sabbath until the Sabbath had passed into the night of Sunday. Then he took the fish and roasted it. The people discovered its smell and came to him and asked him about this, but he turned them away. They did not stop pestering him until he said to them: "This is the skin of a fish which we found." On the next Sabbath he did the same, and when the day passed and it was the night of Sunday, he took it and roasted it. The people discovered the smell and came to him. He said to them: "If you want, construct something as I have." They said: "What have you constructed?" So he told them and they did as he had done until there were many like this. Their city had outskirts which were closed, and then the transformation hit them. Their neighbors, which were from the areas around them, came to them the next day and asked about them but did not find people. They found the city closed to them. They called but no one answered, so they built a fence around the city. As for them being apes, he made apes out of them, transforming them.

*Qurtubi:* There is disagreement regarding the identification of this city. Ibn Abbas, Ikrimah, and Suddi say it is Eilat. On the authority of Ibn Abbas also, it is said that it is Midian, between Eilat and Mount Sinai. Zuhri says Tiberias. Qatadah and Zayd b. Aslam say it is one of the littoral cities of Syria between Midian and Aynun. It is also said to be Maqnah. The Jews used to keep secret this tale because what was in it was a disgrace to them.

*Tabari:* The city is located between Egypt and Medina.

*Ibn Kathir:* This city is Eilat and it is on the shore of the Red Sea.

*Ibn Yazid:* The city is called Muntana, located between Midian and Aynun.

*Husayn b. al-Fadl:* It is related concerning the story in this verse that it took place in the time of David, that Iblis appeared to the people and said: "You are only forbidden from taking the fish on the Sabbath, so therefore make some sort of an enclosure. When the fish swim into the enclosure on Friday, they will remain in it and will not be able to escape because of the paucity of water." Then the people took the fish on Sunday.

*Qurtubi:* There was a group of the Israelites who denounced the sin of hunting the fish and they were separate from the others and prohibited it. It is said that the ones who prohibited it said: "We will not dwell with you," so they partitioned the city. That day, the ones who forbade the fishing went into their meeting hall and did not come out at the request of anyone. When they emerged later they found that everyone else had been transformed into apes. Qatadah says the youths were changed into apes and the old people into pigs. Only those who forbade the practice survived. It is according to this that the Israelites broke into two groups.

*Prophet Muhammad:* Do not perpetuate what the Jews practiced, and thereby be transformed into something forbidden by God on account of artifices.

*Ibn Kathir:* God mentions the people of this city, that they became three groups. One group perpetuated the thing which was warned against because through artifice they hunted the fish on the Sabbath. Another group prohibited this and set themselves apart. A third group kept silent and did not do anything wrong nor prohibit others from doing wrong, but they were punished along with the first group.

*Ikrimah:* I came to Ibn Abbas one day and he was crying. His Quran was in its holder. He did not stop crying until I brought the book and sat. I said: "What are you crying about, Ibn Abbas? May God allow me to help." He said: "These pages in Surah al-A'raf (Q 7). Do you know Eilat?" I said: "Yes." He said: "In it Jews were living and fish would swim to them on the Sabbath, then they would submerge and they would not be able to reach them unless they would dive after them. They used to come to them on the day of their Sabbath openly with white bodies as though they were like milk being churned, struggling in the water. This went on for some time. Then Satan appeared to them and he said: 'It is merely prohibited that you eat the fish on the Sabbath,' so they took them and ate them on another day. It was said that a group of them said: 'You are prohibited from eating them on the Sabbath,' so instead they caught them on the Sabbath but ate them on another day."

*Ibn Abbas:* God had made incumbent on the Israelites a day on which to worship him and refrain from work on account of him on this day. This was Monday. Some evil people changed the day from Monday to Saturday. They said: "It is Saturday." Moses forbade them, but they disagreed with him, so he made Saturday incumbent on them as the Sabbath. He forbade them to work on it and to transgress on it. A man from among them went to gather wood, so Moses took him aside and asked him: "Were you commanded to do this by someone?" He did not find anyone who had commanded him, so his followers stoned him.

## Curse

*Tabari:* God is speaking to his prophet Muhammad: Say to those Christians who describe God in their own image: "Do not exaggerate and make up lies concerning Christ, that which is not true. It is not a lie, the story about the Jews who were cursed by God on account of his prophets and his apostles, David and Jesus son of Mary."

*Ibn Abbas:* They were cursed in the Gospel by the tongue of Jesus son of Mary and they were cursed in the Psalms by the tongue of David.

*Ibn Abbas:* They mixed themselves, after this was forbidden, with their neighbors. God struck the hearts of some of them with others of them. They were cursed by the tongue of David and Jesus son of Mary.

*Mujahid:* They were cursed by the tongue of David and became apes. They were cursed by the tongue of Jesus and became pigs.

*Ibn Abbas:* With every tongue were the disbelieving Israelites cursed: by the covenant of Moses in the Torah, by the covenant of David in the Psalms, by the covenant of Jesus in the Gospel, and they were cursed by the tongue of Muhammad in the Quran.

*Ibn Jurayj:* They were cursed by David's curse. David passed by a group of disbelieving Israelites and they were in the Temple. He said: "What was in the Temple?" They said: "Pigs." So he said: "God, make them pigs," and they were pigs. Then the curse of Jesus came upon them. Jesus said: "God, curse those who lie about me and about my mother. Make them into despised apes."

*Qatadah:* God cursed them with the tongue of David in his time and turned them into despised apes, and in the Gospel with the tongue of Jesus he turned them into pigs.

*Abu Malik:* "Those Israelites who disbelieved were cursed by the tongue of David" refers to those who were transformed by the tongue of David into apes and by the tongue of Jesus into pigs.

*Hasan al-Basri:* As for those who ate the fish, all of them suffered from indigestion from what they ate, and they were punished with a punishment in this world, and greater will be the suffering in the next world. By God, the killing of a believer is a serious thing according to God, judging from the punishment for eating fish.

*Bukhari:* Amr b. Maymun says he saw, in the period before Islam, a group of apes who stoned some other apes. He wrote down the report: "I saw, in the period before Islam, a group of apes who gathered together around other apes who had committed fornication, and stoned them, so I stoned them with them."

# Khidr and Dhu al-Qarnayn

**Q 18:60** When Moses said to his servant: "I will not stop until I reach the meeting place of the two waters, or I will continue forever." **61** When they reached the meeting place of the two waters, they forgot their fish. It took its way into the water by a passage. **62** When they passed onward, he [Moses] said to his servant: "Bring our lunch, for we have reached a stage in this journey of ours." **63** He [the servant] said: "Did you see, when we took refuge at the rock? I forgot the fish. I would not have forgotten to mention it except for Satan. It took its way into the water by a tunnel." **64** He [Moses] said: "This is what we were seeking." So they retraced their steps. **65** They found one of our [God's] servants to whom we had given mercy from us, and to whom we had taught knowledge from us. **66** Moses said to him: "May I follow you, on the condition that you teach me that right guidance you have been taught?" **67** He [the servant of God] said: "You will not be able to be patient with me. **68** "How can you be patient concerning that which your experience does not encompass?" **69** He [Moses] said: "You will find me patient, God willing. I will not disobey you in anything." **70** He [the servant of God] said: "If you follow me, then do not ask about anything until I speak something of it to you." **71** They set out and were riding on a boat when he [the servant of God] scuttled it. He [Moses] said: "Did you scuttle it in order to drown those on it? You have done something stupid." **72** He [the servant of God] said: "Did I not say that you would not be patient with me?" **73** He [Moses] said: "Do not blame me for what I forgot, nor oppress me with difficulty because of what I did." **74** They set out and met a boy when he [the servant of God] killed him. He [Moses] said: "Did you kill an innocent who has not killed anyone else? You have done something vile." **75** He [the servant of God] said: "Did I not say that you would not be patient with me?" **76** He [Moses] said: "If I ask you about anything after this, do not allow me to accompany you. You will have a good excuse from me." **77** They set out and came to the people of a city and asked this people for some food, but they [the people] refused them hospitality. They found in the city a wall which was about to fall down. He [the servant of God] set it up straight. He [Moses] said: "If you had wanted, you could have taken pay for that." **78** He [the servant of God] said: "This is the parting between you and me. I will tell you the interpretation of that about which you were not able to be patient. **79** "As for the boat, it belonged to poor people who worked the water, and I intended to damage it, for behind them was a king who was taking every boat by force. **80** "As for the boy, his parents were believers and feared that he would cause them difficulty through rebellion and disbelief. **81** "I intended that their Lord would give them a substitute, better than he [the first son] in purity and closer in mercy. **82** "As for the wall, it belonged to two orphan boys in the city. Under it was a treasure which belonged to them. Their father had been upright. Your Lord intended that they should reach maturity and then remove their treasure, a mercy from your Lord. I did not do it of my own accord. This is the interpretation of that about which you were not able to be patient."

## Khidr

*Ibn Hajar:* There is disagreement concerning the genealogy of Khidr, whether he was a prophet, how long he lived, and whether he remained alive until the time of the Prophet Muhammad and even after him. It is said that he was a son of Adam. This is the opinion related by Daraqutni, on the authority of Dahhak, from Ibn Abbas, but is considered weak since Dahhak did not transmit reports from Ibn Abbas. Another opinion is that he was the son of Cain. This is mentioned by Abu Hatim on the authority of Abu Ubaydah. Wahb b. Munabbih says his name is Baliya b. Malikan b. Peleg b. Eber b. Shelah b. Arpachshad b. Shem b. Noah. This is also the opinion of Ibn Qutaybah. Nawawi relates the same thing but says "Kaliman" instead of "Malikan" as the name of his father. Ibn Qutaybah also relates the opinion that he was Ama'il b. Eliphaz [Yafaz] b. Esau b. Isaac. Ibn al-Kalbi, on the authority of Ibn Abbas, says that he was from the tribe of Aaron, the brother of Moses. This is far from the case. Even more strange is the opinion of Ibn Ishaq that he is Aramiyah b. Khulfiyah. Tabari rejects this. Muhammad b. Ayyub says he was the son of the daughter of the Pharaoh. Naqqash relates that he was the son of the Pharaoh. Muqatil b. Sulayman relates that he was Elisha but this is also far from the case. Abdallah b. Shawdhab says he was Persian. Tabari mentions this, and also the opinion that he was one of those who believed in Abraham and Hagar, and was with Abraham in Babylon. It is also said that his father was Persian and his mother Roman, or his father Roman and his mother Persian. It is established in Bukhari and Muslim that the reason for his name [i.e., "green"] is that he sat on a white fur and it turned green underneath him. The fur is symbolic of the dry earth. Ahmad b. Hanbal transmits this, on the authority of Abu Hurayrah with the explanation that the fur is dead grass.

*Tabari:* Khidr was among those in the days of Afridun the king, son of Athfiyan, according to the opinion of the majority of the People of the First Book, before Moses b. Imran. It is said that he was over the vanguard of Dhu al-Qarnayn the great, who was in the days of Abraham the friend of God. He was the one who passed judgment in favor of Abraham at Beersheba. It was a well Abraham had dug for his livestock in the desert of Jordan. A group of the people of Jordan claimed the land in which Abraham had dug his well. So Abraham brought them for judgment to Dhu al-Qarnayn, the one about whom it is mentioned that Khidr was over his vanguard during the days of his campaigns in the lands, that while with Dhu al-Qarnayn he came upon the river of life and drank from its water without knowing. Dhu al-Qarnayn and those with him did not know, but Khidr became immortal and he is alive until now.

*Ka'b al-Ahbar:* Khidr rode with a group of his companions until he reached the Indian Ocean, also called the China Sea. He said: "My companions, lower me in." So they lowered him into the sea for many days and nights, and then he came back out. They said to him: "Khidr, what did you see? How has God honored you and preserved you in this ocean?" He said: "One of the angels came to me and said: 'Human being, where are you from and to where are you going?' I said: 'I want to see the depth of this sea.' He said to me: 'How? A man from the time of David the prophet has already begun this descent and has not, to this hour, reached even a third of the way to the bottom. And this was 300 years ago.' "

*Tabari:* Some claim that Khidr was the offspring of someone who believed in Abraham, the friend of God, and followed him, according to his religion, and emigrated with him from the land of Babylon when Abraham emigrated from there. It is said that his father was a great king. Others say the Dhu al-Qarnayn who was in the time of Abraham was Afridun b. Athfiyan, and that Khidr was over his vanguard.

*Abdallah b. Shawdhab:* Khidr is from the offspring of Persia, and Elijah is from the Israelites. They meet every year during the annual festival.

*Ibn Ishaq:* God appointed to rule over the Israelites a man named Josiah b. Amon, and he sent Khidr to them as a prophet. The name of Khidr, according to what Wahb b. Munabbih claims, on the authority of the Israelites, was Jeremiah b. Hilkiah from the tribe of Aaron b. Imran.

## Status as Prophet

*Ibn Hajar:* It is our opinion that Khidr was a prophet, and there is no dispute in this, for how can someone who is not a prophet know more than a prophet? The Prophet Muhammad, related in a sound report, stated that God said to Moses: "No [you are not the most knowledgeable], but rather our servant Khidr." Likewise, how can a prophet follow someone who is not a prophet? There is some disagreement with those who claim he was a prophet with the objection that if he were a prophet, then to whom was he sent? Ibn Abbas and Wahb b. Munabbih say he was a prophet who was not sent. Ibn Ishaq and some of the People of the Book say he was sent to his people and they followed him.

*Abu Hayyan:* Most scholars hold that he was a prophet. His knowledge was gnosis of hidden things, while the knowledge of Moses was of external law. He is a saint to many Sufis.

*Abu al-Qasim al-Qushayri:* Khidr was not a prophet but was only a saint.

*Mawardi:* He was one of the angels who took human form.

*Abu al-Khattab b. Duhiyyah:* We do not know whether he was an angel, a prophet, or an upright servant of God.

## Khidr and Moses

*Tabari:* The opinion of those who say that Khidr was in the day of Afridun and Dhu al-Qarnayn the great, before Moses b. Imran, are more correct except for the opinion of him who says that he was over the vanguard of Dhu al-Qarnayn, the companion of Abraham, who drank the water of life. In this case, he would not have been sent as a prophet in the days of Abraham but during the days of Josiah b. Amon, because Josiah b. Amon, whom Ibn Ishaq mentioned as being king over the Israelites, was during the time of Bishtasb b. Luhrasb. Between Bishtasb and Afridun were eras and times about which there is no ignorance among those who know about the days of people and their history. The opinion of him who says that Khidr was before Moses b. Imran is closer to the truth than the opinion of Ibn Ishaq who related, on the authority of Wahb b. Munabbih, on account of the information which was related on the authority of the Prophet Muhammad by

Ubayy b. Ka'b, that the companion of Moses b. Imran, who was a learned person whom God commanded Moses to seek out when he thought that there was not one in the earth as knowledgeable as he, was Khidr. The Apostle of God was the most knowledgeable of God's creation regarding the being of things past and the being of things that have not yet happened.

*Fakhr al-Din al-Razi:* Most of the scholars hold that the Moses mentioned in these verses is Moses b. Imran, the one who performed signs before Pharaoh and to whom was revealed the Torah. This is on the authority of Sa'id b. Jubayr who said to Ibn Abbas that Nawf al-Bikali, son of the wife of Ka'b, alleges that Khidr was not the companion of Moses b. Imran. Ibn Abbas said: "The enemies of God lie." It is known that Joseph had two sons: Ephraim and Manasseh [Misha]. Ephraim begot Nun and Nun begot Joshua b. Nun. He is the companion of Moses, and he carried on his commission after his death. As for the son of Manasseh, it is said that prophethood came to him before Moses b. Imran. The people of the Torah allege that he is the one who was searching to be taught this knowledge, and that Khidr is the one who scuttled the ship, killed the boy, and fixed the wall, Moses b. Manasseh being with him. This is the opinion of most of the Jews.

*Ubayy b. Ka'b:* The Prophet Muhammad said: "Moses stood among the Israelites to deliver a speech. Someone said: 'Who is the most knowledgeable of people?' Moses said: 'I am.' God reproved him when he did not attribute knowledge to him. God said: 'No, I have a servant who is at the meeting place of the two waters.' Moses said: 'Lord, how can I find him?' God said: 'Take a fish and put it in a basket. When you miss it, he is there.' So Moses took a fish and put it in a basket. He said to his servant: 'When you miss this fish, tell me.' The two set out walking along the shore of the sea until they reached a rock. Moses rested and the fish stirred in the basket, got out, and went into the sea. God held the flow of the water so that it became like an archway, so that it became a passage for the fish. It was a wonder for Moses and his servant. Then they set out again.

"When it was time for breakfast, Moses said to his servant: 'Bring us our breakfast. We are tired from our journey'. Moses did not become tired until he passed where God had commanded him to stop. He said: 'Did you see, when we took refuge at the rock? I forgot the fish. I would not have forgotten to mention it except for Satan. It took its way into the water by a tunnel.' He said: 'This is what we were seeking.' They retraced their steps.

"They came to the rock and there was a man sleeping, covered in his clothes. Moses greeted him, and the man said: 'From whom does this greeting come in our land?' Moses said: 'Me, Moses.' The man said: 'Moses of the Israelites?' Moses said: 'Yes.' The man said: 'Moses, I have knowledge from God, knowledge which God taught me, not which you taught me. You have knowledge from the knowledge of God which God taught you, not which I taught you.'"

## Meeting Place of the Two Waters

*Ibn Kathir:* Qatadah and others say that one of the two waters is the Persian Sea [Indian Ocean] in the east, and the other is the Roman Sea [Mediterranean] in the west. Muhammad b. Ka'b says the meeting place of the two waters is in Tangiers, meaning in the farthest city in the west.

## Dhu al-Qarnayn

**Q 18:83** They ask you about Dhu al-Qarnayn. Say: "I will relate to you something of it." **84** We made him powerful in the earth and gave him ways to all things. **85** He followed a way. **86** When he reached the place where the sun sets he found it setting in a murky spring. He found with it a people. We said: "Dhu al-Qarnayn, either punish or be good to them." **87** He said: "As for the one who does wrong, we will punish him, then he will be returned to his Lord, and he will punish him with an indefinite punishment. **88** "As for the one who believes and acts upright, he deserves a good reward and we will say something easy from our command to him." **89** Then he followed a way. **90** When he reached the place where the sun rises he found it rising over a people for whom we had provided no cover other than the sun. **91** Like this, we understood the matter that was before him. **92** Then he followed a way. **93** When he reached the place between the two mountains, he found beneath them a people who could hardly understand a word. **94** They said: "Dhu al-Qarnayn, Gog and Magog are despoiling the earth. Should we give you tribute on the condition that you would build a barrier between us and them?" **95** He said: "The power with which my Lord has vested me is better. Help me with strength and I will make a dam between you and them. **96** "Bring me blocks of iron." When he had filled up the area between the two mountains he said: "Blow!" When he made it like fire he said: "Bring me iron so that I might pour molten lead over it." **97** They were not able to scale it or dig through it. **98** He said: "This is a mercy from my Lord. When the promise of my Lord comes, he will make it to be dust. The promise of my Lord is true." **99** On that day we will leave them to surge one upon the other. The trumpet will be blown and we will assemble them, all together. **100** On that day we will present Hell, all spread out, to the unbelievers, **101** those whose eyes were hidden from remembering me, who were unable to hear. **102** Do those who do not believe think that they can take my servants as protectors instead of me? We have prepared Hell as a resting place for the unbelievers.

## Name and Genealogy

*Ibn Ishaq:* Foreign sources claim that Dhu al-Qarnayn ["he of the two *qarns*"] was a man from Egypt whose name was Marzban b. Mardabah the Greek. He was a descendant of Javan b. Japeth b. Noah. Khalid b. Ma'dan al-Kala'i reports that when the Prophet Muhammad was asked about Dhu al-Qarnayn, he said: "He was a king who took the earth from its foundations by various means." Khalid said: Umar b. al-Khattab heard a man saying "Dhu al-Qarnayn." Umar said: "Oh God, forgive this. What favor do you have that you would call out the names of prophets, and eventually the names of angels?"

*Qurtubi:* Ali b. Abi Talib heard a man saying "Dhu al-Qarnayn." Ali said: "Is it enough that you call out the names of prophets, and eventually the names of angels?" According to him Dhu al-Qarnayn was the upright servant of a king, who advised him about God and aided him. It is said that he was a prophet sent to conquer the earth by God. Daraqutni says an angel named Rabaqil used to reveal things to Dhu al-Qarnayn. This angel is the one who will traverse the earth on the Day of Resurrection, and fasten the feet of all creatures by night. Suhayli says the angel was the one who watched over Dhu al-Qarnayn who traversed the earth from the east to the west. Others say that the angel was ruling over all of the other angels together, or that he was guardian over the other angels, ruling over the treasury of Hell. He used to come out and devour people and they were not able to escape from him.

*Qurtubi:* Ibn Hisham says his name was Alexander. He was the one who built Alexandria, so it was named after him. Ibn Hisham also says he was Sa'b b. Dhi Yazin al-Himyari, a descendant of Wa'il b. Himyar. Wahb b. Munabbih says he was Roman. Tabari mentions a report from the Prophet Muhammad that Dhu al-Qarnayn was a young man from Rome. Suhayli says: It is evident that there are two Dhu al-Qarnayns: One of them from the time of Abraham, who judged in favor of Abraham when there was a dispute over the well of Beersheba in Syria. The other of them is the one close to the time of Jesus. It is said that

Dhu al-Qarnayn is Afridun who killed Biwarasib b. Arundasib the king in the time of Abraham or before that time.

*Ibn Kathir:* Abu Zur'ah reports that Dhu al-Qarnayn was a prophet but that opinion is not supported. The second Alexander was from Rome. He was the son of Qaylays the Macedonian who lived in the time of Rome. The first one, mentioned by Azraqi and others, is the one who circumambulated the Ka'bah with Abraham. He and his vizier Khidr were the first to believe in Abraham and follow him. As for the second Alexander b. Qaylas the Macedonian, the Greek, his vizier was Aristotle the well-known philosopher. He is the one whose kingdom was near the time of the Romans but before Jesus Christ by about 300 years. It is the first who is mentioned in the Quran, in the time of Abraham. He circumambulated the Ka'bah with Abraham when he had first built it, and made a sacrifice there to God. Wahb b. Munabbih says he was a king who was named Dhu al-Qarnayn because the sides of his head were brass. He also says that some of the People of the Book say he was called this because he was king over Rome and Persia. Others say that there were things on his head resembling two horns [qarnayn]. Abu al-Tufayl asked Ali about Dhu al-Qarnayn. He said: "He was a sincere worshipper of God. He called his people to God but they hit him on his head [qarn]. He died but God resurrected him. Again he called his people to God and they hit him on his head, and he died. So he is called Dhu al-Qarnayn." It is also said that he is called Dhu al-Qarnayn because he reached the east and the west where the sun rises and sets. Some mention that he was called Dhu al-Qarnayn because he reached the two rims [qarnayn] of the sun in the east and the west.

*Abu al-Tufayl:* I heard Ali b. Abi Talib when a group asked him whether Dhu al-Qarnayn was a prophet. He said: "He was an upright worshipper who loved God and God loved him. He was sincere toward God and God was sincere toward him. God sent him to his people and they hit him on his head [qarn] twice, therefore he is called Dhu al-Qarnayn.

*Wahb b. Munabbih:* Dhu al-Qarnayn was a king. The People of the Book disagree concerning him. Some of them say he was the king of Rome and Persia. Others say that on his head were things resembling horns. Others say that he was called this because the two sides of his head were of brass.

*Qurtubi:* As for the difference of opinion concerning the reason for his being named Dhu al-Qarnayn, it is said: that he had two braids in his hair. It is also mentioned that the two braids were like horns on his head. It is said that at the beginning of his reign he looked as though he was Egyptian with the disks of the sun, and it was explained that the sun would rise and set upon him, so they called him Dhu al-Qarnayn. It is said that he was called this because he reached the east and the west as if he had passed beyond the rims of this world. A group of people say that when he reached the rising place of the sun a vision was revealed of the sun's horns, so he was called Dhu al-Qarnayn. Wahb b. Munabbih says he had two horns under his turban.

*Ibn Kathir:* It is reported that a group of disbelievers from Mecca sent for a group of Jews to ask them to test the Prophet Muhammad, saying: "Ask him about the man who circumambulated the earth, about youth, and about the spirit." So God revealed Surah al-Kahf (Q 18).

*Tabari:* Uqbah b. Amir reports that a group of Jews came and asked the Prophet Muhammad about Dhu al-Qarnayn. So he told them that he was a young man from Rome, that he built Alexandria, that his kingship was exalted in the heavens, he went to the wall and saw the faces of the people who had faces like dogs.

*Qurtubi:* It is said that there were four kings of the whole world. Two were believers and two were disbelievers. The believers were Solomon b. David and Alexander. The disbelievers were Nimrod and Nebuchadnezzar.

## Travels

*Ibn Ishaq:* Dhu al-Qarnayn traveled different ways until he reached the ends of the earth in the east and the west. There was no place or people on earth over which Dhu al-Qarnayn did not exercise his authority, from the east to the west and beyond those.

*Ali b. Abi Talib:* God caused a cloud to appear for Dhu al-Qarnayn and prepared a way for him, and spread out for him fire. The night and the day were the same for him.

*Kashani:* Ali b. Abi Talib was asked about Dhu al-Qarnayn, how he was able to reach the east and the west. Ali said: "God gave him clouds and prepared for him ways, and spread out for him a light. The night and the day were equal." Other sources add that Ali said: "It was as if

Dhu al-Qarnayn were so near the sun that he could take it by its tip in the east and the west. When he narrated his vision to his people, he informed them and they called him Dhu al-Qarnayn. He called them to God and they turned to Islam."

*Tabarsi:* Ali b. Abi Talib said: God made clouds for Dhu al-Qarnayn's use and carried him on them. He stretched them out on the ways, and spread out for him the light. The night and the day were equal for him.

*Mujahid:* He followed camps and roads between the east and the west. He followed ways in the earth.

*Ibn Kathir:* God gave him great power in the earth, all that came to kings including might, armies, and weapons of war. This was kingship over all of the earth from the east to the west. Other kings were servants to him. God caused all the ways, meaning roads, to be easy for Dhu al-Qarnayn to conquer all the climes, cities, and lands of the earth. According to Ibn Abbas, Mujahid, Sa'id b. Jubayr, Ikrimah, Suddi, Qatadah, and Dahhak: God gave Dhu al-Qarnayn knowledge. Qatadah says this was specifically knowledge of the lay of the earth and its landmarks. According to Abd al-Rahman b. Zayd God taught Dhu al-Qarnayn all the languages of the earth so that there was no people he conquered whose language he did not know.

## East

*Qatadah:* At the place where the sun rises Dhu al-Qarnayn found a people for whom God had provided no cover because in their land there were no mountains nor trees. They did not have the capacity to build and live in houses but they hid in the water and made tunnels. When the sun ceased to be upon them they came out to their way of life and their fields. These people are the Zanj.

*Hasan al-Basri:* When the sun rose over them the people took refuge in the water. When it set they came out and grazed just as cattle graze.

*Ibn Jurayj:* They had never built buildings nor had any been built for them, so when the sun rose they went into tunnels until the sun set, or they went into the sea. In this land there were no mountains. An army came to them once and the people said to them: "Do not be here when the sun rises." The army said: "We will not go until the sun rises. What is the big deal?" The people said: "These are corpses of the army upon whom the sun rose here, where they died." So the army left, hurrying away.

## Gog and Magog

*Ibn Abbas:* When Dhu al-Qarnayn reached the place between the two mountains, it was two mountains of rubble which were between Gog and Magog. The two mountains were Armenia and Azerbaijan.

*Wahb b. Munabbih:* Dhu al-Qarnayn was a man from Rome, the son of an old man with no other sons. His name was Alexander but he was called Dhu al-Qarnayn because the two sides of his head were of brass. When he reached maturity he became an upright worshipper. God said to him: "Dhu al-Qarnayn, I am sending you to the nations of the earth, nations of different languages, all the people of the earth. Among them are two nations between which is the length of the earth, and among them are two nations between which is the width of the earth. The nations in the middle of the earth include the Jinn, humans, and Gog and Magog. As for the two nations between which is the length of the earth: the nation at the setting place of the sun is called Nasik; the other nation at the rising place of the sun is called Mansik. As for the two nations between which is the width of the earth: the nation in the left quarter of the earth is called Hawil, and the other in the right quarter of the earth is called Tawil." When God said this, Dhu al-Qarnayn said to him: "God, you have called me to a great order of which no one but you is capable. Tell me about these nations to which you are sending me: with what strength can I best them, with what force can I outnumber them, with what scheme can I trick them, with what composure can I evaluate them, with what language can I speak to them, how can I understand their languages, with what hearing can I understand their speech, with what sight can I pierce them, by what proof can I contend with them, by what heart can I comprehend them, by what wisdom can I determine their matters, by what balance can I be just among them, by what steadfastness can I be patient with them, by what knowledge do I make connections among them, by what learning can I be certain of their matters, with which hand do I attack them, with which foot do I stomp them, by what acumen do I dispute them, with what army do I battle them, with what kindness do I treat them? Lord, I do not have any of these things I mention which will stand up to them, overpower them, or contain them. You are the Lord of mercy who does not commission someone who is not up to the task, for you are Merciful and Compassionate." God said: "I will give you the capacity to do what I ask. I will make your heart discerning so that it will encompass everything, and cause you to understand all things. I will spread your tongue so that you may speak everything, open your hearing so that you may hear everything, extend your sight so that you may perceive everything, settle your matters so that you are certain of everything, enumerate for you so that you will not forget anything, cause you to remember so that nothing escapes you, strengthen your back so that nothing breaks you, strengthen your base so that nothing reaches you, strengthen your heart so that nothing scares you. I will make fire and shade subservient to you, and gather them as one of your armies. The light will go before you and guide you, the darkness will conceal you from behind. I will strengthen your reasoning so that nothing will frighten you. I will make easy all that is in your hands so that you can conquer everything, strengthen your might so that you can attack everything, and clothe you with awe so that nothing will challenge you."

When this was said to him, he set out heading toward the nation which was at the setting place of the sun. When he reached them he found them gathered and so numerous that only God could count them, having strength and force which only God could overcome, with different languages, diverse passions, and various hearts. When he saw this, he tried to outnumber them with the darkness. He deployed three armies surrounding them, encompassing them from every direction, and pushed them back until they were gathered in one place. Then he sent the fire upon them and summoned them to God, to the worship of him. Some of them believed in him and some of them did not. He stood his ground to those who turned away from God and caused the darkness to come upon them. It entered their mouths, noses, ears, and stomachs, entered their houses, homes, covered above them, under them, and from every side. They rushed around in the darkness confused, and when they were worried that they would be destroyed in it, they called out to Dhu al-Qarnayn in one voice. He lifted the darkness from them, took them by force, and they accepted his summons to God. Dhu al-Qarnayn gathered a great army from the people of the west, and then set out leading them, the darkness pushing them from behind and guarding all around them, the fire in front of them leading and guiding them.

Dhu al-Qarnayn was heading in the direction of the southern part of the earth, intending to meet the nations in the southern quarter of the earth called Hawil. The people followed him, and when they reached the sea or water, the people built boats from small pieces of wood like sandals, putting them together in an hour. Then he put on the boats all of those nations and armies who were with him, and when they had crossed the rivers and seas each person would disassemble one part of the boat and taken it with him so that it was not too much to carry. They continued like this until they reached Hawil, and he did there as he had done in Nasik. When he was done there he continued to the east until he came to Mansik at the rising place of the sun. He did there and recruited an army there as he had done with the two previous nations. Then he turned toward the north of the earth intending to meet Tawil the nation which was opposite Hawil. They faced each other, between them being the width of the earth. When he arrived there he did there as he had done before, and recruited an army there as he had done before.

When he was finished there he set out for the nations which were in the middle of the earth, the Jinn, the remaining humans, and Gog and Magog. When he was on one of the roads which was bordering on the region of the Turks, close to the east, a nation of upright people said to him: "Dhu al-Qarnayn, between these two mountains are creatures of God. There are many who resemble people but most resemble beasts, eating grass, ravishing the domesticated and wild animals like predatory animals, eating all the vermin of the earth from the snake to the scorpion, and any creature of God which has life on the earth. There is nothing God created which grows as they do in one year nor increases as they increase nor multiplies as they multiply. If they have the time, according to what we see, their growth and multiplication will fill up the earth, no doubt. They will displace the people from the earth and despoil it. A year has not passed for us that we do not fear that we will be overtaken by them. We wait for the first of them to come upon us from between these two mountains. Should we give you tribute on the condition that you would build a barrier between us and them?" (18:94). He said: "The power with which my Lord has vested me is better. Help me with strength and I will make a dam between you and them (18:95). Bring me rocks, iron and brass while I go to their land and learn their learning and measure the distance between their two mountains."

Then he set out toward them and reached the midst of their land. He found them all of one size, male and female, reaching the height of half an average-sized man. They had claws in the place of nails on their hands, teeth like the teeth of predatory animals, strong palates like the palates of camels the movement of which could be heard when they ate like the movements of the cud of a camel or the gnawing of an old stallion or strong horse. They were hairy. There was hair on their bodies which protected them from the heat and cold. Each of them had two great ears: one of them hairy on the inside and outside, the other fuzzy on the inside and outside. Owing to the size of the ears, they clothe themselves with them, rolling up in one of them and spreading out the other, one in the summer and the other in the winter. There were not among them male or female who did not already know the appointed time at which they would die. This is because the males do not die until 1000 children issue from their loins and the females do not die until 1000 children issue from their wombs. When this happens they are certain of death. They are given for sustenance a sea serpent in the spring for which they pray when it is time, just as others pray for rain. One is thrown up for them each year and they eat it for the whole year until another like it comes out the next year. It feeds their multiplication and growth. When it rains, they are made fertile, they live and grow fat. The evidence of this is apparent on them. The women flow with milk and the men become lustful. When it does not rain they become barren and thin, the men abstain from sex, and the women change. They summon each other like pigeons and howl like dogs. They have sex whenever they meet, like beasts.

After Dhu al-Qarnayn saw this he set out back from the area between the two mountains. He measured the distance between them while he was still in the land bordering the land of the Turks near the rising place of the sun, and found it to be a distance of 100 parsangs. When be began his work he dug a hole until he reached water. Then he widened it to 50 parsangs, putting rocks into it, and coating it with brass which he melted down and cast over it so that it became like a tributary of the mountain which is beneath the earth. He raised it, topped it with molten iron and brass, and made its supports from brass so that it became like a fine cloak from the yellow and red of the brass and the black of the iron. When he had finished and strengthened it he set off toward the community of people and Jinn.

While he was traveling he came to an upright community who were rightly guided by the truth and acted justly according to it. He found a fair, just community which shared among themselves equally, judged with justice, were kind and merciful, with one state of being, one speech, their natures similar, their ways straight, their hearts open, their lives good. Their graves were at the doors of their houses and there were no doors on their houses. They had no leaders over them nor did they have judges, riches, kings, or nobles. They did not contend with one another, fight, disagree, have droughts or become stressed. The plagues which befell other people did not befall them. They had longer lives than other people, had no poor or needy among them, nor coarse or rude people. When Dhu al-Qarnayn saw their condition he was amazed at it, and said: "Tell me about yourselves, people, for I have traversed all of the earth from its deserts to its seas, from the east to the west, its fire and shade, and have not found anything like you." They said: "Indeed, ask us about whatever you want." He said: "Tell me, why are the graves of your dead at the doors to your houses?" They said: "Intentionally, we do this so that we might not forget death. Remembering, it will not go out of our hearts." He asked: "Why do the entrances of your houses have no doors?" They said: "There are no suspicious people among us, only trustworthy people." He said: "Why do you have no leaders over you?" They said: "We do not act unjust." He said: "Why do you have no judges?" They said: "We do not litigate." He said: "Why do you not have rich people among you?" They said: "We do not seek to have more." He said: "Why do you not have kings?" They said: "We do not seek to be great." He said: "Why do you not disagree and fight?" They said: "Because of the kindness of our hearts and the uprightness that exists among us." He said: "Why do you not insult and battle one another?" They said: "Because we conquer our natures with resolve and rule ourselves with control." He said: "Why do you have a single speech, and your way is straight and level?" They said: "Because we do not lie nor deceive nor slander one another." He said: "Tell me, how did your hearts become similar and your lives become just?" They said: "Our chests are sound; on account of that dispute and envy are taken from our hearts." He said: "Why do you have no poor or needy among you?" They said: "Because we share among ourselves equally." He said: "Why do you have no coarse or rude among you?" They said: "Because of humility and meekness." He said: "What makes you live longer than other people?" They said: "Because we obey the truth and judge with justice." He said: "Why do you not have droughts?" They said: "We are not mindless of seeking forgiveness." He said: "Why do you not become stressed?" They said: "Because we prepare ourselves for affliction, desire and want, and are free from it." He said: "Why do plagues not befall you as they befall other people?" They said: "We trust only in God, and do not do astrology." He said: "Tell me, is this what you found your forefathers doing?" They said: "Yes, we found our forefathers being merciful to their poor, caring for their needy, forgiving the one who sinned against them, being charitable to the one who was distressed with them, seeking the forgiveness of the one whom they wronged, preserving the times of their prayers, fulfilling their obligations, keeping their promises, not hating their equals nor rejecting their relatives. So God was just with them because of their conduct. He preserved them while they were living and preserves them in their afterlife."

*Abu Saʿid al-Khudri:* I heard the Prophet Muhammad saying: "God, and Magog will break open and come forth upon the people just as the word of God says. From every elevation they will procreate and cover the earth. The Muslims will withdraw from them to their cities and fortresses. They will harvest their livestock and drink the water of the earth. They will pass by the river and drink from it until it is dry. After them a person will pass by this river saying there once was water here. There will not be left a single person who did not withdraw to a castle or city. One of them will say: 'We are finished with these people of the earth. The people of heaven remain.' Then one of them will ready his spear and throw it into heaven, and it will return to him bloody because of the affliction and rebellion. During this time God will send worms into their necks like borers. They will go into their necks and morning will find them dead, not a hiss being heard from them. The Muslims will say: 'Is there a man who will risk himself for us to see what the enemy is doing?' A man from among them will volunteer for this, thinking that he is already dead. He will go out and find them all dead, one on top of the other. He will cry: 'Company of Muslims, spread the good news, God has saved you from your enemy.' They will come out of their cities and fortresses, their livestock will walk freely, with no shepherd but their own flesh."

## Dhu al-Qarnayn and Abraham

*Tabari:* Dhu al-Qarnayn was the one who passed judgment in favor of Abraham at Beersheba. It was a well Abraham had dug for his livestock in the desert of Jordan. A group of the people of Jordan claimed the land in which Abraham had dug his well. So Abraham brought them for judgment to Dhu al-Qarnayn.

*Ibn Kathir:* Dhu al-Qarnayn came to Mecca and found Abraham and Ishmael building the foundations of the Ka'bah from five mountains. He said: "What are you doing?" Abraham replied: "We have been commanded to build this Ka'bah." Dhu al-Qarnayn said: "Then prove it." So five sheep stood up and said: "We bear witness that Abraham and Ishmael are the two who have been commanded to build this Ka'bah." Dhu al-Qarnayn then said: "I am satisfied." And he then joined Abraham in circumambulating the Ka'bah.

# Aaron and Joshua

**Q 5:26** He [God] said: "It [the land] will be forbidden to them for forty years, and they will wander in the earth. Do not be troubled because of this sinful people."

### Aaron

*Ibn Kathir:* The majority of the scholars agree that Aaron died in the Wilderness of Wandering about two years before Moses his brother. After him, Moses died in the Wilderness of Wandering also. He asked his Lord to let him be close to Jerusalem when he died.

*Suyuti:* It is said that Aaron favored his mother only or his father only and was taller than Moses, eloquent of speech, and died after Moses. He was born before Moses, though. In some of the reports of the Prophet Muhammad's Night Journey he is reported to have said: "I ascended into the fifth heaven where I saw Aaron. Half of his beard was white and half was black, and it almost reached his navel. I said: 'Gabriel, who is this?' He said: 'The beloved of his community: Aaron b. Imran.'" Ibn Miskawayh mentions that the meaning of Aaron in Hebrew is "beloved."

### Death of Aaron

*Suddi:* God revealed to Moses that he had prepared a resting-place for Aaron in such-and-such a mountain. So Moses and Aaron set out toward this mountain. When they were resting by a tree they saw a house unlike any they had seen before, within which was a fine bed and a pleasant scent. When Aaron saw this, he was amazed. He said: "Moses, I would love to sleep in that bed." So Moses told him to sleep in it. Aaron said: "But I am afraid that the lord of this house will come and be angry with me." Moses said: "Do not be afraid. The lord of this house prepared it for you, so sleep." Aaron said: "Moses, sleep with me. If the lord of the house comes, he will be angry with both of us together." So Moses slept and death took Aaron. When Aaron perceived this, he said: "Moses, you have cheated me." The house was raised up into the heavens, along with the tree and the bed.

When Moses returned to the Israelites and Aaron was not with him, they said: "Moses killed Aaron because he was jealous of Aaron's popularity." Moses said: "Aaron was my brother and my vizier, so how could I kill him?" Many of the Israelites gathered around him, so he prayed and called upon God. God caused the bed with Aaron on it to descend from the heavens so that all the Israelites could see it, and they believed Moses.

*Tha'labi:* Moses and Aaron died in the Wilderness of Wandering. Aaron died before Moses. They were both outside of the Wilderness of Wandering, by some caves, when Aaron died. Moses buried him and returned to the Israelites. They said: "Where is Aaron?" He said: "He died." They said: "You are lying. You killed him because of his popularity." Aaron was beloved among the Israelites. Moses turned to his Lord, and God revealed to him that he should take the Israelites to the tomb of Aaron. Moses took the Israelites to the tomb and called: "Aaron!" Aaron emerged from his tomb with dust on his head. Moses said to him: "Did I kill you?" Aaron said: "No, I died."

## Joshua

*Ibn Kathir:* He is Joshua b. Nun b. Ephraim b. Joseph b. Jacob b. Isaac b. Abraham. The People of the Book say he is Joshua, son of Ammihud. There is agreement among the People of the Book concerning his prophethood. The Samaritans, who reject the prophethood of anyone after Moses except for Joshua b. Nun, accept him because he is mentioned in the Torah.

*Ibn Ishaq:* Prophethood passed from Moses to Joshua at the end of the life of Moses. Moses met with Joshua and asked him what God had set down in the way of commands and prohibitions. Joshua said to Moses: "You who speaks with God, did I not ask you about what God revealed to you, everything you yourself told me, beginning with your meeting with him?" Because of this, Moses despised life and looked forward to death. This is because, until he died, Moses continued to receive revelations concerning commands and the law, and to speak with God about every circumstance.

*Tabarsi:* All of the representatives who had gone into the land died except for Joshua b. Nun and Caleb. The rest of them died but their offspring flourished and they went out to war against Jericho and conquered it. There is disagreement about who conquered it. It is said that Moses conquered it with Joshua ahead of him, and it is said that Joshua conquered it after the death of Moses. After Moses passed away God appointed Joshua as a prophet. It is reported that while they were fighting, the sun started to go down, so Joshua called upon God to keep the sun up until they conquered Jericho. It is also said that Moses and Aaron died in the Wilderness of Wandering, and that Aaron died a year before Moses. Moses was 120 years old, and Joshua was 126 years old. Joshua remained leader of the Israelites for 27 years after the passing of Moses.

## Conquest of the Land

**Q 2:58**   When we said: "Enter this district, eat from its plenty what you want. Enter the gate prostrated and saying: 'hittah.' We will forgive your sins and will increase those who do good." **59** Those among them who did wrong substituted a different word for what had been said to them. We sent a plague from the heavens against those who did wrong because they continued to be wicked.

**Q 7:161**   When it was said to them: "Inhabit this district, eat from it what you want, say 'hittah' and enter the gate prostrated. We will forgive you your sins and will increase those who do good." **162** Those among them who did wrong substituted a different word for what had been told to them. We sent a plague from the heavens against them because they continued to do wrong.

*Ibn Kathir:* The soundest opinion is that the district mentioned [2:58] is Jerusalem. This is the opinion of Suddi, Rabi'a b. Anas, Qatadah and others. Others say that it refers to Jericho. This is reported on the authority of Ibn Abbas and Abd al-Rahman b. Zayd. This opinion is off track because Jericho was not on their way and they were heading toward Jerusalem not Jericho. Even further off track is the opinion that it refers to Egypt. This happened when they left the wilderness after 40 years, under Joshua b. Nun. God opened the land for them, keeping the sun in the sky for more than a day until they were able to conquer it. When they had conquered it, they were commanded to enter the gate, the gate of the city, "prostrated," meaning thankful to God for the blessings he bestowed upon them in the conquest, victory, marking the return to their land, and their rescue from the wilderness and error.

*Ibn Abbas, Mujahid, Qatadah, Dahhak:* This was the "al-Hittah Gate," one of the gates of Jerusalem. It was the gate facing the direction of prayer.

*People of the Book:* The Jordan river was parted by the Israelites and they stopped in Jericho. It was the most fortified of the cities, with the highest of castles, and the most people. They surrounded it for six months. Then one day they blew horns and each man appeared to be a great force. The walls of the city fell, they entered and took all the livestock they found. They killed 12,000 men and women. They battled many kings. Joshua conquered 31 of the kings of Syria. They did this on Friday when the sun was about to set, and Saturday was about to begin, making it unlawful for them to fight. So Joshua said to the sun: "You are commanded and I am commanded. God, keep it from setting." So God prevented the sun from setting until they were able to conquer the city.

*Abu Hurayrah:* The Prophet Muhammad said: "The sun did not stand still for any human being except for Joshua on the night he entered Jerusalem."

*Ibn Kathir:* This saying of the Prophet Muhammad [that the sun did not stand still for anyone but Joshua] shows the weakness of the report that the sun remained in the sky until Ali b. Abi Talib performed the afternoon prayer.

*Ahmad b. Hanbal:* Abu Hurayrah reports that the Prophet Muhammad said: "One of the prophets set out on a campaign and said to his people: 'A man who has not yet consummated his marriage, a man who has built a house but not yet put a roof over it, and a man who has purchased sheep or pregnant camels and is waiting for their offspring, these men should not follow me.' He campaigned until he drew near to the city, at about the time of the afternoon prayer. He said to the sun: 'You are commanded and I am commanded. God, keep it from setting for some time.' So it was prevented from setting until God caused them to conquer the city. They gathered the booty and brought fire so that it might consume the booty, but it did not. This prophet said: 'Among you is dishonesty. Let one man from each tribe swear allegiance to me.' So they did so, and his hand stuck to the hand of one of the men. The prophet said: 'Among you is dishonesty. Let your tribe swear allegiance to me.' His tribe swore allegiance to him. His hand stuck to the hands of two or three of the tribe, and he said to them: 'You have taken some of the booty.' They brought out some booty which resembled a golden cow head and they placed it with the other booty. Then the fire came and consumed the booty. Booty was not lawful for anyone before us. God knew our weakness and so made it lawful for us [the Muslims]."

## Hittah

*Ibn Abbas:* "Hittah" means asking forgiveness.

*Ikrimah:* They were supposed to say "There is no god except God."

*Awza'i:* Ibn Abbas wrote to a man who had written to him asking about the expression "They said Hittah." He wrote to him that this means they acknowledged their sins.

*Prophet Muhammad:* It was said to the Israelites: "Enter the gate prostrated, saying 'Hittah.'" They entered crawling on their bottoms. They changed the expression and said instead: "A grain [hintah] in the hair."

*Ibn Masud:* Instead of saying "Hittah" they said: "A grain [hintah], a red grain in the hair." They said "Hatta [with soft "h"] saman-an azbat-an mazb-an" which in Arabic means: "A red grain [hintah] with which the black hair is pierced."

## Death of Joshua

*Ibn Kathir:* The Israelites settled in Jerusalem, and Joshua the prophet of God lived there and judged among them according to the Book of God, the Torah, until he was taken by God. He was 127 years old, thus he lived for 27 years after Moses.

# Elijah

**Q 37:123** Elijah was one of the messengers. **124** When he said to his people: "Do you not fear God? **125** "Will you call upon Baal and forsake the best of creators? **126** "God is your Lord and the Lord of your forefathers." **127** They rejected him. They are to be present [on Judgment Day] **128** except for the pure who worship God. **129** We left [this legacy] upon him in later times. **130** Peace to the family of Ya-Sin. **131** Thus do we reward those who do good. **132** He was one of our believing worshippers.

## Elijah

*Ibn Kathir:* Elijah b. Tishbi. It is also said he is Elijah b. Ya-Sin b. Phinehas b. Eleazar b. Aaron. It is also reported that Elijah and Khidr meet every year during the month of Ramadan in Jerusalem, that they perform the Pilgrimage together every year, and that they drink from Zamzam enough to keep them until the next year. It is also said that they meet in ʿArafat each year.

*Suyuti:* Ibn Ishaq says that Elijah is son of Ya-Sin b. Phinehas b. Eleazar b. Aaron the brother of Moses b. Imran. Ibn Asakir says Ibn Qutaybah related that he was of the tribe of Joshua. Wahb b. Munabbih says he lives as long as Khidr lives, which means he remains until the end of time. Ibn Masud says that Elijah is Idris, and he is coming soon. Elijah is a Hebrew name.

*Ibn Saʿd:* The first prophet sent was Idris, then Noah, then Abraham, then Ishmael and Isaac, then Jacob, then Joseph, then Lot, then Hud, then Salih, then Shuayb, then Moses and Aaron the sons of Imran, then Elijah the Tishbi, son of Eleazar b. Aaron b. Imran b. Kohath [Fahth] b. Levi b. Jacob b. Isaac b. Abraham.

*Kaʿb al-Ahbar:* Four prophets are still living, two of which are on the earth: Elijah and Khidr, and two in heaven: Idris and Jesus.

## Elijah's Mission

*Ibn Kathir:* It is said that Elijah was sent to the people of Baalbek, west of Damascus. He summoned them to God, to leave the worship of their idol which they called "Baal." It is also said that Baal was the name of a woman. But the people rejected him and sought to kill him, so he fled from them and hid.

*Ka'b al-Ahbar:* Elijah hid from the king of his people in a cave for ten years until the king died and another was appointed. Then Elijah came to him and presented himself. He converted 10,000 of the finest of his people and ordered them to kill the others.

*Some of the scholars from Damascus:* Elijah fled from his people, hiding in the cave of a mountain for twenty nights, or 40 nights, during which time ravens brought him his nourishment.

*Ibn Ishaq:* After God took Ezekiel, the sins of the Israelites became great. They forgot about the covenant God made with them to the extent that they set up idols and worshipped them instead of God. So God sent to them Elijah b. Ya-Sin b. Phinehas b. Eleazar b. Aaron b. Imran as a prophet. After Moses, the prophets were sent to Israel only to renew what the Israelites had forgotten from the Torah. Elijah was alive during the time of one of the kings of the Israelites called Ahab. The name of his wife was Jezebel. Ahab used to listen to Elijah and believe him, and Elijah would order his affairs. But the rest of the Israelites took an idol and worshipped it instead of God. It was called "Baal." Some scholars say that Baal was nothing but a woman they used to worship instead of God. Elijah started to call them to God but they would not heed anything from him unless it was from this king.

There were, at this time, kings scattered throughout the area, and each king had a region from which he would take tribute. The particular king the affairs of whom Elijah was keeping in order, the king who saw Elijah as rightly guided among all his companions, said to Elijah: "By God, I think that to which you are calling the people is invalid. By God, I do not think that so-and-so and so-and-so (enumerating the kings of the Israelites who had worshipped idols rather than God) are any different than we are, eating, drinking, enjoying themselves, ruling, not losing anything of this world on account of what you claim is invalid. We do not seem to have anything more than they do." It is alleged that Elijah recoiled, and the hair of his head and skin stood on end. Then he fled from the king, and the king did as his companions: worshipped idols and did what they did. Elijah said: "Oh God, the Israelites turn only to rejecting you and the worship of others beside you. Turn your favor away from them."

Elijah received a revelation: "We place the matter of their sustenance in your hands to the extent that you will be the one to decide about this." Elijah said: "Oh God, hold back the rain from them, keep it from them for three years until the beasts of burden, cattle, flying animals, and trees are destroyed; until the people have to struggle very hard." After Elijah called this upon the Israelites he hid himself from them. Wherever he was, sustenance was sent down to him. When people would find the smell of bread in a house they said: "Elijah has just entered that place." The people would seek out Elijah in that house and would persecute whoever was in the house. One night Elijah sought the shelter of an Israelite woman who had a son named Elisha b. Akhtub who was injured. The woman gave Elijah shelter and hid his being there, so Elijah prayed for her son and he was cured from the injury that afflicted him. Elisha followed Elijah, believed in him, took him to be truthful and clung to him, going with him wherever he went. Elijah was old and gray but Elisha was a young boy.

God revealed to Elijah: "You have destroyed many cattle, riding animals, birds, insects and trees which did not disobey me, in addition to the Israelites, the destruction of which I did not intend on account of the sins of the Israelites, by keeping back the rain from the Israelites." Elijah said: "My Lord, allow me to be the one to pray for this for them, me to be the one who brings them relief from this adversity which has afflicted them. Perhaps then they will return and renounce their worship of that which is other than you." It was said to him: "Yes." So Elijah went to the Israelites and said to them: "You have been destroyed, the cattle, riding animals, birds, insects and trees have been destroyed by your sins. You are under the influence of falsehood. If you want to know this, to know that God is angry with you because of this falsehood, to know that it is to the truth that I summon you, then bring out your idols which you worship and which you allege are better than that to which I summon you. If they answer you, then it is as you claim. If they do not do anything, then you will know that you are under the influence of falsehood and should abandon it. I will summon God and he will lift this affliction from you." They said: "You are being fair." So they brought out their idols and that by which they sought God, those things he did not accept. They prayed but the idols did not answer them nor did they lift from them that which afflicted them. So they realized that they were misled and worshipping false gods. Then they said to Elijah: "We are already destroyed. Pray to God on our behalf."

So Elijah prayed on their behalf to lift from them their affliction, that they be given rain. A cloud like the disk of the sun appeared over the surface of the sea by God's permission, while they were watching. Then the clouds were flung toward them and it became overcast. God sent rain and watered them. Their lands were revived, and the affliction was lifted from them. But they did not renounce their old ways nor return to God but continued in the worst of what they had been doing.

When Elijah saw their unbelief, he called upon his Lord to take him and give him rest from the Israelites. He was told: "Wait for such-and-such a day, then go out to such-and-such a city. Ride upon the thing that comes to you but do not fear it." So Elija went out, Elisha b. Akhtub with him, until he reached the city that was mentioned to him in the place that he was commanded. A horse of fire approached and stopped right before him. He jumped on it and it took off with him. Elisha called out: "Elijah, Elijah, what do you command me?" That was their final contact with him. God covered him with feathers and clothed him in fire, and stopped for him the need for the taste of food and drink. He flew with the angels and was part human, part angel, part earthly, part heavenly.

*Wahb b. Munabbih:* When Elijah called upon his Lord to take him from the Israelites who rejected him, a mount came to him the color of fire and he rode on it. God made him feathered and clothed him in fire. He stopped for him the need for the taste of food and drink, and he became part angel, part human, part heavenly, part earthly. He passed on his legacy to Elisha b. Akhtub.

*Anas b. Malik:* We were with the Prophet Muhammad, on a journey, when we stopped at a place and a man in the valley was saying: "Oh God, make me to be of the community of Muhammad." I went into the valley and when the man stood up he was more than 300 cubits tall. He said to me: "Who are you?" I said: "Anas b. Malik, servant of the Messenger of God." He said: "Where is he?" I said: "He is within hearing distance of your voice." He said: "Summon him so that I might greet him with peace. Say to him: 'Your brother Elijah greets you with peace.'" I went to the Prophet Muhammad and told him. He came and met the man and greeted him. Then the two sat down and began talking. Elijah said to him: "Messenger of God, I have not eaten in a year except for one day. This is the day of my breakfast; you and I are eating." Food descended from heaven upon them: bread, fish, and beans. They ate and gave me to eat as the evening arrived. Then he left and I saw him pass on a cloud toward the heavens.

*Wathilah b. al-Asqa:* The meeting between the Prophet Muhammad and Elijah happened during the campaign against Tabuk. Anas b. Malik and Hudhayfah b. al-Yaman were sent by Elijah to the Prophet Muhammad. They said: "The height of his body is two or three cubits." When the Prophet Muhammad met him they ate food from Paradise. Elijah said: "I eat only every four days." The food included bread, pomegranates, grapes, fresh dates, and bean sprouts. The Prophet Muhammad asked him about Khidr. He said: "My meeting with him is at the beginning of the year. If you should meet him before me, greet him with peace for me."

# Elisha

**Q 6:86** Ishmael, Elisha, Jonah, and Lot, all of whom we made more virtuous than the worlds.

**Q 38:48** Mention Ishmael, Elisha, and Dhu al-Kifl, all of them are among the chosen ones.

## Identity

*Suyuti:* Ibn Jubayr says he is son of Akhtub b. Eleazar. Some pronounce the name with two "l"s. It is a foreign name, but it is also said that it is Arabic, derived from a verb.

*Ibn Asakir:* Elisha was Asbat b. Adi b. Shuthelah [Shultam] b. Ephraim b. Joseph b. Jacob b. Isaac b. Abraham. It is also said that he was the nephew of Elijah, and that he was hiding out with Elijah in Mount Qasyun from the king of Baalbek. Then he went with Elijah to Baalbek and when Elijah was lifted up Elisha became God's prophet to his people after him.

*Wahb b. Munabbih:* Someone said that he was Asbat from Baniyas.

## Time of Elisha

*Ibn Ishaq:* After Elijah was Elisha. He was Elisha b. Akhtub. He remained as long as God wished him to remain, calling his people to God, adhering to the program of Elijah and his law until God took him. After him, among the Israelites there was dissension, great were their sins, many were the tyrants. They killed the prophets. Among them was the king 'Anid Tagh. It is said that he was the one whom Dhu al-Kifl guaranteed that if he repented and returned to God he would enter Paradise.

*Tabari:* It was a time of confusion among the Israelites. Great were their sins. They killed more and more prophets. God caused tyrants to oppress them as kings in the place of the prophets. They shed their blood. God also caused their enemies to rule over them. When they used to fight against one of their enemies, they would take with them the Ark of the Covenant which was in the Tent of Meeting. They would be victorious on account of its divine power because in it God had placed the Sakinah and the artifacts of what the families of Moses and Aaron had left behind. It was during one of these battles with the people of Gaza and Ashkelon that the Israelites were defeated, and the Ark was taken from their hands. When the king of the Israelites found out about this, his neck broke and he died of sorrow. The remaining Israelites were like sheep without a shepherd until God sent one of the prophets called Samuel. They asked him to establish a king over them so that they could fight their enemy. From the death of Joshua b. Nun to the sending of Samuel b. Bali was 460 years.

*Wahb b. Munabbih:* After Elijah, command over the Israelites was taken by Elisha. He was made a prophet among the Israelites after Elijah. He remained among them as long as God wanted him to be, then God took him. The people followed after one another and grew great again in their sins. They had the Ark of the Covenant handed down from one elder to the next. In it was the Sakinah and the artifacts of what the families of Moses and Aaron had left. They would meet no enemy while advancing with the Ark that God would not defeat. The Sakinah, according to one of the Israelite scholars, was the head of a dead cat. When it cried out in the Ark with the cry of a cat, victory was assured and conquest came to them.

# Ezekiel

**Q 2:243**  Did you not see those who went out from their homes, by the thousands, for fear of death? God said to them: "Die!" Then he resurrected them. God is full of bounty for people but most of the people are not thankful.

*Tabari:* There is agreement among the scholars that the one set up over the Israelites after Joshua was Caleb b. Jephunneh. Then Ezekiel b. Budhi came after him. He is the one called "Ibn al-Ajuz."

*Ibn Ishaq:* Ezekiel b. Budhi was called Ibn al-Azuj because his mother asked God for a son though she was already old and barren. God gave him to her and so he was called "son of the old woman" [Ibn al-Azuj]. He prayed for the people whom God mentioned in the Book [2:243].

*Wahb b. Munabbih:* A great misfortune afflicted the Israelites at that time. They complained about what afflicted them saying: "Would that we were already dead, and had rest from the affliction in which we are now." God revealed to Ezekiel: "Your people screamed from the affliction, alleging that they would rather die and be at rest. What rest is there for them in death? Do they think that I cannot raise them up again after death? Set out for the plain of such-and-such. There are 4000 of them there." These were the ones God mentioned [2:243] as having fled their homes. God said: "Get up and speak to them!" Their bones were already scattered, the birds and the beasts of prey having scattered them. Ezekiel cried out to them: "Crumbling bones, God commands you to assemble!" and the bones of each person assembled together. Then Ezekiel cried out a second time: "Bones, God commands you to be clothed with flesh!" and they were clothed with flesh, and after the flesh skin, and they became bodies. Then Ezekiel cried out a third time: "Spirits, God commands you to return to your bodies!" and they arose with God's permission and they praised God as one.

*Ibn Masud, on the authority of some of the Companions of the Prophet Muhammad:* In a city called Dawardan, just east of Wasit, a plague occurred. Most of the people fled and settled in an adjacent region. Most of those who remained in the city were destroyed but the others got away and not many of them died. When the plague lifted, these people returned to the city in safety. Those who remained said: "These companions of ours were more resolute than we were. If only we had done as they had done we would remain. If the plague occurs a second time, we will leave with them." A plague did occur in the next year and they fled, 30,000 of them, until they settled in a place which was an expansive valley. An angel called to them from the floor of the valley, and another from the top of it: "Die!" They died and were destroyed. Their bodies decayed.

A prophet named Ezekiel passed by and when he saw them he stopped and began to think about them. He twisted the corner of his mouth with his finger and God revealed to him: "Ezekiel, do you want me to show you how I will resurrect them?" He said: "Yes," thinking only that he would be amazed at the power of God over them. He was told: "Cry out!" So he cried out: "Bones, God commands you to assemble." The bones flew together one to another until they became skeletons. Then God told him to cry out: "Bones, God commands you to be clothed in flesh." They became clothed in flesh and blood, and the clothes in which they died. Then it was said to him: "Cry out!" So he cried out: "Bodies, God commands you to arise." They arose.

*Mujahid:* After being resurrected, these people said: "Praise you our Lord, praise you for there is no God other than you." They returned to their people living and knowing that they had been dead, with the pallor of death on their faces. Their garments became grubby like shrouds. Then they died at the times which had been appointed for them.

*Ibn Kathir:* Once when Umar b. al-Khattab was praying there were two Jews behind him. When Umar went to bow he left an open space and one of the two Jews said to the other: "Is it him?" When Umar finished he said: "What did the one of you mean to the other by: 'Is it him?'" They said: "We find in our book mention of a horn of iron which gave to Ezekiel the power that was given to him, who raised the dead by the permission of God." Umar said: "We do not find Ezekiel in our book and no one raised the dead by God's permission except for Jesus son of Mary." They said: "Do you not find the verse in the book of God: 'Messengers we have not told you about' (2:164)?" He said: "Of course." They said: "As for the resurrection of the dead, we will tell you that the Israelites were afflicted with a plague. A group of them left, and when they were a distance away God killed them, and the people built a wall over them. When their bones had decayed, God sent Ezekiel and he stood over them. He said: 'Whatever God wills.' God raised them for Ezekiel and God revealed concerning this: 'Did you not see those who went out from their homes, by the thousands, for fear of death?'" (2:243).

*Wahb b. Munabbih:* Caleb b. Jephunneh was taken by God after Joshua, and he appointed as successor over the Israelites Ezekiel b. Budhi who was Ibn al-Ajuz. He was the one who summoned the people whom God mentioned in the Book to Muhammad just as we received it.

*Ibn Ishaq:* It reached me that the people fled from outbreak of a plague or from a disease that afflicted the people, afraid of death, in the thousands. They stopped on an elevated part of the land and God said to them: "Die!" So all of them died. The people of that land built an enclosure to keep out predatory animals and then the people left the dead in the enclosure exposed because there were too many of them to cover. Ages passed and they became decayed bones. Ezekiel b. Budhi passed by them, stopped, and wondered about their condition. Mercy for them entered him and it was said to him: "Do you want God to resurrect them?" He said: "Yes." It was said to him: "Say: 'Rotted bones, that have rotted and decayed, return each bone to its companion.'" So he cried this out and watched the bones rush toward one another and assemble. Then it was said to him: "Say: 'Flesh, nerves, and skin, clothe the bones by God's permission.'" He said this and watched the nerves attach to the bones, then the flesh, skin and hair until creatures were completed but without souls. Then he prayed life for them and something from the heavens covered him and distressed him so that he fainted from it. He recovered and found the people sitting and saying: "Glory to God," for God had resurrected them.

*Ibn Abbas:* Umar b. al-Khattab set out for Syria and he met one of the soldiers of Abu Ubayda b. al-Jirah and his companion. They told him about a plague which had befallen Syria, so he mentioned the report concerning the deliberations of the Muhajirin and the Ansar: Abd al-Rahman b. Awf came to him while he was in seclusion. He said: "I have this knowledge which I heard from the Prophet Muhammad: 'When it is in the land and you are in it, do not go out fleeing from it. When you hear about it in the land, do not proceed.'" Then Umar praised God and he left.

*Abdallah b. Amir:* Abd al-Rahman b. Awf reported to Umar while he was in Syria, on the authority of the Prophet Muhammad, that this illness was a punishment for the nations before them: "When you hear about it in the land, do not enter the land. When it happens in the land and you are in the land, do not go out fleeing from it." Then Umar returned from Syria.

# Samuel and Saul

**Q 2:246** Did you not see the leaders of the Israelites, after Moses, when they said to their prophet: "Send us a king so that we might fight for God." He said: "Perhaps, if it is decreed for you to fight, you will not fight." They said: "What is there for us except to fight for God since we have been cast out from our homes and our sons?" When it was decreed for them to fight they refused except for a few of them. God knows those who do wrong. **247** Their prophet said to them: "God has sent Saul [Talut] to you as a king." They said: "How can he be a king when we have more right to kingship than he does? He has not been given an abundance of wealth." He [their prophet] said: "God has chosen him above you, and has added to his capabilities in knowledge and body. God gives kingship to whom he wishes." God is Encompassing, Knowing. **248** Their prophet said to them: "A sign of his kingship is that the Ark will come to you, in which is the Presence [Sakinah] of your Lord and the remains of what the family of Moses and the family of Aaron left behind, borne by angels. This is a sign for you, if you are believers." **249** When Saul left with the army, he said: "God will test you at the river. If a person drinks of it then he is not with me. If a person does not taste it, except for a hand-full, then he is with me." Except for a few, they drank from it. When they crossed it [the river], he [Saul] and those who believed with him, they said: "Today we do not have the force against Goliath and his army." Those who said that they would meet God said: "How many times has a small force conquered a big force by the permission of God. God is with those who are steadfast." **250** When they went out to compete against Goliath and his army they said: "Our Lord, pour patience upon us, keep firm our feet, and cause us to be victorious over the people who are unbelievers." **251** They routed them by the permission of God. David killed Goliath. God gave him kingship, wisdom, and taught him that which he wished. If God had not pushed back some of them with the others, then the earth would be spoiled. But God is Bountiful to the worlds.

## Samuel

*Ibn Kathir:* It is said that the prophet is Samuel b. Bali b. Elkanah [ʿAlqamah] b. Jeroham [Yarkham] b. Elihu [Eliyahu] b. Tohu [Tahu] b. Zuph [Suf]. Muqatil b. Sulayman says he was one of the descendants of Aaron. Mujahid says he was Samuel b. Halfaqa, but did not give his earlier forefathers.

*Ibn Abbas and Ibn Masud:* When the Amalekites conquered the land of Gaza and Ashkelon from the Israelites, killed many of them, and captured many of their sons, prophethood was cut off from the tribe of Levi, and none of the tribe was left except for a pregnant woman. She started asking God to give her a male child. She gave birth to a boy and named him Samuel. The meaning of the name in Hebrew is "Ishmael," that is, "God heard my prayer." When she had weaned him, she sent him to the mosque and he converted to Islam at the hands of an upright man. He stayed with him so that he could learn from his goodness and worship. Samuel was with this man when something came to him while he was sleeping in the night. A voice came from a corner of the mosque. He was afraid and he thought it was the old man calling him. So Samuel asked him: "Did you call me?" He did not want him to be alarmed so he told him: "Yes, now sleep." So he slept. Then the voice called a second time and a third time. It was Gabriel calling him. He came to him and said: "Your Lord has sent you to your people."

## Saul

*Thaʿlabi:* The king is Saul [Talut, "tall one"] b. Kish [Qaysh] b. Abiel [Aniyal] b. Zeror [Sirar] b. Becorath [Lahub] b. Aphiah [Afih] b. Aysh [Arish] b. Benjamin b. Jacob b. Isaac b. Abraham.

*Ikrimah and Suddi:* He was a water-carrier.

*Wahb b. Munabbih:* He was a tanner.

*Ibn Kathir:* It is mentioned that prophethood used to be with the tribe of Levi, and kingship was with the tribe of Judah. When Saul came from the tribe of Benjamin, they found this to be wrong and so refused his rule over them. They said: "We have more right to kingship than he does." They mentioned that he was poor without any extensive wealth, so how could one like him be king?

It is said that God revealed to Samuel that the Israelite who was taller than his rod would be the king. When he found him he was to anoint him with the holy oil from a particular horn, and he would be king. So he went about and measured everyone with this rod. He could not find anyone tall enough except for Saul. When he found him, he anointed him and made him king over the Israelites. It is said that Saul was great in battle, that he was tall, and that he was handsome.

## Ark of the Covenant

*Ibn Kathir:* Among the blessings of the appointment of this upright man as king over them was God's return of the Ark which had been captured from the Israelites by their enemies. They used to be victorious over their enemies because of it. It is said that the "Sakinah" was a basin of gold in which the hearts of the prophets were washed. It is also said that the "Sakinah" was like a spirit and that its voice was like a cat when it bellowed in times of war and ensured the victory of the Israelites. In the Ark were the pieces of the Tablets, and some of the manna which had come down upon the Israelites in the Wilderness of Wandering. Angels bore it to them, and they saw it with their own eyes as a sign from God and proof of the kingship of Saul.

It is also said that when the Amalekites had taken this Ark, in which were the Sakinah, the holy remains, and some say the Torah also, the Amalekites placed it under the idol which they had in their land. When they woke up in the morning the Ark was on the head of the idol, so they put it under the idol again. The next day the Ark was on top of the idol. When this had been repeated, they knew that God had done it. So they sent the Ark out of their cities and to one of their provinces. But a disease struck all of them. When this continued for a long time, they put the Ark on a cart and tied it to two oxen, sending them away. It is said that the angels gave water to the oxen until they came with the Ark to the leaders of the Israelites.

*Tabari:* There are different opinions as to what was in the Ark. Ibn Abbas, Qatadah, Suddi, Rabi', and Ikrimah say in it was the rod of Moses and the pieces of the Tablets. Abu Salih says it was the rod of Moses, the rod of Aaron, the two Tablets of the Torah, and manna. Atiyah b. Sa'd says it was the rod of Moses, the rod of Aaron, the clothes of Moses, the clothes of Aaron, and the pieces of the Tablets. Sufyan al-Thawri says it was the pieces of the Tablets and the shoes of Moses and Aaron. Ibn Abbas also says that when Moses threw the Tablets they broke, part of them was recalled, and he put the rest in the Ark. Ata b. Abi Rabah says the "remains" refers to knowledge and the Torah. Dahhak says that it refers to fighting for God. Because of the Ark the people fought alongside Saul as they had been commanded.

## Sakinah

*Tabari:* Ali b. Abi Talib says the Sakinah was a blowing wind with a face like the face of a man, and also that it had two heads. Mujahid says that Gabriel and the Sakinah guided Abraham from Syria. It had a head like the head of a cat, two wings, and a tail. Wahb b. Munabbih reports that some of the Israelites used to say the Sakinah had the head of a dead cat. It would screech from the Ark like a cat. Ibn Abbas says that the Sakinah was the basin of gold from Paradise in which the hearts of the prophets were washed. Suddi also says it was this basin, and that God gave it to Moses. He also says that with the Sakinah were the Tablets made of pearl, emerald, and crystal. Wahb b. Munabbih also says that the Sakinah was a spirit from God which talked. Whenever the Israelites disagreed about something it spoke and told them the solution. Rabi'a says that the Sakinah was mercy from God.

## River

*Ibn Abbas:* This river is the Jordan river. The command of Saul to his army at this river was a command of the prophet of God from God himself as a test. If a person drank from this river on that day, then he would not participate in this conquest. Only those who did not taste of it, except for a hand-full, would participate.

*Suddi:* The army was 80,000; 76,000 drank from the river, leaving 4000.

*Bukhari:* Bara b. 'Azib says that the companions of Muhammad used to say that the number of warriors at Badr was the same as the number of warriors who crossed the river with Saul. Only a small group of 310 believers crossed with him.

## Goliath

*Suddi:* It is related that David was the smallest of his father's sons. He was a boy of thirteen years old when he heard Saul the king of the Israelites calling the Israelites to fight Goliath and his army. Saul said: "To whomever kills Goliath I will marry my daughter and share with him my kingship." David used to sling pebbles and was very skilled in slinging. When he was with the Israelites a rock called to him: "Take me! With me you will kill Goliath." So he took it. Then another rock did likewise, and another. He took the three and put them into his bag. When the ranks faced off, Goliath came forward and called for someone to challenge him. David went forward and Goliath said: "I regret that I must kill you." David said: "But I look forward to killing you." He took the three stones, put them in his sling and the three stones became one. He slung it at Goliath and it split his head. Goliath's army fled defeated and Saul gave to David what he had promised, married his daughter to him and gave him dominion in his kingdom. David was great among the Israelites. They loved him, more than Saul.

## Saul and David

*Ibn Kathir:* It is said that Saul became jealous of David and wanted to kill him. He tried to do this but was not able to reach him. The scholars forbade Saul from killing David, so he became tyrannical and killed them until only a few of them remained. Then repentance came to him and he regretted what he had done previously. He began to cry, and went out to the cemetery and cried until the ground became wet from his tears. That day a voice called to him from the graves: "Saul, you killed us. We were alive, you harmed us, and now we are dead." This increased his crying and he became very afraid. So he wanted to ask a scholar about his situation, if he had been forgiven. It was said to him: "Have you left a scholar?" Finally he found a woman who took him to the tomb of Joshua. She called upon God and Joshua got up from his grave. He said: "Have I been raised on the Day of Resurrection?" She said: "No, but this is Saul who wants to ask you whether or not he has been forgiven." Joshua said: "Yes. He will be divested of his kingship, and go and fight for God until he dies." Then Joshua returned to being dead. So he left the kingship to David, and went with thirteen of his sons and fought for God until he died.

*Ibn Ishaq:* The prophet who was sent and told Saul about his repentance was Elisha b. Akhtub.

*Tha'labi:* Saul came to the tomb of Samuel, and Samuel scolded him for what he had done after his death.

*Tabari:* The People of the Torah allege that the period from the kingship of Saul to when he was killed with his sons was 40 years.

# David

*Ibn Kathir:* He is David b. Jesse b. Obed ['Awid] b. Bo'az ['Abar] b. Salmon b. Nahshon b. Amminadab [Uwaynadab] b. Aram b. Hezron b. Perez [Farid] b. Judah b. Jacob b. Isaac b. Abraham. He was a servant of God, his prophet, and his vicegerent [khalifah] in the land of Jerusalem.

*Wahb b. Munabbih:* David was small with blue eyes, short hair, a pure heart, and clean.

*Suyuti:* He is the son of Jesse b. Obed b. Bo'az [Ba'ar] b. Salmon b. Nahshon [Yakhshun] b. Amminadab ['Uma] b. Yarib b. Ram b. Hezron [Hadrun] b. Perez b. Judah b. Jacob. In Tirmidhi it is said that he was the most worshipful of all people. Ka'b al-Ahbar says: he had a red face, dark head, white body, and a long beard in which were curls. His voice and appearance were handsome. Prophethood and kingship were united in him. Nawawi says that the historians report that he lived 100 years, that the length of his reign was 40 years, and that he had twelve sons.

## David's Military Ability

**Q 2:251** They routed them by the permission of God. David killed Goliath. God gave him kingship, wisdom, and taught him that which he wished. If God had not pushed back some of them with the others, then the earth would be spoiled. But God is Bountiful to the worlds.

**Q 21:79** We made the mountains subservient to David, singing praises, along with the birds. We are the Doers. **80** We taught him the making of armor for you, so that we might guard you from your own harm. Will you be thankful?

**Q 34:10** We gave excellence from us to David. Mountains and birds echo with him. We made iron soft for him. **11** Make ample coats of mail with balanced perforations. Do what is upright. I have sight of what you make.

*Ibn Kathir:* The Israelites loved David and wanted him to be king over them. Saul ordered this to be so, giving the kingship to him. God united in David both kingship and prophethood, the best of this world and the next. Before him kingship had been vested in one tribe and prophethood in another, but they were brought together in David. It is reported that: "The ruler is the shadow of God on earth."

*Uthman b. Affan:* God establishes with rulers what he does not establish with the Quran.

*Ibn Kathir:* God taught David to make armor from iron to guard against battles with the enemy. God instructed him in its manufacture, and how to do it. It is established in a report: "It is best that a man eats from his earnings. David, the prophet of God, used to eat from the earnings of his hands."

*Hasan al-Basri and Qatadah:* God softened iron for David to the extent that he could work it by hand without need for fire or hammer. He was the first to make armor from chain mail. Before that, armor was made of sheet metal.

*Abdallah b. Shawdhab:* David used to make a suit of armor every day and sell it for 6000 dirhems.

## David's Piety

**Q 38:17** Remember our servant David, possessed of strength. He returned. **18** We made the mountains subservient to him, singing praises in the evening and dawn. **19** The birds assembled. On account of him, all returned. **20** We strengthened his kingship, and gave to him wisdom and sound termination of affairs.

*Ibn Abbas and Mujahid:* "Strength" (38:17) means strength in obedience to God, in worship and doing what is upright.

*Qatadah:* God gave him "strength" in worship and understanding in Islam. It was mentioned that he used to stand vigil all night and fast half of the time.

*Bukhari and Muslim:* The Prophet Muhammad said: "The most beloved prayer to God is the prayer of David. The most beloved fast to God is the fast of David. He used to sleep half the night, then keep vigil for another third of it, then sleep for another sixth. He used to fast for a day, then break the fast for a day. He did not flee when he met an enemy."

*Ibn Abbas:* David was a great faster. He was brave and never fled from facing enemies. He would fast a day and then not fast for a day. The Prophet Muhammad said: "The best fast is the fast of David. He used to recite the Psalms with 70 different voices which were in him. He used to perform bowings and prostrations in the night, crying to himself."

*Ibn Abbas:* David used to fast the first three days of the month, three days from the middle of the month, and the last three days of the month. He started the month with fasting, he spent the middle fasting, and he concluded it with fasting.

## David's Music

*Ibn Abbas and Mujahid:* God had given David a great voice unlike what he had given to anyone else. When he used to recite his book, the birds would stop in the air and reverberate with his song, praising with his praises. Likewise the mountains responded to him, singing praises with him, every morning and evening.

*Awza'i:* Abdallah b. Amir says that David was given an excellent voice unlike anything that had been given before. It was so excellent that the birds and the wild animals used to stay with him until they died of thirst and hunger.

*Wahb b. Munabbih:* Everyone who listened to him had to skip as if they were dancing. He used to recite the Psalms with a voice unlike any heard by ears. The Jinn, people, birds, and animals used to stay near him because of his voice, so long that some of them died from hunger.

*Aishah:* The Prophet Muhammad heard the voice of Abu Musa al-Ash'ari while he was reciting, and said: "Abu Musa has been gifted with one of the Psalms of the family of David."

*Ahmad b. Hanbal:* Abu Hurayrah says that the Prophet Muhammad said: "Recitation was made easy for David. He used to order his mount to be saddled and would recite the Quran before the saddle was on. He only ate from the work of his own hands."

## David's Wives

*Ibn Saʿd:* When the Jews saw that the Prophet Muhammad married more than one woman, they said: "Look at this one who is not satisfied by food, nor, by God, is anything important to him except for women." They were very envious of him because of his many wives, so they tried to shame him for this. They said: "If he were a prophet, he would not desire women." The strongest of them in saying this was Hayy b. Akhtab. But God proved Muhammad's prophethood to them. God revealed: "Or the people who are envious of what God brings to them of his grace" meaning the people envious of the Prophet Muhammad. And God revealed: "We gave to the family of Abraham the Book and wisdom. We gave them great dominion" (4:54). This refers to that which God gave to Solomon b. David. He had 1000 women, 700 wives and 300 concubines. David had 100 wives. Among them was the wife of Uriah the mother of Solomon, whom he wedded after the unrest. This is more than the Prophet Muhammad had.

*Ibn al-Kalbi:* David had 100 women, and Solomon 1000, 300 of which were concubines.

## David's Judgments

**Q 38:21** Has the account of the litigants reached you, when they scaled the walls of the Mihrab? **22** When they came upon David, he was afraid of them. They said: "Do not be afraid. We are litigants, one of whom has wronged the other. Decide the truth between us. Do not deviate from justice, but guide us on the level path. **23** "This is my brother who has 99 ewes, and I have one ewe, yet he says: 'Commit it to my care,' and he overcame me with his proposal." **24** He [David] said: "He has oppressed you in asking for your ewe to be added to his ewes. There are many whose associates cheat one another, except for those who believe and do upright things. Few, are they not?" David thought that we had merely tried him, so he asked his Lord for forgiveness, performed a prostration, and repented. **25** We forgave him for that. He has close access to us, and a fine place of return. **26** David, we made you a vicegerent on the earth, to judge among men in truth, not to follow whims, for they mislead you from the path of God. Those who are misled from the path of God are due a harsh punishment because they forget the Day of Reckoning.

*Ibn Abbas:* Two men came to David concerning a cow. One of them claimed that the other had usurped it from him. The other denied it. So David postponed the matter until the night. During the night, God revealed to David that he should kill the claimant. When the morning came, David said to the claimant: "God has revealed to me that I should kill you. Since I will kill you, what do you say about the claim you are making?" He said: "By God, prophet of God, I am justified in my claim against him, but I had earlier killed his father." So David commanded that he be killed. The status of David among the Israelites was very high, and they respected him greatly.

*Wahb b. Munabbih:* Because there was much evil and false witnesses among the Israelites, God gave David a chain by which to make judgments. Its length was from the heavens to the Rock in Jerusalem. It was of gold. It was used when two men had a dispute over the truth, such as if one claimed he delivered something but the other claimed he never got it. Once a man deposited pearls with another man, and he claimed not to have received them from him. He took a staff and placed the pearls in it. When the two were at the Rock, the claimant reached for the chain. When the other was told to take it with his hand, he reached for the staff in which were the pearls, and the claimant gave it to him, and said: "God, you know that I gave it to him." Then he reached for the chain and took it. The matter was ambiguous for the Israelites, then it was solved quickly in their midst.

*Ibn Kathir:* God addressed David with the intention of making him responsible for the matters and judgment of people. He ordered them with justice and following the truth which was sent down from God, not his own opinions and whims. David was known to be certain in his justice, abundant in worship, having performed many sacrifices, so that not a single hour passed of the night and the beginning and end of the day without the people of his house being in worship.

## Psalms

**Q 4:163** We revealed to you just as we revealed to Noah and the prophets after him. We revealed to Abraham, Ishmael, Isaac, Jacob, the Tribes, Jesus, Job, Jonah, Aaron, and Solomon. We gave Psalms to David. [Another reading: We gave the Quran to David.]

**Q 17:55** We gave Psalms to David.

*Suyuti:* Another reading of Q 4:163 is "We gave the Quran to David."

*Ibn Kathir:* The meaning of "Quran" here is the "Psalms" which were sent down to David and revealed to him. The Psalms are a well-known

book which God sent down during the month of Ramadan. In it are
lessons and wisdom.

## Death of David

*Ahmad b. Hanbal:* Abu Hurayrah says that the Prophet Muhammad
said: David was very jealous. When he left, he would lock all the doors
so that no one could enter into his household until he returned. One
day he had left and locked up the house, and when his wife was going
about the house she came upon a man standing in the middle of the
house. She said to someone in the house: "From where did this man
enter? The house is locked up. By God, we will be reproached by
David." David came and found the man in the middle of the house.
David said to him: "Who are you?" The man said: "I am the one who
does not fear kings, nor does a partition impede me." David said: "By
God, you are the Angel of Death. Welcome by the command of God."
David remained in his place until the angel took his spirit. After he was
washed and wrapped the sun rose over him. Solomon said to the birds:
"Give shade to David!" They gave him shade until the earth was dark.
Then Solomon said to the birds: "Take wing by wing!" Abu Hurayrah
says: The Prophet Muhammad showed how the birds did this. He held
his hand how the falcons covered him that day.

*Ibn Abbas:* David died suddenly. It was Saturday. The birds used to
shade him.

*Hasan al-Basri:* David died when he was 100 years old. He died
suddenly on a Thursday.

*Abu al-Sakan al-Hujri:* Abraham, David, and his son Solomon all died
suddenly.

*Wahb b. Munabbih:* People attended the funeral of David and sat in the
sun on a summer day. A group of 4000 ascetics attended his funeral.
No one among the Israelites, after Moses and Aaron died, caused more
grief than David. The heat caused the people to suffer, so they called
upon Solomon to protect them from the heat. Solomon went out and
called the birds. They responded to him, so he ordered them to shade
the people. The birds gathered from every side until they were blocking
out the air and the people were about to die from suffocation. So they
screamed to Solomon, and he called upon the birds to give the people
shade from the sunny side only and leave open the side with the wind.

They did this and the people were shaded and could enjoy the wind. This was the first that people saw of King Solomon.

*Abu al-Darda:* The Prophet Muhammad said: "David was taken from among his followers but they did not fight or make substitutions. The followers of Jesus remained with his Sunnah and guidance for 100 years."

# Solomon

### David's Heir

**Q 27 : 16** Solomon inherited from David. He said: "Oh people, we have been taught the speech of the birds, and some of every thing has come to us. This is due to He, the Clear Abundance."

*Ibn Kathir:* Solomon inherited prophethood and kingship, but not all of David's property because David had other sons.

*Ibn Asakir:* He is Solomon b. David b. Jesse b. Obed b. Boaz [Abir] b. Salmon b. Nahshon [Nakhshur] b. Amminadab [Umina Adab] b. Aram b. Hezron b. Perez [Qaris] b. Judah b. Jacob b. Isaac b. Abraham. It is said that he is buried in Damascus.

*Jabir b. Abdallah:* The Prophet Muhammad said: "The mother of Solomon b. David said: 'My son, do not sleep too much at night. If you sleep too much at night, your worship will be rebuffed as that of a poor person on the Day of Resurrection.'"

*Suyuti:* Ka'b al-Ahbar says he had a white body and his father instructed him in many things from a young age so that his reason and learning was strong. Ibn Abbas says two believing kings ruled over the whole earth: Solomon and Dhu al-Qarnayn. Two disbelieving kings ruled over the whole earth: Nimrod and Nebuchadnezzar. Historians say that Solomon was a king when he was thirteen years old and he began building the Temple after four years of his kingship had passed. He died when he was 53 years old.

### Speech of Birds

*Abu Malik:* Solomon b. David passed by a male sparrow which was moving around a female sparrow. He said to his companions: "Do you know what it says?" They said: "What does it say, prophet of God?" He said: "It proposes marriage, saying: 'Marry me and live with me in any of the rooms in Damascus that you wish.'" Solomon said: "All the rooms in Damascus are built of rock, so it is not possible for one to live in them, but all suitors are liars." Solomon was also able to understand the speech of other animals and other creatures. This is indicated by God's word: "some of every thing has come to us" (27:16). This means all of the needs of a kingdom had come to him: aids, armies, equipment, groups of Jinn, people, birds, wild animals, demons, sciences, understanding, and the languages of creatures, both words and bodily expressions.

## Solomon and the Ants

**Q 27:17** Gathered around Solomon were his armies of Jinn, people, and birds, all in order. **18** When they came to a valley of ants, an ant said: "Ants, go into your dwelling or Solomon and his armies will crush you without knowing." **19** He [Solomon] smiled and laughed at what it said, and said: "My Lord, order me that I might be thankful for your grace which you bestowed upon me and my progenitors, that I might do what is upright, pleasing to you. Cause me to be included, by your mercy, among your upright worshippers."

*Ibn Kathir:* Solomon went out one day with his army of Jinn, people and birds. The Jinn and the people went with him and the birds flew overhead providing shade from the heat with their wings. None of the ranks would proceed until the ones behind were caught up with them.

*Wahb b. Munabbih:* Solomon and his group passed, on their feet, a valley, as a group. The name of the ant was Jiris. It was from the tribe called the Banu al-Shaysban.

*Zuhri:* Solomon went out with some of his companions to pray for water. He saw an ant standing and raising one of its legs toward heaven, praying for water. He said to his companions: "Return, for you will have rain. This ant has already prayed for rain, and it will be answered."

*Suddi:* Some of Solomon's companions needed rain, so he ordered the people to go out. They saw an ant standing and raising its hand, saying: "God, I am one of your creations. We have no riches from your abundance." God caused the rain to come upon them.

### Solomon and the Hoopoe

**Q 27:20** He [Solomon] reviewed a troop of birds and said: "Why do I not see the Hoopoe, or is he among those who are absent? **21** "I will punish him with a severe punishment or slaughter him unless he brings to me a clear authorization." **22** He [Hoopoe] lingered not far. He said: "I have encompassed what you have not encompassed. I come to you with certain news from Sheba. **23** "I found a woman ruling over them. Some of every thing has come to her, and she has a great throne. **24** "I found her and her people worshipping the sun instead of God. Satan has made their works look good to them and has blocked them from the way. They are not rightly guided, **25** in that they do not worship God who brings forth what is hidden in the heavens and the earth, and knows what you hide and what you make public. **26** "God, there is no God other than he, Lord of the Great Throne." **27** He [Solomon] said: "We will see if you are telling the truth or are one of the liars. **28** "Go, with this letter of mine. Deliver it to them. Then turn away from them and watch to see what they respond."

### Hoopoe Bird

*Ibn Abbas:* When they needed water in the deserts, when they were traveling, the Hoopoe would go and look for them, whether a specific spot had water or not. God had given him this ability, to see water under the surface of the earth. He would indicate the spot to the others and they would dig there.

### Queen of Sheba

**Q 27:29** [The Queen] said: "Oh leaders, delivered to me is a honorable letter. **30** "It is from Solomon: 'In the name of God, the Merciful, the Compassionate. **31** "'Do not think yourself better than I, but come to me submitting.'" **32** She said: "Oh leaders, give me legal advice in my matter. I do not decide any matter until you have testified." **33** They said: "We incline toward strength, and incline toward severe harm, but the matter is up to you, so think about what you are commanding." **34** She said: "When kings enter a district they despoil it and make the mightiest of its people to be the lowest. Like this they do. **35** "I am sending to them a present. Wait and see the return of the messengers." **36** When he [messenger] came to Solomon, he [Solomon] said: "Will you abundantly give me wealth? That which God has given me is better than that which he has given you. Rather, it is you who should be glad about your gift. **37** "Return to them. We shall come to them with armies the like they have not met. We will expel them from there as lowly people, for they are small ones."

*Ibn Kathir:* Solomon sent a letter to Sheba calling upon her to obey God and obey his messenger, and to submit to his kingship and authority. Some of the exegetes mention that the Hoopoe bird carried the letter, came to her castle, and gave it to her while she was alone. Then he waited to one side, watching to see what her response would be to the letter.

*Tha'labi:* After the death of her father, a man who was full of evil ruled over her people. She sent to him and proposed marriage. So he married her. When she came into his room, she served him wine. When he was drunk, she cut off his head and hung it on her door. The people accepted her and she ruled over them. Her name was Bilqis bt. al-Sayrah. It is also said that his name was Sharahil b. Dhi Judan b. al-Sayrah b. al-Harith b. Qays b. Sayfi b. Saba b. Yashjub b. Ya'rub b. Joktan [Qahtan]. Her father was one of the great kings. But he had refused to marry among the people of Yemen, and it is said that he married a female Jinn whose name was Rihanah bt. al-Sakan. She gave birth to Bilqis. It is also reported, on the authority of Abu Hurayrah, that the Prophet Muhammad said: "One of the ancestors of Bilqis was Junayya." It is said that someone had mentioned Bilqis to the Prophet Muhammad, who said: "No people who appoint a woman over their affairs will prosper."

*Bukhari:* The Prophet Muhammad, when news came that the Persians were ruled by the daughter of Khusraw, said: "No people who appoint a woman over their affairs will prosper."

*Ibn Kathir:* When Solomon's reply reached the people of Sheba from the prophet of God, they had no choice but to listen and obey. They answered his call in that same hour, and went to him with the queen, all together, showing obedience. When Solomon heard of their arrival, he gathered his groups of Jinn and made a request of them.

## Throne of Sheba

**Q 27:38** He [Solomon] said: "Leaders, which of you will bring me her throne before they come to me submitting?" **39** An Efrit from the Jinn said: "I will bring it to you before you can get up from your place. I have the strength to do it, am trustworthy." **40** One who had knowledge from the Book said: "I will return it to you in the blink of your eye." When he [Solomon] saw it placed before him, he said: "This is by the abundance of my Lord, to test me, whether I am thankful or disbelieving. If one is thankful, his being thankful is [gain] for his soul. If one disbelieves, my Lord is free from needing anything, Honorable." **41** He said: "Disguise her throne. We will see if she is guided or one of those who is not guided." **42** When she arrived, she was asked: "Is this your throne?" She said: "It is as if it were. Knowledge came to us before this. We are submitting." **43** He blocked her from the worship of others beside God. She was of a people who were disbelievers. **44** She was told: "Enter the tower." When she saw it she thought it was the depth of the sea, so she uncovered her legs. He said: "It is a tower paved with slabs of glass." She said: "My Lord, I have done wrong to myself. I submit, with Solomon, to God, the Lord of the worlds."

*Ibn Kathir:* The throne of Sheba was encrusted with all types of gems, gold, and jewels. Solomon requested that the Jinn bring him the throne of Bilqis, on which she sat when she ruled. The person who is said to have knowledge from the "Book" [27:40] was Asif b. Barkhiyya, the son of Solomon's maternal aunt. It is also said he was a man from the believers of the Jinn who was said to have knowledge of the Great Name of God. It is also said that he was an Israelite, one of their scholars. A fourth opinion is that he was Gabriel.

## High Tower

*Ibn Kathir:* Solomon had ordered the building of a tower from glass, and to make water flow from it. He put slabs of glass on it, and put fish and other water animals in it. She was ordered to enter the tower while Solomon was sitting on his throne in the tower. It is said that the Jinn wanted to make Bilqis look ugly to Solomon, because they were afraid he would marry her. Her mother had been from the Jinn and had ruled over them. When Bilqis uncovered her legs Solomon saw the hair on them and was repulsed.

*Thaʿlabi:* When Solomon planned to marry Bilqis, he took her back to her kingdom in Yemen. He used to have sex with her once a month, and he would stay three days with her, then he would return. So he ordered the Jinn to build him three castles in Yemen: Ghumdan, Salihin, and Baytun.

*Ibn Ishaq:* Wahb b. Munabbih says that Solomon did not marry Bilqis, but he married her to the king of Hamdan. He took her to the king of Yemen. Storms used to plague the kingdom of Yemen, so he built her three castles in Yemen: Ghumdan, Salihin, and Baytun. The first was the best known.

## Solomon and the Horses

**Q 38:30** To David we gave Solomon, excellent in worship. He responded. **31** When there was brought before him, in the evening, the best of running horses, **32** he said: "I prefer the love of the good thing to mentioning my Lord," until it [the sun] was hidden by the veil [of night]. **33** [Solomon said]: "Return them to me," and he suddenly slashed their throats and legs.

## Afternoon Prayer

*Ibn Kathir:* Many say that Solomon was so preoccupied with inspecting these horses that the sun went down and the time for the afternoon [asr] prayer had passed without him performing it. Ali b. Abi Talib relates that he did not miss the prayer intentionally without an excuse, but that it was allowed in their law to delay the prayer for reasons of conquest or the inspection of horses. A group of scholars also report that the Prophet Muhammad delayed the afternoon prayer on the day of the Battle of Khandaq, and that this was legal until such license was abrogated by the institution of the special prayer to be performed when in fear. Shafi'i and others say that it is still legal until now, that it is permitted to delay the prayer for reason of intense battle. Others say that the Prophet Muhammad delayed the afternoon prayer unintentionally.

## Slashing the Horses

*Ibn Kathir:* He cut the tendons of their hamstrings and the veins of their necks. This is the best opinion of Tabari. Wahidi relates on the authority of Ibn Abbas that he slashed the veins and tendons. There is punishment for hobbling animals, or destroying property without cause or blame, but this may have been allowed in their religion. Some scholars rule that when Muslims are afraid they might not gain the upper hand over an infidel because of something to do with sheep or other livestock, it is permitted to slaughter them, as long as they fear God in doing it. It is said that it was one great horse, 10,000 horses, or 20,000 horses.

*Tha'labi:* The best of running horses refers to horses which stand on three legs and put just the hoof of the fourth leg on the ground. It is said that Solomon had prayed the noon prayer and was sitting on his throne when 900 horses were displayed before him. He became so preoccupied with their beauty, number, and majesty that the sun went down and the time for the afternoon prayer passed. No one reminded him of this. So he said: "Return them to me." They brought them back and he cut their hamstrings and necks with a sword. He sacrificed them to God, leaving only 100 horses. The Arabian horses that exist today were from this original 100 that Solomon left.

*Hasan al-Basri:* It was one horse which came out of the sea with wings. When Solomon hamstrung the horse, God replaced it with something better and swifter, the wind which would blow and be calm at his command, however he wished, its morning a month and its evening a month. He would eat lunch in Jerusalem, then go to Istakhar, then the wind would blow him to the houses of Babylon.

*Ibn al-Kalbi:* Solomon conquered the people of Nisibis and extracted from them 1000 horses.

*Muqatil b. Sulayman:* Solomon inherited 1000 horses from his father David. His father had extracted them as tribute from the Amalekites.

*Ka'b al-Ahbar:* There were fourteen horses. Solomon commanded their necks and legs to be cut with a sword, and he killed them. God took away his kingdom for fourteen days because of his injustice in killing the horses.

## Gifts to Solomon

**Q 21:81** For Solomon, the violent wind was made to blow at his command, to the land which we blessed. We are Knowing of all things. **82** Of the demons and divers were some for him. They did other things besides this. We watched over them.

**Q 34:12** To Solomon belongs the wind, its morning a month and its evening a month. We sent him a spring of copper. There were Jinn who worked before him by the permission of his Lord. If one of them turned away from our command, we caused him to taste the punishment of the blazing Fire. **13** They made for him what he wanted: mihrabs, images, basins like reservoirs, fixed cauldrons. Work, family of David, thankfully. Few of my servants are thankful.

**Q 38:34** We tested Solomon. We put a body on his throne. Then he returned. **35** He said: "My Lord, forgive me and give me a kingdom which is not appropriate for anyone after me. You are the Giver." **36** We made the wind subservient to him, going at his command, a gentle breeze, wherever he wanted, **37** demons, all builders, and divers, **38** and others bound in fetters. **39** This is what we gave.

Entrust or keep, without account. **40** He had close access to us and a good place of return.

## Solomon the Prophet-King

*Ibn Kathir:* God gave Solomon what he wanted and allowed him to use it how he wanted [38:39]. God allowed him to do what he wanted and he did not have to account for it to God. These are the circumstances of a prophet-king, in contradistinction to a servant-messenger who can only grant something by the permission of God. It is said that our Prophet Muhammad was given the choice between these two types, and he chose to be a servant-messenger. In some of the reports it is stated that the Prophet Muhammad was asking Gabriel about doing something, and Gabriel instructed him about doing it. God made a division between succession to prophethood and kingship after the Prophet Muhammad, within his community, until the Day of Resurrection.

## Solomon's Test

*Wahb b. Munabbih:* Some scholars say that there was a man named Sidon, a great king, who lived on an island in the sea to which no people could come, but God had given Solomon authority in his kingship, without preventing him from anything, whether on the land or in the sea. So Solomon went out to this land, carried by the wind, arriving with his army of Jinn and people. He killed the king and looted all that was there. Among the loot was a daughter of this king, who was named Jiradah. He had never seen anything as beautiful as she was. So he chose her for himself and called upon her to convert. She converted by his hand, out of fear and with little trust. He loved her more than he loved any of his wives. She had a great dwelling next to him but her sadness and tears would not go away. So Solomon said to her: "Why are you so sad?" She said: "I remember my father, his kingdom and authority and what was in it. This saddens me." He said to her: "God has substituted for you a kingdom greater than his, an authority greater than his, and God has guided you to Islam. It is better for you than everything else." She said: "This may be so, but when I remember it, I cannot help but be sad. Perhaps you can order your demons to fashion for me an image of him in my room, so that I can see him morning and evening, and perhaps my sadness will go away." So Solomon ordered the demons to fashion for her an image of her father in her dwelling. They did, and it was as if she was looking at her father himself except that there was no spirit in it. She stood him up after they made it and clothed it with the clothes he used to wear. Then, when Solomon would leave her dwelling, she would come to the image in the morning with her baby girls, she and they would worship him just as they did during his kingship. Every evening she would go and do the same thing. Solomon did not know anything about this for 40 days.

News of this reached Asif b. Barkhiyya who was righteous. He never used to leave from the door of Solomon. At any hour Solomon wanted to enter his house, Asif would be there. He came to Solomon and said: "Prophet of God, great are my years, feeble is my strength, and short is my life which is now going from me. I wanted to establish a place before my death by which to remember what happened in the past with the prophets of God, so that my knowledge might cause the people to know better the many commands of the prophets of which they are ignorant." He said: "Do it." So Solomon gathered the people to him, and he stood in their midst speaking. He mentioned things from the past prophets of God, praising all of them until he ended with Solomon. He only mentioned praiseworthy attributes of Solomon when he was younger. Solomon became angry, entered his house and summoned Asif: "Asif, you mentioned things about the past prophets of God, and you lauded praises for their good attributes, and when you talked about my praises you only mentioned things I did when I was small. What about later in my life?" Asif said: "Someone other than God has been worshipped in your house for 40 days, because of passion for a woman." Solomon said: "In my house?" He said: "Yes, in your house." Solomon said: "By God, they will return to God. I did not know anything about this except what you have told me."

Then Solomon returned to his house and broke his wife's idol. He punished this woman and her girls. He commanded that pure clothes be brought. These were clothes which were sewn only by virgins, and no menstruating woman had touched them. He put them on and went out to a waterless desert, alone. He ordered ashes and scattered them. Then he turned toward God in repentance, sitting on the ashes, crying and calling upon God to forgive him what happened in his house. He did this for the whole day until it was evening and then returned to his house.

Solomon had a daughter named Aminah. Now whenever something happened, he wanted to settle a matter or wanted to sleep with one of his wives, he would deposit his ring with her until he was pure. He would not touch the ring until he was pure because his ring was of green sapphire and was given to him by Gabriel. On it was written: "There is no god but God, Muhammad is the Prophet of God." His kingdom was in his ring. So he left it with his daughter one day when he was going about his business. A demon, the master of the sea, came to her in the form of Solomon. His name was Sakhran. He asked her for the ring, and she put it in his hand. Then he went and sat on the throne of Solomon, and the birds, Jinn, people, and demons rallied around him.

Solomon returned from his time in the desert and came to Aminah. He did not look like himself and people did not recognize him. He asked his daughter to give him the ring. She said: "Who are you?" He said: "Solomon b. David." She said: "You are lying. You are not Solomon. Solomon has already come and taken the ring. He is sitting on the throne of his kingdom." Then Solomon knew that his sins had caught up to him. So he went up and stood on one of the houses of the Israelites and said: "I am Solomon b. David." They were urging him on, saying: "Look at this madman. What things is he alleging? He says he is Solomon." When Solomon saw this, he left, heading for the sea. He began to transport fish, for fishermen, from the sea to the market. Every day they would give him two fish. When evening came, he sold one of the two fish for some bread, and he would roast and eat the other. He stayed like this for 40 days, which was the same amount of time that the idol was worshipped in his own house. Asif b. Burkhiyya and the Israelite scholars refused to follow the rulings of the demon during these 40 days.

After 40 days, the demon left Solomon's throne. He passed through the sea, taking the ring with him. A fish swallowed him and some fisherman caught the fish. Solomon was working for the fishermen on that day and when it was evening they gave him two fish. One of the two was the fish which had swallowed the ring. He sold for bread the one which did not have the ring in its belly, and he cooked the other one, finding the ring inside of it. He took the ring, put it on his hand and made a prostration. All of the birds, Jinn, people, and demons gathered around him. He went back to his people and returned to his kingship.

*Tha'labi:* When Solomon was tested, the ring fell from his hand. In it was kingship. Solomon took it and returned it to his hand, but it fell off again. When Solomon saw that it would not stay on his hand, he knew it was a test. Asif said to Solomon: "You are being tested because of your sin. The ring will not stay with you for fourteen days." So he cried to God and left in repentance. Asif put the ring on his hand and it stayed. His was the body that was on the throne of Solomon. He was the scribe of Solomon, and had knowledge from the Book. Asif was established in the kingdom of Solomon and ruled in his stead for fourteen days. Then Solomon returned repentant, God returned his kingdom to him, and Asif returned the ring and the throne to Solomon.

*Tha'labi:* Some of the exegetes say that the reason for the test of Solomon was that he was ordered not to marry any women except from the Israelites, but he married a woman from outside, so he was punished.

## Wind

*Hasan al-Basri:* Solomon used to set out in the morning, on the wind, from Damascus and alight in Istakhar for lunch. Then he would go with the wind to the houses of Kabul. Between Damascus and Istakhar is a month's journey. Between Istakhar and Kabul is a month's journey.

*Tha'labi:* It is reported that Solomon traveled from the land of Iraq after breakfast, had lunch in the city of Marw, and prayed the afternoon prayer in the city of Balkh. The wind carried him while the birds provided shade for his horse and his army. He then traveled from Balkh through the cities of the Turks, crossing to the land of China. He stayed to his right with the rising of the sun along the edge of the sea until he came to the land of India. He then left there for Makran and Kirman, passing them until he came to the land of Persia, where he alighted for some days. After breakfast there he ate lunch in Kaskar and returned to Syria. He landed at the city of Palmyra. Before his journey he had ordered the demons to build Palmyra for him. They built it with slabs and pillars of white and yellow marble.

## Building of Jerusalem

*Ibn Kathir:* Ibn Abbas, Hasan, and Qatadah say the body was a satan. Solomon was away, and when he returned he retook control. Tabari says the name of the satan was Sakhran. It is also said that it was Asif. Solomon was away from his throne for 40 days. When he returned he ordered the building of Jerusalem. The first one to build a place of prayer there was Jacob. This is evident from the report in which Abu Dharr says: "Prophet Muhammad, which mosque was first placed?" The Prophet Muhammad said: "The Sacred Mosque [in Mecca]." Abu Dharr said: "Then which?" The Prophet Muhammad said: "The mosque of Jerusalem." Abu Dharr said: "How long was it between them?" The Prophet Muhammad said: "Forty years." It is established that the time between Abraham and David is closer to 1000 than 40 years.

*Amr b. al-As:* The Prophet Muhammad said: "When Solomon built Jerusalem he asked his Lord for three things. He gave him two, and we are hoping to receive the third. He asked him for judgment that would be like the judgment of God, and he gave him that. He asked for a kingdom that was not appropriate for anyone after him, and he gave him that. And he asked that whenever a man left his house, heading to pray in Jerusalem, that God would remove his sins as though it was the day of his birth. We hope that God has given this to us."

*Ibn Kathir:* It is mentioned that the city of Istakhar was also built by the Jinn for Solomon. In it were the remnants of the old Turkic kingdom. This is likewise the case for the cities of Palmyra and Jerusalem, and the Gate of Jayrun and the Gate of Barid which are in Damascus.

## Judgment of Solomon

**Q 21:78** David and Solomon when they gave judgment concerning the field into which the sheep of a certain people had strayed. We were witnesses to their judgment. **79** We gave understanding to Solomon. To both of them we gave wisdom and knowledge. We made subservient to David the mountains praising and the birds. We are the Doers.

*Ibn Kathir:* Some people had a vineyard into which some sheep of another group of people had strayed. The sheep had come by night and eaten up all of its plants. So the people brought the case to David to judge. He judged in favor of the owner of the vineyard, the value of the sheep as compensation. When they left and saw Solomon, he said: "What did the prophet of God rule?" They said: Such-and-such. He said: "If I had been judging it, I would have delivered the sheep to the owner of the vineyard so that he would benefit from their products until his loss had been compensated, and then the sheep would be returned to their original owner." When news of this reached David, he accepted it as the judgment.

*Abu Hurayrah:* The Prophet Muhammad said: "There were two women, each with a son, when suddenly a wolf took one of their sons. They fought over the remaining son. The older one said: 'It took your son.' The younger said: 'No, it took your son.' So they brought the matter to David and he judged in favor of the older one. They went to Solomon who said: 'Bring me a knife and I will cut him into two, a half for each of you.' The younger one said: 'Let her have him, then.' So Solomon granted the son to the younger woman."

## Solomon's Wives

*Ibn Kathir:* It is reported by some of the earlier scholars that Solomon had 1000 women, 700 wives and 300 concubines, or 300 wives and 700 concubines.

*Bukhari:* Abu Hurayrah says that the Prophet Muhammad said: "Solomon b. David said: 'I can stop by 70 women tonight, causing each to give birth to a son to fight for God.' His companion said to him: 'God willing,' but Solomon did not say this. So only one of the women gave birth, and he was a miscreant." The Prophet Muhammad said: "If he had just said 'God willing' then each of them would have given birth to a son to fight for God."

## Death of Solomon

**Q 34:14**    When we decreed his death, nothing indicated his death except an earthworm which ate at his rod. When he fell down, the Jinn understood that if they had been knowledgeable of the unseen, they would not have lingered in the punishment of the humiliated.

*Ibn Abbas:* Solomon the prophet of God used to go into seclusion in Jerusalem for a year or two years, a month or two months, more or less. His food and drink would be brought to him, and he would go out only to pray. When he would go to pray, he used to see a tree growing in front of him. He would say to it: "What is your name?" It would reply: "So-and-so." He would then ask: "For what purpose are you?" If it was for seeds, he would let it go to seed. If it was for curing a disease, he would let it grow. One day when he was praying he saw a tree before him. He said to it: "What is your name?" It said: "Destruction." He said: "For what purpose are you?" It said: "The destruction of this Temple." Solomon said: "God will not destroy it while I am living. You are the thing which heralds my death and the destruction of Jerusalem." So he pulled it out of the ground and replanted it inside of a wall he had. Then he went back into his sanctuary and prayed, leaning on his rod, and he died. The demons did not know that he had died, so they continued to work, afraid that he might emerge from the sanctuary and punish them. After a while, the demons gathered around the sanctuary which had two holes, one in the front and one in the back. One of them decided to go in. He found Solomon sitting without moving or making a sound, and saw that he was dead. He came out and told the people that Solomon had died. They opened up the sanctuary and took him out. His rod had been eaten away by an earthworm, but they did not know for how long he had been dead. So they put an earthworm on his rod and saw how much it would eat in one day. From this they calculated that he had been dead for a year.

*Ibn Kathir:* In the fourth year of his reign, Solomon started building Jerusalem. According to Zuhri he lived for 52 years, and his reign was 40 years. Ibn Abbas says that his reign was twenty years. Tabari says that the total age of Solomon when he died was 50 and some odd years. His son Rehoboam [Rukhaim] was king after him for seventeen years, and after him the kingdom of the Israelites split up.

# Daniel

*Ibn Abi al-Hudhayl:* Two lions harmed Nebuchadnezzar, so he threw them in a pit. Then he brought Daniel and threw him in on top of them. They did not stir but they stayed put by the will of God. Then Daniel longed for food and drink, but God sent a revelation to Jeremiah who was in Syria: "Prepare food and drink for Daniel!" Jeremiah said: "Lord, I am in the land of Jerusalem and Daniel is in the land of Babylon, in Iraq." So God revealed to him again: "Provide what I ordered you. We will send something to carry you and what you are to provide." He did this and sent to him someone to transport him and what he was ordered to bring, until they stopped at the top of the pit. Daniel said: "Who is that?" Jeremiah said: "I am Jeremiah." Daniel said: "What do you bring with you?" Jeremiah said: "Your Lord sent me to you." Daniel said: "My Lord remembered me?" Jeremiah said: "Yes." Daniel said: "Praise God who does not forget those who remember him, praise God who satisfies those who desire him, praise God who protects those who trust in him, praise God who repays goodness with goodness, praise God who repays patience with salvation."

*Ibn Masud and other Companions of the Prophet Muhammad:* When Nebuchadnezzar destroyed Jerusalem he carried off with him the notables and leaders of the Israelites. He carried off Daniel, Eli, Azariah, and Mishael, all of them children of the prophets. He carried off the Exilarch with him. When he arrived in Babylon, Nebuchadnezzar found that Sayha'in had died. He became king in his place. He honored Daniel and his companions, but the Magians were envious of them, so they denounced them: "Daniel and his companions do not worship your God, and they do not eat of your sacrifices." Nebuchadnezzar summoned them and asked them, and they said: "Yes, we have a Lord we worship, and we do not eat of your sacrifices." Nebuchadnezzar ordered the digging of a trench, and six of them were thrown into it. A ferocious lion was thrown in with them to eat them. The people who threw them in said: "Let us go eat and drink." When they returned they found the people sitting and the lion lying down with his paws between them, not having scratched or wounded one of them. They found another man with them. They counted and found seven people with the lion. The king said: "Who is this seventh? There were only six." The seventh came forth, and it was one of the angels. He slapped the king, who then turned into a wild beast and remained that way for seven years.

*Tabari:* Nebuchadnezzar was established in his rule as long as God wished for him to be established, then he saw a vision, and when he saw it it amazed him, but then he forgot it. He summoned Daniel, Hananiah, Azariah, and Mishael who were the seed of the prophets. He said: "Tell me about the vision I saw. Something hit me and I forgot it, and I am perplexed what it is." They said to him: "Tell us about it and we will tell you its interpretation." He said: "I do not remember it. If you do not tell me its interpretation, I will cut you off at your shoulders." So they went from his presence and prayed to God, asking him for help. They asked him to let them know the dream. So he let them know that for which they asked, and they came to Nebuchadnezzar and said to him: "You saw a statue." He said: "You are right." They said: "Its feet and legs were of clay, its knees and thighs of copper, its stomach of silver, its chest of gold, its neck and head of iron." He said: "You are right." They said: "As you were looking at it it amazed you, but God sent a rock from the heavens and it smashed the statue. It is that which made you forget the vision." He said: "You are right, so what is its interpretation?" They said: "Its interpretation is that you saw the king-ship of kings, some were weaker than others, some were better than others, some were more powerful than others. The first kingship was of clay, being the weakest. Then above it was the copper, and it was better and stronger. Then above the copper was the silver and it was better than the copper. Then above that was the gold and it was better than the silver. Then was the iron, your kingdom, the strongest of the kingdoms and more powerful that what came before it. The rock which you saw God send from the heavens is a prophet God is sending from the heavens to smash all of this. Authority will return to God."

### Daniel's Corpse and Signet Ring

*Ibn Ishaq:* Abu al-Aliyah reports: When we entered Tastar we found in the treasury of Ahrimazan a bed on which was a dead man at whose head was the copy of a book. We took the book and conveyed it to

Umar b. al-Khattab who summoned Ka'b al-Ahbar who transcribed it
into Arabic. I was the first Arab to read this, and I read it as I read the
Quran. Abu Khalid b. Dinar asked: "What was in it?" Abu al-Aliyah
said: "Your life, your matters, the mistakes of your words, and its state
in the Hereafter." Abu Khalid said: "What did you do with the man?"
Abu al-Aliyah said: "In the daylight we dug thirteen graves dispersed,
and when it was night we buried him and filled in all the other graves
to keep him protected from the people, so they might not dig him up."
Abu Khalid said: "What would they want of him?" Abu al-Aliyah said:
"When the heavens would hold back from them, they would come out
with his death-bed and it would rain." Abu Khalid said: "Who do you
think this man is?" Abu al-Aliyah said: "A man named Daniel." Abu
Khalid said: "For how long, when you found him, had he been dead?"
Abu al-Aliyah said: "For 300 years." Abu Khalid said: "Had nothing
about him changed?" Abu al-Aliyah said: "Except for the hair on the
back of his head. The flesh of the prophets is not deteriorated by the
earth nor eaten by predatory animals."

*Ibn Kathir:* The date of Daniel's death is preserved as 300 years. He was
not a prophet but rather an upright man, because between Jesus son of
Mary and the Prophet Muhammad there were no other prophets. The
interval between them [Jesus and Daniel] was 400 years. It is also said:
600 years and 650 years. The date of his [Jesus'] death was 800 years,
close to the time of Daniel. Either this was Daniel and he is the same
one mentioned here, or it was another man, whether a prophet or
upright person, but more probable is that it was Daniel because Daniel
was taken by the king of Persia and imprisoned by him.

*Abu al-Ash'ath al-Ahmari:* The Prophet Muhammad said: "Daniel
asked his Lord to let the community of Muhammad bury him." When
Abu Musa conquered Tastar he found a box containing his nerves and
his veins. The Prophet Muhammad had said: "When someone identifies
Daniel it will be announced in Paradise." The one who identified him
was a man named Harqus. Abu Musa wrote to Umar b. al-Khattab
telling him about the find. Umar wrote back to him: "Bury him and
send Harqus to me. The Prophet Muhammad announced him in
Paradise."

*Anbasah b. Sa'id:* Abu Musa found a book with Daniel, a jar with fat in
it, dirhems and a signet ring. Abu Musa wrote about this to Umar: "As
for the book, send it to us. As for the fat, send some of it to us, pass the
rest among you that the Muslims might seek a cure from it, and divide

up the dirhems among them. As for the signet ring, we give it to you as spoil."

*Ibn Abi al-Dunya:* When Abu Musa found the body, they mentioned to him that the corpse was Daniel. So he wrote to Umar telling him about the matter and that he had found some money in this place, close to 10,000 dirhems, and that he had a box containing a book. Umar ordered him to wash the body with water and lotus, to wrap it and bury it in a grave and not to tell anyone about it. He ordered the money to be returned to the treasury and the box containing the book to be conveyed to him. He gave him the signet ring as spoil.

*Ibn Kathir:* It is related by Abu Musa himself that he ordered four to go by night and dig a grave and bury him in it. Then he summoned the four and chopped off their heads so no one but Abu Musa knew the location of the grave.

*Abu Burdah:* This signet ring is of that dead man who the people of this city allege is Daniel, the one that Abu Musa took that day and buried. Abu Musa asked the scholars of that city about the inscription on this seal. They said: "The king who had Daniel under his rule summoned his astrologers and scholars. They said to him that there would be a boy born on such and such a night who would overthrow his kingdom and spoil it. The king said: 'By God, this night all boys must be killed.' But the people took Daniel and threw him in the lions' pit. The lions did not harm him. His mother went to find him and found Daniel with the lions licking him, God protecting him." Abu Musa said: "The scholars of this city said: 'Daniel carved his picture and the picture of the two lions licking him in the stone of this signet ring.'"

*Ibn Abi Burdah:* I saw in the hand of the son of Abu Musa a signet ring, its stone engraved with two lions, between them a man being licked by these lions.

# Ezra and Jeremiah

**Q 9:30** The Jews say that Ezra is the son of God and the Christians call Christ the son of God. This is what they say from their own mouths. They imitate the sayings of those who did not believe before them. God battles them for they are deluded.

### Ezra the Prophet

*Ibn Asakir:* He was Ezra b. Jarwah. It is also said he was son of Surayq b. Amariah [Adiya] b. Ayyub b. Zerahiah [Darzana] b. Uzzi [Uri] b. Bukki [Taqi] b. Abishua [Asbuʿ] b. Phinehas b. Eleazar b. Aaron b. Imran. It is said that he was Ezra b. Sarukha. Some reports say that his grave is in Damascus. Ibn Abbas and Abu Hurayrah report: "I do not know if Ezra was a prophet or not."

*Ibn Abbas:* Ezra was one of those Nebuchadnezzar led into exile when he was a boy. When he reached the age of 40 years God gave him wisdom. There was no one who had memorized more or had more knowledge of the Torah than he. He is mentioned among the prophets but God erased his name when he asked his Lord about his fate.

*Ibn Kathir:* It is well known that Ezra was one of the Israelite prophets, that he was between David and Solomon and between Zechariah and John, that he was the only one who remained among the Israelites who memorized the Torah. He related all of it to the Israelites just as Wahb b. Munabbih says: God commanded an angel to bring down a scoop of fire and to throw it at Ezra so that he transcribed the Torah piece by piece until he had done all of it.

*Ibn Kathir:* Ezra was not a prophet. Ata b. Abi Rabah says there were nine things in that time period: Nebuchadnezzar, the garden of Sanaʿa, the garden of Sheba, the people of the al-Ajdud, the command of

Hasura, the People of the Cave, the People of the Elephant, the city of Antioch, and the command to follow. Hasan al-Basri says: The matter of Ezra and Nebuchadnezzar was in that time period. But Bukhari reports that the Prophet Muhammad said: "I am the first of the people of the son of Mary, and there is no prophet between me and him." Wahb b. Munabbih says he lived between Solomon and Jesus.

*Tirmidhi:* Abu Hurayrah reports that the Prophet Muhammad said: "One of the prophets sat under a tree and it offended him, so he ordered it to provide for him. He went out from under it and it burned with fire. God revealed to him: A single ant." Mujahid on the authority of his father says it was Ezra, as do Ibn Abbas and Hasan al-Basri.

## Ezra the Son of God

*Ibn Asakir:* Ibn Abbas asked Abdallah b. Salam about the word of God "The Jews say that Ezra is the son of God" (9:30). Why did they say that? Ibn Salam mentioned to him what was from his books of the Israelites, the Torah he had memorized. The opinion of the Israelites was: Moses was not able to bring us the Torah except in a book but Ezra brought it to us without a book. A group of them elevated his status and said: Ezra is the son of God.

*Ibn Kathir:* Suddi says that this misperception happened when the Amalekites defeated the Israelites, killing their learned ones and taking their remaining notables into exile. Ezra cried about the fate of the Israelites and because knowledge had gone from them, until his eyelids dropped. That very day he passed by a cemetery where there was a woman crying over a grave. She was saying: "Feeder, clother." Ezra said to her: "Woe to you, who used to feed you before this?" She said: "God." Ezra said: "God still lives and is not dead." She said: "Ezra, who used to teach the learned ones before the Israelites?" He said: "God." She said: "So why do you cry for them?" Then he knew that this was a message, cautioning him. It was said to him: "Go to such-and-such a river, wash in it, and perform a prayer with two sets of bowings and prostrations. You will meet there a Shaykh. Whatever he feeds you, eat it." So Ezra went and did as he was commanded. When the Shaykh told him to open his mouth, he opened his mouth and the Shaykh put something in it like a great live coal, three times. Then Ezra returned and he was the most knowledgeable of the people in the Torah. He said: "Israelites, I bring you the Torah." They said: "Ezra, you are nothing but a liar." So he stood and tied a pen to one of his fingers and wrote the entire Torah with his finger. When the people returned from the exile and the learned returned, the Israelites told them about Ezra. They brought out the copy of the Torah which they had placed in the mountains. They received it and found Ezra's Torah to be complete. Some of the ignorant ones among them said that because Ezra created this, that he was the son of God.

*Tabari:* Suddi says Ezra was only a boy when this happened, and that the Israelites said about his knowledge of the Torah: "God would not give you this unless you were his son."

*Abdallah b. Ubayd b. Umayr:* "The Jews say that Ezra is the son of God" (9:30) was said by a single man. They say his name is Phinehas. They say he is the same one who said: "God is poor and we are rich" (3:181).

*Ibn Abbas:* Sallam b. Mishkam, Nuʿman b. Abi Awfa, Shas b. Qays, and Malik b. al-Sayf [all Jews] came to the Prophet Muhammad and said: "How can we follow you if you renounce that which came before you. You do not think that Ezra is the son of God?" So God revealed to him the verse.

*Qurtubi:* "The Jews say" is general but it means something more specific because not all of the Jews say this, as when God says: "Those people who say" it does not mean all people. What is meant by the Jews here is Sallam b. Mishkam, Nuʿman b. Abi Awfa, Shas b. Qays, and Malik b. al-Sayf. They said this to the Prophet Muhammad. Naqqash says there are no more Jews remaining who say this, for they have died out. It is also said that only one Jew, named Phinehas, said this.

*Qurtubi:* It is related that the cause of this saying is that the Jews killed the prophets after Moses, so God recalled the Torah from them and erased it from their hearts. Ezra went out roaming the earth until Gabriel came to him and said: "Where are you going?" He said: "I am seeking knowledge." So he taught him all of the Torah. Then Ezra came with the Torah to the Israelites and taught it to them. It is said that God caused Ezra to memorize all of it. He said to the Israelites: "God has caused me to memorize the Torah." So they began to study it from him. The Torah had been buried by the learned ones of the Israelites when they were afflicted with catastrophe. Then Nebuchadnezzar killed them and the Torah remained buried until it was found, and it was just the same as what Ezra was teaching. Because of this the people were misled and said: "This could not happen to Ezra unless he was the son of God."

## City in Ruins

**Q 2:259**  Or like he who passed by the city all in ruins down to its roots. He said: "How shall God bring it to life after its death?" God caused him to die for a hundred years, then raised him. He said: "How long did you remain?" He said: "I remained for a day or part of a day." He said: "No, rather you remained for a hundred years. Look at your food and your drink! They have not aged. Look at your donkey! in order that we might make of you a sign to the people. Look at the bones! how we bring them together then clothe them in flesh." When this was made clear to him, he said: "I know that God has control over everything."

## Ezra at the City in Ruins

*Abdallah b. Salam:* Ezra was the servant whom God killed and then resurrected after 100 years.

*Wahb b. Munabbih:* Ezra was an upright and wise worshipper. He went out one day to an estate of his to check it out. When he returned he came to a ruin while it was still standing but on fire. He entered the ruin on his donkey and then alighted from his donkey. With him was a container of figs and a container of grapes. He descended into the shade of this ruin, got out a large bowl he had with him and began making juice from the grapes he had with him in the bowl. Then he took out some dry bread, dipped it into the juice in this bowl to make it wet and then eat it. Then he lay down his head and stretched out his feet to the wall and looked at the roofs of those houses. He saw what was in them, standing on their roofs, as the inhabitants perished. He saw the bones deteriorate and said: "How shall God bring it to life after its death?" (2:259). He was not doubting that God could bring it back to life but expressing amazement. God sent the Angel of Death and he took Ezra's soul. God caused him to die for 100 years.

When 100 years was up God sent an angel to Ezra to wake up his heart and eyes so that he might see the Israelites and know how God had revived them. So he rode on this creature and saw. Their bones were clothed with flesh, hair and skin, then the spirit was breathed into them. All this he saw and knew while he was sitting. The angel said to him: "How long were you gone?" He said: "I was gone a day, or part of a day." The angel said to him: "You were gone for 100 years. Look at your food and drink," meaning the dried bread and his juice which he made in the bowl. They were in the condition they were before without changing. This is the word of God "they have not aged" (2:259). Likewise, the container and the grapes were fresh and nothing had changed from their condition, as if what happened before had been canceled. The angel said to him: "Do you doubt what I said to you? Look at your donkey!" So he looked at his donkey, the bones of which had deteriorated and become decayed. The angel called out to the bones of the donkey. They responded and came back together. As Ezra watched, the donkey was clothed with nerves and sinews then with flesh, skin and hair. Then the angel breathed into it and the donkey stood upright and raised its head and brayed toward the heavens.

So he rode his donkey until he came to his home town. The people did not know him, he did not know the people and he did not know his place. So he set out until he came to his place, where he saw an old blind woman sitting who had been part of the community for 120 years. Ezra left the community when she was twenty years old and she knew him. Ezra said to her: "Is this the place of Ezra?" She said: "Yes, this is the place of Ezra," and she cried, "I have not seen anyone from this place mention Ezra for years. The people have forgotten him." He said: "I am Ezra. God caused me to die for 100 years then raised me." She said: "Glory to God. We missed Ezra for 100 years and did not hear him mentioned." He said: "I am Ezra." She said: "Ezra was a man who used to visit the sick and be a companion to the afflicted. So call upon God that he might return my sight to me so that I can see if you are Ezra." He called upon his Lord and wiped his hand over her eyes, and they were healed. Then he took away his hands and said: "By the authority of God, get up!" God made her legs whole and she stood up, looked at Ezra and said: "I witness that you are Ezra."

She went out to the camp of the Israelites while they were sitting around. A son of Ezra was an old man of 118 years old. She called to them and said: "This is Ezra who came to you and whom you rejected. I am so-and-so, your patron. His Lord summoned me, returned my sight to me and made my legs whole. He claims that God caused him to die for 100 years and then raised him up." So the people rose up and looked at Ezra. His son said: "My father had a black birthmark between his shoulders," so Ezra uncovered his shoulders and it was known that he was Ezra. The Israelites said: "There is not among us a single person who memorized the Torah as it was passed down to us except for Ezra." Nebuchadnezzar burned the Torah and nothing remained of it except that which was memorized by men who wrote it down for us. His father Sarukh had buried the Torah in the days of Nebuchadnezzar in a place that no one but Ezra knew. So he took them to that place, dug up and took out the Torah. The pages were worn and the book studied.

Ezra sat in the shade of a tree, the Israelites around him, and renewed for them the Torah. Two shooting stars fell from the sky and entered his heart. The Torah was remembered and renewed among the Israelites. After that the Jews said: Ezra is the son of God, because of the shooting stars, his renewal of the Torah, and his reestablishing of the Israelites. The one who renewed the Torah for them in the land of Iraq was Ezekiel. The city in which he died was called by them Sayirabbadh.

*Ibn Abbas:* "We will make you a sign to people" (2:259) means to the Israelites. This is because he would sit with his sons who were old men while he was still a young man, because he died when he was 40 years old and then God raised him as a youth as he was on the day he died.

## Jeremiah

*Ibn al-Kalbi:* Nebuchadnezzar found Jeremiah the prophet in the Israelite prison. God had sent him as a prophet to the Israelites. He warned them about Nebuchadnezzar and taught them that God would bring a power upon them to kill their fighting men and capture their offspring unless they repented and renounced their evil deeds. Nebuchadnezzar said to him: "What is your story?" Jeremiah told him that God sent him to his people to warn them about what was going to happen to them, but they rejected him and imprisoned him. Nebuchadnezzar said: "An evil people, they defied the messenger of their Lord." So he released Jeremiah and was kind to him. The weakened Israelites who remained gathered together said: "We have done evil and were wrong. We repent to God for what we have done. Call upon God to accept our repentance." So he called upon his Lord and he revealed to Jeremiah that they were not doing what they were saying: "If they are truthful, let them stay with you in this city." Jeremiah told them what God had ordered him and they said: "How can we stay in this city after it has been destroyed and God has poured out his anger on its people?" They refused to remain.

Nebuchadnezzar wrote to the king of Egypt: "Some of my slaves have fled from me to you. Return them to me or I will conquer you and the cavalry will attack your country." The king of Egypt wrote back: "They are not your slaves, but free men and the sons of free men." So Nebuchadnezzar attacked and killed him, took the people of Egypt captive and kept going into North Africa until he reached its farthest point. Then he set back with the captives from Palestine and Jordan. With them were Daniel and others of the prophets. At this time the Israelites were dispersed: some of them to the Hijaz, Yathrib, Wadi al-Qura, and other places. God revealed to Jeremiah: "I am rebuilding

Jerusalem, so go and settle there." So he went out and when he arrived it was in ruins. He said to himself: "Glory to God. God commanded me to settle in this city, he told me he was rebuilding it. When will he rebuild it, when will he revive it after its death?" He laid down his head and slept. With him was his donkey and a container of food. He remained sleeping for 70 years until Nebuchadnezzar had died and the king who was above him, Luhrasb whose reign lasted 120 years, was succeeded by his son Bishtasb. Word reached Bishtasb that the cities of Syria were in ruin, that predatory animals had multiplied in the land of Palestine, and that there was not a single person remaining there. So he announced to the Israelites in Babylon: "If anyone wants to return to Syria, he may return." He made a man from the house of David king over them and ordered him to rebuild Jerusalem and its Temple. The people returned and rebuilt Jerusalem. Then God opened Jeremiah's eyes and he saw the city, how it had been repopulated and rebuilt. He had remained in this sleep until he was 100 years old, then God raised him and he thought that he was sleeping not more than an hour. He remembered the city in ruin and desolation. When he looked at it he said: "I know that God is capable of all things."

*Wahb b. Munabbih:* When Nebuchadnezzar was returning to Babylon with the captive Israelites, Jeremiah came on his donkey, with grape juice in a vessel and a container of figs. When he reached Jerusalem he stopped, saw that it was in ruins, and doubt entered his mind: "How will God revive this after its death?" So God caused him to die for 100 years. His donkey, juice, and basket of figs were with him when God caused him to die, so God caused his donkey to die with him. God hid him from people so that no one could see him. Then God raised him up. He looked at his donkey, the one that had died with him, and saw how piece by piece the veins and the nerves were joined together, then how it was clothed with flesh and filled with spirit, and finally stood up and brayed. Then he looked at his juice and figs. They were in the condition they were in when he set them down, unchanged. He said: "I know that God is capable of all things." Then God gave long life to Jeremiah after that, and he is the one who is seen in the open spaces of the land and the cities.

# Zechariah and John the Baptist

**Q 19:1** Kaf, Ha, Ya, 'Ayn, Sad. **2** [The] Mention of a mercy from your Lord to his worshipper Zechariah. **3** When he cried to his Lord in hiding. **4** He said: "My Lord, the bones of my body are weak, the hair of my head is gray, but I have not been unhappy in my calling upon you, my Lord. **5** "I fear for my relatives after me but my wife is barren, so give me an heir from you, **6** one to inherit from me and inherit the family of Jacob. Make him, my Lord, one with whom you are pleased." **7** "Zechariah, we give you good news of a son, whose name is John. We have not made any by that name before." **8** He said: "My Lord, how can I have a son when my wife is barren and I am decrepit from having reached old age?" **9** He said: "Like this: your Lord says it is an easy thing for me. I created you before when you were nothing." **10** Zechariah said: "My Lord, give me a sign." God said: "Your sign is that you will not speak to people for three nights, while being still the same." **11** Zechariah went out to his people from the Mihrab. He signaled them to praise in the morning and evening. **12** "John, take the Book with strength." We gave him wisdom, while he was still a youth, **13** compassion from us, and purity. He was God-fearing, **14** pious toward his parents, and he was not overbearing or disobedient. **15** Peace upon him, the day he was born, the day he dies, and the day he will be raised up alive.

**Q 3:38** There Zechariah called upon his Lord, saying: "My Lord, give me good progeny from you, for you are Hearing of prayer." **39** While he was standing in prayer in the Mihrab, the angels called to him: "God gives you good news of John, confirming the truth of a word from God, noble, chaste, and a prophet from among the upright." **40** He said: "My Lord, how can I have a son, having reached old age, my wife being barren?" God said: "Like this: God does what he wants." **41** Zechariah said: "My Lord, give me a sign." God said: "Your sign is that you will not speak to people for three days except with signs. Remember your Lord many times, praising him in the evening and morning."

**Q 21:89** Remember Zechariah when he called upon his Lord saying: "My Lord, do not leave me childless. You are the Best of Inheritors." **90** We responded to him and gave to him John. We healed his wife for him. They were quick in good works, calling on us in yearning and awe. They humbled themselves before us.

## Zechariah

*Ibn Asakir:* He is Zechariah b. Berechiah. It is also said that he is Zechariah b. Dan.

*Ibn Ishaq:* After the return of the Israelites to Jerusalem from Babylon they flourished but they sinned and God sent messengers to them. They rejected some of them and killed some of them until the last prophets sent to them were Zechariah, John b. Zechariah, and Jesus son of Mary. They were descendants of David. John was son of Zechariah b. Iddo b. Meshullam b. Zedekiah b. Berechiah b. Shephatiah b. Fakhor b. Jorum [or Shallum] b. Jehoshaphat b. Asa b. Abijah [Abiah] b. Rehoboam b. Solomon b. David.

*Suyuti:* He is one of the descendants of Solomon b. David. He was killed after his son was killed. On the day the birth of his son was announced to him he was 92 years old. It is also said 99 or 120 years old. Zechariah is a non-Arabic name pronounced five ways in the Quran.

*Wahb b. Munabbih:* Did Zechariah die or was he killed? There are two traditions. One is that he fled from his people and entered a tree. They came and took the tree and began to saw it. When the saw reached his ribs God revealed to him: "If your wailing does not stop, the earth and those upon it will be overturned." So he stopped his wailing until he had been cut in two. Another is that the tree was split open for him but he died.

## John

*Tabari:* The Christians claim that Jesus was born to Mary 303 years after the time of Alexander's conquest of the land of Babylon. They allege that John b. Zechariah was born six months before Jesus, and mention that Mary bore Jesus when she was thirteen years old. They report that Jesus lived until he was taken up 32 years and some days old, and that Mary lived after his ascension another six years, altogether her life was 50 years. They allege that John and Jesus met at the river Jordan when he was 30 years old, that John was killed before the ascension of Jesus. Zechariah b. Berechiah was the father of John b. Zechariah, and Imran

b. Mathan was the father of Mary. Both of them were married to two sisters: the mother of John was married to Zechariah and the mother of Mary was married to Imran b. Mathan. Imran b. Mathan died when the mother of Mary was pregnant with her. When Mary was born, Zechariah looked after her after the death of her mother because her aunt, the sister of her mother, was with him. The name of Mary's mother was Hannah bt. Faqud b. Qabil. The name of the sister of Mary's mother, the name of John's mother, was Elizabeth bt. Faqud. Zechariah was guardian of Mary when she became engaged to Joseph b. Jacob b. Mathan b. Eleazar b. Eliud b. Achim b. Zadok b. Azor b. Eliakim b. Abiud b. Zerubbabel b. Shealtiel b. Jechonia b. Josiah b. Amon b. Manasseh b. Hezekiah b. Ahaziah b. Jotham b. Uzziah b. Joram b. Jehoshaphat b. Asa b. Abijah b. Rehoboam b. Solomon b. David. To Zechariah was born John, the son of the great-aunt of Jesus, the son of Mary. He came to Syria calling the people to God. Then John and Jesus met and they parted after John baptized Jesus. It is said that Jesus sent John b. Zechariah with twelve disciples to teach the people. Among what they taught was the prohibition of marriage to a niece.

*Suyuti:* He was the first named John according to the text of the Quran. He was born six months before Jesus. He was a prophet young and was killed unjustly. God gave authority, on account of his being killed, to Nebuchadnezzar and his armies. John is a non-Arabic name, but it is also said it is Arabic. Kirmani says he was named John [Yahya] because God revived [ihiya] him in faith. It is also said because in him lived [hayya] the mercy of his people. It is also said because he was martyred and the martyrs are raised to life.

## Destruction of Jerusalem

**Q 17:4** We decreed for the Israelites, in the Book, that they would despoil the earth twice and exalt themselves as being great. **5** When the first of these two promises came to pass, we sent upon them one of our servants, strong in battle. He entered into the inmost parts of their homes. If was a fulfilled promise. **6** Then we granted victory over them: We extended your wealth and sons, and made you to have more men. **7** If you did good, you did it for yourselves. If you did evil, you did it against yourselves. When the other promise came to pass, they disfigured your faces and entered your temple just as they had entered it the first time, and they destroyed all that they could. **8** Perhaps your Lord is to show you mercy. If you revert, then we will return and make Hell a prison for those who disbelieve.

*Ibn Abbas:* Jesus son of Mary sent John b. Zechariah with twelve disciples to teach the people. Among what they taught was the prohibition of marriage to a niece. Their king had a niece who amazed him and he wanted to be married to her. She had a desire that he carried out every day. When her mother heard about this she said to her daughter: "When you come to the king, and he asks you about your desire, say: 'My desire is that you kill John b. Zechariah for me.'" When she came to the king he asked her about her desire and she said: "My desire is that you kill John b. Zechariah for me." He said: "Ask me something else." She said: "I will not ask you for anything but this." So he summoned John and called for a bowl, and then he killed him. A drop of John's blood fell on the earth and did not stop boiling until God sent Nebuchadnezzar against them. An old Israelite woman came and showed this blood to Nebuchadnezzar. God put it in his heart to kill the Israelites on account of this blood, until it would stop boiling. So he killed 70,000 of them who were of the same age, and the blood stopped boiling.

*Ibn Masud:* A man from among the Israelites saw in his sleep that Jerusalem would be destroyed and the Israelites killed at the hands of an orphaned boy, the son of a widow among the people of Babylon, called Nebuchadnezzar. The people believed and their vision came to pass. The man began to ask about the boy until finally he came to the boy's mother while he was gathering wood. When he arrived with a pile of wood on his head, he threw it and then sat at the side of the house. The Israelite man talked with him and then gave him three dirhems, saying: "Buy some food and drink with this." For a dirhem he bought meat. For a dirhem he bought bread, and for a dirhem he bought wine. They ate and drank. The second day he did the same thing and on the third day he did the same thing. Then the Israelite said: "I would like to write for you a guarantee of safety for me if you would someday become king." The boy said: "You are ridiculing me." The Israelite said: "I am not ridiculing you but what would it be for you to take my hand over this?" The mother talked to her son, saying: "What is it to you? If it happens you have lost nothing." So he wrote a guarantee of safety for him. The Israelite said: "How will you recognize me if you come and the people are all around me, separating me from you? Make me a sign by which you will recognize me." He said: "Lift your document of guarantee on a pole and I will recognize you by it." So he clothed him and gave him gifts.

The king of the Israelites honored John b. Zechariah. He favored John's company and asked John's advice on his affairs and never made a decision without him, but the king desired to marry his niece. He asked John about this, and John forbade him to marry her. He said: "I do not approve of her for you." When news of this reached her mother, she hated John for forbidding the king to marry her daughter. She went to the girl when the king sat to drink, clothed her in fine clothes, perfumed her, clothed her in jewels, and put a black kiswa over her. Then she sent her to the king and commanded her to serve him drink and offer herself to him. If he desired her she was to refuse until he granted her what she asked. When he gave her that, she was then to ask for the head of John b. Zechariah to be put in a basket. So she did this and began serving the king and offering herself to him. When he took of his drink he desired her and she said: "I will not do it unless you grant me what I ask." He said: "What do you ask of me?" She said: "I ask you to send for John b. Zechariah and bring me his head in this basket." He said: "Ask me something else." She said: "I do not want to ask anything but this." When she refused him, the king sent and brought John's head. The head was talking right until it was placed in the king's hands. It was saying: "She is not allowed for you." When the king arose, the blood of John was boiling. The king ordered dust to be thrown over the blood but it rose above the dust and boiled. He threw more dust on it but the blood rose again. He continued to throw dust on it until it reached the wall of the city and it was still boiling.

News of this reached Sayha'in, who called on the people: "I want to send an army to you and appoint a man over you." Nebuchadnezzar came to him and said: "What you sent the other time was weak, but I have entered the city and listened to the people talk. So send me." So he sent him. Nebuchadnezzar went until he arrived at that place, but the people had fortified their cities against him, and he was not able to defeat them. The situation became harsh and his companions were hungry and wanted to return when one of the old women of the Israelites came out and said to him: "Where is the commander of the army?" They brought her to him and she said: "It has come to my attention that you intend to return with your army before conquering this city." He said: "Yes, my stay has been extended and my companions are hungry. I am not able to continue with this." She said: "What if I were able to open the city for you? Would you grant me what I ask? and kill whomever I order you to kill? and stop when I order you to stop?" He said: "Yes." She said: "When morning comes apportion your army into four units and set up one at each of the four corners. Then raise your hands into the heavens and call out: 'We ask for you to help us conquer, God, on account of the blood of John b. Zechariah.' The city will fall."

So they did it and the city fell. They entered it from every side. The old woman said to him: "Hold your hand. Kill over this blood until it stops boiling." She took him to the blood of John which was covered with a lot of dust. He killed over it until it rested. He killed 70,000 men and women when the blood finally rested. She said: "Stop your hand. When a prophet is killed God is not satisfied until the one who killed him is killed, and the one who sanctioned the prophet's killing."

# Jesus

Q 3:33 God chose Adam, Noah, the family of Abraham, and the family of Imran above all the worlds, 34 offspring, one from the other. God is Hearing, Knowing. 35 When the wife of Imran said: "My Lord, I vow to you that which is in my belly as a sacred trust. Accept from me for you are the Hearing, the Knowing." 36 When she delivered it, she said: "My Lord, I have delivered a girl." God knows best that which she delivered. "The male is not like the female. I have named her Mary. I ask you to protect her and her offspring from the stoned Satan." 37 Her Lord accepted her well. He caused her to grow well. Zechariah was her guardian. Every time he came upon her in the Mihrab he found that she had sustenance. He said: "Mary, how does this come to you?" She said: "It is from God. God sustains whom he wants without measure."

## Mary

*Ibn Ishaq:* The wife of Imran was the mother of Mary. The daughter of Imran was the mother of Jesus, son of Mary. The name of Mary's mother was Hannah bt. Faqud b. Qutayl. Her husband was Imran b. Yashaham b. Amon b. Manasseh b. Hezekiah b. Jotham [Ahriq] b. Uzziah [Yuwaym] b. Jorum [Yuzam] b. Jehoshaphat b. Ashabaraban b. Rehoboam b. Solomon b. David b. Jesse. Hannah made the vow [3:35] because Zechariah and Imran married two sisters. The mother of John married Zechariah and the mother of Mary married Imran. Imran died while his wife was pregnant with Mary, but she remained a fetus in her womb. The child had been withheld from her until she grew old. While Hannah was sitting under a tree she saw a bird feeding its chick, and she wanted a child, so she asked God to give her one. She gave birth to Mary and Imran was killed. When she knew that a fetus was in her womb, she vowed it to God, to the service of God. She made the child a servant in the Temple so that it would not be related to the things of this world.

*Abu Hurayrah:* The Prophet Muhammad said: "Every person born is attacked by Satan and is thus prone to desire, except for Mary the daughter of Imran. When Hannah gave birth to her, she said: 'Lord, I put her and her offspring in your protection from the stoned Satan.' A veil was placed around her, and Satan attacked it."

*Ali b. Abi Talib:* The Prophet Muhammad said: "The best of women were Mary bt. Imran and Khadijah bt. Khuwayld."

*Anas b. Malik:* The Prophet Muhammad said: "The best women of the worlds are four: Mary bt. Imran, Asiyah wife of Pharaoh, Khadijah bt. Khuwayld, and Fatimah bt. Muhammad."

*Mu'awiyah b. al-Qurrah, on the authority of his father:* The Prophet Muhammad said: "There were many perfect men but only three perfect women: Mary bt. Imran, Asiyah wife of Pharaoh, and Khadijah bt. Khuwayld. The virtues of Aishah are as far above those of other women as the virtues of *tharid* [meat dish] are above all other food."

## Birth of Jesus

**Q 3:42**   When the angels said: "Mary, God has chosen you and purified you, chosen you above the women of the worlds. **43** "Mary, be devout to your God, prostrating and bowing down with those who bow down in prayer." **44** This is some of the news of the hidden we reveal to you. You were not with them when they casts lots with pens to determine which of them would be the guardian of Mary. You were not with them when they disputed with one another. **45** When the angels said: "Mary, God brings you good news of a word from him. His name is Christ Jesus, son of Mary, regarded among those near [to God] in this world and the next. **46** "He will speak to the people in childhood and maturity, and is among the upright." **47** She said: "My Lord, am I to have a son when no human has touched me?" He said: "Like this, God creates what he wants. When he decides a matter he only needs to say to it 'Be' and it is."

**Q 19:16**   Mention, in the Book, Mary when she withdrew from her family to an eastern place. **17** She separated herself from them with a veil, and we sent our spirit to her. He appeared to her as a regular human being. **18** She said: "I seek refuge in the Merciful from you, if you fear God." He said: "I am merely a messenger from your Lord to give you a sanctified son." **19** She said: "Am I to have a son when no human being has touched me and I am not unchaste?" **20** He said: "Like this, your Lord says: 'This is easy for me, to make him a sign for the people, a mercy from us. It is a decreed matter.'" **22** She became pregnant with him and withdrew with him to a far place. **23** The pains of child-birth caused her to go to the trunk of a palm tree. She said: "Would that I had died before this. Would that I had been a forgotten thing." **24** A voice called to her from beneath the tree: "Do not be sad, your Lord made you a stream beneath the tree. **25** "Shake the trunk of the palm tree and fresh dates will fall upon you. **26** "Eat and drink, and find pleasure. As for if you see a single human being, say: 'I made a vow to the Merciful to fast. Therefore I will not talk with any person today.'"

*Tabari:* Mary and her cousin Joseph b. Jacob were attached to the service of the Temple [kanisah]. When Mary ran out of her water, and Joseph his water, each one of them would take a vessel and set out for the cave in which was the water which they found to be sweet. They filled their vessels and returned to the Temple. When it was the day on which Gabriel met Mary, the longest and hottest day of the year, her water ran out. She said: "Joseph, would you go with us to get a drink?" He said: "I have a surplus of water, enough to last today and tomorrow." She said: "But, by God, I have no water." So she took her vessel and set out alone until she reached the cave. She found Gabriel there, but God had caused him to appear to her as a regular human being. He said to her: "Mary, God sends me to you to give you a sanctified son." She said: "I seek refuge in the Merciful from you, if you fear God" (19:18) for she thought that he was an ordinary person. He said: "I am merely a messenger from your Lord." She said: "Am I to have a son when no human being has touched me and I am not unchaste?" He said: "Like this, your Lord says: 'This is easy for me, to make him a sign for the people, a mercy from us. It is a decreed matter'" (19:19–21). A "decreed matter" means that God had decided that this would be the case. When he said this, she submitted to the decree of God. He breathed into her bosom, then he left and she filled her vessel.

*Wahb b. Munabbih:* When God sent Gabriel to Mary, he appeared to her as a regular human being. She said: "I seek refuge in the Merciful from you, if you fear God" (19:18). Then he blew into an opening in her clothing so that the breath reached her womb. She conceived Jesus. One of her relatives was with her, called Joseph the carpenter. They set out together for the place of prayer [masjid] which was on Mount Zion. In those days, that place of prayer was among the greatest places of prayer. Mary and Joseph used to serve in this place of prayer at this time. Service there was a great virtue, and they both desired to do this. They were attached to the services: burning incense, sweeping it, and purifying it, all the work that was done for it. Among the people of that time there was not known anyone more devoted to striving and worship than these two.

The first to disavow the pregnancy of Mary was her companion Joseph. When he saw she was pregnant he was greatly distressed and did not know how to explain the situation. Joseph was ready to make an accusation against her when he remembered that she was upright and pious, and that she was never gone from him for even an hour. He wanted to exonerate her, seeing what had happened, and when these thoughts became overwhelming, the first words he said to her were: "Your condition has occurred to me and although I was intent on being silent and keeping it to myself, it overcame me and I decided to talk about it and lift it from my heart." She said: "Say a kind word." He said: "I want to say nothing but that. Tell me, can crops grow without a seed?" She said: "Yes." He said: "Does a tree grow without it being rained upon?" She said "Yes." He said: "Can there be a child without a penis?" She said: "Yes. Do you not know that God caused the crops to grow on the day of their creation without a seed? The seed was from the crops which God caused to grow without a seed. Do you not know that God caused the tree to grow without rain, that he made, by this ability, the rain to be life for the tree after he created each one of them on their own? Do you say that God is not able to cause the tree to grow until it is watered? If it were not for the water, is he not able to make it grow?" Joseph said to her: "I do not say that, for I know that God is able to do what he wants. He says 'Be' and it is." Mary said to him: "Do you not know that God created Adam and his wife without male or female?" He said: "Yes." When she said this, it occurred to him that this was something from God and that he would stop asking her about it, only thinking that she was concealing something. Then Joseph returned to the service of the place of prayer, sparing Mary, and doing himself all of the work which was required. He did this because he saw the delicate character of her body and its yellow color, the darkening of her face and the growth of her belly, the weakening of her strength, and her persistent gaze. This was not how Mary used to be.

### East

*Zamakhshari:* Mary left for worship in a place which was adjacent to the east of Jerusalem, or she went from her house in seclusion from the people. It is said that she left the sanctuary in order to wash herself from menstruation, that this was a separation required on account of menstruation or on account of something that came over her. She used to reside in the Temple, and when she was menstruating she would walk around the Temple by herself. When she had become pure, she returned to the Temple. She was washing herself when the angel came in the form of a man, a beardless youth, with a shining face, and curly hair, appearing like a human being. There was nothing diminished from the human image, and the image was good, the best of creation. But he appeared to her in the image of a person, in order that she would understand his words and not be afraid of him. If he had appeared in an angelic image, she would have been afraid and not able to listen to his words.

*Ibn al-Jawzi:* According to the Arabs, the east is a good place compared to what is in the west. Concerning the verse "She separated herself from them with a veil" (19:17), there are three opinions: The first of them is that she constructed a screen. This is the opinion of Abu Salih on the authority of Ibn Abbas. Second is that the sun shaded her and none of them could see her. This is how God covered her. This meaning is transmitted on the authority of Ibn Abbas also. Third is that she took cover behind the walls. This is the opinion of Suddi on the authority of his teachers. Concerning the reason for her separating herself, there are two opinions. The first is that she separated herself to purify herself from menstruation and to comb her hair. This is the opinion of Ibn Abbas. Second is that she separated herself in order to delouse her head. This is the opinion of Ata b. Abi Rabah.

*Qatadah:* She separated herself to a far, remote place. But it is also said that she merely went to a place on the way to where the sun rises, because what borders on the east is good compared with what borders on the west. That east is better than west is similar to a saying of the Arabs.

*Zamakhshari:* It is also said that at this time, she was in the place of the husband of her sister, Zechariah, and the Mihrab was on her side of the dwelling. When Zechariah would go out, he would lock the door for her. She was content to find it empty in the mountain so that she could delouse her head. At this time, her roof suddenly broke and she went outside and sat in the sanctuary behind the mountain, then the angel came to her. It is said that the Christians took the east as their direction of prayer because Mary forsook her family to a place in the east.

*Ibn Abbas:* The People of the Book prescribed for themselves prayer toward the Temple and pilgrimage there. They continued to do these two things until it was said by God: "She separated herself from them with a veil." Then they prayed toward the rising of the sun.

### Conception

*Tabari:* The spirit was Gabriel. God named him his spirit on account of the love he had for him and his closeness, just as you say to your loved one: you are my spirit. Some read this as "our refreshment [rawh-na]" with a fatha [instead of ruh-na] because they reasoned that it was a reference to the refreshment of the worshippers.

*Suddi:* Her outer dress came off of her when Gabriel said this to her. He took her by the palms of her hands and then he blew into the sleeve of her arm. It was open at the front. The breath entered her chest and she became pregnant. She went to her sister, the wife of Zechariah, in the night and visited her. When she opened the door for her, she clung to her. The wife of Zechariah said: "Mary, I think that I am pregnant." Mary said: "I also think that I am pregnant." The wife of Zechariah said: "I felt what is in my stomach bow down to what is in your stomach." This is like the word of God "fulfilling the word from God" (3:39).

*Ibn Jurayj:* They say that he blew into the sleeve of her arm and hand.

### Satan and Jesus

*Wahb b. Munabbih:* At the time of the birth, the idols which people were worshipping instead of God became overturned and toppled on their heads in all of the earth. The demons were afraid but they did not know the cause of this. So they went to Iblis who was sitting on his throne in the abyss of the green sea, resembling the throne which was on the water. He was veiled like the veils of light before the Merciful. They came to him while there were still six hours left of the day. When Iblis saw them gathered together he was frightened, for he had not seen them assembled together before now, since the time when he divided them. He had only seen them in small bands. He asked them and they told him about what had happened in the earth. The demons were concerned because they used to enter into the idols and direct people to do things. Now they were afraid that the people would not worship the idols. Iblis was concerned about the situation, so he flew away and was gone for three hours, during which time he passed by the place where Jesus had been born. When he saw the angels surrounding this place he knew that this was what had happened. Iblis wanted to approach from above but the angels' heads reached into the heavens. Then he tried to approach from below the earth, but the feet of the angels were set below where he intended to go. Then he tried to enter among the angels but they kept him from doing this. So Iblis returned to his companions and told them about the birth of the Christ. He said to them: "This matter was kept secret from me. Before this, no child was conceived without my knowing it and none has given birth without my being present. I hope to mislead him more than he can be rightly guided. Before him, no prophet has ever been more difficult for me and for you."

## Wise Men

*Wahb b. Munabbih:* The night of Jesus' birth a group who believed in him went out because a star appeared which they did not know. Before this, they had discussed that the rising of this star was one of the signs of the nativity in the Book of Daniel. They went out toward the star, bringing with them gold, myrrh, and frankincense. They passed by one of the kings of Syria and he asked them where they were heading. They told him about the star. He said: "But why do you bring gold, myrrh, and frankincense to give to him, from among all things?" They said: "This is appropriate for him, because gold is the most noble of things to be possessed, and this prophet is the most noble of the people of his time. With myrrh wounds and cuts are healed, and this prophet will be a physician to all the ailing and sick. The frankincense because its smoke reaches the sky like the smoke of no other thing, and this prophet God will raise to the sky like no other in his time was raised." When they said this, the king decided to himself to kill the child. He said: "Go, and when you find the place, send the information to me, for I desire what you desire in this matter." So, they set out and offered the gifts they had with them to Mary. They had intended to return to the king, to tell him about the place of Jesus, but an angel appeared to them and said: "Do not return to him, and do not tell him about the place, because he only desires this so that he can kill the child." So they returned to their place by a different road.

## Flight

**Q 23:50** We made the son of Mary a sign to his mother. We gave them refuge on the height with a resting place and springs.

*Wahb b. Munabbih:* When the time of her parturition was close, God revealed to her: "Go from the land of your people, for if they see you they will hate you and kill your child." She went to her sister while her sister was pregnant, having been given the tidings of John. When the two met, the mother of John found that within her belly her fetus was bowing its head in recognition of Jesus. Joseph carried Mary to the land of Egypt on his donkey. There was nothing between her and the saddle during the ride on the donkey. Joseph set out with her until they reached a place close to the land of Egypt, cut off from the cities of her people, when Mary felt birth pangs. She took refuge on the donkey's provision bag beside the trunk of a palm tree. This was during the winter and the delivery was hard upon Mary. When she found it difficult, she took refuge under the palm tree. Angels surrounded her and stood in rows around her. When she delivered and was sad, it was said to her: "Do not be sad, your Lord made you a stream beneath the tree. Shake the trunk of the palm tree and fresh dates will fall upon you. Eat and drink, and find pleasure. As for if you see a single human being, say: 'I made a vow to the Merciful to fast. Therefore I will not talk with any person today'" (19:24–26). The ripe dates fell upon her even though it was the winter at that time.

## Egypt

*Wahb b. Munabbih:* Mary carried Jesus on the donkey while Joseph was with her until they arrived at the land of Egypt. This is what is meant by "the height" in God's word: "We gave them refuge on the height with a resting place and springs" (23:50).

Mary stayed in Egypt twelve years, hiding Jesus from the people and not revealing him to anyone. She did not trust anyone to watch over him or raise him. She used to glean grain when she heard of a harvest. She used to carry the cradle on her shoulder and carry the grain on the other. This continued until Jesus was twelve years old. The first miracle of his seen by the people was when his mother was lodging at the home of a dignitary of the Egyptian people. This dignitary had his treasure stolen from him, and nothing but poor people lived in his house, but he did not accuse them. Mary was sad because of the misfortune of the dignitary, and when Jesus saw that she was sad he said to her: "Mother, do you want me to show him where his treasure is?" She said: "Yes, son." He said: "Tell him to gather the poor people of his house to me." Mary told the dignitary this and he assembled the poor people of his house. When they had assembled, Jesus stood in front of two of them. One of them was blind and the other lame. Jesus put the lame around the neck of the blind and said to him: "Get up with him." The blind said: "I am too weak to do this." Jesus said: "How were you able to do this the day before?" When the people heard him saying this, they raised the blind up until he was holding up the lame.

When he stood up carrying the lame, the lame led the blind down into the opening of the treasury. Jesus said: "This is how they cheated the dignitary the day before: the blind used his strength and the lame his eyes." The lame and the blind said: "You are right." They returned the dignitary's property to him, he placed it back in his treasury and said: "Mary, take half of it." She said: "I am not created for such things." The dignitary said: "Give it to your son." She said: "He is greater than I in this matter."

Then the dignitary's son had a wedding and made a great feast to which all of the people of Egypt gathered. When this feast was finished a group of people from Syria visited the dignitary without warning. They alighted to stay with him but he had no drink with him that day. When Jesus saw him concerned about this he went into one of the houses of the dignitary in which were two rows of jars. Jesus passed his hand over the tops of the jars and touched them. Every jar over which his hand passed was full of drink, to the last one. He was twelve years old at this time, and when he did this the people knew that he was something special and that God had given him this power.

## Prophethood of Jesus

**Q 3:48** "He [God] will teach him the Book, the Wisdom, the Torah, and the Gospel **49** and, [make him] a messenger to the Israelites: 'I have come to you with a sign from your Lord. I create for you, from clay, the image of a bird, breathe into it, and it becomes a bird by the permission of God. I heal the blind and leprous. I resurrect the dead by God's permission. I related to you what you eat and what your store in your houses. In this is a sign for you if you believe. **50** "'[I come as] a fulfillment of the Torah which is before you, to allow for you some of what was forbidden to you. I come to you with a sign from your Lord. Fear God and obey me. **51** "'God is my Lord and your Lord. Worship him. This is the straight path.'" **52** When Jesus noticed that among them was disbelief, he said: "Who will be my helpers for God?" His disciples said: "We are the helpers of God, we believe in God. Bear witness that we are those who submit. **53** "Our Lord, we believe in what you revealed and follow the messenger. So write us with those who bear witness." **54** They plotted and God plotted. The best of the plotters is God. **55** When God said: "Jesus, I will take you and raise you to me, and purify you from those who disbelieve. I make those who follow you above those who disbelieve on the Day of Resurrection. Then to me will you return. I will judge between you concerning that about which you disagree. **56** "As to those who disbelieve, I will punish them with a harsh punishment in this world and the next. They will not have anyone helping them. **57** "As to those who believe and do upright things, God will reward them, but God does not love those who do wrong.

**58** "This we recite to you from the signs and the message of Wisdom." **59** The likeness of Jesus is with God just as the likeness of Adam he created from the earth. Then he said to him: "Be" and he was. **60** The truth is from your Lord, so be not among those who doubt. **61** If a person disputes with you regarding this, after what knowledge has come to you, say: "Come, let us father our sons and your sons, our women and your women, ourselves and yourselves, then let us make supplication and make the curse of God to be upon those who are liars." **62** This is the true story. There is no god other than God. God is He, the Mighty, the Wise. **63** If they turn back, God knows about those who despoil.

**Q 19:27**   She came with him to her people, carrying him. They said: "Mary, you bring a strange thing. **28** "Sister of Aaron, your father was not an evil man nor was your mother unchaste." **29** She pointed to him [the baby] and they said: "How can we talk to one who is in the bed of a child?" **30** He [Jesus] said: "I am a servant of God. He gave me the Book and made me a prophet. **31** "He made me blessed wherever I am, has bequeathed prayer and alms-giving upon me as long as I am alive. **32** "[He made me] pious toward my progenitor, nor did he make me to be giant or unblessed. **33** "Peace is upon me the day I was born, the day I die, and the day I am raised up living." **34** This was Jesus the son of Mary, a word of truth about which they dispute. **35** God does not take a son, glory be to him. When he decides a matter, he merely says to it "Be" and it is. **36** God is my Lord and your Lord. Him we worship. This is the straight path. **37** The sects disagree among themselves. Woe to those who disbelieve, who will witness the Great Day.

**Q 5:110**   When God said: "Jesus son of Mary, mention my favor upon you and upon your mother when I helped you with the Holy Spirit causing you to speak to the people from the cradle and in old age. When I taught you the Book, the Wisdom, the Torah, and the Gospel. When you created from clay an image in the likeness of a bird by my permission, and you breathed into it and it was a bird, by my permission. You healed the blind and lepers, by my permission. When you brought forth the dead by my permission. When I held back the Israelites from you, when you brought them signs." The ones among them who disbelieved said: "This is only clear magic." **111** When I revealed to the disciples to believe in me and my messenger. They said: "We believe and witness that we are those who submit."

*Tabari:* God revealed to Jesus' mother Mary to set out with him for Syria. She did what she was commanded and did not settle in Syria until he was 30 years old. The revelation came when he was 30 years old. His prophethood was three years, then God raised him up to him.

*Yahya b. Zakariya:* Some of the early Muslims say that Jesus used to wear hair and ate the leaves of trees. He had no house, no family, and no property, and he never saved any food for meals.

*Sha'bi:* When the Hour was mentioned to Jesus, he used to scream. It was said: It is not possible for one to mention the Hour to the son of Mary and keep him quiet.

*Ja'far b. Burqan:* Jesus used to say: "God, I am not able to defend against what I despise, not able to do what I want. I am by the command of another, and I am merely the instrument for my work. There is no one poorer than I am. God, my enemy rejoices at my misfortune and my friend does evil to me. Do not put my misfortune in my religion. Do not let rule over me one who does not have mercy for me."

*Hasan al-Basri:* Jesus will be the head of the ascetics on the Day of the Resurrection. The fugitives with their sins will gather around Jesus on the Day of the Resurrection. One day Jesus was sleeping on a rock. He was using it as a pillow, and found it pleasant for sleeping. Iblis came by and said: "Jesus, do you not want anything from this world? This rock is from this world." So Jesus stood up, took the rock and threw it at Iblis, saying: "This is for you, along with this world."

*Mu'tamir b. Sulayman:* Jesus went out to his disciples, wearing a wool cloak and covering, barefoot, crying, and disheveled. He was yellow from hunger, his lips parched from thirst. He said: "Greetings, Israelites. I am the one who sent down this world in its place, by the permission of God, without wonder or self-praise. Do you know where is my house?" They said: "Where is your house, Spirit of God?" He said: "My house is the places of prayer, my blessing is water, my food is hunger, my light is the moon at night, my prayer is in the winter at the rising of the sun, my sweet herbs are the wild plants of the earth, my clothing is wool, my feelings are fear of the mighty Lord, my sitting partners are worldly and poor. Tomorrow comes and I have nothing. Yesterday, I had nothing. But I am good of soul and without distress. Whoever is richer than I am is more beset with hassles."

*Abu Abdallah al-Sufi:* Jesus said: "Seeing this world is like wanting a drink of sea water, for the more you drink the more thirsty you become until you die."

*Ibrahim al-Taymi:* Jesus said to his disciples: "Truly I say unto you, whoever seeks Paradise, will have bread of barley and sleep in a dunghill with many dogs."

*Ibn Kathir:* The disciples said to Christ: "Christ, look at the place for God's worship, what is better than it?" He said: "Amen, amen. Truly I say unto you, God will not leave one stone of this place of worship standing, but it will be destroyed by the sins of its people. God will not rebuild it with gold, silver, or these rocks which amazed you. More beloved to God than all of these things are upright hearts with which God inhabits the earth."

*Ibrahim al-Taymi:* Jesus said: "My disciples, store up your treasures in heaven. The heart of man is where he stores his treasure."

## Disciples of Jesus

**Q 5:112** When the disciples said: "Jesus son of Mary, is your Lord able to send down to us a table from heaven?" He said: "Fear God, if you are believers." **113** They said: "We want to eat from it and satisfy our hearts, to know that you have been truthful with us, so that we might be witnesses of it." **114** Jesus son of Mary said: "Oh God, our Lord, send down to us a table from heaven, so that the first and last of us might have a feast as a sign from you. Sustain us, for you are the best of those who provide sustenance." **115** God said: "I will send it down to you. If, after that, anyone of you disbelieves, I will punish him with a punishment unlike I have punished anyone from among the worlds."

**Q 61:14** You who believe are helpers of God just as Jesus son of Mary said to the disciples: "Who is a helper of God?" The disciples said: "We are helpers of God." A group of the Israelites believed and another group disbelieved. We helped those who believed against their enemies. They were exposed.

*Tabari:* Among the disciples and followers of Jesus who were in the land after them were: Peter the disciple, and Paul who was a follower but not a disciple; they went to Rome. Andrew and Matthew went to the land whose inhabitants eat people, in which are the Blacks. Thomas went to the land of Babylon in the east, Philip to Qayrawan and Carthage, that is North Africa. John went to Ephesus, the city of the People of the Cave. James went to Jerusalem, that is Aelia. Bartholomew went to Arabia, the land of the Hijaz. Simeon went to the land of the Berbers outside of North Africa. Judas, who was not a disciple, went to Ariobus. He took the place of Judas Iscariot after he did what he did.

*Ibn Kathir:* It is said that the Gospel was transmitted from Jesus in four versions: Luke, Matthew, Mark, and John. Among these four gospels are many differences with respect to each version, many additions, and many deletions. Two of these four are from those who knew and saw Christ: Matthew and John. Two of them are from his disciples: Mark and Luke.

Among those in Damascus who believed in Christ was a man named Dina. He used to hide in a cave inside the eastern gate, near the Crusader church, out of fear from Paul the Jew. Paul was oppressing all those who followed Christ. He had shaved the head of the son of his brother when he believed in Christ, and walked around the city with him. Then he stoned him until he died. When Paul heard that Christ had headed for Damascus, he readied his mule and left to kill him. On the way, he was met by something that looked like a star. When he turned toward the disciples of Christ an angel came to him and beat him on his face with the tip of his wing and blinded him. When this happened, the truth of Christ came upon his soul and he asked forgiveness for what he had done, believed in him, and accepted him. He asked that his sight might be returned, so he was told: "Go to Dina who is in Damascus, at the end of the market on the eastern side. He will call to you." So he went, Dina called to him and restored his sight. The faith of Paul in Christ was great. He believed that he was a servant of God and his messenger. Churches were built for him, in his name. The church of Paul was well known in Damascus from the time his followers founded it until it was destroyed.

## Table from Heaven

*Ibn Kathir:* Jesus had ordered the disciples to fast for 30 days. When they had completed the fast, they asked Jesus to have a table sent down to them from heaven, so that they could eat from it, and to satiate their hearts that God had accepted their fast and would answer their request. This was also so that they would establish a feast for breaking the fast, and a feast that would suffice for the first and last of them, the rich and the poor. Jesus cautioned them against this, for he was afraid that they would not be thankful. But when they would not stop asking, Jesus got up to go to his place of prayer. He bowed his head in silence and his eyes filled with tears, asking God to give them that for which they asked. So God sent down to them a table from heaven. The people saw it descend between the clouds as it came down a little at a time. It continued to come closer until it alighted in the hands of Jesus. It was wrapped in a cloth. Jesus stood up and uncovered it, saying: "In the name of God, the best of those who provide sustenance." On the table were seven fish and seven loaves. It is also said that it was vinegar, pomegranates, and fruits. It had a very strong aroma. God said: "Be", and it existed.

Jesus ordered them to eat, but they said: "We will not eat until you eat." So he said: "But you are the ones who asked for it in the first place," but they refused to eat from it first. So Jesus ordered the poor, needy, sick, and lame to eat from it. There were close to 1800 there eating from it. All who were sick, lame, infirm, or ill were healed from eating it. It is also said that the table used to come down once a day and the people would eat from it. The first and the last of them ate from it up to, it is said, 7000 people. It used to come down day after day just as the she-camel of Salih used to give milk to drink day after day. God ordered Jesus to make the food only for the poor and needy and not the rich. This angered many people, and the hypocrites began to plot against him. It was these people that God transformed into pigs.

*Ammar b. Yasir:* The Prophet Muhammad said: "The table came down from heaven with bread and meat. It was not allowed for the faithless and those who store up food to eat, who were transformed into apes and pigs."

*Ibn Kathir:* There is disagreement about the table: Did it come down or not? The majority hold that it came down, just as is indicated in the reports, and this is also clear from the Quran. Tabari reports that Mujahid and Hasan b. Abi al-Hasan al-Basri say that it did not come down, for the disciples withdrew their request after God said: "If, after that, anyone of you disbelieves, I will punish him with a punishment unlike I have punished anyone from among the worlds" (5:115). This supports the Christians who claim that they do not know the story of the table, and that it is not mentioned in their Bible.

## Walking on Water

*Bakr b. Abdallah al-Muzanni:* The disciples of Jesus were told to head toward the sea. So they set about, looking for Jesus. When they arrived, they saw Jesus walking on the water. One wave would lift him up, and another would put him down. When he arrived at the place of the disciples, one of them, perhaps the best of the disciples, said to him: "Can I come out to you, prophet of God?" Jesus said: "Yes." So he put one of his feet on the water and then started to walk, putting the other foot down. He said: "I am going to drown, prophet of God!" Jesus said: "Take my hand, fortress of faith. If a person has certain faith, he can walk on water."

## Jesus as Son of God

**Q 4 : 171**  People of the Book, do not exaggerate in your religion. Do not say of God anything but the truth. Christ Jesus son of Mary was only the messenger of God, and his word which a spirit from him bestowed on Mary. Believe in God and his messengers. Do not say "Trinity." Stop! It is better for you. God is an only God. Glory to him [that he is above] having a son. What is in the heavens and what is on the earth are his. Sufficient is God as a guardian. **172** Christ will not disdain to be a worshipper of God, nor do the attending angels. He who disdains his [God's] worship is arrogant. He [God] will gather them together to him to make an account. **173** As for those who believe and do upright acts, he will reward them their due and increase them from his bounty. As for those who disdain and are arrogant, he will punish them with a great punishment. They will not find for themselves anyone besides God as their protector or help.

**Q 5 : 17**  They disbelieved, those who said: "God is Christ son of Mary." Say: Who would have power from God over anything if he intended to destroy Christ son of Mary, his mother, who on all the earth? To God is dominion of the heavens and earth, and what is between them. He created what he wants, for over all things God has Power.

**Q 5 : 73**  They disbelieved, those who said: "God is one of the trinity." There is no god other than the only God. If they do not cease from what they are saying, a grievous punishment will befall those among them who disbelieve. **74** Why do they not repent to God and ask his forgiveness? God is Forgiving, Merciful. **75** Christ son of Mary was only a messenger. The messengers that were before him passed away. His mother was truthful. They both used to eat food. See how he made clear signs of them. Then see how they [others] are deluded.

**Q 5 : 116**  When God said: "Jesus son of Mary, did you say to people: 'Take me and my mother as two gods beside God?'" He said: "Glory to you, it is not possible for me to say what I have no right to say. If I had said it, you would know it, for you know what is in my soul, but I do not know what is in your soul. You know the hidden things. **117** "I only said to them what you commanded me to say: Worship God, my Lord and your Lord. I was a witness for them as long as I was with them. When you took me, you were watching over them. You are a witness to all things. **118** "If you punish them, they are your servants, but if you forgive them you are the Mighty, the Wise."

**Q 6 : 100**  They make God to associate with the Jinn, though he created them, and they falsely attribute sons and daughters to him without knowledge. Praise be to him, who is exalted above how they describe him. **101** Originator of the heavens and the earth, is he to have a son when he has no consort? He created all things. Of all things he is Knowing. **102** That is God, your Lord. There is no god other than he, creator of all things. Worship him for he is Guardian of all things. **103** No vision can know him, for he controls vision. He is Subtle, Aware.

**Q 9:30**   The Jews say that Ezra is the son of God and the Christians call Christ the son of God. This is what they say from their own mouths. They imitate the sayings of those who did not believe before them. God battles them for they are deluded.

**Q 10:68**   They say: "God took a son." Glory be to him. He is sufficient. To him belong what is in the heavens and what is on the earth. You do not have authority in this. Do you speak about God concerning what you do not know? **69** Say: Those who create a lie against God will not prosper. **70** Enjoyment in this world, then to us will be their return. Then we will make them to taste the severe punishment on account of their having been liars.

**Q 17:111**   Say: Praise to God who did not take a son, nor has an associate in his dominion, nor [does he need] protection from debasement. Say: He is Great.

**Q 18:4**   So that he might warn those who say that God takes a son. **5** They have no knowledge of it nor had their fathers. It is a serious word that issues from their mouths. What they say is only lies.

**Q 19:88**   They say: "The Merciful took a son." **89** You bring something preposterous. **90** The heavens are on the verge of bursting from it, the earth splitting open, and the mountains falling down in ruin. **91** That they attributed a son to the Merciful. **92** It is not consistent for the Merciful to have taken a son. **93** There is nothing in all the heavens and the earth that does not come to the Merciful as a servant. **94** He takes account and enumerates their number. **95** All of them come to him alone of the Day of Resurrection.

**Q 21:26**   They say: "The Merciful took a son." Glory to him, they are but honored servants. **27** They do not precede him in speech and they act according to his command. **28** He knows what is before them and behind them. They do not intercede except for him with whom God is well pleased. They are anxious and fearful of him. **29** If one of them says: "I am a god other than he" this one we will reward with Gehennah. Like this we reward those who do wrong.

**Q 37:149**   Ask them: Does your Lord have daughters and they have sons? **150** Or we created the angels female and they witnessed it? **151** From their own mouths they say: **152** "God begot," for they are liars. **153** Did he prefer daughters to sons? **154** How do you judge this? **155** Will you not be reminded? **156** Or do you have clear authority? **157** Bring your book if you are truthful. **158** They created a genealogy between him and the Jinn. The Jinn already know that they will be present [before God]. **159** Glory to God, above what they ascribe. **160** Unlike the servants of God, the chosen ones.

**Q 39:4**  If God had wanted to take a son, he could have chosen what he wanted from that which he created. Glory to him, he is God, the One, the Vanquisher. **5** He created the heavens and the earth in truth. He makes the night to overlap the day and the day to overlap the night. He causes the course of the sun and the moon. Each follows a course specified for it. He is the Mighty, the Forgiving.

**Q 43:81**  Say: If the Merciful had a son, I would be the first worshipper. **82** Glory to the Lord of the heavens and the earth, Lord of the Throne, above what they ascribe to him.

**Q 112:1**  Say: He is God, One, **2** God the Eternal. **3** He did not beget nor was he begotten. **4** There is nothing like unto him.

*Ibn Kathir:* The polytheist Arabs allege, in their ignorance, that the angels are the sons of God, that they are in-laws of the Jinn. The unbelievers from among the philosophers, polytheist Arabs, Jews, and Christians allege, without knowledge, that God had a son.

*Wahb b. Munabbih:* When Iblis saw Jesus on the Day of Temptation he could not make him do anything. Iblis made himself like an old man in appearance, and two demons who looked just like him went with him. They mingled among the crowd of people. God gathered the sick around Jesus in a crowd of 50,000. If people could reach him, they would. If they could not, Jesus came to them and touched them. He healed them by praying to God. Iblis came to him in a dazzling shape, and when the people saw it they began to follow him. He began to tell them about the miracles: "This man is a wonder. He spoke in the cradle, he raises the dead, he prophesies about hidden things, he heals the sick. This is God." One of the companions of Iblis said: "You are ignorant, old man. What you say is wrong. It is not consistent with God that he would reveal himself to worshippers nor does he live in the womb or in the hollows of women. Rather, this is the son of God." The third companion of Iblis said: "What you two say is wrong, and you are ignorant. It is not consistent with God that he would take a son, but he is a deity along with God." Then they all left and this was the last seen of them.

*Ibn Kathir:* In Surah Al Imran (Q 3) God revealed 83 verses against the Christians for their imprecation of God, for they allege that God had a son. God is greater and higher than what they ascribe to him. This was before the massacre of Christians at Najran, when they began to allege that God was one of three: the Divine Essence, Jesus, and Mary. God revealed the heart of Surah Al Imran to demonstrate that Jesus was one of the worshippers of God. God created his image in Mercy just as he created others of his creation, but he created him without a father just as he created Adam without a father or mother. God said to him: "Be" and he was, Glory be to God, the Exalted. It also explains the basis of this birth to his mother Mary, how he ordered her and how she carried her son Jesus. This is also explained in Surah Maryam (Q 19).

## Jesus as Seal of the Israelite Prophets

**Q 7 : 157**   Those who follow the Messenger, the Gentile Prophet about whom they find written in the Torah and the Gospel. He commands them what is good and forbids them what is evil. He allows them the good things and prohibits what is impure. He releases them from their heavy burdens and yokes which were upon them. Those who believe in him, honor him, help him, and follow the light which was revealed with him, they are those who will prosper.

**Q 61:6**   When Jesus son of Mary said: "Israelites, I am the messenger of God to you, fulfilling that which is in my hands of the Torah, good news of a messenger to come after me, his name being Ahmad." When he came to them with signs they said: "This is clear magic."

*Ibn Kathir:* Jesus was the seal of the Israelite prophets.

## Crucifixion and Ascension

**Q 4 : 155**   Their breaking of their covenant and rejection of the signs of God, their killing of the prophets without right, their saying "our hearts are wrapped" but God has placed a seal upon them in their disbelief for they are not believers, except for a few. **156** Their rejection and saying a great false charge against Mary. **157** Their saying: "We killed Christ Jesus son of Mary the messenger of God." They did not kill him nor crucify him, but it only appeared that way to them. Those who disagree about it are in doubt about it. They do not have knowledge but only follow conjecture. They certainly did not kill him. **158** Rather, God raised him up to him. God is Mighty, Wise. **159** There are no People of the Book except those who believe in him before his death. On the Day of Resurrection he will be a witness against them.

*Wahb b. Munabbih:* When Jesus son of Mary was told by God he was about to leave this world, he feared death and was sad. He called his disciples and prepared food for them. He said: "Come to me tonight, for I have something to tell you." When they came that night, he fed them, and when they finished he began to wash their feet. They thought it was a grievous thing and were disturbed. Jesus said: "Whoever rejects what I do tonight is not with me, and I am not with him." They waited until he had finished and he said: "What I did with you tonight, serving the meal, and washing your feet, is to make you equal with me. You think I am the best of you, so do not be arrogant with one another. Give up yourselves for one another just as I give up myself for you. I ask you to call out to God: ask him to delay my end." They went to pray but fell asleep and did not pray. He started to wake them up saying: "Praise be to God, can you not watch for one night to help me?" They said: "By God, we do not know what happened. We were keeping watch but were not able to stay awake. When we tried to pray, we could not." Jesus said: "The shepherd is taken away and the flock disperses."

Jesus began to talk about his death, and said: "One of you will deny me three times before the cock crows, and one of you will sell me for a few coins, and he will eat my price." The disciples left, and the Jews were looking for Jesus. They found Simeon, one of the disciples and said: "This is one of his disciples," but he denied it and said: "I am not his disciple." Another found him and he denied it. Then another found him, but he denied it again, and he heard the cock crow, and cried.

In the morning, one of the disciples came to the Jews and said: "If I give you Christ, what will you give me?" They gave him 30 pieces of silver, he took the silver, and led the Jews to Jesus. They took him, chained him, tied him with rope and began to lead him away, saying: "You raised the dead, chased away the devil, and cured the possessed. Can you not now set yourself free?" They spat on him and put thorns on him, and brought the wood on which they intended to crucify him. But God raised him up to himself and they crucified "only a likeness." A week passed when his mother and the woman whom Jesus healed and cured from demons came crying at the place of the crucifixion. Jesus came to them and said: "Why are you crying?" They said: "Because of you." So he said: "God raised me up to himself, and only good has happened to me. Only a likeness of me was shown to them. Tell the disciples to meet me at such and such a place." The disciples met him at the place, eleven of them, since the one who had betrayed Jesus was missing. Jesus asked about the missing disciple and they told him that he hanged himself. Jesus said: "Had he repented, God would have forgiven him." He told them to go and speak in the languages of the people, warning them and calling them to God.

*Wahb b. Munabbih:* God allowed Jesus son of Mary to die at the third hour of the day, and then he raised him to himself.

*Ibn Ishaq:* The Christians allege that God allowed him to die for seven hours of the day, then he resurrected him. God said to him: "Descend and go to Mary Magdalene on her mountain, for no one wept for you as she wept, and no one was as sad for you as she is sad. Let her assemble for you the disciples, and then send them into the land calling the people to God, for you have not done this." So God caused him to descend to her. The mountain was glowing with light when he descended. She gathered his disciples and he sent them, commanding them to tell people, from him, what God ordered. Then God raised him up to himself. He covered him in feathers and clothed him in light. He cut off from him the need for food and drink. He flew with the angels around the Throne. He was human and angelic, heavenly and earthly. The disciples separated as they were ordered. On this night on which he descended, the Christians burn smoke.

*Suyuti:* God created him without a father. He was carried for an hour. It is also said three hours, six months, eight months, or nine. It is said that Mary was nine years old, or fifteen. Jesus ascended when he was 33 years old. According to reports he will descend and kill the Anti-Christ [Dajjal] and will get married and have a son. He will stay on the earth for seven years and then be buried next to the Prophet Muhammad. Bukhari records that he was red as if he had come out of a steam-bath. The name Jesus is Hebrew or Syriac. Ibn Abbas says no prophet had two names except Jesus and Muhammad.

## Tomb of Jesus

*Zuraqi:* One of our women made a vow to appear at the top of al-Jamma, a mountain in Aqiq near Medina. I appeared with her, and when we stood on the top of the mountain there was a great tomb upon which was two great stones, one at the head and one at the feet. On them was writing in an ancient script [musnad] which I did not know. I took the two stones with me and when I was part of the way down the mountain they were too heavy for me. I threw one of them and kept going with the other. I showed it to some people who spoke Syriac asking if they knew its writing. They did not know it. So I showed it to a Yemenite who wrote Psalms, and a person who wrote in the ancient musnad script, but they did not know it. When I could find no one who knew it, I threw it under a coffin of ours, where it stayed for years.

Then some people from Media, from Persia, visited us seeking pearls. I asked them if they had writing, and they said yes. So I brought out the stone for them and when they read it, it said: "This is the tomb of the Messenger of God, Jesus son of Mary, upon him be peace, to the people of this land." They were the people of the land in that time and he died among them and was buried at the top of the mountain.

## Second Coming

*Abu Hurayrah:* The Prophet Muhammad said: "All the prophets are brothers. Their mothers are different but their religion is one. I am the first of people with Jesus son of Mary, for there was no prophet between him and me. He will descend. When you see him, you will recognize him to be a man of medium size, with skin of red and white. He has lank hair as if his head is dripping. He will break all crosses, kill the pigs, and abolish the tax on non-Muslims until all who are not under Islam will perish. In his time, God will destroy the Anti-Christ, and will establish security on the earth so that the camel and the lion will graze together, the tiger and the cow, the wolf and the sheep. Children will play with snakes without being harmed. He will remain for 40 years, then he will be buried and prayed over by Muslims."

*Ibn Kathir:* Jesus will descend on the white minaret in Damascus just as the dawn prayer is happening. This is the easternmost minaret in Damascus which is built of white rock. It was built in the place of the one destroyed by the Christians. Jesus will descend, kill all the pigs, break the crosses, and no one will accept anything but Islam. He will remain for 40 years and then he will die and be buried with the Prophet Muhammad and his two companions Abu Bakr and Umar b. al-Khattab.

*Tirmidhi:* Written in the Torah is the description of Muhammad and Jesus son of Mary who will be buried with him.

*Ibn Kathir:* The time between Jesus and Muhammad is said to be 600 years. Qatadah says 560 years. It is also said 540 years. Dahhak says 430 years. But it is well known that it is 600 years. There are also those who say 620 lunar years which would be 600 solar years.

## Three Apostles

**Q 36:13** Give to them, as an example, the Companions of the City [qaryah], when those messengers came to it. **14** When we sent two to them, they rejected both of them, so we strengthened them with a third. They [messengers] said: "We are messengers to you." **15** They [people] said: "You are only human like us. The Merciful does not send down anything. You are nothing but liars." **16** The [messengers] said: "Our Lord knows that we are messengers to you. **17** "Incumbent upon us is nothing but the clear message." **18** They said: "We augur evil for you. If you do not stop, we will stone you, we will inflict a grievous punishment upon you." **19** They [messengers] said: "Your augury of evil is with you, if you remember, it is rather you who are a transgressing people." **20** Then, from the farthest part of the city, came a man, running. He said: "My people, follow the messengers! **21** "Follow him who does not ask you for a recompense, [you] who are rightly guided. **22** "What do I have if I do not worship him who caused me to come into being, and to whom you will return? **23** "Should I take a god other than he? If the Merciful should intend for me some hardship, their intercession will not keep anything from me, nor will they deliver me. **24** "Then, I would be in clear error. **25** "I believe in your Lord. Listen!" **26** It is said that he entered into Paradise and said: "If only my people would know, **27** "for what my Lord has forgiven me and placed me among the honorable." **28** After him, we did not send down to his people any conscript from the heavens. We are not among those who keep on sending. **29** It was only a single scream when they were made extinct.

## Antioch

*Ibn Kathir:* It is well known among many of the earlier scholars and their successors that this city was Antioch. Ibn Ishaq transmits this on the authority of Ibn Abbas, Ka'b al-Ahbar, and Wahb b. Munabbih. These people report that they had a king named Antiochus b. Antiochus, who used to worship idols. God sent three messengers to him. They were: Sadiq, Masduq, and Shallum. He rejected them. Qatadah claims that they were apostles of Christ. This is also the opinion of Ibn Jurayj, on the authority of Wahb b. Munabbih and Shuayb al-Jaba'i: The names of the first messengers were: Simeon and John, and the third was Paul. The city was Antioch.

*Tabari:* There are those who say that these verses (Q 36:13–29) refer to three messengers sent by God, that these three were prophets and apostles sent to one of the kings of Rome, named Antiochus, and that the city to which they were sent was Antioch. Others say that they were the apostles of Jesus son of Mary. They were not apostles of God but were apostles of Jesus son of Mary. Jesus sent them to the city, and since Jesus was acting according to God's word in this, his sending of them was also according to God's word.

*Ibn Kathir:* The interpretation which identifies these verses with the followers of Jesus is very weak because the people of Antioch, when Christ sent three of his disciples to it, was the first city to believe in Christ at that time. This was one of the four cities in which there was a Christian Patriarch: Antioch, Jerusalem, Alexandria, and Rome. Then, after them, Constantinople. And they were not destroyed. The inhabitants of this city mentioned in the Quran were destroyed just as it says in the last part of the story. But, rather, it is that the three messengers mentioned in the Quran were sent to the inhabitants of ancient Antioch. The people rejected the messengers and God destroyed them. Then the city was resettled after that. In the time of Christ the people believed in his apostles sent to them. It is also evident from the story that the messengers were sent from God.

*Tabarani:* On the authority of Mujahid, on the authority of Ibn Abbas: The Prophet Muhammad said: "There are three precursors: Moses came before Joshua b. Nun, Jesus came before the People of Ya-Sin, and Muhammad came before Ali b. Abi Talib."

### Believer

*Sufyan al-Thawri:* The name of the man who believed was Habib b. Mara.

*Tabari:* There was a man who lived in Antioch, whose name was Habib, and he was a silk merchant. He was sick and had become leprous. His house was near the farthest city gate. But he was a believer and gave alms. Every evening he used to divide his earnings into two piles, feeding his family with one, and giving the other as alms. He did not worry about his sickness, his work or his weakness, for he was pure of heart and his disposition was upstanding. In the city of Antioch in which he lived was one of the Pharaohs who was called Antiochus b. Antiochus b. Antiochus. He used to worship idols and was a polytheist, so God sent messengers: Sadiq, Saduq, and Shallum. God first sent two of them to the people of the city but they rejected them, so then he reinforced them with a third.

*Ibn Kathir:* It is said that the man who believed was a carpenter, that he was a weaver, that he was a shoemaker, that he was a fuller. It is said that he used to worship in a cave there.

*Ibn Abbas:* Habib was a carpenter who had been taken suddenly by leprosy. He was very charitable but his people did not like him. When they killed him, God caused him to enter Paradise.

*Ibn Masud:* The people trampled the believer with their feet until his intestines came out his rear. God said to him: Enter Paradise!" and he entered it still living. God caused the sickness of this world, its sadness, and its disease to go from him.

## Punishment

*Ibn Kathir:* The exegetes say God sent Gabriel who took the two sides of the gates of their city. Then he screamed a single scream and they were extinct. Their voices were extinguished and their movements ceased. Not even an eyelash remained from them.

# Muhammad

**Q 2:129** [Abraham said]: "Our Lord, raise up a messenger in their midst, from among them, to recite to them your signs, teach them the Book and Wisdom, and purify them. You are the Mighty, the Wise."

**Q 61:6** When Jesus son of Mary said: "Israelites, I am the messenger of God to you, fulfilling that which is in my hands of the Torah, good news of a messenger to come after me, his name being Ahmad." When he came to them with signs they said: "This is clear magic."

## Prophet Muhammad Foretold

*Amr b. Murrah:* Five were named before they came: Muhammad [61:6], John [19:7], Jesus [3:45], and Isaac and Jacob [11:71].

*Abu Zur'ah b. Sayf b. Dhi Yazan:* At the time when Sayf b. Dhi Yazan was over the Ethiopians, before the birth of the Prophet Muhammad, a delegation of Arabs, the most honored and knowledgeable among them came to him to greet him, a delegation from the Quraysh. Among them was Abd al-Muttalib b. Hashim [grandfather of Muhammad]. They came to him, with his permission, in the head castle called Ghumdan. The king said to Abd al-Muttalib: "Oh Abd al-Muttalib, I bring to you, from my secret knowledge, a matter that I would not reveal to anyone other than you. I reveal it to you because you are its origin, so that it might be to you a secret thing until God permits it to be known. I found in the hidden book and the guarded knowledge, which we keep to ourselves and hide from others, awesome information and a great danger, concerning the honor of living, the virtue of death, to all people, to your group as a whole, and to you especially: When he is born in the Tihamah, a boy between whose shoulders is a birthmark, he will have authority and leadership over all of you until the Day of Resurrection. When this time comes in which he is born, his name will be Muhammad. His father and mother will be dead, and he is to be raised by his grandfather and uncle. We have already seen him born several times, and God makes his mission public, and will make us to be helpers for him, strengthening with them his followers and weakening those who are against him, turning the people from error, and making the honorable people of the land to worship God, to shun Satan, extinguish Hell fires, and break idols. His word is final, judgment just, he commands by what is known and what he does, forbidding the evil and its empty results."

## Recovery of the Well

*Ibn Ishaq:* While Abd al-Muttalib was sleeping in the sanctuary at Mecca, something came to him and ordered him to dig Zamzam. It had been buried between the Quraysh's idols Isaf and Na'ilah, at the Quraysh's place of immolation. The Jurhum had buried it when they left Mecca. It is the well of Ishmael b. Abraham from which God gave him water when he was thirsty as a child. His mother went to find him water but could not find any, so she climbed up Safa and called upon God, asking him to help Ishmael. Then she came to Marwah and did the same thing. God sent Gabriel who dug out for him a place in the earth with his heel, and water appeared. His mother heard the sounds of predatory animals and was thus afraid for her son. She came back and found him scratching with his hand in the water under his cheek, drinking. So she made him a small hole.

*Ali b. Abi Talib:* Abd al-Muttalib said: I was sleeping in al-Hijr when something came to me and said: "Dig Tibah!" I said: "What is Tibah?" Then it went away from me. I went back to my bed and slept in it. It came to me again and said: "Dig Barrah!" I said: "What is Barrah?" Then it went away from me. When the next day came I returned to my bed and slept in it and it came to me and said: "Dig Madnunah!" I said: "What is Madnunah?" Then it went away from me. The next day I returned to my bed and slept in it, and it came to me and said: "Dig Zamzam!" I said: "What is Zamzam?" It said: "It will never stop nor run dry, it will water the great pilgrim company. It is between the dung and the blood, by the nest of the white-winged crows, by the nest of the ants." When the matter of Zamzam was made clear to him, and its location pointed out, and he knew that it was true, he and his son Harith b. Abd al-Muttalib set out with an ax, for he had no other son at that time, and began to dig. When the hiding place appeared, Abd al-Muttalib praised God.

The Quraysh knew that he had uncovered the well, so went up to him and said: "Abd al-Muttalib, this is the well of our father Ishmael. We have a claim to it, so share it with us." He said: "I will not do that, for the command specified me to find it and not you." They said: "Do what is right, for we are not leaving until we litigate with you about this." He said: "Appoint anyone of your choosing to judge between you and me." They said: "A soothsayer of the Banu Saʿd b. Hudhaym." He said: "Agreed." She lived in the highlands of Syria. Abd al-Muttalib and a band of the sons of his father from the Banu Abd Manaf rode with representatives of each of the tribes of the Quraysh. The land there was wilderness. They set out until, somewhere in this wilderness between the Hijaz and Syria, Abd al-Muttalib and his companions ran out of water. They were so thirsty they thought they would perish, so they asked for water from the tribes of Quraysh, but they refused. They said: "We are in the wilderness and we are afraid that what happened to you might happen to our companions." When Abd al-Muttalib saw this, he turned to his companions and asked: "What do you think?" They said: "We don't know except to follow your lead." He said: "Then I think that each man should dig a hole for himself with what strength he has left. Whenever a man dies, his companions can bury him in the hole he dug until we are down to the last man, for it is better that one man is exposed than the whole riding company." They agreed and each of them got up and dug his hole, then sat thinking that death was coming. Then Abd al-Muttalib said to his companions: "By God, let us not meet this death by our own hands, not looking for water in the land nor desiring to help ourselves, for perhaps God will provide us with water in one of the cities. So mount up!" They mounted up while one of the representatives from the tribes of Quraysh watched what they were doing. Abd al-Muttalib got up to mount his horse and when it got up a spring of water flowed from under its hooves. Abd al-Muttalib and his companions praised God, they dismounted, drank, and filled their water skins. Then he called out to the tribes of Quraysh: "Come to the water which God has provided us, drink and water your beasts." Then they said: "By God, Abd al-Muttalib, God has decided in your favor and we will not dispute your claim to Zamzam ever, for he who has given you drink in this wilderness is the one who has given you the drink of Zamzam. Return to your task of giving water in righteousness."

*Ibn Ishaq:* It is claimed that when Abd al-Muttalib asked about Zamzam he was told that it was near the nest of ants and where the crows would peck on the next day. Abd al-Muttalib went out the next day with his son Harith, who was his only son at this time, and found the nest of ants and crows pecking between the two idols Isaf and Na'ilah at the immolation place of the Quraysh. He had an ax and began to dig where he had been commanded. When the Quraysh saw him they told him not to dig between their two idols at their place of immolation. Abd al-Muttalib told his son Harith to protect him while he continued to dig. When they saw that he was not stopping they left. He continued to dig until he uncovered the hiding place. He praised God and knew that he had been right about where to dig. He continued to dig and found two gazelles of gold. These gazelles were those buried by the Jurhum when they left Mecca. He found in it swords from Qal'ayah and armor.

### First Revelation

**Q 96:1**   Recite in the name of your Lord who created, **2** created the human being from a blood-clot. **3** Recite! your Lord is the Most Noble.

*Aishah:* The beginning of the revelations to the Prophet Muhammad was when a vision was revealed to him in his sleep. Each time he saw it, it would seem like the breaking of the day. At that time, he liked seclusion and would spend time secluded in the cave of Hira. He would practice acts of piety there, going there nightly until he would yearn for his family, return for provisions, and then return to Khadijah [his first wife]. He continued like this until the truth came to him while he was in the cave of Hira. The angel came to him and said: "Recite!" Muhammad said: "What should I recite?" So the angel began to press him to his utmost limit and then released him and said: "Recite!" Muhammad said: "What should I recite?" So the angel began to press him a second time until he reached his limit, then released him and said "Recite!" Muhammad said: "What should I recite?" So the angel began to press him a third time and then released him, and said: "Recite in the name of your Lord who created the human being from a blood-clot! Recite! your Lord is the Most Noble." The Prophet Muhammad repeated it, his heart beating in fear. Then he returned to Khadijah, and said: "Cover me with cloths!" So she covered him until he overcame his anxiety. He told Khadijah what had happened. She said: "God will never disgrace you."

Then Khadijah took him to her cousin Waraqah b. Nawfal. He had become a Christian in the period before Islam. He used to write the Hebrew Bible and write from the Gospel in Hebrew what God wanted him to write. He was a great man. Khadijah said to him: "Uncle, listen to your cousin!" Waraqah said to Muhammad: "Cousin, what did you see?" So the Prophet Muhammad related to him what he saw, and Waraqah said to him: "This is the Law which God revealed to Moses. Oh, if I were a young man, if I could be alive when your people drive you out." The Prophet Muhammad asked: "Will I be driven out by them?" He said: "Yes. There has not yet come a man with what has come to you who was not treated as an enemy."

## Washing of the Prophet's Heart

**Q 94:1** Did we not open your chest? **2** and remove your burden from you **3** which injured your back?

*Aishah:* The Prophet Muhammad vowed that he would make a retreat for a month. He and Khadijah his wife agreed that it be the month of Ramadan. He left that same night and heard: "Peace be upon you." He said: "I thought that it was the sudden appearance of a Jinn, so I went away quickly until I found Khadijah. Khadijah said: 'What is the matter?' I explained to her what had happened and she said to be glad for the greeting was a good sign. So I left another time and suddenly I was with Gabriel on the sun with a wing in the east and a wing in the west. I was afraid of him, so I went away quickly but he was already between me and the door. He spoke with me until I felt at ease. Then he made me a promise and I came to him. He moved slowly and I wanted to return home when suddenly I was with him and Michael on the edge of the horizon. Gabriel left and Michael remained between the heavens and the earth. Then Gabriel took me, opened my chest and took out my heart. He removed from it that which God wanted removed. He washed it in a basin with water from the well of Zamzam, and then returned my heart to its place. Then it was bandaged. Gabriel turned me around just as he turned around the basin and made a seal on my back because I had the touch of the seal in my heart."

*Ibn Ishaq:* A group of the Prophet Muhammad's companions said to the Prophet Muhammad: "Prophet of God, will you tell us about yourself?" He said: "Yes. I am that for which Abraham prayed, and the good news of Jesus. When my mother was pregnant with me, she saw that a light came out of her which illuminated for her the castles of Syria. I was nursed among the Banu Sa'd b. Bakr. When I was with a brother of mine, behind our houses, shepherding a flock of ours, two men in white clothes came upon me with a basin made out of gold, filled with snow. They took me, opened my torso, and removed my heart. They opened my heart and removed from it a black blemish which they discarded. Then they washed my heart and torso in the snow until it was clean. One of them said to the other: 'Weigh him against ten of his own community.' So he weighed me with ten of them, and I outweighed them. Then he said: 'Weigh him against 100 of his own community.' So he weighed me with 100 of them, and I outweighed them. He then said: 'Leave him be, for, by God, if you were to weigh him against his whole community, he would outweigh them.'"

*Anas b. Malik:* Gabriel came to the Prophet Muhammad while he was playing with two boys. The angel took him, lifted him up, opened his chest, and removed his heart. Then he opened his heart and removed a blemish from it. Gabriel said: "This is your portion of Satan." Then Gabriel washed it in a basin made of gold with water from the well of Zamzam. He bandaged him up and returned him to his place. The two boys ran off to his mother, that is, his wet-nurse, and said: "Muhammad has been killed." They came back and found him alive and infused with color.

*Sa'ib b. Yazid:* My aunt went with me to the Prophet Muhammad and said: "Prophet of God, my nephew is in pain." So the Prophet wiped my head and invoked a blessing for me. Then he performed ablutions and I drank from the water in which he performed his ablutions. I stood up behind him and saw the seal between his shoulders. It was like the pommel of the Hajalah bird.

*Israil:* I saw the seal between his shoulders like the body of a white pigeon.

*Anas b. Malik:* I saw the mark of the stitches on the Prophet's chest.

## Night Journey

**Q 17:1** Glory to the one who took his servant on a journey by night from the sacred place of prayer [al-masjid al-haram] to the farthest place of prayer [al-masjid al-aqsa] whose surroundings we blessed, in order that we might show him our signs. He is the Hearing, the Seeing. **2** We sent Moses the Book, and we made it a guide to the Israelites: "Do not take a protector other than me."

*Tabari:* Then the Prophet said, wondering at the creation of God: How wonderful is the power concerning that than which we have not seen anything more wonderful? This is the word of Gabriel to Sarah: "Do you wonder about the command of God?" (11:73). This is that God created two cities: one of them in the east and the other in the west. The people of the city in the east are from the remnants of Ad, the descendants of those who believed in Hud. The people of the city in the west are from the remnants of Thamud, the descendants of those who believed in Salih. The name of the one in the east in Syriac is Marqisiya, and Jabalq in Arabic. The name of the one in the west in Syriac is Barjisiya, and Jabars in Arabic. Both of the cities have 10,000 gates, a parsang being between every two gates. Each day, 10,000 men from the guards, armed with weapons, take turns guarding each of the gates of these two cities. They will continue this until the day of the blowing of the Trumpet. By him in whose hand is the soul of Muhammad, if there were not so many of those people and their voices were not so loud, then the people of this world would hear the crash of the setting of the sun when it rises and when it sets. Behind them are three nations: Mansak, Tafil, and Taris; and before them are Gog and Magog. Gabriel took me to them during my Night Journey from the Sacred Mosque to the Farthest Mosque, and I called upon Gog and Magog to worship God but they refused to heed me. Then he took me to the people of the two cities, and I called them to the religion of God, and to his worship. They consented and turned toward God. They are our brothers in religion. He who is good among them is like he who does good among you, and he who is evil among them is with those of you who are evil. Then he took me to the three nations, and I called them to the religion of God, to worship him, but they denied that to which I had called them. They disbelieved in God and considered his messengers to be liars. They are, together with Gog and Magog, and the rest who disobeyed God, in the Fire.

*Anas b. Malik:* The Prophet Muhammad was sleeping in the mosque of the sanctuary at Mecca when three angels came to him. His eyes were asleep but his heart was not sleeping, as is the case with all the prophets: their eyes sleep but their hearts do not. The angels did not speak to him until they first took him and placed him by the well of Zamzam. Gabriel opened the Prophet Muhammad's chest, removed his heart and washed it in the water of Zamzam by hand until it was clean. Then he brought a gold basin in which was a dressing of faith and wisdom. He dressed his chest and sewed it up. Then the Prophet Muhammad rode on Buraq and traveled until he reached Jerusalem. There he led all the prophets and messengers in prayer. After that Gabriel took the Prophet Muhammad and ascended into the heavens with him until they arrived at the gate of the heavens.

When the inhabitants of the first heaven learned that the Prophet Muhammad was with Gabriel they welcomed him and spread the news among the inhabitants of heaven. In the first heaven was found Adam. Gabriel told the Prophet Muhammad: "This is your father Adam." Adam greeted the Prophet Muhammad. Then they passed to the second heaven where there were two driving rivers. Gabriel explained that these were the headwaters of the Nile and the Euphrates. Then they passed to the third heaven where there was a river on the banks of which were domes and castles of pearl, crystals, and sapphires. Gabriel explained that this was the river Kawthar which God kept for the Prophet Muhammad. Then they passed through the fourth, fifth and sixth heavens until they reached the seventh heaven. In each of the heavens were different prophets. Idris was in the second heaven, Aaron was in the fourth, another in the fifth, Abraham in the sixth, and Moses in the seventh. Moses said: "My Lord, I did not think that anyone would be raised higher than I am." Then God raised the Prophet Muhammad higher than this until he reached the Lotus Tree, and he was next to the great door of the Mighty Lord himself. He was the distance of two bow lengths or less from God when God revealed things to him.

God revealed to the Prophet Muhammad that his community would pray 50 times all day and night. Then the Prophet Muhammad went down until he reached Moses who asked him what God had said. The Prophet Muhammad explained about the 50 prayers. Moses said: "Your community will not be able to do that. Return and ask God to lessen the requirement." So the Prophet Muhammad returned and said to God: "My Lord, lessen the requirement. My community is not able to do this." So God lowered it by ten prayers, and the Prophet Muhammad returned to Moses. Moses kept telling him to return until finally the number of prayers was five. Moses said: "Muhammad, by God, the Israelites rebelled against me with less than five. They were weak and abandoned God. Your community is weaker of body, heart, sight, and hearing. So return and ask your Lord to lessen the requirement." So the Prophet Muhammad returned to God and said: "Lord, my community is weak of body, heart, sight, and hearing, so lessen the requirement." God said: "Muhammad!" The Prophet Muhammad said: "Here I am." God said: "I will not substitute the word I gave you according to what I wrote for you in the Mother Book [Umm al-Kitab], but for you each prayer will count as ten. In the Mother Book is fifty prayers but for you it is five." So the Prophet Muhammad returned to Moses and told him what had happened. Moses said: "By God, the Israelites rebelled with less than that, and renounced God. Return and ask God to lessen the requirement again." The Prophet Muhammad said: "Moses, by God I am ashamed to disagree with my Lord again." Moses said: "Go in peace." When the Prophet Muhammad awoke, he was in the Sacred Mosque of Mecca.

*Abu Hurayrah:* Gabriel and Michael came to the Prophet Muhammad with a gold basin filled with the water of Zamzam. Gabriel told Michael to open Muhammad's chest and wash his heart three times. Michael washed it in three basins of water from Zamzam and removed the blemish from it. He filled Muhammad with forbearance, knowledge, faith, belief, and submission [Islam]. Then he sealed him up with the seal of the prophets between his shoulders.

Then Muhammad was brought a riding animal and rode upon it. Every one of its steps reached the edge of the horizon, as far as the eye could see. Muhammad and Gabriel traveled until they came upon a people who farmed one day and harvested the next. Each time they harvested the crops returned just as they had been. Muhammad asked: "What is this?" Gabriel said: "They are those who struggle [mujahidun] for God. Goodness is multiplied 700-fold for them. They do not run out of anything which is not replaced with the best of provisions."

Then they came upon a people smashing their heads with a rock. Each time they smashed them, their heads would return just as they had been. They had no break from doing this thing. Muhammad said: "Who are they?" Gabriel said: "They are those who find it too heavy a burden to bow their heads for the required prayers."

Then they came to a people with only a piece of cloth covering their genitals and a piece of cloth covering their behinds, grazing like camels and livestock, eating from the trees of Dari'a [88:6] and Zaqqum [37:62, 44:43, 56:52], and the brimstones of Hell. Muhammad said: "Who are they?" Gabriel said: "They are those who did not give a tithe from their wealth, but God did not treat them wrong in any way, for God does no harm to worshippers."

Then they came to a people each with a pot sitting in front of them with a piece of well-cooked meat and a piece of dirty, raw meat. They would eat from the raw meat but ask for the good, cooked meat. Muhammad asked: "Who are they?" Gabriel said: "They are men from your community. Each has a wife allowed and good but he goes to a bad woman and sleeps with her until morning. The woman who has an allowed and good husband goes to the bad man and sleeps with him until morning."

Then they came to a piece of wood in the road around which only a small piece of cloth could fit. Nothing could pass without being torn. Muhammad said: "What is this?" Gabriel said: "This is like the people of your community who sit on the road and are robbers." He recited: "Do not sit on every road, threatening and blocking" (7:82).

Then they came to a man who had gathered a big bundle of faggots but was unable to carry it, and he was adding more to it. Muhammad said: "What is this?" Gabriel said: "This is a man from your community who has the trust of the people but is not able to carry it out, and more is added upon him. He wants to bear it but is not able to do so."

Then they came to a people who were cutting their tongues and their mouths with iron scissors. Each time they would cut them, their tongues would be just as they had been, and they did not cease to do this. Muhammad said: "Who are these?" Gabriel said: "They are those who are the speakers of your community, preaching strife by saying not to do anything."

Then they came to a small hole with a great bull trying to get out of it. The bull wanted to leave but he could not. Muhammad asked: "What is this?" Gabriel said: "This is the man who speaks with big words, then he regrets what he said but is not able to retract it."

Then they came to a valley in which was a pleasant, cold wind. In the wind was musk, and Muhammad heard a sound. He said: "What is this pleasant, cold wind, this wind which is like the scent of musk. And what is that sound?" Gabriel said: "That sound is Paradise. The inhabitants are saying: 'Lord, grant me what you promised me, multiply my portion, brocades, silk, sarcenet, colorful carpet, pearls, corals, silver and gold, my cups, dishes, utensils, my apples, dates, pomegranates, milk, and wine. Bring me what you promised.' God says: 'This is what is due each male and female Muslim, male and female believer, whoever believes in me and my messengers, those who are upright, who do not associate anything with me, and do not take anything as my equal. He who fears me is safe, he who calls upon me is strong, he who asks of me is given, he who eats from me is satisfied. I am God. There is no god other than I. I give benefit to the believers. The blessings of God are great for all creation.'"

Then they came to a valley and heard a disagreeable sound, and there was a rotting smell. Muhammad said: "What is that smell and what is that sound?" Gabriel said: "That is the sound of Hell. The inhabitants are saying: 'Lord, grant me what you promised me, multiply my chains, fetters, blazing fire, hellfire, the Dari'a tree, boiling fluid, and my punishment. Make my pit deep and intensify my heat. Bring me what you promised.' God says: 'This is what is due each male and female who associates other things with me, each male and female who disbelieves, each male and female bad person, every giant who does not believe in the Day of Reckoning.'"

Then they came to Jerusalem. Muhammad dismounted and tied his mount to the Rock. Then he entered and prayed with the angels. When the prayer was completed the angels asked about who was with Gabriel. When they learned it was Muhammad they greeted him. Then Muhammad met the spirits of the prophets and they praised their Lord. Abraham said: "Praise God who took me as his friend, gave me a great kingdom, made me a people who fear God and follow my example, who saved me from the fire making it cold and peaceful." Then Moses praised his Lord: "Praise God who spoke words to me, destroyed the house of the Pharaoh, saved the Israelites by my hand, made my community a people guided by the truth and acting with justice." Then David praised his Lord: "Praise God who made me a great king, taught me the Psalms, made the mountains and birds subservient to me, gave me wisdom and a great ability in public speaking." Then Solomon praised his Lord: "Praise God who made the spirits subservient to me, the devils subservient to me teaching me what I wanted, who taught me augury, who gave me all things in abundance, who made the armies of devils, men and birds subservient to me, who gave me a great kingdom and made my kingship a good kingship." Then Jesus praised his Lord: "Praise God who gave me his word and made me as Adam was made from the earth. God said to him: 'Be,' and he was. He taught me the Book, the Wisdom, the Torah, and the Gospel. He allowed me to create birds from clay and breath life into them so that they would be birds by the permission of God. He allowed me to heal the sick and raise the dead. He raised me and saved me and my community from Satan."

*Abu Sa'id al-Khudri:* The Prophet Muhammad said: "God raised me to the second heaven and I was with Joseph surrounded by followers from his community. His face was like a full moon at night. He greeted me. Next I passed to the third heaven where I was with John and Jesus. Each of them looked like the other, their clothes and hair. They greeted me. Next I passed to the fourth heaven and I was with Idris. He greeted me. Then I passed to the fifth heaven and I was with Aaron surrounded by many followers from his community. He had a long beard. He greeted me. Next I passed to the sixth heaven and I was with Moses b. Imran. He had a lot of hair, as though it were a shirt on him. Next I passed to the seventh heaven and I was with Abraham. He was sitting with his back against the Inhabited House. He greeted me: 'Greetings, upright prophet.' Then I entered the Inhabited House and prayed in it. Every day 70,000 angels enter it, and this does not stop until the Day of Resurrection. Next I stopped when I was at a tree the leaves of which were covering for the community and at its base was a spring which flowed out into two branches. I said: 'What is this?' Gabriel said: 'This one is the river of mercy, and this one is the river of Kawthar which God gave you.' I washed in the river of mercy and it cleansed me from all my sins in advance. Then I went beyond Kawthar until I entered Paradise. In it are things no eye can see, no ear can hear, and no human heart can sense. There are pomegranates like the humps of a camel, and birds like the Bukht camel."

## Seal of the Prophets

**Q 33:40**  Muhammad was not the father of one of your men, but he is the messenger of God, the Seal of the Prophets. God is Knowing of all things.

*Ibn Kathir:* The Prophet Muhammad was commissioned to realize the message and transmit it to the people of the east and the west, then he bequeathed the role of transmitter to his community after him. The highest of those established after him were his Companions. They transmitted from the Prophet Muhammad just as he had commanded them in all of his sayings, actions, and circumstances, during his days and nights, his being at home and traveling, what he kept private and what was public. Then it was bequeathed to all who followed these predecessors up to our own time. The Prophet Muhammad whom God sent, the one whom God honored by making the Seal of the Prophets and the messengers, the perfection of the *hanif* religion. God related, in his great Book, that there was no prophet after Muhammad so that people would know that anyone claiming this position after him would be a liar, leading people astray.

*Ibn Kathir:* It is prohibited to say "Zayd b. Muhammad" because Muhammad was not his father, even if he had adopted him, because the Prophet Muhammad did not have a male child who lived until he reached puberty. He had three sons by Khadijah: Qasim, Tayb, and Tahir, who died as infants. He also had Ibrahim from Mariyah the Egyptian, but he also died while still nursing. He had four daughters by Khadijah: Zaynab, Ruqiyah, Umm Kulthum, and Fatimah. Three of them died during his life. Fatimah died six months after him.

*Ubayy b. Ka'b:* The Prophet Muhammad said: "My place among the prophets is like a man who builds a house, making it beautiful and complete. But he leaves a place for one brick which he does not lay. The people begin to walk around the bricks and wonder at it, saying:

'Would not the placement of this brick make it complete?' My place among the prophets is the place of this brick."

*Jabir b. Abdallah:* The Prophet Muhammad said: "My place among the prophets is like a man who builds a house, making it complete and beautiful except for the place of one brick. It is on the inside, and when he sees it he says: 'Only the placement of this brick would make this better.' I am the placement of this brick. With me the prophets are sealed."

*Anas b. Malik:* The Prophet Muhammad said: "The message and prophethood have come to an end. There is no messenger after me, and no prophet." The people were distressed at this, so he said: "But there is good news." They asked: "Prophet of God, what good news?" He said: "The vision of a Muslim man is one part of prophethood."

*Jubayr b. Mut'im:* I heard the Prophet Muhammad say: "I have names: I am Muhammad, Ahmad. I am the blotter with which God blots out disbelief. I am the assembler who assembles the people beneath my feet. I am the last, after whom there are no more prophets."

# Glossary of Interpreters and Transmitters

**Abd al-Aziz b. Rufay**   Abu 'Abdallah 'Abd al-'Aziz b. Rufay' (d. 130) is known as a reliable transmitter of hadith reports from the first generation of the Followers of the Prophet Muhammad's Companions. He came from Ta'if but settled in Kufah. He reported hadith reports on the authority of Ibn Abbas, Ibn Umar, Anas b. Malik, Zayd b. Wahb, and Ubayd b. Umayr.

**Abd al-Ghaffar**   Abu Salih 'Abd al-Ghaffar b. Mihran b. Ziyad (140–224) was a well-respected scholar of hadith reports who lived in Haran and Egypt. Many of the compilers of the six authoritative collections of prophetic hadith reports transmit hadith on his authority.

**Abd al-Rahman b. Awf**   'Abd al-Rahman b. 'Awf al-Sahabi (d. 31) was an early Meccan convert to Islam from the Banu Zuhra. He emigrated to Ethiopia and then to Medina, and fought at the main battles with the Muslims. He is said to be one of ten people whom the Prophet Muhammad assured of Paradise.

**Abd al-Rahman b. Zayd**   'Abd al-Rahman b. Zayd b. Aslam al-'Umari (d. 182). He is known for his knowledge of the Quran and its interpretation. His interpretation of the Quran is said to have been collected, as were his writings on the abrogation of the Quran. He is reported to have transmitted on the authority of his father and Ibn al-Munkadr.

**Abd al-Razzaq**   Abu Bakr 'Abd al-Razzaq b. Hammam (126–211) was a transmitter of hadith reports and Quran interpreter. He is known for a collection of hadith reports he assembled, and a commentary on the Quran he wrote, both of which are extant only in part.

**Abdallah b. Amir**   Abu Muhammad 'Abdallah b. 'Amir b. Rabi'ah al-'Anzi (d. 85) was a Medinan born in the year of the Battle of Hudabayah. He transmitted hadith reports from several of the Prophet Muhammad's closest Companions such as Umar b. al-Khattab, Uthman, and Abd al-Rahman b. Awf.

**Abdallah b. al-Harith** ʿAbdallah b. al-Harith b. ʿAbd al-Muttalib b. Hashim b. ʿAbd al-Manaf (d. 78), brother of Rabiʿah b. al-Harith left Mecca and went to join the Prophet Muhammad in Medina before the conquest of Mecca. He is said to have been buried in the gown of the Prophet Muhammad.

**Abdallah b. Salam** Abu Yusuf ʿAbdallah b. Salam b. al-Harith (d. 43) was a Companion of the Prophet Muhammad whose transmission of hadith reports is highly respected and cited by many later scholars.

**Abdallah b. Shawdhab** Abu ʿAbd al-Rahman ʿAbdallah b. Shawdhab (86–156). Born in Balkh or Khurasan, Abdallah moved to Basrah and finally settled in Jerusalem. He was of the first generation of the Followers, and was considered to be trustworthy in his transmission of hadith reports from Hasan al-Basri, Ibn Sirin and others.

**Abdallah b. Ubayd b. Umayr** Abu Hashim ʿAbdallah b. ʿUbayd b. ʿUmayr al-Laythi (d. 113) was son of Ubayd b. Umayr, the well-known transmitter of hadith reports. Ibn Jurayj and al-Awzaʿi trans-mitted hadith reports on his authority.

**Abdallah b. Uthman b. Khuthaym** Abu ʿUthman ʿAbdallah b. ʿUthman b. Khuthaym (d. 144) was a Quran scholar from Mecca. He is considered to have been a sound transmitter of hadith reports from many well-known figures such as Abu al-Tufayl, Abu al-Zubayr, and Mujahid.

**Abdallah b. Zamʿah** ʿAbdallah b. Zamʿah b. al-Aswad (d. 80) was the son of Qaribah the elder, daughter of Abu Umayyah b. al-Mughirah and of Atikah bt. Abd al-Muttalib, the aunt of the Prophet Muhammad.

**Abu Abdallah al-Sufi** Abu ʿAbdallah Ahmad b. al-Hasan b. ʿAbd al-Jabbar al-Sufi is known to have transmitted from al-Harith b. Surayj and al-Harith b. Asad al-Muhasibi. Among those who transmitted on his authority is Abu al-Walid Hassan b. Muhammad b. Ahmad al-Nisapuri (270–349).

**Abu al-Aliyah** Abu al-ʿAliyah Rufayʿ b. Mihran al-Riyahi (d. 90 or 96). A freed slave of the Banu Riyah, he belonged to the first generation of the Followers in Basrah. He is known as a transmitter of the Quran and of hadith reports, and a commentary on the Quran is attributed to him but not extant. He is considered a sound transmitter of hadith reports, primarily from Umar and Ubayy b. Ka'b, and is the source of the transmission of many hadith reports from Qatadah, Dawud b. Abu Hind, Asim al-Ahwal, and others.

**Abu al-Ash'ath al-Ahmari**   Abu al-Ash'ath Sharahil b. Adah al-San'ani (d. after 100), originally from Yemen, was one of the foremost scholars of Damascus who transmitted hadith reports from Abu Hurayrah and others.

**Abu al-Darda**   Abu al-Darda' al-Ansari al-Khazraji (d. 32). One of the Companions of the Prophet Muhammad, who became a Muslim following the Battle of Badr. His hadith reports are well known by Sufis because of his renown as an ascetic [zahid] and sage [hakim] in the early Muslim community. He collected the Quran during the lifetime of the Prophet Muhammad and later taught it while serving as a judge in Damascus.

**Abu al-Khattab b. Duhiyyah**   Abu al-Khattab b. Duhiyyah 'Umar b. Hasan b. 'Ali (546 or 548–633) was a well-known hadith scholar of later generations with other expertise in grammar. He is said to have memorized the whole of Bukhari's collection of hadith reports.

**Abu al-Layth al-Samarqandi**   Abu al-Layth Nasr b. Muhammad al-Samarqandi (d. 373 or 375). A well-known Hanafi jurist, Abu al-Layth al-Samarqandi is author of a number of works in diverse fields. Along with his Quran commentary, Samarqandi is known for his compendium of Hanafi fiqh *Khizanat al-Fiqh*, his collection of fatwas on various issues, a work on hadith transmission, and works on various aspects of Muslim piety. His Quran commentary is significant for the Central Asia perspective it preserves.

**Abu al-Qasim al-Balkhi**   Abu al-Qasim 'Abdallah b. Ahmad b. Mahmud al-Ka'bi al-Balkhi (d. 319) was a Mu'tazili scholar of the Quran. He is reported to have written a Quran commentary in twelve volumes which is not extant but is cited by later scholars such as Fakhr al-Din al-Razi.

**Abu al-Qasim al-Qushayri**   Abu al-Qasim 'Abd al-Karim b. Hawzin b. 'Abd al-Malik (375–465) was a famous Sufi writer from Khurasan. He is also respected for his knowledge of Islamic law, Quran interpretation, hadith reports, and literature.

**Abu al-Sakan al-Hujri**    Abu al-Sakan al-Hujri transmitted hadith reports from Jabir b. Abdallah from the Prophet Muhammad, and Abd al-Samad b. Abd al-Warith transmitted hadith reports on his authority.

**Abu al-Tufayl**    Abu al-Tufayl ʿAmir b. Wathilah b. ʿAbdallah al-Kinani (d. 100–110) was born sometime after the Hijrah and transmitted hadith reports from Abu Bakr, Umar b. al-Khattab, Ibn Masud, and Ali b. Abi Talib. He is said to have been witness to the Prophet Muhammad, though he would have been very young, perhaps only eight years old, when the Prophet Muhammad died.

**Abu Bakr**    Abu Bakr ʿAbdallah b. Abi Quhafa (d. 13) was one of the first converts to Islam, one of the Prophet Muhammad's closest Companions, and was the first Caliph. The Prophet Muhammad married the daughter of Abu Bakr.

**Abu Burdah**    Abu Burdah ʿAmir b. ʿAbdallah b. Qays al-Ashʿari, brother of Abu Musa al-Ashʿari (d. 103–107). One of the first generation of Followers in Kufah, he transmitted hadith reports from a number of prominent Companions of the Prophet Muhammad including his father, Aishah, Abu Hurayrah, and Ibn Umar.

**Abu Dharr**    Abu Dharr Jundab b. Junadah b. Sufyan (d. 80) is said to have been the fifth person to convert to Islam. He came to Medina only after the battles of Badr, Uhud and the Ditch. He is described as black and hairy with white hair and a beard. He is credited with the origins of many ascetic attitudes in early Islam.

**Abu Hayyan**    Abu Hayyan al-Tawhidi ʿAli b. Muhammad b. al-ʿAbbas (c. 310–414) was a well-known philosopher who studied grammar and law, and frequented Sufi masters. He traveled widely and wrote books, some of which he burnt himself before his death. He is highly respected for his style of Arabic prose.

**Abu Hurayrah**    Abu Hurayrah ʿAbdallah al-Dawi al-Yamani (d. 58). He came to Medina in the year 7 and converted to Islam, and was with the Prophet Muhammad for roughly four years. He is well known as the transmitter of many hadith reports, and it is estimated that more than 800 people transmitted on his authority. It is said that the Prophet Muhammad caused him never to forget anything he heard from him.

**Abu Jaʿfar al-Baqir**    Abu Jaʿfar Muhammad b. ʿAli al-Husayn b. ʿAli al-Baqir (56–114 or 117) was the great-grandson of the Prophet Muhammad, through the Prophet Muhammad's daughter who married Ali b. Abi Talib, and was the fifth Shi'i Imam. He transmitted hadith reports from the Prophet Muhammad, Ali b. Abi Talib, Hasan, Husayn, Ibn Abbas, Aishah, and other prominent figures. Many prominent figures of the next generation, such as Ata b. Abi Rabah, Zuhri, and Ibn Jurayj transmitted hadith reports on his authority.

**Abu Kurayb**    Abu Kurayb Muhammad b. al-'Ala' b. Kurayb (161–248) was a prominent and trusted Kufan hadith scholar who is said to have known upwards to 300,000 hadith reports. He is often cited in the six authoritative collections of hadith, and by other respected scholars such as Abu Zur'ah, Abu Ya'ala and Abu Hatim.

**Abu Malik**    Abu Malik al-Ash'ari is known for transmitting reports from the Prophet Muhammad about the drinking of wine, musical instruments, and the punishment of God turning sinners into apes and pigs.

**Abu Musa al-Ash'ari**    Abu Musa b. Qays al-Ash'ari (d. 42) was a Companion of the Prophet Muhammad, joining him at the time of the expedition against Khaybar in the year 7, although he is also said to have been one of the emigrants to Ethiopia before the Hijrah. He was appointed governor of Basrah under Umar b. al-Khattab, and to him is attributed a variant codex of the Quran which is still attested.

**Abu Nujayh**    Abu Nujayh 'Aribad b. Sariyyah al-Sulami (d. 75) was a Companion who settled in Homs, and reported hadith from the Prophet Muhammad and the well-known Companion Abu Ubaydah b. al-Jarrah.

**Abu Sa'id al-Khudri**    Abu Sa'id al-Khudri Sa'd b. Malik (d. 63) was a well-known Companion who transmitted hadith reports from the Prophet Muhammad, Abu Bakr, and Umar b. al-Khattab. Many important Followers transmitted on his authority, and he was widely regarded as an expert in legal affairs.

**Abu Salih**    Abu Salih Muhammad b. Yahya al-Qattan (d. 223) was a Basran transmitter of hadith reports on the authority of his father and Sufyan b. Uyaynah. He is used as a source by a number of important hadith scholars such as Abu Zur'ah, Bukhari, Muslim, and Abu Dawud.

**Abu Ubaydah**    Abu 'Ubaydah 'Amir b. 'Abdallah b. al-Jarrah (d. 18) was a close Companion of the Prophet Muhammad, one of the earliest converts to Islam, and one of the commanders during the conquests before his death in Palestine. He emigrated to Ethiopia before the Hijrah and is said to have been given the title "Amin" or "Trustworthy" by the Prophet Muhammad himself.

**Abu Ya'ala**   Abu al-Ya'ala Ahmad b. 'Ali (210–305) was a well-known hadith scholar from Mosul. He is author of a collection of hadith reports called the *Musnad* which was used as an authoritative source of hadith reports by many later scholars.

**Abu Zur'ah**   Abu Zur'ah 'Ubaydallah b. 'Abd al-Karim b. Yazid (d. 211) was a famous hadith scholar from Rayy. He transmitted hadith reports from a number of well-known Followers, and is said to have memorized something like 100,000 hadith reports.

**Ahmad b. Hanbal**   Ahmad b. Muhammad b. Hanbal (d. 241) is called the "Imam of Baghdad" or "Imam Ahmad." The *Musnad* of Ibn Hanbal contains roughly 30,000 hadith reports, organized according to the Companions of the Prophet Muhammad who first circulated the report. He is well known as the eponymous founder of the Hanbali school of fiqh scholarship.

**Aishah**   'A'ishah bt. Abi Bakr (d. 58). The third wife of the Prophet Muhammad, she is credited with transmitting many hadith reports, some 300 of which are preserved in Bukhari and Muslim. She is also reported to have had her own codex of the Quran.

**Ali b. Abi Talib**   Abu al-Hasan 'Ali b. Abi Talib b. 'Abd al-Muttalib b. Hashim b. 'Abd al-Manaf b. Qusayy (d. 40). The Prophet Muhammad's paternal cousin, his son-in-law, and the fourth Caliph (r. 35–40), Ali is regarded by many Shi'i Muslims as the first in a line of Imams which succeed the Prophet Muhammad. Because of the importance of this position, many of Ali's sayings are included in Shi'i commentaries but not in non-Shi'i commentaries.

**Ali b. Rabah**   Abu Musa 'Ali b. Rabah b. Qusayr (d. 114–117) was one of the foremost scholars of the first generation of the Followers. It is said that he was born in the year of the Battle of Yarmuk (34) and that he was the confidant of several Umayyad Caliphs.

**A'mash**   Abu Muhammad Sulayman b. Mihran al-A'mash (60–148) was known in Kufah as a transmitter of hadith reports, and scholar of the Quran. He transmitted reports from Zuhri and Anas b. Malik. He studied the readings of the Quran with Mujahid and Nakha'i. His "reading" of the Quran followed that of Ibn Masud and Ubayy b. Ka'b, and is considered one of fourteen authoritative readings.

**Ammar b. Yasir**  Abu al-Yaqzan 'Ammar b. Yasir b. 'Ammar b. Malik (d. 37) was a Yemeni Companion who transmitted hadith reports from the Prophet Muhammad and Hudhayfah b. al-Yaman. Many prominent figures, including Ibn Abbas, Abu al-Tufayl, and Abu Musa al-Ash'ari, transmitted hadith reports on his authority. He was killed with Ali b. Abi Talib at the Battle of Siffin.

**Amr b. al-As**  Abu 'Abdallah 'Amr b. al-'As b. Wa'il (d. 43) was a well-known military commander and Companion of the Prophet Muhammad. He is best known for his conquest of Egypt, where he remained for some time as governor.

**Amr b. Kharijah**  'Amr b. Kharijah b. al-Muntafiq al-Ash'ari was a Companion who transmitted hadith reports from the Prophet Muhammad, but only a small number of hadith reports are attributed to his transmission.

**Amr b. Maymun**  Abu 'Abdallah 'Amr b. Maymun (d. 74–76) converted to Islam during the time of the Prophet Muhammad, and subsequently moved to Kufah, where he was known for transmitting hadith reports on the authority of prominent Companions such as Umar b. al-Khattab, Ali b. Abi Talib, Ibn Masud, Abu Hurayrah, and others.

**Amr b. Murrah**  Abu 'Abdallah 'Amr b. Murrah (d. 118) was a Kufan authority in Islamic law.

**Amr b. Qays**  Ibn Umm Maktum 'Amr b. Qays (d. 80) was an early convert to Islam in Mecca. He was blind and went to Medina after the Prophet Muhammad left Mecca. In Medina, he lived with other reciters of the Quran. He is said to have been the muezzin for the Prophet Muhammad, and to have carried the Muslim banner in the Battle of Qadisiyyah.

**Anas b. Malik**  Abu Hamza Anas b. Malik (d. 91 or 93). One of the most widely cited transmitters of hadith reports, he was ten years old when he was given to the Prophet Muhammad as a servant following the Hijrah. Dhahabi mentions that Bukhari and Muslim record 278 reports on the authority of Anas b. Malik.

**Anbasah b. Sa'id**    Abu Ayyub 'Anbasah b. Sa'id b. al-'As was a Qurayshi of the Umayyad family. He transmitted hadith reports from several prominent Companions of the Prophet Muhammad such as Anas b. Malik, Umar b. Abd al-Aziz and Abu Hurayrah. He is cited in Bukhari, Muslim, and Abu Dawud.

**Ata b. Abi Rabah**    'Ata' b. Abi Rabah (d. 114 or 115). A Nubian, born in Yemen, and raised in Mecca as a client of the Abu Maysara b. Abi Khuthaym family, Ata was a well-known representative of Islamic law in Mecca. Many hadith reports are attributed to him, said to be obtained through his personal contact with many Companions of the Prophet Muhammad such as Abdallah b. Umar and Aishah.

**Atiyah al-Awfi**    Abu al-Hasan 'Atiyah b. Sa'd b. Junadah al-'Awfi (d. 111) was a transmitter of hadith reports and Quran interpretation, and is closely linked with the early Shi'ah.

**Awn b. Abi Shaddad**    Abu Ma'mar 'Awn b. Abi Shaddad al-'Aqili al-Basri transmitted hadith reports from a number of prominent figures such as Anas b. Malik and Hasan al-Basri, and is considered to be sound as a transmitter.

**Awza'i**    Muhammad b. 'Ali b. al-Husayn Abu 'Amr 'Abd al-Rahman b. 'Amr al-Awza'i (d. 150 or 157) lived in Beirut and was well known as a scholar of Islamic law and of hadith reports. He is regarded as the founder and primary proponent of the "Syrian" law school.

**Bakr b. Abdallah al-Muzanni**    Abu 'Abdallah Bakr b. 'Abdallah b. 'Amr al-Muzanni (d. 106 or 108) transmitted hadith reports from well-known Companions of the Prophet Muhammad such as al-Mughirah b. Sha'bah, Ibn Abbas, Ibn Umar, and Anas b. Malik.

**Bara b. 'Azib**    Abu Umarah al-Bara' b. 'Azib (d. c. 64–72) became a Companion of the Prophet Muhammad in Medina, and was responsible for the conquest of Rayy. He is reported to have sided with Ali b. Abi Talib against Mu'awiyah and he later lived in Kufah, where he died during the governorship of Mus'ab b. al-Zubayr.

**Bukhari**    Abu 'Abdallah Muhammad b. Isma'il b. Ibrahim b. al-Mughirah b. Barbizbah Abu 'Abdallah al-Ju'fi al-Bukhari (d. 256) collected the most widely authoritative collection of prophetic hadith reports in his *Sahih*. This work is a standard reference for many later scholars. Numerous commentaries have been written on the *Sahih* of Bukhari, the best known being those of Ibn Hajar and Qastillani.

**Dahhak**   Abu al-Qasim Dahhak b. Muzahim (d. 105) was considered an expert on the Quran and is said to have lived in various places in Iraq and Central Asia.

**Daraqutni**   Abu al-Hasan 'Ali b. 'Umar b. Ahmad al-Daraqutni (306–385) was considered to be the foremost Baghdadi scholar of the Quran and hadith reports of his time. He is reported to be the first to compile all the various readings of the Quran, and is often cited by later authorities.

**Dawud b. Abi Hind**   Abu Bakr Dawud b. Abi Hind (d. 138) was from Khurasan and later lived in Basrah. He was known for his knowledge of the Quran, its recitation and interpretation, and as an authority in Islamic law.

**Fakhr al-Din al-Razi**   Abu 'Abdallah Muhammad b. 'Umar b. al-Hussain Fakhr al-Din al-Razi (543–606). One of the most famous intellectuals of his time, Fakhr al-Din al-Razi lived on the eve of the Mongol invasions. One of his best-known teachers was Majd al-Din al-Jili, the teacher of the famous Sufi philosopher Shihad al-Din Yahya al-Suhrawardi (d. 587). His Quran commentary has been condemned by scholars such as Ibn Taymiya and praised by others like Subki for its inclusion of philosophical and theological perspectives. The commentary is organized according to different "questions" [masa'il] much like other rational-theological works. Some scholars believe Fakhr al-Din al-Razi died before the completion of his commentary, and that it was finished by his disciples. He was known as a defender of Ash'ari Sunni doctrines.

**Farra**   Abu Zakariya Yahya b. Ziyad al-Farra' (144–207) was a famous Kufan grammarian and reputed founder of the "Kufan School" of Arabic grammar. He wrote a number of extant works on Arabic grammar including a treatise on the grammar of the Quran.

**Hakam**   Abu Muhammad or Abu 'Abdallah al-Hakam b. 'Utaybah (d. 112) transmitted many hadith reports and was respected for his knowledge of Islamic law. It is reported that he was of the opinion that Ali b. Abi Talib was better qualified than Abu Bakr and Umar to be Caliph.

**Hakim**    Abu ʿAbdallah b. al-Bayyiʿ Muhammad b. ʿAbdallah b. Muhammad al-Hakim al-Nisaburi (321–405) was a respected hadith scholar who traveled and wrote many works on the study of hadith. He is said to have heard hadith reports from about 2000 people. He is the author of a well-known commentary on the collections of Bukhari and Muslim.

**Harith**    Harith b. Hassan b. Kaladah al-Bakri was a Companion who transmitted hadith reports from the Prophet Muhammad. Among those who transmitted on his authority were Abu Waʾil and Asim b. Bahdalah (d. 127).

**Hasan al-Basri**    Abu Saʿid b. Abi al-Hasan Yasar al-Basri (21–110). Born in Medina after his father was taken prisoner during the Muslim conquest of Sasanian Iraq, Hasan was of the first generation of Followers of the Companions of the Prophet Muhammad. He was famous for his preaching which criticized accumulation of worldly goods. He is also credited with some unusual readings of the Quran and the transmission of hadith reports.

**Hudhayfah**    Abu ʿAbdallah Hudhayfah b. al-Yaman a well-known Companion of the Prophet Muhammad and military leader during the conquests. He is said to have murdered someone of his own tribe and so fled to Medina where he became an ally of the Banu Abd al-Ashhal, part of the Aws.

**Humayd b. Abd al-Rahman**    Humayd b. ʿAbd al-Rahman was a Basran scholar who transmitted hadith reports from a number of Companions such as Abu Hurayrah and Ibn Umar. Ibn Sirin was among those who transmitted hadith reports on his authority.

**Husayn b. al-Fadl**    Abu ʿAli al-Husayn b. al-Fadl b. ʿUmayr al-Balkhi (180–282) was a Quran commentator, linguist, and hadith scholar. He is known as one of the greatest Quran commentators of his age in Nishabur, where he lived and taught for the latter part of his life.

**Ibn Abbas**    ʿAbdallah b. ʿAbbas b. ʿAbd al-Muttalib b. Hashim b. ʿAbd Manaf b. Qusayy (d. 68). Cousin and companion of the Prophet Muhammad, Ibn Abbas is one of the greatest authorities on Quran interpretation. Ibn Abbas was thirteen years old when the Prophet Muhammad died. When Ibn Abbas died, at the age of 73, he was buried in Taʾif. His sayings are one of the most important sources for hadith and Quran interpretation, and he is often credited with being the founder of the science of Quran interpretation. Because of the extensive Israiliyyat traditions attributed to him, Ibn Abbas is sometimes called the "Rabbi of the Arabs." His sayings are also responsible for establishing the significance of pre-Islamic Arabic poetry for understanding the Quran.

**Ibn Abi al-Dunya**  Ibn Abi al-Dunya Abu Bakr ʿAbdallah b. Muhammad b. ʿUbayd b. Sufyan (208–281) was the tutor of several Abbasid princes who later became Caliphs. He is known for his ascetic life, and numerous scholars have transmitted hadith reports on his authority. He is reported to have written around 100 books, not all of which are extant.

**Ibn Abi al-Hudhayl**  Abu al-Mughirah ʿAbdallah b. Abi al-Hudhayl was a Kufan Follower who transmitted hadith reports on the authority of important Companions such as Abu Bakr, Umar and Ubayy b. Kaʿb.

**Ibn Abi Burdah**  Saʿid b. Abi Burdah (d. 167) was a Kufan Follower who transmitted hadith reports from his father, Anas b. Malik, Abu Waʾil and others. Among those who transmitted on his authority are Qatadah and al-Masʿudi.

**Ibn Abi Hatim**  Abu Muhammad ʿAbd al-Rahman b. Abi Hatim (240–327). Son of the famous Rayy hadith scholar, Ibn Abi Hatim was well known for his work in hadith criticism which helped to establish the standards for evaluating the authority of different reports from the Prophet Muhammad. He is said to have produced a commentary on the Quran, and works on Islamic law.

**Ibn Abi Khaythamah**  Ibn Abi Khaythamah Abu Bakr Ahmad b. Zufayr (185–279) is the author of a respected work on history. He was the student of Ahmad b. Hanbal, and was also known for his study of genealogy and literature.

**Ibn Abi Najih**  Abu Bakr Muhammad b. al-ʿAbbas b. Najih (263–345) was a hadith scholar from Baghdad who reported on the authority of several Baghdadi scholars. His transmission of reports is considered to be sound.

**Ibn al-Jawzi**  Abu al-Faraj ʿAbd al-Rahman b. ʿAli b. Muhammad b. al-Jawzi (510–597) was the author of a well-known commentary on the Quran. He lived and taught in Baghdad, where he was in contact with many famous scholars of the sixth century. His Quran commentary is roughly nine volumes and is written in an abbreviated style so that it summarizes the main points of traditional interpretations on each verse.

**Ibn al-Kalbi** Abu al-Mundhir Hisham b. Muhammad b. al-Saʾib al-Kalbi (d. 204 or 206) was a well-known Kufan scholar of genealogies. His father Abu al-Nadr Muhammad b. al-Saʾib is credited with a Quran interpretation which included materials from Sufyan al-Thawri and Ibn Ishaq.

**Ibn Asakir** ʿAli b. Abi Muhammad al-Hasan b. ʿAsakir (499–571) is one of the best known of a famous Damascus-based family of Shafiʿi scholars. He studied with many prominent scholars of his time in Syria, Iraq, Hijaz, Iran, and Central Asia. He is best known for his monumental history of Damascus which includes an extensive biographical dictionary of Syrian scholars.

**Ibn Damrah al-Saʿdi** ʿUtayy b. Damrah al-Saʿdi (d. 47) transmitted hadith reports from Ubayy b. Kaʿb and Ibn Masud. Among those who transmitted on his authority were Hasan al-Basri and his son Abdallah b. Utayy.

**Ibn Dawud** Abu Bakr Muhammad b. Dawud b. ʿAli (d. 297) is the well-known author of a book on literature, culture, and poetry. He also transmitted hadith reports.

**Ibn Hajar** Shihab al-Din Abu al-Fadl Ahmad b. Nur al-Din ʿAli b. Hajar al-ʿAsqalani (773–852). Considered one of the greatest hadith scholars, Ibn Hajar wrote a number of biographical dictionaries devoted to the Companions of the Prophet Muhammad and later transmitters of hadith reports. He is perhaps best known for his lengthy commentary on the hadith collection of Bukhari, compiled from his lectures over about 25 years.

**Ibn Hibban** Abu Bakr Muhammad b. Hibban al-Tamimi (270–354). During his travels from North Africa to Central Asia, Ibn Hibban compiled a well-regarded collection of hadith reports. He was a judge in Samarqand for a time. He produced a work, used by Dhahabi and Ibn Hajar, evaluating the probity of different hadith transmitters. al-Khatib al-Baghdadi recommends for study 40 books written by Ibn Hibban, though most of these are not extant.

**Ibn Hisham** Abu Muhammad ʿAbd al-Malik b. Hisham (d. 213 or 218) was of a family originally from Yemen. He is famous for his edition of Ibn Ishaq's biography of the Prophet Muhammad. He also produced a book on the history of South Arabia containing much information that is sometimes found in Quran interpretation.

**Ibn Hubayrah** Abu Hubayrah 'Abdallah b. Hubayrah al-Saba'i (d. 126) was considered a trustworthy transmitter of hadith reports from figures such as Ikrimah and Abd al-Rahman b. Ghanam.

**Ibn Ishaq** Muhammad b. Ishaq b. Yasar al-Muttalabi al-Madani (85–150) is well known as a historian, responsible for writing the earliest, most widely known and cited biography of the Prophet Muhammad. The first section of his biography, no longer extant but cited extensively in later sources, is an account of the prophets and other figures from Adam leading up to the Prophet Muhammad. He is said to have transmitted information from his father and his paternal uncles Musa and Abd al-Rahman from the Prophet Muhammad. Ibn Ishaq also traveled widely, collecting information from prominent scholars on the history of the Prophet Muhammad and earlier prophets.

**Ibn Jurayj** 'Abd al-Malik b. 'Abd al-'Aziz b. Jurayj (80–150) was a respected Meccan scholar and transmitter of hadith reports from many of the best-known Companions of the Prophet Muhammad including Ata b. Abi Ribah. He is said to have been among the first to compile books of Islamic learning, and many prominent scholars of the next generation including al-Awza'i and Sa'id b. Abd al-Aziz transmitted on his authority.

**Ibn Kathir** Isma'il b. 'Umar b. Kathir (700–774). Born in Syria under the Mamluks, Ibn Kathir studied in Damascus with the famous al-Mizzi (d. 742) and Ibn Taymiyyah. Ibn Kathir was director of the Dar al-Hadith al-Ashrafiyyah, a place of pilgrimage because it enshrined one of the Prophet Muhammad's shoes. He was named a professor in Quran commentary at the Umayyad University. Like Tabari, Ibn Kathir also wrote a world history and a Quran commentary. Ibn Kathir's commentary is regarded as one of the soundest in terms of its reliance upon authoritative hadith reports, though he also incorporates historical material from non-Muslim sources, and is always careful to comment on his evaluation of earlier opinions from scholars like Tabari and Fakhr al-Din al-Razi.

**Ibn Majah** Ibn Majah Abu 'Abdallah Muhammad b. Yazid (209–273) is the compiler of one of the six authoritative collections of hadith reports, credited with writing more than 30 books on hadith, history, and Quran interpretation.

**Ibn Mardaweh** Abu Bakr Ahmad b. Muhammad b. Abi Bakr (409–498) was a well-known scholar and transmitter of hadith reports who lived in Isfahan. He is said to have authored many works, not all of which are extant.

**Ibn Masud** ʿAbdallah b. Ghafil b. Habib b. Hudayl b. Masud (d. 32) was a Companion of the Prophet Muhammad and transmitter of the Quran. He was one of the earliest converts to Islam, and was entrusted to carry the Prophet Muhammad's shoes and gather the plants used for the ritual toothpick sticks. Most of those who transmitted hadith reports from Ibn Masud were in Kufah, and he is most frequently cited by Tirmidhi. Ibn Masud's Quran differed from the Uthmanic version in variant readings and in the order of the surahs. His comments on the Quran are sometimes regarded as having Shiʿi tendencies because of his use of allegorical exegesis [taʾwil].

**Ibn Qutaybah** Abu Muhammad b. Qutaybah ʿAbdallah b. Muslim al-Dinawari (213–276) was an erudite and prolific scholar of third-century Iraq, writing many works on the Quran, hadith, theology, astronomy, and general encyclopedias. He is considered one of the earliest writers of Arabic prose after Ibn al-Muqaffa and al-Jahiz.

**Ibn Saʿd** Abu ʿAbdallah Muhammad b. Saʿd b. Maniʿ al-Basri al-Hashimi (d. 230) was born in Basra and died in Baghdad. Known as a collector of hadith reports, he traveled widely and studied under the well-known historian al-Waqidi (d. 207). He also studied genealogy with the famous Hisham al-Kalbi. The *Tabaqat* of Ibn Saʿd consists of a series of biographies, beginning with the Prophet Muhammad and continuing through his Companions and their Followers to later generations.

**Ibn Sirin** Abu Bakr Muhammad b. Sirin (d. 105) was a client of Anas b. Malik and is reported to have been deaf. It is also reported that he fathered 30 children from the same woman but only one of the children survived, his son Abdallah b. Muhammad. He is credited as being the first renowned Muslim interpreter of dreams.

**Ibn Umar** Abu ʿAbd al-Rahman ʿAbdallah b. ʿUmar (d. 132), son of the Caliph and prominent Companion Umar b. al-Khattab, was regarded as an example of piety, honesty, and the learning of hadith reports. He was appointed governor of Iraq by the Umayyad Yazid II but was eventually imprisoned by Marwan II in Haran, where he died.

**Ibn Yazid** ʿUbaydallah b. Abi Yazid al-Makki (d. 220) was considered a trustworthy transmitter of many hadith reports from important figures such as Ibn Abbas, Ibn Umar, Ibn Zubayr, and Ali b. Abi Talib.

**Ibn Zayd**  Muhammad b. Zayd b. al-Muhajir was considered a trust-worthy transmitter of hadith reports by many later scholars. Figures such as Zuhri and Malik b. Anas reported on his authority.

**Ibrahim al-Taymi**  Abu Asma' Ibrahim b. Yazid al-Taymi (d. 92–94) transmitted hadith reports on the authority of his father, Anas b. Malik, and Aishah. He was killed by al-Hajjaj b. Yusuf before he reached the age of 40, but is considered to be among the trustworthy transmitters of hadith reports.

**Ikrimah**  Abu 'Abdallah 'Ikrimah (d. 105 or 115), the client of Ibn Abbas, is the best known of those who transmitted on the authority of Ibn Abbas, though some scholars doubt his probity. He was widely respected for his learning in Islamic law, Quran, exegesis, and hadith reports. Some scholars explain that the suspicion regarding the reports given on his authority is related to the allegation that Ikrimah adhered to Khariji beliefs, and thus attributed them to Ibn Abbas.

**Ismail b. Abi Uways**  Abu 'Abdallah Isma'il b. Abi Uways 'Abdallah b. 'Abdallah b. Uways (139–226) is known as a Quran scholar and transmitter of hadith reports. He is cited by Bukhari, Muslim, Abu Dawud, Tirmidhi, and others.

**Israil**  Abu Yusuf Isra'il b. Yunus b. Abi Ishaq 'Amr (d. 160–162) was a scholar of the Quran and hadith reports from Kufah. His transmission of hadith reports is considered sound by most scholars.

**Jabir b. Abdallah**  Abu 'Abdallah Jabir b. 'Abdallah b. 'Amr b. Haram (d. 78) was one of the 70 who swore an oath to the Prophet Muhammad at Aqabah. He is said to have participated in more than half of the raids from Medina with the Prophet Muhammad, but did so only after his father died at the Battle of Uhud.

**Ja'far b. Burqan**  Ja'far b. Burqan al-Kilabi (d. 150 or 151) was a well-known and respected transmitter of hadith reports from significant figures including Waki, Ata, and Zuhri.

**Jawaliqi**  Abu Mansur Mawhub b. Ahmad b. Muhammad (466–539) was a respected Baghdadi scholar of Arabic literature, student of the famous al-Tibrizi in Arabic language and literature at the Nizamiyah university in Baghdad. He is known for his lexicon which preserved words of foreign origin used in the Arabic language.

**Jubayr b. Mut‘im**    Abu Muhammad Jubayr b. Mut‘im b. ‘Adi settled in Medina and converted to Islam before the conquest of Mecca. He transmitted many reports from the Prophet Muhammad. His father, Mut‘im b. Adi, was a noble of the Quraysh who protected the Prophet Muhammad. His son, Muhammad, was also well known as a transmitter of hadith reports and as a historian of the Quraysh.

**Ka‘b al-Ahbar**    Abu Ishaq Ka‘b al-Ahbar b. Mati‘ (d. 32) was one of the most famous Jewish converts to Islam and regarded as the oldest and most authoritative transmitter of Israiliyyat traditions. He came to Medina from Yemen during the caliphate of Umar and sat with the Companions of the Prophet Muhammad, where he would relate reports from the Bible and Jewish traditions.

**Ka‘b b. Ujrah**    Ka‘b b. ‘Ujrah al-Salimi (d. 52) was a Companion of the Prophet Muhammad, and transmitted hadith reports in Kufah and Basrah to a number of important figures such as Rabi‘a, Ibn Sirin, and his sons Sa‘d and Muhammad.

**Kashani**: Mulla Fath Allah Muhsin al-Malaqqab al-Ghayd Kashani (d. 996). Very little is known about Kashani, though he is known as a jurisprudent, theologian, and Quran commentator. He is known for his work *Nahj al-Balaghah*, which is taken to be a collection of discourses from the first Imam, Ali b. Abi Talib. Kashani wrote two Quran commentaries in Persian and one in Arabic. The Arabic contains Shi‘i traditions along with references from Zamakhshari, Baydawi, and Tabarsi.

**Khalid b. Ma‘dan**    Khalid b. Ma‘dan al-Kala‘i (d. 103) was of the first generation of Followers, said to have been a contemporary of 70 of the Prophet Muhammad's Companions, and respected as a jurist. He was of Yemeni origins but lived and died in Syria. It is said that he died while fasting.

**Kirmani**    Abu al-Qasim Burhan al-Din Mahmud b. Hamzah (d. 505) is famous for his expertise on the different recensions of the Quran which is found in his commentary on the Quran. His work is a major resource for later Quran scholars such as Zarkashi and Suyuti.

**Kisa’i**    Muhammad b. ‘Abdallah al-Kisa’i (fl. 500s) is the name attributed to the unknown author of a certain *Stories of the Prophets* book which includes much information not found in earlier works, nor repeated in later exegesis. Kisa’i often expands on earlier exegesis by elaborating a fuller narrative story line.

**Makhul**   Abu 'Abdallah or Abu Ayyub Makhul (d. 110–118) was one of the foremost scholars of Syria. He transmitted hadith reports from a number of Companions of the Prophet Muhammad such as Ubayy b. Ka'b, Abu Hurayrah, and Aishah, and from the first generation of the Followers.

**Malik b. Anas**   Abu 'Abdallah Malik b. Anas b. Malik b. Abi 'Amir al-Asbahi (90 or 97–179). The eponymous founder of the Maliki law school centered in Medina, Malik was one of the Followers of the Prophet Muhammad's Companions, on the authority of many of whom he transmitted hadith reports. He is best known for the compilation of Islamic law attributed to him, the *Muwatta*, which includes many hadith reports from the Prophet Muhammad and his Companions.

**Mawardi**   Abu al-Hasan 'Ali b. Muhammad b. Habib al-Mawardi (364–450) was a respected scholar of Islamic law and author of an extant Quran commentary. He was appointed to judgeships by Abbasid Caliphs, and was sent on a number of diplomatic missions. In addition to Quranic studies, Mawardi produced an important work of political theory and a work on Arabic grammar.

**Maymun b. Mihran**   Abu Ayyub Maymun b. Mihran (d. 177) was known as a leading scholar of the Quran and Islamic law in northern Iraq.

**Mu'awiyah**   Abu 'Abd al-Rahman Mu'awiyah b. Abi Sufyan (d. 60) founder of the Umayyad dynasty and Companion of the Prophet Muhammad.

**Mu'awiyah b. al-Hakim**   Mu'awiyah b. al-Hakim was a Companion from Medina who transmitted hadith reports from the Prophet Muhammad.

**Mu'awiyah b. al-Qurrah**   Mu'awiyah b. al-Qurrah b. 'Iyas was the son of the well-known Companion Qurrah b. Iyas who was killed in the Battle of al-Azaraqah in the time of the first Umayyad Caliphs. He is known for his transmission of hadith reports on the authority of his father.

**Mubarak b. Fadalah**   Ibn Abi 'Umayyah Mubarak b. Fadalah (d. 165). Considered one of the greatest of the Basran transmitters of hadith, he was a client of the family of Umar b. al-Khattab. Some scholars indicate that his transmission of hadith reports is not altogether reliable, and some classify his transmission as unsound.

**Muhammad b. Ka'b**  Abu Hamzah Muhammad b. Ka'b b. Hayyan al-Qurazi (d. 112) was from one of the Jewish tribes of Medina defeated by the Prophet Muhammad. He converted to Islam and settled in Kufah, and later Medina. Some report that he was born during the life of the Prophet Muhammad, but many scholars dispute this. He is considered to be a trustworthy transmitter of hadith reports and one of the early leaders in Quran interpretation.

**Muhammad b. Qays**  Muhammad b. Qays b. Makhramah b. al-Muttalib b. 'Abd al-Manaf transmitted hadith reports from people such as Abu Hurayrah and Aishah, and is said in his youth to have known the Prophet Muhammad before his death.

**Muharib b. Diththar**  Abu Kurdush Muharib b. Diththar b. Kurdush b. Qirwash (d. 116) was a Follower who transmitted hadith reports from a large number of earlier figures such as Ibn Umar, Jabir, and A'mash. He is considered a trustworthy transmitter by many later scholars.

**Mujahid**  Abu al-Hajjaj Mujahid b. Jabr (d. c. 100) is one of the most famous of Quran exegetes and Quran reciters. Mujahid was the client of al-Sa'ib b. Abi al-Sa'ib al-Makhzumi or Abdallah b. al-Sa'ib. Many prominent scholars reported on his authority, including Ikrimah, Ata, Amr b. Dinar, Abu al-Zubayr, and Ibn Abi Najih.

**Muqatil b. Sulayman**  Abu al-Hasan Muqatil b. Sulayman al-Balkhi (80–150) is author of one of the earliest extant Quran commentaries, one which preserves some material not found in later commentaries. His sources include Companions of the Prophet Muhammad and their Followers such as Ata b. Abi Rabah, Dahhak, Zuhri, Ibn Sirin, Ikrimah, and Qatadah.

**Mus'ab**  Abu 'Abdallah Mus'ab b. al-Zubayr (d. 72) was a horseman, one of the nobles of the Quraysh, and under his brother Abdallah b. al-Zubayr, was governor of Iraq, where he was killed by the Umayyad Abd al-Malik.

**Muslim**  Abu al-Husayn Muslim b. al-Hajjaj b. Muslim (202–261) was a famous hadith scholar from Nishapur responsible for the *Sahih Muslim*, one of the best known of the six authoritative books of hadith reports. He is said to have compiled some 300,000 reports, and his compilation, along with that of Bukhari, is considered by many to be the most authoritative of the six books.

**Mu'tamir b. Sulayman** Abu Muhammad al-Mu'tamir b. Sulayman al-Taymi was the son of the well-known Basran historian and transmitter of hadith reports, Sulayman b. Tarkhan. Sulayman is said to have transmitted about 200 hadith reports, and his reports are considered some of the most authoritative of those coming from Basrah.

**Naqqash** Abu Ja'far Muhammad b. 'Isa al-Naqqash was a Baghdadi hadith scholar who settled in Damascus and transmitted hadith reports on the authority of Yazid b. Harun, Yahya b. Abi Kathir, and others.

**Nawawi** Abu Zakariya Muhyi al-Din Yahya b. Sharaf al-Nawawi (631–676) was a well-known scholar of hadith and law from northern Syria. He studied in Damascus, where he stayed for a long time. He is author of many books including a famous commentary on Bukhari's collection of hadith reports.

**Nawf** Nawf b. Fadalah al-Bikali (d. 161) was the son of Ka'b al-Ahbar's wife. He was originally from Yemen but lived in Egypt and Syria where he gained a reputation as a teller of stories, a transmitter of reports from the Prophet Muhammad, and a prayer leader.

**Qatadah** Abu al-Khattab Qatadah b. Di'amah b. Qatadah al-Sadusi (60–117). Although blind from birth, Qatadah is credited with an excellent memory and knowledge of genealogies, lexicography, history, Quran exegesis, variant readings of the Quran, and hadith reports. He was a student of the well-known Hasan al-Basri and Ibn Sirin. He lived mostly in Basrah, though he is said to have died in Wasit.

**Qazwini** Zakariyah b. Muhammad b. Mahmud al-Qazwini (600–682). A famous geographer and author of a well-known work on the "wonders of creation" which was the first systematic exposition of Islamic cosmography. During his studies and travels he met the mystic Ibn al-Arabi and the historian Ibn al-Athir.

**Qummi** Abu al-Hasan 'Ali b. Ibrahim b. Hashim b. Musa b. Babwayhi (d. 328) studied under al-Kulini (d. 328) and is author of one of the earliest Imami Shi'i Quran commentaries. His commentary contains much that is peculiar to Shi'i exegesis of the Quran not found in earlier non-Shi'i Quran commentaries.

**Qurtubi**   Muhammad b. Ahmad al-Qurtubi (d. 671). Born in Spain, al-Qurtubi traveled to Upper Egypt, where he eventually died and was buried. He was a well-known scholar of Maliki jurisprudence and studied with one of Cordova's foremost hadith scholars who wrote a commentary on Muslim's *Sahih*. Qurtubi's commentary is known for its inclusion of numerous hadith reports, many of which were not mentioned by Tabari. Unlike Tabari, Qurtubi is more interested in the content of the hadith reports than the process of their transmission. Qurtubi's commentary does focus on the legal implications of the Quran but has original commentary on narrative passages including the Israiliyyat.

**Rabi'a b. Anas**   al-Rabi'a b. Anas b. Ziyad al-Bakri (d. 139). A prominent Follower of the first generation, he transmitted from Abu al-Aliyah, al-Riyahi, and Hasan al-Basri. He was considered during his time the foremost scholar of Marw, where he met Sufyan al-Thawri, and is also said to have been imprisoned for 30 years.

**Rabi'ah**   Rabi'ah b. al-Harith b. 'Abd al-Muttalib b. Hashim b. 'Abd Manaf (d. 80). A cousin of the Prophet Muhammad, Rabi'ah joined the Muslims only after the Battle of Badr, during the Battle of the Ditch, and subsequently participated in the Battle of Hunayn.

**Sa'd b. Abi Waqqas**   Abu Ishaq Sa'd b. Abi Waqqas Malik b. Wuhayb b. 'Abd Manaf (d. 50 or 58). A leading Companion of the Prophet Muhammad and commander of the armies in Iraq under Umar b. al-Khattab. Sa'd is said to be one of ten Companions the Prophet Muhammad promised entry into Paradise, as one of the first ten converts to Islam. Sa'd was instrumental in the founding of Kufah and was its first governor. He died near Medina and was buried in the cemetery there.

**Safiyah bt. Shaybah**   Umm Mansur Safiyah bt. Shaybah b. 'Uthman b. Abi Talhah (d. c. 80) transmitted reports directly from the Prophet Muhammad, from Aishah and from other wives of the Prophet Muhammad.

**Sa'ib b. Yazid**   Sa'ib b. Yazid b. Sa'id b. Thumamah (d. 82–100) was a Medinan transmitter of hadith reports who transmitted reports from the Prophet Muhammad, his father, and other Companions of the Prophet Muhammad.

**Sa'id b. Abi al-Hasan**   Sa'id b. Abi al-Hasan Yasar (d. 100) was the brother of the famous Hasan al-Basri, and considered one of the trustworthy transmitters from the generation of the Followers. He transmitted hadith reports from Abu Hurayrah and Ibn Abbas among others.

**Saʿid b. al-Musayyab**   Abu Muhammad Saʿid b. al-Musayyab (d. 94). He was a respected Medinan scholar of Islamic law, Quran, history, and genealogy. It is reported that he was imprisoned for refusing to give allegiance to the sons of the Umayyad Caliph Abd al-Malik. He transmitted hadith reports on the authority of Ubayy b. Kaʿb, Abu Dharr, Ali b. Abi Talib, Uthman, Aishah, Abu Hurayrah, Ibn Abbas, and others.

**Saʿid b. Jubayr**   Abu Muhammad Saʿid b. Jubayr b. Hisham (d. 95). One of the Followers who lived in Kufah. Among those from whom he transmitted hadith reports are Ibn Abbas, Abdallah b. Mughaffal, Aishah, Abu Musa al-Ashʿari, Abu Hurayrah, Anas, Abu Saʿid al-Khudri, and Abu Abd al-Rahman al-Sulami.

**Salim b. Abi al-Jaʿd**   Salim b. Abi al-Jaʿd al-Ashjaʿi (d. 100–109) transmitted hadith reports from many prominent Companions of the Prophet Muhammad including Anas b. Malik, Jabir b. Abdallah, and Ibn Abbas.

**Salman al-Farisi**   Abu Abdallah Salman al-Farisi (d. 80) was a famous Companion of the Prophet Muhammad, and is credited with the idea of digging the ditch against the attack of the Quraysh during the Battle of the Ditch. It is said that although he received a large sum of money from the conquests he continued to live a simple life.

**Samurah**   Abu Mahdhurah Samurah b. ʿUmayr b. Lawdhan b. Wahb (d. 59) was known as the "Muezzin" of Mecca. He is said to have refused to cut his hair after the Prophet Muhammad blessed it. He transmitted reports from the Prophet Muhammad.

**Shaʿbi**   ʿAmir b. Sharahil b. ʿAbd al-Shaʿbi (d. 105), from a Yemeni family, was a famous Kufan legal theorist and transmitter of poetry, hadith, and accounts of battles.

**Shafiʿi**   Muhammad b. Idris al-Shafiʿi (150–204), the eponymous founder of the Shafiʿi school of Islamic law, is credited as the architect of much of the theoretical framework for later Islamic thought and legal interpretation of the Quran.

**Shahr b. Hawshab**   Abu Saʿid Shahr b. Hawshab (d. 98) was a Follower of several prominent Companions from whom he transmitted hadith reports including Abu Hurayrah, Aishah, Ibn Abbas, Abdallah b. Amr,

Umm Salmah and Abu Saʿid al-Khudri. Those who transmitted hadith reports from him include Qatadah and Abd al-Rahman b. Thabit.

**Shimr b. Atiyah**   Shimr b. ʿAtiyah al-Asadi (d. c. 115) was considered a trustworthy transmitter of hadith reports from a number of earlier figures including Abu Waʾil. Among those who transmitted on his authority was Aʿmash.

**Shuayb al-Jabaʾi**   Shuʿayb b. al-Usud al-Jabaʾi was a Follower from Yemen on whose authority Salamah b. Wahram and Wahb b. Sulayman transmitted hadith reports.

**Suddi**   Abu Muhammad Ismaʿil b. ʿAbd al-Rahman b. Abi Karimah al-Suddi (d. 127) is widely cited as an interpreter of the Quran who transmitted hadith reports from important figures such as Anas b. Malik and Ibn Abbas.

**Sufyan al-Thawri**   Abu ʿAbdallah Sufyan b. Saʿid b. Masruq al-Thawri (94–161) was a famous legal scholar and hadith transmitter. He was the one scholar primarily responsible for the Basran school of law, which did not survive along with the other classical Sunni schools. Among those from whom he transmitted hadith reports are his father, Abu Ishaq al-Shaybani, and Muharib d. Diththar.

**Suhayli**   ʿAbd al-Rahman b. ʿAbdallah b. Ahmad al-Suhayli (508–581) was known as a scholar of the Quran, Arabic language, and the biography of the Prophet Muhammad. Among his written works is a commentary on the biography of the Prophet Muhammad by Ibn Hisham and several works devoted to the explication of the Quran.

**Suyuti**   Jalal al-Din ʿAbd al-Rahman b. Abi Bakr b. Muhammad al-Suyuti (849–911) is one of the most respected of Quran scholars. He is well known for his works in a number of fields related to the study of the Quran including his famous compendium of Quranic Studies and a voluminous Quran commentary. It is said that his written works number around 600.

**Tabarani**   Abu al-Qasim Sulayman b. Ahmad b. Ayyub al-Tabarani (260–360) was one of the greatest of Arab historians. He was originally from Syria but traveled to the Hijaz, Yemen, Egypt, Iraq, and Iran, where he died in Isfahan. Among his written works is a commentary on the Quran, a collection of hadith reports, and a work devoted to prophethood.

**Tabari**   Muhammad b. Jarir al-Tabari (224 or 225–310). Tabari is author of one of the earliest and best-known commentaries on the Quran and histories of early Islam (from creation until his time). He is said to have memorized the Quran by age seven, and traveled widely for study in Rayy, Baghdad, Basrah, Kufah, Cairo, and parts of Syria. He founded his own school of law, called the Jaririyyah, which did not survive past the fifth century. Tabari was a popular teacher in Baghdad, and it was said that, divided over his entire lifetime, he wrote an average of fourteen pages a day. His Quran commentary is particularly important as it preserves the first two and a half centuries of Muslim exegesis, and is known for its close dependence on hadith reports (often multiple, with differing interpretations).

**Tabarsi**   Abu ʿAli al-Fadl b. al-Hasan al-Tabarsi (d. 548). A noted theologian and jurist, Tabarsi was a master of Arabic learning. His commentary on the Quran is considered authoritative by Sunni and Shiʿi scholars alike. Although Tabarsi was a Shiʿi and he gives special prominence to Shiʿi interpretations, he includes the views of all the major exegetes in a comprehensive fashion, including some Muʿtazili exegetes. His commentary includes both lexical and grammatical questions, and a discussion of the different views of earlier exegetes.

**Tabatabaʾi**   Muhammad Husayn Tabatabaʾi (1321–1403). An Iranian scholar who died in 1982 CE, just a few years after the revolutionary events in Iran, Tabatabaʾi was educated in Tabriz and later at Najaf. In the realm of jurisprudence, he is said to have been one of the foremost Mujtahids. Alongside his Quran, hadith, and legal scholarship, Tabatabaʾi also commented on the Sufi philosophical works of Ibn Sina and Mulla Sadra (d. 1050). He taught Quran commentary and philosophical Sufism. Tabatabaʾi's Quran commentary, completed in 1392/1972, is very large (20 volumes). It relies heavily on the commentaries of Qummi and Tabarsi, treats verses in collective units rather than individually, and treats Shiʿi and Sunni hadith material after a general overview of the passages.

**Thaʿlabi**   Abu Ishaq Ahmad b. Muhammad b. Ibrahim al-Thaʿlabi al-Nisaburi (d. 427) is known for two works: a Quran commentary which draws heavily on earlier works such as Tabari, and a "Stories of the Prophets" book which grows out of his Quran commentary. This latter work includes important materials not found in Tabari's works but does not include some of the more fantastic elements found in the works of Kisaʾi.

**Tirmidhi**   Abu 'Isa Muhammad b. 'Isa b. Sawrah al-Tirmidhi (210–279). Tirmidhi is well known as the compiler of one of the six authoritative collections of hadith reports. He was from the city of Bugh in the district of Tirmidh on the banks of the Balkh river near Khwarazmia. He is also said to have written other books on history and asceticism which are not extant.

**Tusi**   Muhammad b. al-Hasan al-Tusi (385–413). Born in Tus but later settling in Baghdad, Tusi is known for his Shi'i scholarship. Two of Tusi's books number among the four canonical books of the Imami Shi'ah. In Baghdad, Tusi studied with al-Mufid and al-Murtada, whom Tusi succeeded as intellectual leader of the Shi'i community. Tusi's commentary on the Quran is one of the earliest Shi'i commentaries and includes some unique exegetical features which helped to establish later conventions for Shi'i commentaries: variant readings, etymology, word meaning, meaning of phrases, syntax, and reports the occasions of the revelations.

**Ubayd b. Umayr**   Ibn Qatadah 'Ubayd b. 'Umayr (d. 74) was born during the lifetime of the Prophet Muhammad and transmitted hadith reports from his father, Umar b. al-Khattab, Ali b. Abi Talib, Abu Dharr, Aishah, and Ibn Abbas. Many well-known figures transmitted on his authority, such as his son Abdallah b. Ubayd, and Ata b. Abi Rabah.

**Ubayy b. Ka'b**   Abu al-Mundhir Ubayy b. Ka'b b. Qays (d. 32) was a Medinan convert to Islam, known as the secretary of the Prophet Muhammad. Attributed to him is knowledge of earlier revealed books, and he is said to have helped in the collection of the Quran after the Prophet Muhammad's death.

**Umar b. Abd al-Aziz**   'Umar b. 'Abd al-'Aziz b. Marwan b. al-Hakim (d. 101). One of the Umayyad Caliphs, renowned for his piety and knowledge of Islam.

**Umar b. al-Khattab**   Abu Hafs 'Umar b. al-Khattab b. Nufayl b. 'Abd al-'Uzzah (d. 23) was an early convert to Islam and became the second Caliph following the Prophet Muhammad's death. According to some, it was the People of the Book who gave Umar b. al-Khattab the nickname "al-Faruq."

**Umm Hani**   Umm Hani bt. Abi Talib b. 'Abd al-Muttalib was the sister of Ali b. Abi Talib and cousin of the Prophet Muhammad. Before he began receiving revelations, the Prophet Muhammad asked to marry

Umm Hani but Abu Talib married her to Hubayrah. Later, Umm Hani converted to Islam and was estranged from her husband. The Prophet Muhammad again asked to marry her but she refused. She outlived the Prophet Muhammad and transmitted hadith reports from him.

**Uqbah b. Amir**    Abu 'Amr 'Uqbah b. 'Amir al-Juhani was a well-known Companion of the Prophet Muhammad known for his poetry, his transmisson of hadith reports, and his recension of the Quran which differed from the standard Uthmanic codex.

**Urwah b. al-Zubayr**    Abu 'Abdallah 'Urwah b. al-Zubayr b. al-'Awwam (d. 93, 94 or 101) was the son of Zubayr b. al-'Awwam the famous Companion and nephew of the Prophet Muhammad. He reported hadith from his father, his mother the daughter of Abu Bakr, his aunt Aishah, Ali b. Abi Talib, and other eminent figures.

**Urwah b. Ruwaim**    Abu al-Qasim 'Urwah b. Ruwaim (d. 135 or 140) was a legal and hadith scholar from Jordan. He transmitted reports from Anas b. Malik and Abu Dharr which are considered to be sound.

**Utbah b. al-Nuddar al-Sulami**    'Utbah b. al-Nuddar al-Sulami (d. 84). A Companion of the Prophet Muhammad who setted in Damascus. Both Khalid b. Ma'dan and Ali b. Rabah are said to have transmitted hadith reports on his authority.

**Uthman b. Affan**    'Uthman b. 'Affan (d. 35), the third Caliph, was the cousin and son-in-law of the Prophet Muhammad. He was a close Companion of the Prophet Muhammad and responsible for transmitting hadith reports from him. He was also instrumental in establishing the standard text of the Quran.

**Uthman b. Ata al-Khurasani**    Abu Mas'ud 'Uthman b. 'Ata' b. Muslim al-Khurasani (d. 155) transmitted hadith reports from his father and other figures of the earlier generation though many later scholars consider his reports unreliable. He is said to have been one of those who wrote down his hadith reports rather than memorizing them.

**Wahb b. Munabbih**    Abu 'Abdallah al-Abnawi Wahb b. Munabbih b. Kamil b. Sayij (34–114) is widely cited as a Follower, and regarded as a sound transmitter of hadith reports. He reported on the authority of Ibn Abbas, Abu Hurayrah, Abu Sa'id, Nu'man b. Bashir, Jabir, and Abdallah b. Amr b. al-As. Many of his stories and interpretations of the Quran originate in Israiliyyat and the scriptures of the People of the Book.

**Wahidi**   Abu al-Hasan ʿAli b. Ahmad al-Wahidi al-Nisaburi (d. 468) is author of a well-known work cataloging the historical circumstances surrounding the revelation of various verses from the Quran.

**Waki**   Abu Sufyan b. al-Jirrah b. Malih b. ʿAdi (129–196) was an Iraqi hadith scholar from Kufah who transmitted on the authority of most of the best-known figures of the earlier generation. He is known for his ascetic ways.

**Wathilah b. al-Asqa**   Abu Qirsafah Wathilah b. al-Asqaʿ (d. 83) was one of the poorer Companions of the Prophet Muhammad. He was from the Kinani clan of the Banu Layth.

**Yahya b. Zakariya**   Abu Saʿid Ibn Abi Zaʾidah Yahya b. Zakariya (110–183). Regarded as trustworthy by all accounts, he transmitted hadith reports from a number of well-known figures. He is said to have been the first to compile books in Kufah and was appointed a judge by Harun al-Rashid.

**Yaqub b. Abi Salamah**   Abu Yusuf Yaʿqub b. Abi Salamah (d. 164) was a Baghdadi legal theorist. It is said that the Caliph al-Mahdi attended his funeral and said the funerary prayer.

**Yaqut**   Shihab al-Din Abu ʿAbdallah Yaqut b. ʿAbdallah al-Hamawi (d. 626) is the author of a well-known geographical dictionary. He was born in Roman territory to non-Arab parents, was later captured and sold as a slave to a merchant in Baghdad for whom he traveled. After he was manumitted, Yaqut traveled extensively and spent time researching geographical lore in libraries, especially in Aleppo, where he died. His dictionary includes information on real geography and on place names found in the Quran and Muslim exegesis.

**Zajjaj**   Abu Ishaq Ibrahim b. Muhammad al-Zajjaj (d. 311). Recognized as the greatest grammarian of his time, Zajjaj wrote a number of books among which was one defining words in the Quran. He was well respected by scholars from many disciplines.

**Zamakhshari**   Mahmud b. ʿUmar al-Zamakhshari (467–538). Born in Khwarazmia, Zamakhshari studied there and later traveled to Bukhara, Samarqand and Baghdad. He was strongly influenced by Mahmud b. Jarir al-Isbahani (d. 507) one of the best-known grammarians and lexicographers of Arabic. Later he moved to Mecca and stayed there long enough to gain the nickname "Jar Allah" (neighbor of God). Because he is a Mu'tazili, Zamakhshari and his Quran commentary have been subject to scrutiny by other scholars. Zamakhshari's commentary is known for its reliance on reason rather than hadith reports, but also for its excellent study of philology and syntax. It is also well regarded as a reference for apparent lexical and grammatical irregularities in the text of the Quran. An expurgated version (removing obvious Mu'tazili views) of the commentary was made by al-Baydawi (d. 685 or 692).

**Zayd b. Aslam**    Abu Usamah Zayd b. Aslam (d. 136). An interpreter of the Quran and reciter of the Quran, Zayd b. Aslam was a client of the house of Umar b. al-Khattab. He is said to have relied on opinion (ra'y) in his interpretations of the Quran.

**Zayd b. Mu'awiyah**    Zayd b. Mu'awiyah al-Numayri was a Companion from the tribe of Numayr. He was the paternal uncle of Qurrah b. Du'maws. Among those who transmitted on his authority is Aidh b. Rabi'ah.

**Zuhri**    Muhammad b. Muslim b. 'Ubaydallah b. 'Abdallah b. Asghar b. Shihab al-Zuhri (d. 124) was a Medinan transmitter of hadith reports, and was considered an expert on the history of the campaigns of the Prophet Muhammad, the history of the Quraysh, and the Medinan Muslims.

**Zuraqi**    Abu 'Ayyash Zayd b. 'Ayyash al-Zuraqi transmitted hadith reports from Sa'd b. Abi Waqqas, and Abdallah b. Yazid transmitted hadith reports on his authority. Most later scholars regard his reports as reliable.

# Suggestions for Further Reading

### Reference

For the Quran the best resource is the multi-volume *Encylopedia of the Quran*, ed. Jane McAuliffe (Leiden: E. J. Brill, 2001–) now in publication. Less comprehensive but complete is Mustansir Mir, *Dictionary of Quranic Terms and Concepts* (New York, 1987). Older but still useful is John Penrice, *A Dictionary and Glossary of the Quran* (Lahore: Law Publishing Company, 1873). For an English concordance see Hanna E. Kassis, *A Concordance of the Quran* (Berkeley: University of California Press, 1982).

General references for Islam can be located in the *Encyclopaedia of Islam*, first edn, ed. M. T. Houtsma and others, 4 vols (Leiden: E. J. Brill, 1913–34); second edn, ed. H. A. R. Gibb and others, 11 vols (Leiden: E. J. Brill, 1960– ). Note that the second edition of this encyclopedia is still in publication, and readers may need to consult the first edition for entries coming at the end of the alphabet. Readers not familiar with the original terminology used for the entries may wish to consult the separately published *Index of Subjects*, ed. P. J. Bearman (Leiden: E. J. Brill, 1998) and *Index of Proper Names*, ed. E. van Donzel (Leiden: E. J. Brill, 1998). The text along with searching tools is also now available on CD-ROM.

For the Bible and related topics, see *The Anchor Bible Dictionary*, ed. David Noel Freedman and others, 6 vols (New York: Doubleday, 1992). Many of the entries also include bibliographical references which are relevant to the Quran and Muslim exegesis. For Jewish topics, including many biblical references, see the *Encyclopaedia Judaica*, ed. C. Roth and others, 16 vols (New York, 1971–72) and the older *The Jewish Encyclopedia*, ed. I. Singer and others, 12 vols (New York, 1901–06; reprinted, 1964). Some relevant articles may also be located in the *Encyclopedia of Religion*, ed. Mircea Eliade and others, 17 vols (New York: Macmillan Publishing, 1987).

For a recent reference work on prophets in Islam and Judaism with emphasis on the Ancient Near East and Bible, see Scott Noegel and

Brannon Wheeler, *Historical Dictionary of Prophets in Islam and Judaism* (London: Scarecrow Press, 2002).

## Quran

There are a number of English translations of the Quran, of varying qualities and aimed at different types of audiences. This is not the place to give a comprehensive overview of these publications, nor is there space to mention them all. One of the most readily available translations is that by N. J. Dawood, *The Koran* (New York: Penguin Books, 1956; fifth edn, second revision, 1995). The English is clear and readable but some scholars have questioned the consistency of the translation. The verses are not numbered separately but do follow the Egyptian standard edition. In earlier editions of this translation (first–fourth), Dawood has rearranged the order of the surahs, making their location more difficult. The translation of Arthur J. Arberry, *The Koran Interpreted*, 2 vols (New York: George Allen and Unwin, 1955) is well regarded for its careful rendering of the Arabic and attempt to retain the poetic form of the verses. Subsequent editions of Arberry are reprinted in a single volume but verses are only numbered in groups of five and verse divisions are based on the Arabic text reconstructed by Gustav Fluegel (Leipzig, 1841).

Another popular translation is Mohammed Marmaduke Pickthall, *The Meaning of the Glorious Koran: An Explanatory Translation* (London: George Allen and Unwin, 1930), which includes explanatory introductions to the surahs, and individually numbers each verse, though following Fluegel's text. Pickthall's use of archaizing language is distracting and the translation has been accused of some dubious modernizing interpretations. Considered to be more exact in translation is that of Richard Bell, *The Quran*, 2 vols (Edinburgh: T. and T. Clark, 1937). Bell's translation is best avoided by first-time readers since he has rearranged not only the surahs but individual verses and even parts of verses according to his own historical reconstruction of the text.

There are a number of English translations of the Quran published in South Asia and the Middle East, the most widely available being Abdullah Yusuf Ali, *The Holy Quran* (Lahore: Muhammad Ashraf, 1938) and Muhammad Ali, *The Holy Quran*, fourth edn (Lahore: Ahmadiyyah Press, 1951). Both of these translations use archaizing language, and both include footnotes explaining the text from modern perspectives. These publications also contain the Arabic text of the Quran. Another English translation prepared by a number of Muslim scholars and published in Medina is *The Holy Quran: English Translation of the Meanings and Commentary* (Medina, 1413 AH).

For a translation which draws heavily on Muslim exegesis, see *The Quran: A New Interpretation*, trans. Colin Turner with textual exegesis by Muhammad Baqir Behbudi (Richmond, Surrey: Curzon Press, 1997). This translation is very readable but there is no way to distinguish the additional exegetical comments from what is actually found in the text of the Quran. Perhaps the best English translation of the Quran, though still in progress, is that found in Mahmoud Ayoub, *The Quran and Its Interpreters*, 2 vols to date (Albany: State University of New York Press, 1984, 1992). Volume 1 covers the first two surahs, and volume 2 the third surah. Ayoub provides an accurate and clear translation of the Quran along with copious translations from Arabic of Muslim exegesis on almost every verse. Surahs 78–114 have also been translated into English by Mahmoud Ayoub, *The Awesome News: Interpretation of Juz' 'Amma – The Last Part of the Quran*, second edn (Hiawatha, IA: Cedar Graphics, 1997).

## Quranic Studies

The classical Muslim tradition of Quranic Studies has produced some important compendia, some of which have been translated or paraphrased into English. For an overview of this discipline in English, see Ahmad von Denffer, *'Ulum al-Qur'an: An Introduction to the Sciences of the Quran*, revised edn (Leicester: Islamic Foundation, 1983). A Shi'i approach can be found in al-Sayyid Abu al-Qasim al-Musawi al-Khu'i, *The Prolegomena to the Qur'an*, trans. Abdulaziz Sachedina (Oxford: Oxford University Press, 1998). The best short overview of the Quran and its importance in Islam is Michael Cook, *The Koran: A Very Short Introduction* (Oxford: Oxford University Press, 2000).

Among the better-known Western studies of the Quran, see Theodore Nöldeke, *Geschichte des Qorans*, ed. F. Schwally, G. Bergsträsser, and O. Pretzl, 3 vols (Leipzig: Dieterich'sche Verlagsbuchhandlung, 1909, 1919, 1938). Volume 1 is on the origin of the Quran, volume 2 on the collection of the Quran, and volume 3 on the history of the Quranic text. Also of interest in the attempt to reconstruct the history of the Quran text is Richard Bell, *Introduction to the Qur'an* (Edinburgh: University of Edinburgh Press, 1953). More recently, see the exacting work of Angelika Neuwirth, *Studien zur Komposition der mekkanischen Suren* (Berlin: Walter de Gruyter, 1981). Much of this scholarship is reviewed and expanded upon in Neal Robinson, *Discovering the Qur'an: A Contemporary Approach to a Veiled Text* (London: SCM Press, 1996).

Critical studies on the text of the Quran are numerous in Arabic, and some of this has been used by Western scholars in their scholarship.

See, for example, the project started in Arthur Jeffery, *Materials for the History of the Text of the Quran* (Leiden: E. J. Brill, 1937). Also see his *The Foreign Vocabulary of the Qur'an* (Baroda: Oriental Institute, 1938) and his *The Qur'an as Scripture* (New York: Arno Press, 1980). Also see the verse-by-verse commentary of Rudi Paret, *Der Koran: Kommentar und Konkordanz* (Stuttgart: Verlag W. Kohlhammer, 1971). Some of the recent scholarship in this area can also be found in *The Qur'an as Text*, ed. Stefan Wild (Leiden: E. J. Brill, 1996). Readers should also be aware of the wide-ranging work of John Wansbrough, *Quranic Studies* (Oxford: Oxford University Press, 1977).

Much earlier Western scholarship on the Quran has focused on tracing "influences" and determining the "sources" of the Quran. The origins of this approach can be found partially with Abraham Geiger, *Was hat Mohammed aus dem Judentum aufgenommen*, second edn, (Leipzig: M. W. Kaufmann, 1902), which has received much criticism since its publication. Along these same lines is Israel Schapiro, *Die haggadischen Elemente im erzählenden Teil des Korans* (Leipzig: Gustav Fock, 1907). More sophisticated and less provocative is Heinrich Speyer, *Die biblischen Erzählungen im Qoran* (Graubünden, 1931; reprint, Hildesheim: Georg Olms Verlagsbuchhandlung, 1961). Useful but also of this same approach is Josef Horovitz, *Jewish Proper Names and Derivatives in the Koran* (Cincinnati: Hebrew Union College, 1925). More recently, see the approach of John Kaltner, *Ishmael Instructs Isaac: An Introduction to the Qur'an for Bible Readers* (Collegeville, MN: Liturgical Press, 1999).

For an overview of more recent Western scholarship on the Quran, see *The Qur'an: Formative Interpretation*, ed. Andrew Rippin, Formation of the Classical Islamic World Series 25 (Brookfield: Ashgate, 1999). This collection includes a number of influential articles by well-known Quranic Studies scholars. Additional scholarship can be found in *Approaches to the History of the Interpretation of the Qur'an*, ed. Andrew Rippin (Oxford: Clarendon Press, 1988).

Interpretations of the Quran from a thematic perspective are very common in more recent years. Perhaps the best overview of the Quran from this perspective remains Fazlur Rahman, *Major Themes of the Qur'an*, second edn (Minneapolis: Bibliotheca Islamica, 1989). Also see Faruq Sherif, *A Guide to the Contents of the Qur'an* (Reading, UK: Garnet Publishing, 1995), Muhammad Abdel Haleem, *Understanding the Qur'an: Themes and Style* (New York: I. B. Tauris, 1999), and Mohammad Abu-Hamdiyyah, *The Qur'an: An Introduction* (New York: Routledge, 2000). From a more comparative perspective, see Toshihiko Izutsu, *Ethico-Religious Concepts in the Quran* (Montreal, 1966), a revision of his *The Structure of the Ethical Terms in the Koran* (Tokyo, 1959). Also see his

*God and Man in the Koran: Semantics of the Koranic Weltanschauung* (Tokyo, 1964).

Attempts to translate traditional Muslim commentary on the Quran have been uneven and many remain unfinished. An ambitious attempt is Taqi al-Din Hilali and Muhammad Muhsin Khan, *Interpretation of the Meanings of the Noble Quran: A Summarized Version of al-Tabari, al-Qurtubi, and Ibn Kathir with Comment from Sahih al-Bukhari*, 9 vols (Lahore, 1989–92). On a smaller scale see Helmut Gätje, *The Qur'an and Its Exegesis: Selected Texts with Classical and Modern Muslim Interpretations*, trans. and ed. Alford Welch (Berkeley: University of California Press, 1976), which is organized thematically but does not include a translation of the Quran text upon which the comments are made. For a slightly different approach to the Quran by a well-known medieval figure, see Abu Hamid Ghazali, *The Jewels of the Quran (Kitab jawahir al-Quran)*, trans. Abul Qasem (Kuala Lumpur, 1979).

A unique but very important work for understanding the Quran is Syed Muzaffar-ud-Din Nadvi, *A Geographical History of the Qur'an*, second edn, (Lahore: Sh. Muhammad Ashraf, 1968). Part one includes an overview of Arabian geography, and part two provides chapters on the history of the ancient Arabs and includes chapters on the Ad, Thamud, Jurhamites, Minaeans, Lihyanites, and others. Also relevant along these lines are I. Eph'al, *The Ancient Arabs: Nomads on the Borders of the Fertile Crescent, 9th–5th Centuries B.C.* (Jerusalem, 1982), J. F. A. Sawyer and D. J. A. Clines, *Midian, Moab and Edom: The History of Archaeology of Late Bronze and Iron Age Jordan and Northwest Arabia* (Sheffield, 1983), and F. V. Winnett, *The Arabian Genealogies in the Book of Genesis* (Nashville: Abingdon Press, 1970).

## Stories of the Prophets

For English translations of other texts related to the stories of the prophets in Islam, see the first four volumes of the 39-volume *The History of al-Tabari*: Volume 1: *From Creation to the Flood*, trans. Franz Rosenthal (Albany: State University of New York Press, 1989); Volume 2: *Prophets and Patriarchs*, trans. William Brinner (1987); Volume 3: *The Children of Israel*, trans. William Brinner (1991); Volume 4: *The Ancient Kingdoms*, trans. Moshe Perlmann (1987). The non-extant portion, dealing with the stories of the prophets, of Ibn Ishaq's biography of the Prophet Muhammad has been reconstructed and translated by Gordon Newby, *The Making of the Last Prophet: A Reconstruction of the Earliest Biography of Muhammad* (Columbia: University of South Carolina Press, 1989).

The *Stories of the Prophets* of al-Kisa'i, containing much additional folkloric materials, has been translated by Wheeler Thackston, *The Tales of the Prophets of al-Kisa'i* (Boston: Twayne Publishers, 1978). A later and larger thirteenth-century Chagatai work by Nosiruddin Burhonuddin Rabghuzi devoted to the stories of the prophets has been translated by H. E. Boeschoten and others, *The Stories of the Prophets* (Leiden: E. J. Brill, 1995).

There are also English translations of many authoritative Arabic Islamic texts made primarily for Muslims who do not read Arabic. Some of these contain sections dealing with Quran interpretation and other stories related to the prophets, such as the various English translations of Bukhari, Muslim, and Abu Dawud. A heavily edited version of Ibn Kathir's *Stories of the Prophets* has been translated into English by Sayed Gad, *Stories of the Prophets*, ed. Hadeer Refat Abo El-Nagah (Cairo: Dar al-Manarah, 2000). Other English translations of this text also exist. Readers must take care with the uneven quality of the English translations and be aware that additions and expurgations from the original are not often indicated in the translations.

For a somewhat different approach to the stories of the prophets, one emphasizing the spiritual and mystical aspects of the stories, see the English translation of Ibn al-Arabi's text by R. W. J. Austin, *The Bezels of Wisdom* (New York: Paulist Press, 1980).

Secondary studies on certain prophets and stories in the Quran and Muslim exegesis are not numerous but have been appearing steadily during the past decade or so. Among the more notable book-length studies published, see Cornelia Schöck, *Adam im Islam: ein Beitrag zur Ideengeschichte der Sunna* (Berlin: Klaus Schwarz Verlag, 1993). On the prophet Salih and the people of Thamud, see Jaroslav Stetkevych, *Muhammad and the Golden Bough: Reconstructing Arabian Myth* (Bloomington: Indiana University Press, 1996). On Abraham, see Reuven Firestone, *Journeys in Holy Lands: The Evolution of the Abraham–Ishmael Story in Islamic Exegesis* (Albany: State University of New York Press, 1990), which does not completely replace the more contentious Y. Moubarac, *Abraham dans le Coran* (Paris: J. Vrin, 1958). On Moses and the Israelites, see Brannon Wheeler, *Moses in the Quran and Islamic Exegesis* (Richmond, Surrey: Curzon Press, 2002). On Solomon and the Queen of Sheba stories, see Jacob Lassner, *Demonizing the Queen of Sheba: Boundaries of Gender and Culture in Postbiblical Judaism and Medieval Islam* (Chicago: University of Chicago Press, 1993). A wide-ranging interesting work covering many of the stories of the prophets, but one which must be used with some caution, is Haim Schwarzbaum, *Biblical and Extra-Biblical Legends in Islamic Folk-Literature*, Beiträge zur Sprach- und Kulturgeschichte des Orients 30 (Walldorf-Hessen, 1982).

## Bible and Ancient World

Muslim exegesis often interprets the Quran with reference or allusion to the Bible and other texts closely related to biblical tradition. For an overview of biblical traditions relating to the stories in the first five books of the Bible, see James Kugel, *Traditions of the Bible* (Cambridge, MA: Harvard University Press, 2000), which covers a wealth of ancient, late antique, and some medieval materials. Kugel presents translations of small portions of texts with brief analyses reflecting on various characters, themes, and motifs in the biblical text. Some additional ancient Near Eastern materials relevant to the Bible can be found in the survey and English translation of texts edited by James Pritchard, *Ancient Near Eastern Texts Relating to the Old Testament*, third edn, (Princeton: Princeton University Press, 1969).

Much additional material related to the Bible is collected in *The Old Testament Pseudepigrapha*, ed. James Charlesworth, 2 vols (New York: Doubleday, 1983). A number of the texts included in this collection are especially pertinent to Muslim Quran interpretation. This does not entirely replace *The Apocrypha and Pseudepigrapha of the Old Testament in English*, ed. R. H. Charles, 2 vols (Oxford: Oxford University Press, 1913). For the New Testament, see *New Testament Apocrypha*, ed. E. Hennecke and W. Schneemelcher, trans. R. Wilson, 2 vols (London: Westminster, 1963–65). The Armenian apocrypha can be found in *Armenian Apocrypha Relating to Adam and Eve*, ed. and trans. Michael Stone (Leiden: E. J. Brill, 1996) and *Armenian Apocrypha Relating to the Patriarchs and Prophets*, ed. and trans. Michael Stone (Jerusalem: Israel Academy of Sciences and Humanities, 1982). Also see the selection of translated texts included in *The Other Bible*, ed. Willis Barnstone (San Francisco: Harper and Row, 1984).

The collection of texts known as the Dead Sea Scrolls contains many texts related to the Bible. For translations of the Dead Sea Scrolls, see Florentino Garcia Martinez (ed.), *The Dead Sea Scrolls Translated*, second edn (Grand Rapids, MI: Eerdmans, 1996). Also worth mentioning is the latest edition of Geza Vermes, *The Complete Dead Sea Scrolls in English* (New York: Penguin, 1998). Some additional non-canonical materials related to "gnostic" interpretations of the Bible can be found in *The Nag Hammadi Library in English*, ed. James Robinson (San Francisco: HarperCollins, 1990). A number of pseudepigraphical texts not found in other collections can be found in the Society of Biblical Literature Texts and Translations Pseudepigrapha Series, edited by Robert Kraft and Harold Attridge (Scholars Press).

Containing a thick overview of biblical and Jewish history from

Creation to the Second Temple period, see Josephus (c. 37–100), *The Antiquities of the Jews*, translated by William Whiston in *The Works of Josephus*, new edn (Peabody, MA: Hendrickson Publishers, 1987). The works of Philo (c. 20 BCE–c. 40 or 50 CE), which focus on Genesis, have also been translated into English by C. D. Young, *The Works of Philo*, new edn, (Peabody: Hendrickson Publishers, 1993). Also see some of the various authors and texts collected in *Greek and Latin Authors on Jews and Judaism*, ed. D. Stern (Jerusalem: Israel Academy of Sciences, 1974–84).

Multiple recensions of the Bible are available in English translation, some of them containing significant variations from the Greek and Hebrew manuscripts from which most translations of the Bible are made. Some of the various Jewish Aramaic recensions of the Bible have been published in English: see the volumes published in the Aramaic Bible series by Michael Glazier and the Liturgical Press. For the Samaritan Aramaic Bible, see Abraham Tal, *The Samaritan Targum of the Pentateuch*, 3 vols (Tel Aviv: Tel Aviv University, 1980–83).

## Judaism

An overview of Jewish traditions from Adam and Eve to Esther, one which draws heavily on late antique and medieval sources, can be found in Louis Ginzberg, *The Legends of the Jews*, 7 vols (Philadelphia: Jewish Publication Society of America, 1909–38; reprinted, Baltimore: Johns Hopkins University Press, 1998). Ginzberg's work is monumental in scope, but readers must be careful to consult the notes in volumes 5 and 6 to determine the original sources from which Ginzberg draws his material.

There are several late antique and medieval collections of Jewish exegesis and other texts relating to the Bible available in English translation. One of the earliest and closely related to Muslim exegesis is the *Pirke de Rabbi Eliezer*, trans. Gerald Friedlander (London, 1916; reprint, New York: Sepher-Hermon Press, 1981). The *Midrash Rabbah*, trans. Harry Freedman and others, 10 vols (London: Soncino Press, 1939) is one of the largest and most significant collections of early rabbinic Bible exegesis. The first section of Buber's redaction of the *Midrash Tanhuma*, covering the book of Genesis, is translated into English by John Townsend (New York: Ktav Publishing, 1989). Also see the *Midrash Tanhuma-Yelammedenu*, trans. Samuel Berman (New York: Ktav Publishing, 1996) on Genesis and Exodus.

The two recensions of the *Abot de Rabbi Nathan* have been translated into English. Version A: *The Fathers According to Rabbi Nathan*, trans.

J. Goldin (New Haven: Yale University Press, 1955); Version B: *The Fathers According to Rabbi Nathan*, trans. Anthony Saldarini (Leiden: E. J. Brill, 1975). This work is in the form of a commentary on the mishnaic tractate of Abot, and contains many references to biblical interpretation. Also see the materials collected in the *Sefer ha-Massiyot* translated as *The Exempla of the Rabbis*, trans. Moses Gaster (1924; reprinted, New York: Ktav Publishing, 1968). Much of the material in the *Sefer ha-Massiyot* concerns rabbinic figures, but there are numerous references to biblical and other stories which are relevant to the Bible and Quran interpretation.

Among some of the later medieval pseudepigraphical Jewish works relevant to biblical stories, see the *Sefer ha-Yashar*, trans. by M. M. Noah, *The Book of Jasher* (New York: M. M. Noah and A. S. Gould, 1840). Also see the *Sefer ha-Zichronot*, trans. by Moses Gaster as *The Chronicles of Jerahmeel* (London, 1899; reprinted in 2 vols, New York: Ktav Publishing, 1971). Both of these texts include material not found in other accounts on biblical history and on various biblical characters.

Works of some individual medieval Jewish Bible exegetes have been translated into English. Rashi's commentary on the first five books of the Bible can be found in *The Torah: With Rashi's Commentary Translated, Annotated and Elucidated*, trans. Yisrael Isser Zvi Herczeg and others, 5 vols (New York: Mosorah Publications, 1995). For Ramban's commentary on the first five books of the Bible, see *Ramban (Nachmanides): Commentary on the Torah*, trans. Charles Chavel (New York: Shilo Publishing, 1976). Rashbam's commentary on Exodus has been translated into English by Martin Lockshin, *Rashbam's Commentary on Exodus* (Atlanta: Scholars Press, 1997).

Traditions related to rabbinic Bible interpretation can also be found in *The Babylonian Talmud*, 35 vols (London, 1935–48; reprinted in 18 vols, London, 1961) and *The Talmud of the Land of Israel*, trans. Jacob Neusner, 25 vols (Chicago, 1982– ). Miscellaneous traditions can also be found in Moses Gaster, *Studies in Texts in Folklore, Magic, Mediaeval Romance, Hebrew Apocrypha, and Samaritan Archaeology*, 3 vols (New York: Ktav Publishers, 1971).

## Christianity

In addition to the texts already cited above, there are a number of Christian works which draw upon and inform Jewish exegesis, and contain materials related to the Quran and Muslim exegesis. There are a number of general Christian historical texts which recount biblical history from Adam and Eve until the time of Jesus and beyond. Some of these reflect traditions which appear to have been shared with Muslim exegetes. Among these, see the translations from the Syriac of *The Book of the Cave of Treasures*, trans. E. A. W. Budge (London: Religious Tract Society, 1927) and *The Book of the Bee*, trans. E. A. W. Budge (Oxford: Clarendon, 1886). Much of the same material is also presented in the thirteenth-century work of Bar Hebraeus, ed. and trans. E. A. W. Budge as *The Chronography of Gregory Abu'l Faraj the Son of Aaron, the Hebrew Physician, Commonly Known as Bar Hebraeus* (London: Oxford University Press, 1932). The work of Eusebius, *The History of the Church*, trans. G. A. Williamson (New York: Penguin Books, 1965) also has numerous references to biblical history and Christian interpretation of the Bible.

Some sermons and Bible commentaries of Syriac Christians have been published in English: such as those of Aphrahat: see *The Homilies of Aphraates the Persian Sage*, trans. William Wright (London: Williams and Norgate, 1869) and *Demonstrations*, trans. Kuriakose Valavanolickal (Changanassery: Catholic Theological Studies in India, 1999). Numerous publications exist of the works of Ephraim Syrus: see, for example, *Selections*, trans. Edward Matthews and Joseph Amar (Washington, DC: Catholic University of America Press, 1994). Also see *The Early Syriac Fathers on Genesis*, ed. and trans. Abraham Levene (London: Taylor's Foreign Press, 1951). Many of the Eastern Christian texts, some of which are translated into English, can be found in the Corpus Scriptorum Christianorum Orientalium series; these include editions and translations of texts in Arabic, Armenian, Coptic, Ethiopic, Georgian, and Syriac along with subsidiary volumes.

Some of these writings and those of many other early Christian scholars which bear directly on particular passages of the Bible can also be found in English in the single collection of *The Early Church Fathers*, ed. Philip Schaff and Alexander Roberts, 38 vols (Peabody, MA: Henrickson Publishers, 1989). Some of the works of Greek and Latin authors related to the Bible and early Christianity can also be found translated in the Loeb Classics Series published by Harvard University Press.

# Works Consulted

Abū Dāʾūd, Sulayman b. al-Ashʿath. *Sunan Abī Dāʾūd*. Beirut: Dār Ihyā al-Turāth al-ʿArabī, n.d.

al-Azraqī, Muhammad b. ʿAbdallāh. *Akhbār Makkah*. Ed. F. Wustenfeld, *Chroniken der Stadt Mecca*. 2 vols. Leipzig, 1858. Reprint, Beirut, n.d.

al-Bayhaqī, Ahmad b. al-Husayn. *Dalāʾil al-nabūwah maʿarifah ahwāl sāhib al-sharʿīyah*. Ed. ʿAbd al-Muʿatī Qalʿajī. Beirut: Dār al-Kutub al-ʿIlmīyah, 1405.

al-Damīrī, Muhammad b. Mūsā. *Hayāt al-hayawān al-kubrā*. Cairo: Maktabat Mustafā al-Bābī al-Halabī, 1386.

al-Dārimī, ʿAbdallāh b. ʿAbd al-Rahmān. *Sunan al-Dārimī*. Ed. Khālid al-Sabʿ al-ʿAlamī. Beirut: Dār al-Kitāb al-ʿArabī, 1407.

al-Dhahabī, Shams al-Dīn. *Siyar aʿlām al-nubalāʾ*. Ed. Shuʿayb al-Arnaʾūt and Husayn al-Asad. 25 vols. Beirut: Muʾassasat al-Risālah, 1981–88.

Fakhr al-Dīn al-Rāzī. *al-Tafsīr al-kabir*. 32 vols. Cairo: al-Matbaʿah al-Bahlyah, n.d.

Ibn Abī Hātim. *al-Jarh wa al-taʿdīl*. 8 vols. Hyderabad, 1941–53. Reprint, Beirut, n.d.

Ibn al-Athīr. *al-Kāmil fī al-taʾrīkh*. Ed. C. Tornberg. Leiden: E. J. Brill, 1867. Reprint, Beirut: Dār al-Sādir, 1965.

Ibn al-Athīr. *Usd al-ghābah fī maʿrifat al-sahābah*. 7 vols. Cairo, 1970–73.

Ibn Hajar, Ahmad b. ʿAlī b. Muhammad. *Fath al-bārī bi-sharh Sahīh al-Bukhārī*. 13 vols. Beirut: Dār Ihiyā al-Turāth al-ʿArabī, 1408/1988.

Ibn Hajar, Ahmad b. ʿAlī b. Muhammad. *al-Isābah fī tamyīz al-sahābah*. Ed. ʿĀdil Ahmad ʿAbd al-Mawjūd and ʿAlī Muhammad Muʿawwad. 8 vols. Beirut: Dār al-Kutub al-ʿIlmīyah, 1415/1995.

Ibn Hajar, Ahmad b. ʿAlī b. Muhammad. *Tahdhīb al-tahdhīb*. Hyderabad, 1325.

Ibn Hajar, Ahmad b. ʿAlī b. Muhammad. *Lisān al-mīzān*. 6 vols. Beirut, 1407.

Ibn Hanbal, Ahmad b. Muhammad. *Musnad*. 6 vols. Cairo, 1313/1895. Reprint, Cairo, 1969.

Ibn Ḥibbān, Muḥammad. *Ṣaḥīḥ Ibn Ḥibbān*. Beirut: Muʾassasat al-Risālah, 1984.

Ibn Hishām, ʿAbd al-Mālik. *Kitāb al-tijān*. Hyderabad: Majlis Dāʾirat al-Maʿārif al-ʿUthmanīyah, 1347.

Ibn Hishām, ʿAbd al-Mālik. *al-Sīrah al-nabawīyah*. Ed. Ṭaha ʿAbd al-Rūf Saʿd. Beirut: Dār al-Jīl, n.d.

Ibn al-Jawzī, Abū al-Faraj ʿAbd al-Raḥmān b. ʿAlī. *al-Muntaẓam fī taʾrīkh al-mulūk wa al-umam*. Ed. Muhammad ʿAbd al-Qādir ʿAtā and Mustafā ʿAbd al-Qādir ʿAtā. Beirut: Dār al-Kutub al-ʿIlmīyah, n.d.

Ibn al-Jawzī, Abū al-Faraj ʿAbd al-Raḥmān b. ʿAlī. *Zād al-masīr fī ʿilm al-tafsīr*. 9 vols. Beirut: al-Maktab al-Islāmī li al-Ṭibāʿah wa al-Nashr, 1384–88.

Ibn Kathīr, Ismāʿīl. *al-Bidāyah wa al-nihāyah fī taʾrīkh*. Cairo, 1351–58.

Ibn Kathīr, Ismāʿīl. *Qiṣaṣ al-anbiyāʾ*. Beirut: Dār Ibn Kathīr, 1312/1992.

Ibn Kathīr, Ismāʿīl. *Tafsīr al-Qurʾān al-ʿaẓīm*. Beirut: Dār al-Jīl, n.d.

Ibn Mājah, Muḥammad b. Yazīd. *Sunan*. Ed. Muḥammad Fuʾād ʿAbd al-Bāqī. 2 vols. Cairo: Dār al-Kutub al-Misrīyah, n.d.

Ibn Mākūlā, ʿAlī b. Hibat Allāh. *al-Ikmāl fī rafʿ al-irtiyāb ʿan al-maʾtalif wa al-mukhtalif min al-asmāʾ wa al-kunā wa al-ansāb*. Ed. ʿAbd al-Raḥmān b. Yaḥyāʾ al-Muʿallimī al-Yamānī. 6 vols. Hyderabad, 1962.

Ibn Saʿd, Muḥammad. *Kitāb al-ṭabaqāt al-kabīr*. Ed. Eduard Sachau and others. 9 vols. Leiden: E. J. Brill, 1904–40.

al-Kāshānī, Muḥsin al-Malaqqab al-Ghayḍ. *Tafsīr al-ṣāfī*. Tehran: Maktabat al-Sadd, n.d.

al-Kisāʾī. *Qiṣaṣ al-anbiyāʾ*. Ed. Isaac Eisenberg. Leiden: E. J. Brill, 1922.

Mālik b. Anas. *Muwaṭṭāʾ*. Ed. Muḥammad Fuʾād ʿAbd al-Bāqī. Beirut: Dār al-Kutub al-ʿIlmīyah, n.d.

al-Mizzī, Yūsuf b. al-Zākī ʿAbd al-Raḥmān. *Tuḥfat al-ashrās bi maʿrifat al-atrāf*. Ed. ʿAbd al-Samad Sharaf al-Dīn. 12 vols. Bombay: al-Dār al-Qayyimah, 1965–82.

Muqātil b. Sulaymān. *Tafsīr Muqātil b. Sulaymān*. Ed. ʿAbdallāh Maḥmūd Shiḥātah. Cairo: al-Hiyaʾah al-Misrīyah al-ʿĀmmah li-l-Kitāb, 1979.

Muslim. *Ṣaḥīḥ*. Beirut: Dār al-Maʿrifah, 1994.

al-Nasāʾī. *Sunan*. Beirut: Dār al-Kutub al-ʿIlmīyah, n.d.

al-Nīsābūrī, Abū al-Ḥasan ʿAlī b. Aḥmad. *Asbāb al-nuzūl*. Beirut: al-Maktabah al-Thiqāfīyah, 1989.

al-Nīsābūrī, al-Ḥākim Muḥammad b. ʿAbdallāh. *al-Mustadrak ʿalā al-Saḥīḥayn*. 4 vols. Hyderabad, 1342.

al-Qazwīnī, Zakarīyā b. Muḥammad. *ʿAjāʾib al-makhlūqāt wa gharāʾib al-mawjūdāt*. Second edn, Ed. Fārūq Saʿd. Beirut: Dār al-Āfāq al-Jadīdah, 1977.

al-Qummī, ʿAlī b. Ibrāhīm. *Tafsīr al-Qummī*. Beirut: Dār al-Surūr, 1411/1991.

al-Qurṭubī, Muḥammad b. Aḥmad. *al-Jāmiʿ li-ahkām al-Qurʾān*. 20 vols. Beirut: Dār Iḥiyā al-Turāth al-ʿArabī, 1405/1985.

al-Samʿānī, ʿAbd al-Karīm b. Muḥammad. *al-Ansāb*. Ed. ʿAbdallāh ʿUmar al-Bārūdī. Beirut: Dār al-Jinān, 1988.

al-Shawkānī. *Fath al-qadīr*. Ed. Hishām al-Bukhārī and Khuḍr ʿIkārī. Beirut: al-Maktabat al-ʿAṣrīyah, 1417.

al-Subkī, Tāj al-Dīn ʿAbd al-Wahhāb b. ʿAlī. *Ṭabaqāt al-Shāfiʿīyah al-kubrā*. Ed. ʿAbd al-Fattāh Muḥammad al-Hilw and Maḥmūd Muḥammad al-Tināḥī. 10 vols. Cairo, 1964–76.

al-Suyūṭī, ʿAbd al-Rahmān b. Abī Bakr. *al-Darr al-manthūr fī tafsīr al-maʾthūr*. Beirut: Dār al-Kutub al-ʿIlmīyah, 1421/2000.

al-Suyūṭī, ʿAbd al-Rahmān b. Abī Bakr. *al-Ittiqān fī ʿulūm al-Qurʾān*. Ed. Muṣṭafā Dīb al-Bughā. 2 vols. Beirut: Dār Ibn Kathīr, 1416/1996.

al-Suyūṭī, ʿAbd al-Rahmān b. Abī Bakr. *al-Madhdhāhīb fī-mā waqaʿ fī al-Qurʾān min al-ʿArab*. Beirut: Dār al-Kutub al-ʿIlmīyah, n.d.

al-Ṭabarī, Muḥammad b. Jarīr. *Jāmiʿ al-bayān fī tafsīr al-Qurʾān*. Beirut: Dār al-Maʿarifah, n.d.

al-Ṭabarī, Muḥammad b. Jarīr. *Taʾrīkh al-rusul wa al-mulūk*. Ed. M. J. de Goeje. 16 vols. Leiden: E. J. Brill, 1879–1901.

al-Ṭabarsī, ʿAlī al-Faḍl b. al-Ḥasan. *Majmaʿ al-bayān fī tafsīr al-Qurʾān*. Beirut: Dār Maktabah al-Ḥayyāh, n.d.

al-Ṭabaṭabāʾī, Muḥammad Hussayn. *al-Mīzān fī tafsīr al-Qurʾān*. Ed. Hussayn al-Aʿlamī. 21 vols. Beirut: Muʾassisah ʿIlmī li-l-Matbūʿāt, 1411/1991.

al-Ṭayālisī, Sulayman b. Dāʾūd. *Musnad*. Ed. Muḥammad b. ʿAbd al-Muhsin. 4 vols. Cairo: Dār al-Muhandisīn, 1999.

al-Thaʿlabī, Ahmad b. Muḥammad. *Qiṣaṣ al-anbiyāʾ: ʿArāʾis al-majālis*. Beirut: Dār al-Fikr, 1420/2000.

al-Tirmidhī, Muḥammad b. ʿIsā. *al-Jāmiʿ al-Ṣaḥīḥ*. Beirut: Dār al-Turāth al-ʿArabī, n.d.

Yāqūt, Shihāb al-Dīn Abū ʿAbdallāh. *Muʿjam al-buldān*. 5 vols. Beirut: Dār Ṣādir, 1957.

al-Zamakhsharī, Maḥmūd b. ʿUmar b. Muḥammad. *al-Kashshāf ʿan haqāʾiq ghawāmiḍ al-tanzīl wa ʿuyūn al-aqāwīl fī wujūh al-taʾwīl*. Ed. Muḥammad ʿAbd al-Salām Shāhīn. Beirut: Dār al-Kutub al-ʿIlmīyah, 1315/1995.

al-Zarkashī, Badr al-Dīn Muḥammad b. ʿAbdallāh. *al-Burhān fī ʿulūm al-Qurʾān*. Ed. Muḥammad Abū al-Faḍl Ibrāhīm. Cairo: Dār Iḥyāʾ al-Kutub al-ʿArabīyah, 1376/1957.

# Index of Quran Citations

# Index of Interpreters and Transmitters

# General Index

Moses  19, 27, 29, 32, 53,
58, 62, 83, 106, 107, 114,
115, 127, 128, 132, 143,
144, 148, 154–5, 157, 158,
166, 167, 172, 173–227,
238, 239, 240, 243, 249,
254, 256, 257, 264, 285,
286, 319, 325, 326, 331
Moses b. Manasseh  127
mosque  99, 101, 134, 142,
171, 208, 255, 276, 327, 329
Mosque of Abraham  34
Mosque of Salih  78
mosquitoes  93
Mosul  58, 168
Mother Book  328
Mount Judi  50, 58, 61, 62
Mount Nod  56
Mount of Olives  32
Mount Qasyun  248
Mount Thabir  103
Mount Zion  299
mouse  55
Mu'awiyah  67
Mu'awiyah b. Bakr  69,
70, 71
Mu'awiyah b. Numayr  132
Mu'tafikah  98, 124
Mu'tazili  11
Muhajirin  252
Muhallab  54
Muhammad  17, 29, 30, 40,
46, 47, 61, 68, 81–2, 95,
98, 101, 103, 104, 105,
107, 108, 128, 129, 135,
143, 149, 155, 167, 180,
199, 208, 214, 215, 216,
218, 220, 221, 223, 230,
238, 241, 246, 247, 252,
257, 261, 262, 271, 273,
274, 282, 286, 298, 316,
317, 319, 321–33
mujahidun  329
Mujalith  136
Mulgham  148
Muntana  219
Mus'ab  132
music  261
Muslims  61, 69, 105, 123,
132, 143, 171, 172, 215,
218, 237, 242, 271, 282,
317, 330, 333

musnad  316
Muthawwib b. Yaghfur
71
Muzahim  175
Muzdalifah  26
myrtle  185

Na'ilah  322, 324
Naamah  42
Nabeth  153
Nabu  136
Naftali  114
Nahor  84, 93, 113, 120,
121
Nahshon  266
Nahshun  259
Nakhshur  266
Naphish  111
Nasik  232, 234
Nasimah bt. Ishamel  114
Nasr  52, 54
Nawfal  324
Nebaioth  110
Nebuchadnezzar  84, 214,
230, 266, 280, 281, 284,
286, 288, 289, 293, 294,
295
Negus  166
Nesmah  111
Night Journey  46, 47, 135,
149, 191, 238, 326–32
Night of Fate  3
Nile  175, 212, 328
Nimrod  84–5, 89, 91, 92,
93, 230, 266
Nineveh  168
Nisibis  272
Noah  27, 32, 34, 43, 46,
47, 48, 49–62, 63, 65, 66,
68, 76, 77, 83, 84, 88, 94,
101, 109, 116, 120, 132,
147, 157, 158, 164, 190,
223, 228, 243, 263, 297
Nod  25, 32, 42, 56
North Africa  289
Nu'man b. Abi Awfa  286
Numayr  132
Nun  211, 213, 226, 239,
240, 249, 319
Nur  129
Nuwayb  148

Obed  259, 266
Og  58, 211–12
olive tree  185
Oman  65
"Original Arabs"  66
oxen  256

Palestine  98, 114, 120,
210, 289, 290
palm tree  299, 304
Palmyra  276, 277
Paradise  16, 18, 19, 20,
23–30, 39, 48, 71, 100,
103, 107, 108, 111, 135,
148, 160, 165, 185, 200,
209, 213, 248, 257, 282,
307, 318, 320, 330, 331
Paran  102
patriarch  319
Paul  318
Peleg  84, 223
pen  45, 46, 47
People of the Book  40,
105
People of the Cave  284
People of the Elephant
284
People of Moses  214–16
People of the Well  153,
164–7
People of Ya-Sin  319
Perez  259, 266
perfume  26, 27
Persia  91, 229, 276, 282,
317
Persians  60, 84, 91, 169,
223, 224, 227, 269
Pharaoh  62, 67, 94, 120,
164, 166, 173–97, 198,
204, 223, 226, 298, 319,
331
Phinehas  243, 284, 286
pigeons  200, 235, 326
pigs  55, 218, 219, 220,
221, 317
pilgrim  322
Pilgrimage  31–2, 36, 38,
61, 97, 99, 167, 243, 301
Place of Abraham
99–101, 104
plagues  190, 192–5, 235,
236, 240, 250, 252